ISBN 978-1-5279-4457-2
PIBN 10947151

1 MONTH OF
FREE
READING

at

www.ForgottenBooks.com

By purchasing this book you are eligible for one month membership to ForgottenBooks.com, giving you unlimited access to our entire collection of over 1,000,000 titles via our web site and mobile apps.

To claim your free month visit:
www.forgottenbooks.com/free947151

English
Français
Deutsche
Italiano
Español
Português

www.forgottenbooks.com

Mythology Photography **Fiction**
Fishing Christianity **Art** Cooking
Essays Buddhism Freemasonry
Medicine **Biology** Music **Ancient
Egypt** Evolution Carpentry Physics
Dance Geology **Mathematics** Fitness
Shakespeare **Folklore** Yoga Marketing
Confidence Immortality Biographies
Poetry **Psychology** Witchcraft
Electronics Chemistry History **Law**
Accounting **Philosophy** Anthropology
Alchemy Drama Quantum Mechanics
Atheism Sexual Health **Ancient History**
Entrepreneurship Languages Sport
Paleontology Needlework Islam
Metaphysics Investment Archaeology
Parenting Statistics Criminology
Motivational

PROCEEDINGS AND DEBATES

OF THE

CONVENTION

OF THE COMMONWEALTH OF PENNSYLVANIA, *Const Conr.*
1737-38

TO PROPOSE

AMENDMENTS TO THE CONSTITUTION,

COMMENCED AT HARRISBURG, MAY 2, 1838

VOL. VIII.

Reported by JOHN AGG, Stenographer to the Convention:

ASSISTED BY MESSRS. WHEELER, KINGMAN, DRAKE, AND M'KINLEY.

HARRISBURG:

PRINTED BY PACKER, BARRETT, AND PARKE.

1838.

CONVENTION HELD AT PHILADELPHIA.

WEDNESDAY, December 27, 1837.

Mr. Bedford, of Luzerne, moved that the convention do now proceed to the second reading and consideration of the resolution, offered by him on the 26th instant, in the words following, viz:

Resolved, That the following new rule be adopted, both in convention, and in committee of the whole, viz:

" That when any twenty delegates rise in their places, and move the question on any pending amendment, it shall be the duty of the presiding officer to take the vote of the body on sustaining such call, and if such call shall be sustained by a majority, the question shall be taken on the amendment without further debate."

The question being put, the motion was agreed to.

Mr. Bedford said he had offered this resolution for the purpose of accelerating the business of the convention. We have now adopted a resolution fixing the period for an adjournment, *sine die*, and it becomes important to adopt some measure to expedite the business before us. It is now six weeks since there has been a single vote taken in the committee of the whole on any of the articles. The committee to whom the seventh article was referred, reported no amendment to the section now under discussion. An amendment was offered, and an amendment was offered to that amendment: and although both had been fully discussed, and every one's mind was made up, still the majority, being in favor of neither the one proposition or the other, could not get the previous question: attempts had been made to do so without effect. If the call for the previous question were sustained, the amendments would be cut off, and then the original constitution would stand; and this prevented a majority from sustaining the call for the previous question. Thus this debate had been continued for a considerable time without the possibility of cutting it short. He believed such a change in the rules as he now proposed to be absolutely necessary to be carried into effect, before the convention could be able to adjourn *sine die*. The resolution was offered before the resolution to adjourn was adopted; and he believed it to be more necessary now. We have spent six weeks on a single article in the committee of the whole; and within the short space of five weeks which we have before us, we cannot get through our business unless we adopt a rule of this character. Gentlemen say, that, if we cannot get through our business by the second of February, we can extend the time. He had voted against the resolution not because he did not wish to terminate the session, but he wished to see some evidence that we could get through what had been committed to us by the people to perform. Unless this rule shall be adopted, we may not only have to extend the term for the convention to sit, for a few days, but for weeks, and perhaps months. The resolution to adjourn means nothing more than that we will adjourn on that day, if we are ready to adjourn. Those who are anxious to finish the labors of this body by the 2d day of Februry, will be willing to adopt such rules as may enable us to get through our business; more especially, he presumed would the gentleman, who was so anxious to adjourn *sine d e*, and who opposed the resolution, be desirous to devise some mode of expediting the business.

Mr. DICKEY, of Beaver, expressed regret, that he should have to disappoint the gentleman from Luzerne. The rule which the gentleman had introduced was one entirely new, and unknown to legislation. If gentlemen had not wished to consume the time of the convention, they ought not to have offered amendments, which they knew would not be adopted, and which would be withdrawn. The previous question was a sufficient check, whenever the sense of the house was in favor of sustaining it. He did not know whether the previous question would be considered a privileged question, if this were adopted. All the objects which it is desirable to accomplish, can be accomplished by the previous question. The gentleman from Luzerne would not like to vote for the previous question, because he was in favor of the ten dollar note system, and the previous question would cut that off. He believed, however, that the previous question was quite sufficient, and he was therefore opposed to this resolution.

Mr. DARLINGTON, of Chester, asked if the adoption of this rule would not lead to the interruption of a speaker, in the midst of his speech?

Mr. BEDFORD replied, that such was not his intention, and he believed that such would not be the effect of the adoption of the resolution.

Mr. MERFDITH, of Philadelphia, said, that we had already adopted so many new rules, that no one could tell what the rules of order are. He did not know however, whether it would not be necessary to adopt some such provisions, to enable us to adjourn on the second day of February; because, from the course pursued yesterday, it appears, that, although sent here for the purpose of deliberation, we are to be a body deciding the most important questions without debate. Every one who wishes to deliver his views, is to be limited to one hour. We must resort to some mode of sitting out every question in the best mode we can. He moved to postpone the further consideration of this resolution for the present, in order that we may see how the other rules operate. He afterwards withdrew the motion.

Mr. INGERSOLL, of Philadelphia, said, he understood there were three gentlemen, who had in their power to move a reconsideration of the vote by which the resolution of yesterday was adopted, and he hoped they would do so. He would, however, move to amend the resolution now offered, by adding to the end of it, the words following, viz :

" And that the resolution adopted yesterday, fixing the day for the adjournment *sine die* of this body, may be rescinded, or altered, at any time, by a vote of a majority of the convention.

The PRESIDENT decided that this motion was not in order.

Mr. MEREDITH, then renewed his motion, to postpone the further consideration of this resolution for the present. The resolution to adjourn, he added, might be repealed or rescinded at any time.

The question was then put, on the motion of Mr. MEREDITH, and decided in the affirmative—yeas 61.

SEVENTH ARTICLE.

The convention again resolved itself into a committee of the whole, Mr. REIGART in the chair, on the report of the committee to whom was referred the seventh article of the constitution.

The question being on the motion of Mr. FULLER, of Fayette, to amend the amendment offered by Mr. READ, as modified by him, by adding to the end thereof the words following, viz:

" No bank shall issue any bill, check, note or paper credit of a less denomination than ten dollars."

Mr. BARNITZ, of York, had no disposition, as he said, at this time, to enter the wide field of discussion, which had been opened on the questions now pending ; but there were two or three points in which he felt peculiar concern, and upon which he desired to submit some remarks.

As to the causes of the suspension of specie payments, he would say nothing; that question had been discussed. He was satisfied himself, and he thought others were satisfied. He would leave that question in the hands of the people ; they had already decided it in a number of the states, and especially in the empire state, where they had spoken in terms not to be misunderstood.

As to the mode and manner and the necessity of that suspension, he contended that it was a measure of absolute necessity—for the safety of the banking institutions of the state, as well for the convenience and security of the vast number of our fellow citizens who had their engagements with the banks in various modes. It had been asserted by the delegate from Susquehanna, who opened the question, that the suspension of specie payments was a conspiracy by the banks of the country to promote their own interests at the expense of the interests of the country. Mr. B. denied this charge, not in the way of idle declamation or partisan warfare, but upon facts and reasons that no candid or liberal man would deny or dispute. The delegate from Susquehanna, on being pressed for reasons or explanations, with the courtesy that belongs to him disclaimed any improper charge against the individuals who were officers of the banks, but that the charge was made against the corporations.

Sir, (said Mr. B.) this distinction is not easy to understand; but if the gentleman gives it so, we are bound to take it. . But this charge has been given to the winds; it must be met, and, if it can be done, shown to be without the least foundation. The delegate from Susquehanna as well as Mr. B., was at Harrisburg when the mails of the day brought the information of the suspension in Philadelphia and New York. The dismay and embarrassment it occasioned was felt by all.

Meetings were immediately called at Harrisburg, of those who had the managing of the banking institutions there, and the result was a declaration, that the only step by which the safety of these institutions, and of the thousands connected with them as debtors could be assured—the only alternative was to follow the example of New York and of this city—that is to say, to suspend specie payments. But nothing could be further from the opinions and knowledge of one and all of these gentlemen, than any thing like previous combination, or even a suspicion of what was about to take place. I take this fact as a standard, in relation to all the institutions of the state of Pennsylvania, and I feel that I am fully warranted in doing so. It had an influence, so far as character goes, upon all the institutions of our state. Upon the day after the occurrence, to which I have just alluded, I was in York—the place where I reside. A bank has existed there since the year 1814. I was a director of that bank. Information had arrived the evening before of the suspension of specie payments. The directors were immediately called together, and they, like the directors of the banking institutions of Harrisburg, determined also, upon a suspension of specie payments. But I assert confidently, in regard to the directors there, as well as at Harrisburg, so far from their having been a combination, there did not even exist a suspicion, that such an event was about to take place. It had never entered the minds of these gentlemen.

Here, sir, are facts coming home to the understanding of every man, showing nothing like pre-concert, nothing like combination. Sir, the suspension of specie payments on the part of the banks, was an act of stern and absolute necessity, like that which compels the commander of a vessel of war, to throw his guns overboard, that he may save his ship and the lives entrusted to his charge. It was a terrible necessity which compelled them to adopt that measure, although they saw embarrassment and difficulty on every side. No other plan presented itself to them; no other measure could have saved the banks, and those whose vital interests were so intimately connected with them. But even if there had been any other way to save themselves, let me ask the gentleman from Susquehanna, (Mr. Read) where could have been the motive for this conspiracy which he charges against the banks? Here is a measure charged upon them, which must bring with it embarrassment, danger to their charter, and in fact, every evil which they would be most desirous to avert. I do not know for what purpose these charges have been made, unless it may be to aid in the consummation of a work which is going on elsewhere, and that is, to break down these institutions—to sweep them from the surface of the earth.

In relation to the effects of this suspension, gentlemen have brought forward here as one of the calamities which have resulted from that meas-

ure, that all the specie has been absorbed by the banks. In this particular, they are certainly in error. At the time the suspension took place,
the currency existed of notes of the banks and of a certain amount of specie.
Where is it now ? The banks have not got it. Where, then, is it ?
I answer, it is among the people who have themselves suspended specie
payments.

The banks have acquired some since that time. There may, indeed,
be some slight increase as to some few of the banks, but it is by no
means general. Thus we see that this argument falls at once to the
ground, so soon as we come to compare it with facts as they are known
to exist.

But, sir, delegates on this floor who have supported the amendment
offered by the gentleman from Susquehanna (Mr. Read) in the first instance,
and subsequently by my friend on the right, (Mr. Fuller) have accused
myself and others, who take the opposite side of the question to themselves, with being opposed to all reform, to all regulation or restriction of
the banking system. This accusation—that we are opposed to all reform
—has been loudly and repeatedly made; and, sir, it places us in a false
position. One and all of the gentlemen who have taken the same
ground in relation to the banks, that I have taken, admit that there
are defects in the present system, which might, with great propriety, be
remedied. But, the great point of difference between us is, that we say,
that these are defects which must be regulated by the legislature, and
which cannot be regulated by any act on the part of this convention.
They attempt to constitute this body into a legislative assembly, and we,
on the other hand, while we admit the existence of the defects in the
system, say that it is the province of the legislature, and of the legislature
alone, to remedy those defects.

But, there is another point, Mr. Chairman, to which I would call the
attention of the committee for a moment. I allude to the strange inconsistency to which gentlemen on the other side are compelled to
resort, in order to support their own propositions. All the leading debate
on their part has been such as was calculated to destroy the banks, by the
use of every opprobrious epithet which the gentlemen could devise. This
has been the same from beginning to the end of this discussion. I will
not repeat their language ; its character was such that it could not escape
the observation of all who heard it. The gentlemen have all closed their
remarks with the same song—" we are the friends of these institutions, we
do not wish to destroy them;" like the man who would give the vital
stab, and afterwards with a composed air, assure his victim he meant him
no harm—that he only wished to regulate his system. The whole tenor
of the remarks of the gentlemen has tended entirely and directly to have
the effect to destroy every banking institution in the state. I do not say that
such was their design, I merely say that this would be the effect. This
would be the inevitable result, and as to speaking of reform, you might
just as well attempt to resuscitate a dead man after you had destroyed him,
as attempt to reform a system from which you have taken the vital
support away. What is the life blood of these institutions—in the
absence of which they can have no vitality—no existence? It is public
confidence and the public good will. The gentleman from Allegheny

(Mr. Forward) put the matter upon the only true principle ; they must have public confidence and good will, and public opinion at all times in their favor. If this is not so, they are of no avail—they are absolutely useless ; they can do no good either to themselves or others.

But, Mr. Chairman, among other epithets which have been applied to these institutions, they have been spoken of by the strong name of aristocracies and monopolies. Now, I take the opposite ground and I say, that the very nature and object of a bank is to prevent this very monopoly of which such grievous complaints are made. Banks are distributors of money. Monopolies bring together the money of wealthy individuals, for works of private interest peculiar to themselves. Banks, on the contrary, are the means by which capital is distributed ; they are the very antipodes of monopolies. Their object is to make capital useful in every branch of trade and business. I would say, in short, that banks are legal institutions under legal restrictions, by which the wealth and capital of the country are distributed and made subservient to the demands of those who require it, to make industry or skill more productive and profitable. This is my definition of a bank.

But, gentlemen speak also of banks, being aristocratic institutions. I assert, on the other hand, that they are the very offspring of democracy—yes, sir, the very children of democracy. When had we more democracy among us than in the time of Simon Snyder ? At that day, the people, with scarce an exception; were all democrats. And what was the veto on the banks ? It was an old federal measure which had been condemned as a measure of John Adams, the elder, to strengthen the hands of government. What was the result, when Governor Snyder objected to the establishment of banks ? Why, sir, the people would have them, whether the governor was willing or not, and those banks were chartered by a majority of three-fourths of the legislature of your state. Here was your democracy of numbers. From their very nature, banks are democratic. And, here let me say a word in reply to my friend from the county (Mr. Brown) who is not now in his seat, and who made a reference to the extraordinary political revolution which has recently taken place in New York. If I understood the gentleman correctly, he attributed this singular change to bank influence. Sir, this is only carrying out the idea of Mr. Van Buren, in his message, to the congress of the United States. I, for one, disagree entirely with both these gentlemen. I say, that it was not corruption, that it was not improper bank influence, which has produced these great results in New York, but that it was the people coming to the rescue of their own institutions. Such a charge as this, even when it brings with it the weight of the endorsement of the President of the United States, can not gain credence with those who are willing to know the truth, and to judge by the truth alone. The great secret of that revolution, no doubt was, that the people saw their own institutions were in danger and they resolved to come to the rescue. The United States Bank, as we all know, was allowed to go down. The leaders of a powerful party took their stand against it, and it fell. But, that institution stood upon a very different footing from our own state institutions. It had no sympathy with the people, and it fell at once, because it had no sympathy with the people. But, when the leaders of a party, which had become desperate endeavor:d to drive this destruction home to our state institutions, then you find that the matter assumes a very different aspect. The people found that an attack on one interest would bring with it an attack upon another. They rose at once and stayed the hand of the destroyers, who care little for the real interests of the people, provided they can make their favor a means of obtaining office. Sir, let me assure gentlemen, that they have entirely mistaken the ground in this respect—they will find, if they do not already know, that these institutions are so intimately blended with the happiness and the prosperity of the people, that all attempts to interfere with, or destroy them, will, in the end, meet with signal defeat.

I must now, Mr. Chairman, allude briefly to the course of the gentleman from Fayette, (Mr. Fuller.) He introduced a resolution of a very singular character, in connexion with the subject. I refer to the resolution, the object of which was to exclude any member of this body, who might be a stockholder in any banking institution, from voting upon any question connected with the interest of banks. I believe, I state correctly the purport of the resolution. Now, I admit that in a case where a question of right between man and man is to be decided, it is judicious and proper, if not indispensably necessary, that he who has an interest in the decision, shall not be allowed to take any part in the matter. But, this principle never could be exerted to represent active deliberations. Such a principle would be in direct opposition to that which the gentleman from Fayette himself maintains—that is to say : that a representative, in his character as such, represents his constituents, and that all his opinions are the opinions of his constituents.

For my own part, I do not go quite so far ; still that is the principle maintained by the gentlemen from Fayette. Instead, therefore, of this being an objection, it should be otherwise, in connecting his interest with theirs, and thus giving an additional reason for his fidelity in the discharge of those duties which his constituents have imposed upon him.

Suppse that you were to apply the principle contained in that resolution, to legislative acts, I will ask any gentleman whether a single question could come up before a legislative body, in which every member has not himself a direct pecuniary interest? Every law which is adopted by the legislature affects every individual in some way or other ; especially all law in relation to taxes, revenue, and the financial affairs of the country. Each man has to pay his quota under these laws. Sir, I shall pay no regard to such a principle. I feel myself beyond the control of that resolution, or of this body, in regard to any vote which I may think proper to give upon any matter touching the interests of my constituents.

But, there is another point of view which shews that the gentleman from Fayette is interfering with the garments of others, while his own skirts are by no means clear. It is the supposition here that these banking privileges have generally belonged to the people—that they have been granted to individuals as so much of the people's property ; and, it is the desire of gentlemen who array themselves here in opposition to the banking system, to get back to the people these rights and privileges which they say have been improperly granted.

Now, sir, if I am a stockholder in one of these institutions, I hold a portion of these privileges under the charter by which that institution was incorporated; and, if the gentleman from Fayette holds some, he is one of the people. It is, then, a mere question of *meum* and *tuum*. Is he not as much interested in taking this away from me, as I am in keeping it? If I am to be excluded from holding it at all, it follows, by necessary consequence, and for the same reason, that he would be excluded as one of the people from taking it from me. There is, therefore, just as much interest on the one side as there is on the other.

Such, it appears to me, Mr. Chairman, is the position in which gentlemen on the other side have placed themselves by the course of argument they have adopted. They are equally interested.

I come now to say a few words in relation to the immediate question before us. If I understand it, the amendment which has been offered or assumed by the gentleman from Susquehanna, is this;—in the first place, recogniziug the 3d section of the 7th article of the constitution of 1790, as it now stands—adding to it a clause in relation to double legislation operating upon bank charters—and then, added to that, is the proposition of the gentleman from Fayette, (Mr. Fuller) prohibiting the banks from issuing notes of a less denomination than ten dollars. This, I believe, is precisely the state of the question at the present moment.

In regard to the first branch of the amendment, we, of course, can have no objection.

In regard to the second part of that which requires the double action of the legislature in the part of a bank charter,—although I do not think it is very important as applicable to the future—still, it appears to me to be objectionable upon several grounds. I am not able to discover any reason why, in granting a mere private petty corporation, the action of two successive legislatures should be made requisite; especially when we know that a single legislature has power to decide upon the dearest rights of property and of life. Where the reason is to justify this difference, I cannot tell. Perhaps some gentleman on the other side may be good enough to enlighten me.

But there is another reason why I am opposed to it. According to my view of the matter, it conveys a direct sanction—it gives an unequivocal endorsement to the strange and wild accusations which have been made, as well in this body as out of it, against the legislative assembly of our state. It would to a certain extent, directly sanction the declaration which has gone abroad, that the representatives of the people are unworthy to be trusted. I am unwilling, by any word or act of mine, to sanction that idea in the slightest degree. I, therefore, cannot vote for it.

In regard to the last provision—that which proposes to restrict the banks from issuing any notes of a less denomination than ten dollars, there are two or three objections which, to my mind, appear so strong, that I think no member can be so blind as not to see them.

In the first place, then, what is this proposition? It is nothing more than an ingenious attempt to annul, to expunge that very important resolution which was passed by so large a vote in this body, some four or five weeks ago. That resolution, in my opinion, was the most important act which has been done by this convention. I allude to the resolution introduced by the gentleman from the city of Philadelphia, (Mr. Meredith) declaring the inviolability of bank charters. Now, gentlemen were well aware that they could not, by any direct means, accomplish the purpose they had in view—of destroying that resolution, and here is an ingenious mode of doing it in an indirect manner. If the amendment prohibiting the issue of notes of a less denomination than ten dollars, is decided in the way they desire that it should be decided, of course the resolution you have adopted, is a nullity. Adopt this amendment and you at once, by a constitutional provision, take away from these banking institutions one of the most important rights derived under their charters—that is to say, the right of issuing notes of the denomination of five dollars. This is a most important and a most useful part of their rights. I do not know whether such is the design, but it is manifest that, if this amendment succeeds, the certain result will be to destroy—to blot out of existence, to all practical intent and purpose, the resolution adopted at Harrisburg. Sir, it is gone—absolutely annihilated. We all know that, in the general bank law, there is a reservation that charters of banks may be altered, reformed, or even annulled if the public interests should require it. Here is a reservation on the part of the legislature; and although the legislature may alter, reform, or even annul those charters, if the interests of the people should require it, yet no other body can exercise that power, no more than any corporation of any borough town can exercise it. We have the constitution of the United States, which protects contracts of this kind, and here would be an answer to it. I trust, therefore, that gentlemen will see at once, that the direct operation of this amendment would be such as I state.

Let every man refer to the benefits which these banking institutions have every where diffused. Let him look to the state of Pennsylvania! Let him reflect on the high eminence which she has attained among her sister states of the Union. And to what is all this to be traced? I answer to no other source than to the aid which she has received from the banks. Your public works have depended almost entirely on the co-operation and assistance of the banks; from the loans granted by the banks from year to year, and although individuals have contributed a portion, still we are mainly indebted to the loans of the banks for the progress of our public improvements. A few years ago, when the credit of the commonwealth was such that loans could scarcely be obtained, requisitions were made upon the banks, which were complied with, and our public works were continued for another year. But we can go still further back. We can go to the improvements connecting the eastern with the western part of our state. I refer to the turnpike roads between Pittsburg and Philadelphia. Without the aid of the banks, even these roads could not have been made.

But we can go even further. Our commonwealth has, in fact, subsisted on the revenues derived from the banks. At an early day a part of the funds of our government were placed in certain banks of the commonwealth, and for a period of twenty-five years, the government was supported by the dividends arising from those funds.

But look to the effects of these institutions upon common life. The mass of our citizens are operatives throughout the commonwealth, and almost every man depends upon his daily occupation for the means of support in life. The mechanic and the manufacturer and the merchant receive their returns for their labor not at the time the work is done, but at a certain future and stated period. What are the people to do in the mean time, for the necessaries of life, or for such comforts or luxuries as their circumstances may justify, unless the means are obtained in this way.

The mechanic obtains all necessaries from the merchant in the district upon credit, founded on the returns of his industry which he is yet to receive. Where does the merchant obtain his credit? From the merchant in the city. And where does the merchant in the city obtain his credit? From the banks. So that, the accommodation effected by the banks, comes thus imperceptibly, almost to every man's home and fireside; and, although it is not obtained, yet its influence is extended to almost every man in the community. I am, therefore, opposed, upon every principle, to the amendment of the gentleman from Fayette, and also to the amendment originally offered by the gentleman from Lancaster, and I shall vote against both.

Permit me, Mr. President, before I take my seat, to offer a few remarks in reply to what fell from the delegate from the city, on Saturday, in reference to our meeting here. Coming, as it did, from that time-honored source, and with his peculiar feelings and eloquence, it produced an impresion with every member, not soon to be forgotten; and, I am sure, that in expressing my own feelings, I express the feelings of my fellow members from the interior, when I say, that whatever may be the results of our official deliberations, we shall carry with us to our homes, and to our constituents, a deep and abiding sense of the liberal spirit, the kindness, the hospitality of this city.

Sir, its noble institutions of every character—benevolent, literary, scientific and useful, have all been thrown open to us, in a manner most gratifying to our feelings; and more than this, the hearts of the citizens have been thrown open to us in all that kindness and hospitality could offer, to alleviate the privations of the stranger—separated from his family, his friends and his home. Besides, sir, we have had the gratifying opportunity of witnessing the industry, the great works, the vast business concern and the great progress in the useful arts of life, which so eminently adorn and distinguish this, our own great metropolis.

Sir, if no other result should be derived from our adjournment to this place, I trust, and I say so with peculiar pleasure, coming from the district I represent, I trust it will tend to confirm and to perpetuate that liberal and enlightened sentiment of policy, that the interests, the prosperity, the happiness of the fair portion of our great and growing commonwealth, is essentially and intimately connected with the interest, the prosperity and the happiness of every other part.

Mr. COPE, of Philadelphia, said:

I shall doubtless incur the charge of temerity, by engaging in a debate already exhausted, and before an audience whose patience must be worn out; and were I to consult my own feelings only, I should certainly not make the attempt. I will, however, proceed at once to the discussion of the subject before the committee.

That branch of the resolution before us which proposes to restrict the banks from issuing notes of a smaller denomination than ten dollars, is, I presume, a matter of comparative indifference to the traders of Philadelphia. Our merchants receive and pay mostly in checks on the banks. To another,.and a very respectable portion of our citizens, our manufacturers and mechanics, it is of more consequence. Some of these pay weekly, in wages to their workmen, from five hundred to three thousand dollars. Supposing a man's wages to be less than ten dollars a week, notes of that amount would be much more inconvenient, both to the payer and receiver, than notes of a smaller denomination; and if the parties prefer five dollar notes, what good reason can be assigned for refusing to gratify them? Five dollar bills are more convenient to the market people, to travellers, and to the country population generally.

It has been stated by a delegate from the county, that originally the Bank of North America did not issue notes of a less denomination than ten dollars. Assume it to be so, for the sake of argument, and what follows? Why, that the public convenience demanded notes of a smaller denomination—for most certainly that bank, like all others, has for many years issued five dollar notes.

But I have it in my power to furnish some curious and authentic information for the member from the county, (C. J. Ingersoll,) on this subject, derived from an examination of the minutes of the board of directors of the Bank of North America, which I will take the liberty of reading, viz:

"BANK OF NORTH AMERICA, } August 6th, 1789. }

" Mr. Richard Bache moved, upon the recommendation of Dr. Benjamin Franklin, that this bank should now issue small tickets or notes, to supply the call of the public for change, during the present interruption to the circulation of copper coin; and presented a sheet of paper of a very peculiar fabric, as most suitable for the purpose—of which paper the Doctor had only two reams, which he would spare the bank for this particular use.

" Wherepuon the board resolved that Benjamin F. Bache print a number of tickets of the denomination of three ninetieths of a dollar, equal to three pence specie, and also a number of tickets of the denomination of one ninetieth of a dollar, equal to one penny specie."

The minutes of October 1, 1789, contain the copy of a letter from Thomas Willing, Esq. president of the bank, to Alexander Hamilton, secretary of the treasury, from which I have taken the following extract:

" We find, and daily experience convinces us, that there is much less risk of imposition by the counterfeiting of our paper, than of gold and silver now current in America; of which there are so many base pieces well made, and current, that it is hardly possible for a person to receive it without loss, though ever so well informed. It is a truth, that we have destroyed, the last three years, to the full amount of twenty thousand dollars, offered to us in payment as gold and silver."

These extracts furnish us with the experience of our forefathers on the subject of paper and specie, which it will be well for us to remember in the course of this discussion.

The resolution before the committee, if intended as a measure of hostility to the banks, will prove abortive; the arrow will fall short of its mark. The banks will not issue one dollar less on that account, since all who borrow of them, if they cannot obtain five dollar notes, will be glad to get ten dollar notes.

When the Bank of England was chartered in 1694, the same cry of monopoly was urged against its creation. This cry was raised, not by the people, but by the proud barons, who foresaw, in the measure, an abridgement of their overwhelming power. They perceived that its tendency was to elevate the commoners in wealth and influence to a level with themselves. They were right. The commerce of the country, which they were too slothful, or too aristocratic to cultivate, was then at a low ebb; but by the stimulus to industry, which the bank soon diffused over the whole nation, manufactures began to flourish, and the canvass of Great Britain to whiten every ocean, in every quarter of the globe. From that period to this, the wealth, the power and the greatness of the British empire, has been constantly on the increase, until they have attained an eminence surpassed by no nation on earth.

A bank, in its simple elements, is but an association of individuals, for the purpose of lending money. A charter guaranties to the stockholder, that he shall not be made liable for more than the stock he subscribes; and is as much a matter of convenience to the public, as to himself, since claimants on the bank can, with greater facility and certainty, assert their claims, by suing an unit, which a corporation is, than by pursuing individuals difficult to be designated.

A bank is invaluable to young traders of fair reputation. It enables them to enter into competition with their more wealthy neighbors, for fortune and for fame. Were it not for the facility thus afforded to merit and enterprise, the business of the country would be confined to a few capitalists, who would purchase on their own terms, and sell only for extravagant profits. The farmer would receive less for his produce, and pay higher for those necessaries he wants in return.

Banks prevent robberies. It is no doubt within the recollection of others beside myself, on this floor, that for some years before the estab. lishment of the old Bank of the United States, in 1791, robberies were of such frequent occurrence, that two or three burglaries in a single night, were not uncommon. Our highways were infested by thieves, and our farm houses frequently despoiled. The Bank of North America was then the only one in existence, and as it was but little understood, people were not in the habit of depositing their money in its vaults for safe keeping.

When that bank was re-chartered in 1787, the late Judge Breckenridge was a representative from Allegheny in the legislature, whose ses.

sions were then held in Philadelphia.   He left home a determined enemy of the bank.   He and his constituents had formed those horrible ideas of its wickedness, which many now think, or affect to entertain, of the banks of the present day.   Some imagined that it was composed of a band of banditti, who inhabited caves on the banks of the Delaware, from whence they sallied forth to rob hen roosts, and to perpetrate other depredations on the lives and property of their quiet neighbors.   From their supposed residence on the margin of the Delaware, was derived, in the conception of these honest country people, the name of banks.   The representative I have named, pursued his slow and cautious course towards the city, inquiring, as he advanced, into the doings of this young monster.   But Breckenridge was not a man to be long imposed upon; he remained but a short time in the infected city, when maugre the instructions and fears of his constituents, he became one of the most powerful advocates for re-chartering the bank; and it was accordingly re-chartered.

The banks have been courteously called robbers, by members of this convention.   If after having paid for their privileges, and they do not transcend their powers, they should be forcibly deprived of their charters, who are then the robbers?   The banks, or those who despoil them of their rights?   But, say these members, we don't want to destroy, but only to regulate the banks.   That is, I suppose, only to cut off their arms and legs, and then let them run, if they can.

But we have other propositions than the one now under consideration, placed on our files, for future action, and emanating from the same quarter, from the " woods of Susquehanna !"—We are to have, it seems, but ten banks in the state, with a capital of three millions each ; thus cutting off nearly one half of our present circulation,   Now, have gentlemen reflected on the effects of this measure ?   On the misery and loss to individuals, and to the public, which must result from calling out of circulation so many millions of our currency ?   It is scarcely possible to believe that the advocates of this ruinous project can be serious.   But where are the ten banks to be located?   One will doubtless be allotted to Susquehanna county, and it may be convenient for the delegate from that county, (A. Read) to be its cashier.   Another will doubtless go to Indiana county ; and one may find its way to Wilkesbarre, to gladden the heart of the delegate from Luzerne.   But where will you plant the remaining seven?   None can be expected to domesticate in this city of abominations—this " bank bound city of speculators and robbers"—this " gang" of foul spirits—this city of " merchants, whose counting houses are their churches, whose money is their God, and whose legers,—defaced legers of course, the delegate from Indiana will understand me,— whose legers are their Bibles."   Allow me once for all, to observe, that the inhabitants of this same wicked city, have thirty millions of dollars invested in your internal improvements—your turnpikes, rail roads, canals, &c. &c.—and no small portion of the revenue of the state, is drawn from the same source.   I could name an individual, now on this floor, who, besides other investments of the kind, that produce him some remuneration, has one hundred thousand dollars invested in improvements of acknowledged utility to the state, from which he derives not one cent of income.   I might also point your attention to our charitable institutions, our numerous associations, for the promotion of knowledge and science, and for the relief of suffering humanity. To these and other works of disinterested benevolence, not a few of the "gang," so called, devote nearly the whole of their time ; and for the promotion of such objects, give away more than some of their envious slanderers are worth, or ever will be. Yet such is the city, and these are the men, to whom are ascribed, by the delegates from Susquehanna, Indiana and Luzerne, the opprobrious epithets which I have quoted.

But the banks have stopped specie payments ! the wicked ingrates ! But have not the people ? and has not the government ?

The delegate from the county, (C. J. Ingersoll,) stated in his place, that thirty per cent had lately been paid for money. Then are our banks the best remedy for usury, for they cannot charge more than six per cent.

It is made the subject of complaint that the issues of the banks are irregular, that they sometimes lend profusely, and then very sparingly. As well may gentleman complain of the variations of the seasons, and that our winters do not yield crops of cotton and grain, as well as our summers. When produce is brought to market, money is wanted to pay for it ; when the season for business is over, money ceases to be in equal demand. About twelve to fifteen hundred thousand bales of cotton are brought annually to our seaports. The banks are then called on, and they lend to accommodate the demand. The shippers draw upon their European correspondents, and the banks are repaid. As a further exemplification, the state of Kentuckey sends, annually, to the Atlantic states, live stock, such as horses, mules, &c., to the value of two millions of dollars. The banks there furnish the means of payment, to a class of men, who purchase of the farmers. The banks are repaid by drafts on eastern merchants, who in turn, are provided for by the arrival of the stock. In a single establishment, in Cincinnati, one thousand hogs are slaughtered daily, during the season, and in that city there are several of these extensive establishments. Money is of course wanted for these operations, and the same process takes place. So with our millers ; they want money to buy wheat, and reimburse the banks by the sale of their flour. When money is wanted, the banks lend—when it is not wanted, they cannot lend. It is contrary to their interests to keep their means unemployed.

But the monster, the Bank of the United States ! that bane of our prosperity. That same monster was going on very usefully and harmlessly, in the pursuit of its lawful occupations, when General Jackson took it into his head to confer a head on the Portsmouth branch, and to signify, through his friends, his desire for other changes in the administration of its concerns. He was not gratified. He had previously spoken well of the bank—he now became its determined enemy—he first flattered, and then asked for favors. But the lady was coy, she had no fancy for a more intimate connexion, and then came the declaration of war. "It must be admitted," said the President, "the bank has failed in the great end for which it was established—a uniform and sound currency." But our domestic exchanges were then, on an average, throughout the country, at about one half of one per cent, and it afterwards gradually rose to five per cent, ten per cent, and twenty per cent. and from Tennessee, remittances to Philadelphia reached twenty-five per cent, premium. The removal of the deposits gave the first impulse, and the suspension of specie payments added to the troubled wave. But General Jackson had sworn a tremendous oath, that he would wring off the neck of the bank —and he seldom wavered in his purpose. A gentleman, who had been his intimate friend for years, and who was also my friend, said of him— "I never, in all my life, knew that man undertake any thing, good or bad, that he would not persevere in, without regard to consequences." He did so persevere, until his measures destroyed the best currency any nation ever was blessed with, and brought ruin on thousands.

This little matter of neck wringing was a very natural conception. The General was known to be game, and had long sustained the reputation of being one of the best cock fighters in this christian community.

It was long ago charged upon the bank that it lent money to the printers; and the crimination has been revived on the floor of this house. And why, let me ask, should not the loans of the bank be extended to printers, as well as to any other class of our fellow citizens? The bank assuredly did not apply to the printers, but the printers, like all other borrowers, applied to the bank, and were treated in the same manner. If they offered satisfactory paper, they were accommodated ; if not, their applications were rejected. I believe that the bank has suffered no loss by them, but that the sums borrowed were regularly repaid. As a former director of that institution, I here emphatically bear my testimony to the integrity of all these operations. I recollect that one of those printers accompanied his application with a written declaration that he was opposed to the bank, and whether the loan were granted or declined, he should continue his opposition. He obtained what he asked, and was as good as his word. He remains to this day, its open, consistent and avowed enemy. But a delegate has reminded us that large loans were made to Thomas Biddle ; implying, of course, that the borrower had been improperly favored. The facts of that case are these : The government had paid off a large amount of its stock, held by the bank, and it became a matter of concernment to find some immediate employment for this addition to the funds of the bank. Several persons were applied to, among others T. Biddle. He was a broker, of high reputation, was in the habit of employing large sums in his business, and a gentleman, on whose probity, means and punctuality, the utmost reliance could be placed. To him, therefore, a temporary loan was made, and ample security obtained. When the regular business of the bank enabled the directors to use these funds, in ordinary discounts, the money was demanded and returned, together with the interest. In this transaction the bank was as much obliged to Thomas Biddle, as Thomas Biddle was to the bank. A loan to Charles Biddle has likewise been the subject of criticism. It is sufficient for me to say in relation to that loan, that he was at the time a director of one of our city banks, and that the money he borrowed was for the use of that bank, at a period of public pressure—the Bank of the United States, at all times willing to render necessary assistance to any of the other banks. On another occasion, a considerable loan was made to a person who held a high station as a public officer. He called at the bank and alleged that congress had risen without making an appropriation, to enable him to pay a stipulated sum to certain Indians, with whom he had negociated a treaty for their lands, and with whom he apprehended difficulty, as he would not be able to make them comprehend why he could not pay them according to contract. The amount required was advanced by the bank, which waited until congiess, at their next session, made the necessary appropriation, when it was repaid. Another loan was made to a gentleman who now holds an office of high trust and confidence in the government, who was, at the time, and I believe has always been, one of the bank's opponents.

I should not feel myself warranted thus to speak of these several loans, had it not been for the charges of partiality and political favoritism, so often urged against the institution ; and I am sure if the parties were now in my hearing, they would excuse the liberty I take in thus referring to these transactions.

Another fact it may not be improper to mentiou. A majority of the directors of the bank were originally Jackson men, and had actually given their votes for this noted person. If they became otherwise, it was his fault, not theirs. It should be remembered also that the administration appointed five out of the twenty-five of which the board consisted. But politics formed no part of the business of the bank. In [their loans, and in their appointments to office, the inquiry never was as to the political opinions of any man, but always as to his responsibility and fitness.

Permit me here to state a fact, strongly illustrative of the inestimable value of confidence and credit.

At the first meeting of the trustees of the late Stephen Girard's Bank, of which I was one, and which meeting was held immediately after his decease, we found to our amazement, that the whole amount of specie in his bank was but $15,673 80, one half of which sum was in uncurrent coin. On making this unpleasant discovery, I was deputed by my colleagues to call on the Bank of the United States, to make known our situation and to solicit its aid. The directors forthwith tendered us the loan of $100,000. As however, money soon came into our hands from the debtors of the Bank, we did not avail ourselves of this generous offer. I mention the circumstance as another instance of the liberal spirit in which the affairs of the Bank of the United States, has ever been administered, and of how much may be accomplished where, as in the case of Stephen Girard, confidence and credit were neither suspected nor impaired.

But it is asserted the bank employed the press to political purposes. Such an imputation, in the absence of all proof, is only to be met with a flat denial. When charged with impure motives and base actions, it certainly caused the truth to be published in its own defence : this is the whole truth of the matter. The President had, however, resolved on its destruction. He thought of the bank as the farmer thought of his pig. " Have I not fed you and fattened you, till you have become. sleek and wanton ?—you most ungrateful scoundrel—that you must make such a squealing, now that I want to cut your throat ?"

It has been contended on this floor that if we dispense with paper currency, specie will flow into the country to supply its place. Such an idea is fallacious in the extreme.   We must get specie as we get every thing else, by giving the value.   If we discharge our pockets of our bank notes, we shall wait long before their place will be supplied by gold or silver, unless we have something to give, as an equivalent.

Are we never to be done with crude experiments, and rash experimenters ?   Gentlemen now tell us, that by reducing the amount of our currency, we can make one dollar go as far as four.   Granted, and I will tell you what more you may do.   By reducing it, still further, you may make one dollar go as far as ten.   But what follows ?   Why the laborer, who now gets his dollar a day, would then get ten cents, and the farmer, who has his land mortgaged, for $5,000, will have to pay $60,000, while the salaried officers of your government will have their incomes increased in the same proportion.   Secretary Woodbury for instance, who now receives six thousand dollars a year, will receive sixty thousand !   And the President, who receives twenty-five thousand, will receive two hundred and fifty thousand ! ?   It will indeed be a glorious golden age, a millenium for the office holders, but I guess, it will prove a little worse than purgatory, to some other folks.

I will tell you what further you may do : you may affix such heavy burdens on your banks, by curtailing them of their earnings, and by subjecting the existence of their charters, to the caprice of the popular will, which like the wind, bloweth as it listeth, and no man knows whence it cometh or whither it goeth, that no prudent man will invest capital in them. You may by your folly, drive away capital from your state, and cause it to enrich your rival neighbors.   But I will tell what you cannot do. After driving this capital away, you cannot get it back again, when you want it.   A man may very easily set his barn on fire, but he can't quite so easily put it out.

The delegate from the county, paid a sort of left handed compliment to the directors of the Bank of the United States, after saying of the bank, that it had fallen like Lucifer, to rise no more. He called the attention of the house, to the splendid dwellings of some of the directors.   In doing this, his object was, perhaps, merely to give pungency to his eloquence, perhaps to round a period, or perhaps to intimate his suspicion, that they had made a free use of the money of the institution, but of such an insinuation, I do not accuse him.   Whatever motive may have had the preponderance for the time in his fruitful intellect, I can assure him, and the house, that having served in that board for many years, and consequently had much intercourse with the members, and with the business of the bank, I can say, that to my certain knowledge, the directors were not large borrowers ; that they were men of intelligence, and spotless integrity ; that they were selected from among our most respectable citizens, and were incapable of using the funds of the bank, to any sinister purpose whatever ; and as to myself, that I never borrowed a dollar from the bank, or had the use of any of its funds, while a director, nor at any other time. I may add, that I am not now in the direction, having relinquished my seat, on becoming a member of this convention.

It has been insinuated also, that the Bank of the United States, was more devoted to the accommodation of the wealthy, than of the middle class of our fellow citizens.   This charge, like others, is without foundation. So far from this is the fact, that I have a distinct recollection, that for twelve years, during which time I was a director, we regularly continued the discount of one note in particular, which, in its origin was, I think, for thirty dollars, and afterwards reduced to twenty, at which latter rate it was renewed, from time to time, and remained unpaid when I left the institution. One such instance will probably suffice. Have we any other bank in the city, that discounts paper of smaller denomination? If so, let that bank be designated.

We have it constantly sung in our ears, and the delegate from Susquehanna, having caught the note, has been pleased to amuse himself and the house, with the harmony, that we have now in the United States, eighty millions of dollars in specie. How does he know this fact? Yes, I ask these "men of the woods," I do not say "babes in the woods," no I wish they were half as innocent—I ask then, these "men of the woods," who kindly undertake to instruct us on financiering and banking, how they know that we have these eighty millions? I tell them they are perfect babes upon this subject. They may know the amount that has been imported—and I acknowledge it to be great—because that is matter of record, no ship being permitted to discharge her cargo, or to break bulk, until she is regularly entered at the custom house, and a permit obtained. But no man, I repeat it, can know what sums have been exported. No entry of that need be made. Tens of thousands, and hundreds of thousands may be shipped off, and are shipped off, without being reported at all, so that even these very men of the woods of Susquehanna, who are to teach us, and put us to rights, according to the promised intimation of their delegate, will find their skill and information, on this subject, entirely unavailing.

Ship owners, for obvious reasons, do not let their ship's crews know what specie is on board, or that there is any on board; and, even the owners, and captains, may be ignorant of the sums stowed away by passengers among their baggage.

But, Gen. Jackson, forsooth, imported specie! I know he imported the French indemnity in gold. It was the property of the deeply injured and suffering merchants. He did not consult them on the subject, but they were nevertheless charged five per cent commissions, &c. for the favor, when, had it been left to their own management, they could have realized to themselves, a profit of ten per cent. But, it may be asked, did he not give them the gold on its arrival? No, he knew better what was good for them than they did. Some small portion was doled out to them, and the balance!—Perhaps the office holders can tell what became of that.

But, it is triumphantly asked, did not the gold bill bring specie into the country. It certainly did, and I know one merchant, who made eighty thousand dollars, by importing the precious article. How much was made by others, it is difficult to calculate. It opened a wide door for profitable speculation. Let us remember, by the way, that although this government demands specie of its debtors, it is very scrupulous of paying in specie, and precious little seems to escape from its strong box. Indeed, they do not appear ever to have been in the habit of paying away much specie. I speak with positiveness, when I say that they never placed a dollar of it in the United States Bank, not even of their original subscription of seven millions of the stock. The whole seven millions was paid by the government in certificates of the public debt, bearing an interest of five per cent. Not a farthing was paid in coin.

Specie, as a circulating medium, is expensive and inconvenient, for large transactions. The annual loss, by mere use, that is, by actual wear and friction, has been shewn to be very great, though scarcely noticed by the public, and ten, twenty or thirty per cent, loss in value, on an article of constant demand, becomes a very serious affair.

Again, suppose I wished to purchase in New Orleans, five thousand bales of cotton, which are probably worth two hundred and fifty thousand dollars. It would take a month, perhaps, to convey the money to that city. There would besides, be the hazard of accidents and robbery, by the way. Against these, I might insure, but not without paying a premium. Supposing, after all risks had been incurred, the price of cotton should have risen so high, as to render a purchase imprudent. I must, in that case, travel back with my load, at the same cost and risk, which I incurred in the outward journey, with the loss of interest in the bargain. Suppose on the other hand, instead of taking specie, I simply write to my correspondent, directing him to make the purchase, and draw on me for the amount. Whether he succeed or not, I lose no time, and I incur neither hazard nor expense. But, could not this be done, if we had no banks?—yes, doubtless—but either I must do as I have stated, or I must pay somebody else for doing it; for without some system of paper exchange, the transportation of coin could not be avoided. This might further be exemplified; but, I will waste no more of your time on so plain a matter. I may, however, observe, that if the specie in the case supposed, should never reach New Orleans, I should entirely forego my purchase, and all advantages connected with it, for before I could recover from the underwriters, the season might pass away, and my object in the purchase be frustrated.

The all powerful love, the people! The dear people! How patriotic thus openly to profess it. Many seem to love them so ardently, as to be willing to do almost every thing to serve themselves, out of this pure love. Marat loved the people. Robespiere loved the people. Napoleon loved the people—and may I say it? Andrew Jackson loved the people. They all in turn professed a reverence for republicanism, and it would be curious to trace their manner of shewing it. I will not attempt that. Don't you remember the caption of the first consul's edicts?

"French republic, one and indivisible."

"Liberty, equality, fraternity."

"I, Napoleon Buonaparte, decree."

Our form is more simple—

"I, Andrew Jackson, take upon me the responsibility."

We, of the convention, have a different mode of expressing our love and confidence, for and in the dear people. We proclaim aloud, as on the house top, that we are willing to trust the people with all power,

WEDNESDAY AFTERNOON, December 27, 1837.

SEVENTH ARTICLE.

The convention again resolved itself into a committee of the whole, Mr. Reigart in the chair, on the report of the committee to whom was referred the seventh article of the constitution.

The question being on the motion of Mr. Fuller, of Fayette, to amend the amendment offered by Mr. Read, as modified by him, by adding thereto the words following, viz :

" No bank shall issue any bill, check, or paper credit, of a less denomination than ten dollars."

Mr. Chauncey, of Philadelphia, said he was opposed to the amendment under consideration, offered by the gentleman from Fayette, to the modified amendment of the gentleman from Susquehanna. It consisted of provisions for the restriction of the issues of notes of a less denomination than ten dollars. He was opposed to the provision by itself; and, he was also opposed to it in connexion with the proposition of the gentleman from Susquehanna, and in connexion with other propositions which had been offered of similar import to this. He was opposed to the system which was submitted to the consideration of the committee; a system, as it had been avowed, of hostility to the banking institutions of the state. If this system was carred into effect, there was an end to the banking system; and, it was scarcely more than necessary to refer to the amendment to see that no other consequence could follow. It proposed to reduce the whole capital of the banks to thirty millions, to denominate the number of banks, to compel a limitation of the profits to seven per cent; to provide for the individual liability of stockholders; and, it farther placed these institutions at the will of the legislature. Was he not right, therefore, in supposing such a system—a system which reduces the capital of the institutions, limits the profits, makes the stockholders liable, and places them at the will of the legislature, a measure of hostility against the banks ? These are declared to be wholesome restrictions, offered in friendship, and for the purpose of preserving them in existence. But, when we had seen the axe put to the root of the tree; when we had seen the attempt to place these institutions, not on the footing of the law or the constitution, but at the will of the legislature, this was not the kind of friendship which the banks wished to receive. For his single self, he could not doubt that the certain operation of the system would be the total destruction of the banking system.

What should we say to the policy of this system ? The gentlemen on the other side of the question had deprecated the introduction of party feelings into this discussion. They wish to leave all party feelings out of the question; and, to bury all political considerations. But, it appeared to him that this appeal was not made in sincerity. No man could deprecate more than himself, that party feeling which destroys all freedom of action and reflection, and reduced men to mere machines. If he understood it, this was a question of political economy, in relation to which different views are entertained by the different parties which divide the community.   No matter if the subject is discussed on party grounds or not, because the question is essentially a party question.   It is insisted that restrictions shall be imposed, which will be destructive of the banking system.   This is evident from the tone of the various propositions themselves : from the course of argument in the committee ; and, from the avowed policy of the general government, with which all these movements are in perfect harmony.   By the reduction of capital, and of the number of banks ; by subjecting the stockholders to personal liability ; and, making the banks dependent on the legislative will, this result is made most clear.   The course of argument which has been pursued here is not to be reconciled with any principle but that of the destruction of the banks, the whole argument goes on the supposition that the banks are corrupt and under a system of wicked administration.   It takes it for granted that this is the fact ; that, from their very nature, they must be productive of evil to the mass of the community ; and, that they have built up, and continued to sustain a moneyed aristocracy in the country.   If gentlemen are sincere in these statements ; if they believe the evils to be such as they represent them to be, they must come to the conclusion that the system ought to be destroyed.   This was clear in the whole of the argument of the gentleman from Susquehanna, on every page of his speech ; therefore, there could be no doubt that his proposition to restrict, looked to the destruction of the system.

If gentlemen contemplate the destruction of the banks, it is idle, worse than idle, to talk of alleviating the existing evils by restrictions.   Let them come forward and state that the system should be for ever abandoned, because restrictions can never cure the existing evils.   A more efficient remedy must be found, in order to cure the great evils of which they complain, if these evils really exist.   Therefore, he contended that the gentlemen on the other side must be intent on the destruction of the banking system.   But, their arguments are also in accordance with the open and avowed course of the administration of the general government, which he took to be avowed hostility to the banks.   Let us (said Mr. C.) take a view of the policy of the general government in reference to this matter.   It may throw some light on the subject.   The policy, which is now pursued, commenced in the cabinet of the late president of the United States.   Previous to that, the whole policy of the government had been favorable to the banking system.   When the late president came into office, that system was in full operation, all minds had become shaped to it.   The credit system was incorporated with it.   When General Jackson came into office he found the country in a prosperous condition, and the people happy.   The whole page of history, from the fall of man to the present hour, never exhibited a more perfect scene of national happiness than was exhibited here.   This was not an overcharged description.   Such was the condition of the country, when General Jackson came into office.   What was the picture ?   The prosperity in every situation of life was unexampled.   The currency flowed in an even stream, and performed its office.   It performed the office of a currency more perfectly than had ever been known in any age or country.

Foreign exchanges were looking up; and, such was the equality of domestic exchange, that the difference in the cost of articles in different sections of the country, was of no account. If any one is disposed to deny the accuracy of this picture, let him put his finger on any page of history, and shew wherein this representation differs from the fact. The system had produced the happiest results; and, having called into action the industry of the country, and secured to labor its due compensation, had brought about universal prosperity. He would have been deemed a lunatic indeed, who, seeing the condition of the country, at the moment when General Jackson came into office, would have predicted that in so short a space of time, such results could have been produced as those which we had witnessed. A disastrous and sudden change came over us, and it became evident that there was in the government a greater power to do evil, than to do good. The general government determined on a change of the system; and, commenced an experiment for the purpose of ascertaining if there was sufficient pliability and subservience to its power, to enable it to carry this change into effect. It commenced a war against the bank by a movement against the branch of the Bank of the United States, at Portsmouth, in New Hampshire He would venture to assign as a reason, because no man ever attempted to assign any other reason for the removal of the public funds from that branch—

Mr. EARLE, of Philadelphia county, here asked if the gentleman was in order.

The CHAIR decided, that the discussion was in order, and directed the gentleman to proceed.

Mr. CHAUNCEY resumed :

The only reason that had been assigned was that the officers of this branch of the United States Bank had shewn themselves to be too unbending, and too upright, to lend themselves and the institution to the promotion of political objects. The President of the United States, then waged war against the institution, and it was known to all of us how that war had resulted. This man was the idol of the people, and disregarded the votes of congress, and the decision of the highest talents in the land, adopted his own constitutional construction, and broke down that beautiful fabric which the wisdom and virtue of our fathers had created, and which had been committed to us for preservation, and the people cheered what he did. It was to the hostility of this individual that the extenuation of the Bank of the United States was to be attributed. and the dissolution of that great corporation. The great capital of that institution was thus withdrawn from circulation.

The legislature of Pennsylvania, with great wisdom, and with great advantage to the citizens, granted a charter to this company, and secured the advantage of its great capital to the people of the state. The state received most timely and efficient aid to its financial resources, and, more than all, it founded a system of public instruction for its youth; and, it had, in short, the wisdom to establish an institution which, I predict will be of incalculable advantage as a probation to the business, and the currency of the country. But, Mr. Chairman, a proclamation went forth against this bank that it must be destroyed, and every effort has been made, and will continue to be made, to destroy it ; but, in vain, as I confidently believe. Sir, I shall not dwell upon the means any further than may be necessary, nor will I waste the valuable time of this body, by discussing the point whether the measures now before us are a part of the plan by which this object is to be accomplished, or whether they are connected with any scheme to build up any thing else.

The United States Bank had the public deposits taken away from it, before its charter expired. The government had cast upon itself the necessity of supplying the place of that institution. That bank was a part of the machinery of our financial system, and it was necessary that its place must be supplied. For this purpose, there were two projects set before the people ; the one being to create a metallic currency, and the other, to use the state banks as the fiscal agents of the government. One word only as to this scheme for a metallic currency.

I have never been able to persuade myself that there is any man, in the present state of the world, who has any knowledge of the business of the world, and of the quantity of the precious metals on the earth—who believes that we could have a metallic currency. Sir, there is no such thing on the face of the earth. The world is too old—or from some other cause, it happens that there is no such thing. You have heard of hard money states. France and Spain have been cited. But, is this an entire hard money currency ? A very small part of the business of the world is done by means of the precious metals. Even in such states, the currency is composed of various ingredients, embracing a great variety of articles. But, there is no longer any such thing in the world as a metallic currency. This is a dream ; it is not even a vision, and I will not waste more of your time in discussing such a matter.

The other scheme was to use the state bank as the fiscal agents of the government. A very short space of time was required to develope the difficulty of this system. At this time, no man believes in it from one end of the country to the other. These were the two favorite schemes of the government, to supply the place of that perfect fiscal agent, the United States Bank. No man, I say, believes in them now. But, the administration had other offices to perform in this work. While this clamour was heard through the country in relation to a metallic currency, it was thought proper to give some semblance of reality, some shew of sincerity to its professions, and the government, therefore, set itself to work to import specie. It caused gold to be imported from abroad at a time when there was a heavy debt due from the United States to Europe. It caused gold to be imported. It caused the French indemnity to be imported in gold. It was to be brought from a country, too, where gold is the basis of the currency, and into a country which was the debtor of Europe. In addition to this, the government caused the precious metals to be taken from the sea board where they were wanted, to the interior of the country where they were not wanted.

But, it is said, Mr. Chairman, that these were not the causes of the distresses which we have witnessed ; it is said, that these were not the causes of the suspension of specie payments on the part of the banks throughout the Union ; and, we are told that the true causes are overtrading, speculation, and overissues. I do not undertake to say, that evil has not arisen from overtrading, overissues and speculation. But, to my mind, it is clear that if the only evils which we have endured arose from the last mentioned causes ; and, from them alone, they would have been remedied in the same manner as evils of a similar description have been remedied in times past ; and, that nothing has produced these evils, but the unwise measures of the administration. I intend to prove the truth and soundness of this position.

At the time alluded to, the currency of the country was equal, and it was in the power of the Bank of the United States, as well as in accordance with its interests, to keep it so. Nothing can be clearer to my mind, than that the establishment of such an institution, is the only possible mode of regulating the financial concerns of this nation, in such a manner as to prevent a constant recurrence of the disastrous state of things, which we now witness. In the internal commerce of this country, inequality naturally arises ; and at one moment the products of the south and west are sold to the east and north, and are to be paid for. The debtor must find the means of payment, he has not got the means. Again—the account is reversed, and the same necessity exists on the other side, to provide for these payments.

It is a matter of gain which will inevitably be easily arranged, if this matter rests in the right hands. To provide these means, there is only one mode to produce equality—by the power of a unique interest ;—a *power* which shall gain with one hand, what it loses with the other. This is a simple operation, and will preserve every thing in its right place. But there is no other mode, which so presents itself to the mind as worthy of example, as that of a national bank with branches. This is the real mode, and our experience teaches us that it is the only rational mode by which the desired end can be obtained.

The government went astray from this principle, and went astray, too, at the moment when this principle was in full operation ; when the country was deriving advantages and blessings from it ; and at a time when it was obvious, that no man could find out an improvement in the system. And, sir, the government went on a false principle. The state banks are independent of each other in point of insterest ; they are, to each other, as so many individuals, and each seeks its own gain, without reference to its neighbor. The state banks did not equalize the exchanges—the state banks could not do it. The adoption of this new system, brought with it nothing but mischief. It has had an experiment, and those who brought it into existence have ungratefully repudiated their own offspring.

And here, Mr. Chairman, was the miserable end of this experiment. At the present moment, we have no system—we have no currency, and the government, in its extremity, has abandoned the course. I think I am justified in using this language. I say the government in its extremity, because it has tried its schemes—it has tried to administer the financial concerns of the nation through the state banks, and we all know what the result has been.

They have talked about a metallic currency, and they have imported a large quantity of gold for the purpose of trying the experiment; but they have never entered upon it. They have abandoned the course in extremity, because they found that the mode which had commended itself, to the judgment of wise men, and which they had dismissed from their councils, was the only mode in which the financial affairs of the country could be administered.   And now, to cover the retreat of the administration, it is declared that the government has no business with the currency; that it should have no connexion with banks, that it should conduct its own monetary concerns, as a private man does, and that it should keep its money in its own closet.

Sir, this abandonment of the currency on the part of the general government, is a matter of deep interest to the people of this country.   For my own part, I am not able to understand how the government is to divorce itself from the great national concern; I say, I am not able to understand how the government is to divorce itself from this great national public concern.   Is the currency of the country a matter of state, or of national interest?   Does any man doubt?   I ask for an answer to this inquiry—does any man say that a state can regulate the currency of this great country?   Or that all the states of this Union upon any possible supposition of harmony and concord of action, can regulate it?   I should like to see the process by which it is to be done.   I should like any man to point out to me, by what means the currency of this great country can be regulated, either by separate or joint action on the part of the states.   A state, I am aware, may do much for its own currency, but nothing beyond it.   Its power is limited to its own borders, and beyond these borders the subject is not within its control.   In the very nature of the thing, the matter belongs to the national government, and no where else, and if that government does not possess the requisite power, it must be given to it; for no where else can that power exist in such a manner as to accommodate itself to the wants and necessities of the people.

Sir, the present administration of the government attempts to cast off this *duty*; and the friends of that administration undertake to shape the whole system of our financial operations upon the supposition that the power belongs to the states.   To do this, they begin with the state banks, and undertake to put them under certain restrictions.   I think—looking to the source from which the series of resolutions which have been brought up for the consideration of this body, emanated—I think that this is to destroy all the banks.   My intention is to treat this as what it purports to be.   There is, to be sure, in these resolutions, a mixture of two subjects—a mixture of currency, and a mixture of questions in relation to bank restrictions, but my first objection to this system of currency and banking, is that it is premature.   The people have yet to decide whether this new principle of divorce, as it is termed, shall prevail or not.   I say, it is premature.   This great question is to be settled by the people of this country.   The people are to say whether the government is justified or not, in attempting to abandon this matter of a national currency.   I think that the indications are against it.   The people, according to present appearances, will have, as they ought to have, an administration which will take care of this great national concern; and not attempt to cast it from them as a matter with which they have nothing to do.

The necessity for state action has not arisen, and, in my opinion never will; but the matter will be left, where it ought to be left, with the gen-

sion from their course here—that the banks are under a moral obligation to have in their vaults, an amount of specie, equal to their notes in circulation.

This seemed to be the inevitable conclusion from the arguments of gentlemen on the other side. If it be not so, where is the foundation for the charge of dishonesty and fraud, on the part of these institutions. If it be not so, that they consider the banks under a moral obligation, to keep in their vaults, an amount of specie, equal to their paper in circulation, and the deposits made with them, where is the foundation for the charge of fraud against these institutions. Does any gentleman seriously believe that it is in the contract, that it is in the bond, or, that it is an implied understanding even with these institutions, that they were to keep an equal amount of specie in their vaults, with their notes in circulation ? Has any gentleman, who has ever seen a bank statement, believed for a single instant, that this was a part of the obligation of the banks ?

No, sir, every gentleman knows that it is neither an express or implied contract, according to the understanding of any one. No man who had the slightest knowledge of the subject of banking, could suppose for a moment, that banking could be conducted on that plan. The state of the world, is such as to render it necessary, that banking should be conducted on the most liberal system. The business of the world was of such a nature, that it must be carried on upon credit, and he thought we lived in an age of the world, when that was no longer an open and debateable question. The business of the world was now conducted upon credit ; and, do gentlemen wish to reverse the whole order of things ? It was as well known that the business of the world was transacted on credit, as it was that the sun was shining ; and, it was also known, that the business of the world could not be carried on with the precious metals. The precious metals are confined within a limited sphere. They have a certain office to perform, and that is but in a small way connected with the business transactions of the world.

In these days of credits, the precious metals were used but for some three or four purposes. In the first place, they were used in this country, in a species of manufactures, and they being used in this way, caused the precious metals of this country to diminish no little, and he did not believe it was in the power of legislation to prevent this. They are also used as change in the common transactions of life ; they were also used, to no inconsiderable extent and amount, in the settling of balances between different states, when these balances cannot be settled in any other way, except by the use of the precious metals. He believed he had now stated pretty much all the uses to which the precious metals are now, or were likely to be used for.

Now, sir, the circulation or currency of the country is paper, and a paper, too, which has answered our purposes well. It was the best kind of paper, and, as had already been shewn to the committee, it had answered the purposes of a country, with more safety, more certainty, and more stability, than the public paper of the government. The great object of both the rulers and the people, is, or should be, to suffer the specie to remain at rest for all other purposes, than those which he had just mentioned.

But, sir, the repose of what is justly called the specie basis, may be disturbed. It has been disturbed, by the unwise measures of the government, and the experiments which have been going on in relation to the currency.

Now, he would ask how the resolution before the committee was to extend the specie basis? If we have a right understanding of what is meant by the specie basis, he would ask gentlemen how this amendment was to extend it? He should think it would diminish it. Yes, sir, he should think that this amendment would diminish the specie basis. It was intended by the amendment, and, as was avowed by gentlemen in their arguments, to put more specie in circulation among the people, and consequently, it will diminish the basis. Besides this, it will be putting it more readily in the hands of those who desire to take the specie out of circulation for any purposes which they may desire. What are the reasons on which the passage of this amendment is grounded? He believed that two reasons were urged in its favor. First, that it will contract the issues of the banks; and, secondly, that it will put more specie in circulation. It was meant by this amendment, that where you now have notes under ten dollars, you should have specie or nothing. More coin and less paper, that is the text. It may be so, but the question still occurs, to what good purpose does this tend. Who is the gainer by this, if the notes can be converted into specie, at the pleasure of the holder? Are the notes not more convenient than the specie? The answer is obvious. Will not this measure diminish the quantity of specie wanted in the banks, as a basis. Will it not make it more convenient for those who are disposed to take it out of circulation, to do so?

But, says the gentleman from Luzerne, in speaking in support of this proposition, we will have a currency for the working man, which will be to him on Monday morning, what it was on Saturday night. The gentleman also told us, he believed in his conscience that this was the currency which the framers of the constitution designed for the mass of the people. He further said, that it was that currency of which the people are robbed. The banks take it from the hard hand of labor and put in place of it, worthless paper trash; and, that the persons who did this, were gamblers and speculators.

If this be argument, he (Mr. C.) confessed he could not see it. It was language, according to his sober judgment, not proper to be addressed to such a body of men as this. It may have its place, but he thought it to be out of place here. This language about robberies of the people, was merely figurative. It is a mere fancy sketch, and the picture is too striking for this deliberative body. The plain matter of fact is, that it differs not to the laborer, nor to any man, whether he receives his money in bank notes, convertible into specie, or in the specie itself. The hard hand of labor will draw exactly the same sustenance from the one as from the other.

Does the delegate from Luzerne, in his conscience believe, that the framers of the constitution decided what should be the currency for the mass of the people? If so, might he be permitted to ask the gentleman for his reasons?

Sir, the framers of the constitution said nothing like this. It is improbable that they meant it. If they meant it, why did they not say so? They were men who were every way competent to express their meaning, and nothing could be more easy than to have done so.

The CHAIR here stated to the gentleman that the hour which the rule fixed for members to speak, had expired.

Mr. SERGEANT would ask whether the gentleman was not entitled to the time which he had lost, when he was interrupted by the gentleman from the county of Philadelphia.

The CHAIR replied that he would be entitled to it.

Mr. HEISTER then moved that the gentleman have leave to proceed, and on that motion, called for the yeas and nays, which were ordered, and were yeas 62, nays 51, as follows:

YEAS—Messrs. Agnew, Ayres, Barndollar, Barnitz, Biddle, Bonham, Carey, Chambers, Chandler, of Philadelphia, Clarke, of Beaver, Cline, Cochran, Cope, Cox, Craig, Cummin, Cunningham, Darlington, Denny, Dickey, Dickerson, Doran, Dunlop, Far elly, Fleming, Forward, Harris, Hays, Helffenstein, Henderson, of Dauphin, Hiester, Hopkinson, Houpt, Ingersoll, Jenks, Konigmacher, Maclay, Martin, M'Dowell, M'Sherry, Meredith, Merrill, Miller, Pennypacker, Pollock, Porter, of Northampton, Purviance, Reigart, Royer, Russell, Scott, Serrill, Sill, Sterigere, Stevens, Sturdevant, Taggart, Wiedman, Woodward, Sergeant, *President* —62.

NAYS—Messrs. Banks, Barclay, Bedford, Bell, Bigelow, Brown, of Northampton, Brown, of Philadelphia, Clark, of Dauphin, Clarke, of Indiana, Cleavinger, Coates, Crain, Crawford, Crum, Curll, Darrah, Dillinger, Earle, Foulkrod, Fry, Fuller, Gamble, Gearhart, Gilmo e, Grenell, Hastings, Hayhurst, Hyde, Keim, Kennedy, Krebs, Magee, Mann, M'Cahen, Merkel, Montgomery, Nevin, Overfield, Read, Ritter, Saeger, Scheetz, Sellers, Seltzer, Shellito, Smith, of Columbia, Smyth, of Centre, Snively, Stickel, Todd, Weaver—51.

So the motion for leave was decided in the negative, not two-thirds voting therefor.

A motion was made by Mr. CHAUNCEY, that the committee now rise, Which motion was not agreed to.

Mr. STERIGERE rose and said, that as the committee had refused to give the gentleman from the city of Philadelphia, leave to proceed, he (Mr. S.) would resume the argument he had commenced this morning, and which he was precluded from finishing by the expiration of the hour allotted to each delegate by the rule.

Mr. S. here gave way to

Mr. INGERSOLL, who said that he was desirous to address one word to the good sense and the good feelings of the members of this body. It is obvious, said Mr. S., much confusion and difficulty will arise—

Mr. EARLE here rose, and called the gentleman from the county of Philadelphia (Mr. Ingersoll) to order.

The CHAIR said, that the gentleman from the county of Philadelphia, (Mr. Ingersoll) was perfectly in order.

Mr. EARLE appealed from the decision of the Chair,

And, after some conversation, the question on the appeal was taken, and the decision of the Chair was affirmed.

Mr. INGERSOLL then proceeded :

I was about to say, Mr. Chairman, at the time I was called to order, that much confusion and difficulty would arise from the enforcement of this new and very inconvenient rule, limiting the members to the short space of one hour, and that I hope I may be able to prevail upon the committee, to go into convention for a few minutes, with a view to see if we cannot get rid of it. I am authorized to say, that many of the members of this body, doubt the constitutional right of this convention, to impose such a restriction upon the power of speech—on the freedom of debate. I ask the committee to rise for the purpose of considering this question in convention.

i Mr. BELL here rose and inquired of the Chair, if this was a debateable question.

The CHAIR said, it was not.

Mr. BELL submitted, that he understood the gentleman from the county of Philadelphia, (Mr. Ingersoll) as proceeding to debate it.

Mr. INGERSOLL: Oh! no—I did not debate it—I merely premised it.

Mr. EARLE said, he did not precisely know whether his colleague from the county, (Mr. Ingersoll) had submitted a motion that the committee rise, or had merely made an appeal to the committee to do so. He (Mr. E.) was desirous, however, to move an amendment, and " to premise it " with a speech.

Mr. DENNY called the gentleman from the county of Philadelphia (Mr. Earle) to order.

The CHAIR said, there was no question now pending before the Chair, except the motion that the committee rise.

Mr. EARLE said, he was only going to submit an amendment, and "'to premise it " with a speech.

The CHAIR said, the delegate from the county of Philadelphia was out of order.

Mr. DICKEY rose, and demanded the previous question, and appealed to the committee to sustain him in this motion.

Mr. WOODWARD rose and inquired : " Does the gentleman from Beaver (Mr. Dickey) intend to violate the agreement made with me upon the floor ? I will thank him to answer this question."

Mr. EARLE : I call the gentleman from Luzerne (Mr. Woodward) to order.

Mr. DICKEY : I trust that the committee will give me the privilege to reply to the inquiry put to me by the gentleman from Luzerne.

Mr. EARLE : I call the gentleman from Beaver (Mr. Dickey) to order,

And, the question being then taken, the demand for the previous question was seconded by the requisite number of delegates.

Mr. BELL rose to a point of order. He submitted whether a piece of trickery was to cheat the members of this body, out of an intention which they honestly entertained, to—

Mr. STEVENS called the gentleman from Chester (Mr. Bell) to order.

Mr. BELL said, he had understood that a motion was pending that the committee rise. Pending that motion, the previous question had been called; the effect of which would be not only to get rid of the motion that the committee rise, but of all amendments to the resolution under discussion, in committee. That subject had been debated a long time, and at the very moment when he was under the impression that the question was about to be taken, the previous question was demanded. He submitted to the Chair, whether that demand was in order at this time.

The CHAIR said, that the motion, in the opinion of the Chair, was in order at this time.

Some further conversation ensued on a point of order,

And on the question,

Shall the main question be now put ?

The yeas and nays were required by Mr. SMYTH, of Centre, and nine-teen others, and are as follows, viz :

YEAS—Messrs. Agnew, Ayres, Baldwin, Barnitz, Biddle, Carey, Chambers, Chand-ler, of Philadelphia, Chauncey, Clark, of Dauphin, Cline, Coates, Cochran, Cope, Cox, Craig, Cummin, Cunningham, Darlington, Denny, Dickey, Dickerson, Doran, Dunlop, Farrelly, Forward, Hays, Henderson, of Dauphin, Hopkinson, Houpt, Inger-soll, Jenks, Konigmacher, Maclay, M'Dowell, M'Sherry, Meredith, Merrill, Penny-packer, Pollock, Royer, Scott, Serrill, Sill, Sterigere, Stevens, Weidman, Young, Sergeant, *President*—49.

NAYS—Messrs. Banks, Barclay, Barndollar, Bedford, Bell, Bigelow, Bonham, Brown, of Northampton, Brown, of Philadelphia, Clarke of Beaver, Clarke, of Indiana, Cleavinger, Crain, Crawford, Crum, Curll, Darrah, Dillinger, Earle, Fleming, Foulk-rod, Fry, Fuller, Gamble, Gearhart, Gilmore, Grenell, Harris, Hastings, Hayhurst, Helffenstein, Hiester, Hyde, Keim, Kennedy, Kerr, Krebs, Magee, Mann, Martin, M'Cahan, M'Call, Merkel, Miller, Montgomery, Nevin, Overfield, Porter, of North-ampton, Purviance, Reigart, Read, Ritter, Russell, Seager, Scheetz, Sellers, Seltzer, Shellito, Smith, of Columbia, Smyth, of Centre, Snively, Stickel, Sturdevant, Tag-gart, Thomas, Todd, Weaver, Woodward—68.

[Mr. STERRIGERE, here resumed and concluded his remarks, for which see APPENDIX.]

Mr. WOODWARD having addressed the committee until the expiration of the hour allowed by the rule of the committee of the whole on that subject.

[The remarks of Mr. WOODWARD, not having been returned in time for insertion in their proper place, will be given in the APPENDIX.]

A motion was made by Mr. WOODWARD,

That in this instance the rule be dispensed with, and that leave be granted him to proceed with his remarks.

And on the question,

Will the committee of the whole agree to the motion ?

The yeas and nays were required by Mr. Bell and nineteen others, and are as follows, viz:

Yeas—Messrs. Baldwin, Bonham, Chambers, Clarke, of Indiana, Craig, Cunning, ham, Denny, Dickey, Dillinger, Donagan, Doran, Dunlop, Flaming, Forward, Gamble, Hastings, Helffenstein, Hiester, Hopkinson, Ingersoll, Keim, Krebs, Maclay, Martin, M'Dowell, M'Sherry, Merrill, Nevin, Porter, of Lancaster, Porter, of Northampton, Purviance, Read, Royer, Scheetz, Serrill, Shellito, Sterigere, Stickel, Taggart, Weidman. —40.

Nays—Messrs. Agnew, Ayres, Banks, Barndollar, Barnitz, Bedford, Rell, Biddle, Bigelow, Brown, of Northampton, Carey, Chandler, of Philadelphia, Chauncey, Clarke, of Beaver, Clarke, of Dauphin, Cleavinger, Cline, Coates, Cochran, Cope, Cox, Crain, Crawford, Crum, Cummin, Curll, Darlington, Darrah, Dickerson, Earle, Fry, Fuller, Gearhart, Gilmore, Grenell, Harris, Hayhurst, Hays, Henderson, of Dauphin, Houpt, Jenks, Kerr, Konigmacher, Mann, M'Cahen, M'Call, Merkel, Miller, Montgomery, Over-field, Pennypacker, Pollock, Reigart, Ritter, Russell, Saeger, Scott, Sellers, Seltzer, Sill, Smith, of Columbia, Smyth, of Centre, Snively, Stevens, Sturdevant, Todd, Weaver, Young—67.

So the question was determined in the negative.

Mr. Agnew, of Beaver, rose and said, that the principle of this amendment had been acted on already, in convention, at Harrisburg. At that time, the subject had undergone an ample discussion, and time was given for every gentleman to express his opinions. The convention had then come to a decision, and such as his judgment was willing to rest on. And when we saw the course pursued by gentlemen in introducing into the discussion—

Mr. Woodward rose to a point of order.

Mr. Stevens called the gentleman from Luzerne to order.

Mr. Agnew demanded the previous question, which was sustained by the number required by the rule.

And on the question,
Shall the main question be now put?

The yeas and nays were required by Mr. M'Cahen, and nineteen others, and are as follow, viz:

Yeas—Messrs. Agnew, Ayres, Baldwin, Barndollar, Barnitz, Biddle, Carey, Chambers, Chandler, of Philadelphia, Chauncey, Clarke, of Beaver, Clark, of Dauphin, Cline, Cochran, Cope, Cox, Craig, Crum, Cunningham, Darlington, Denny, Dickey, Dickerson, Dunlop, Farrally, Forward, Harris, Hays, Henderson, of Dauphin, Hiester, Houpt, Jenks, Kerr, Konigmacher, Maclay, M'Call, M'Sherry, Meredith, Merrill, Merkel, Montgomery, Pennypacker, Pollock, Porter, of Lancaster, Purviance, Reigart, Royer, Russell, Saeger, Scott, Serrill, Sill, Snively, Stevens, Thomas, Todd, Weidman, Young, Sergeant, President—59.

Nays—Messrs. Banks, Barclay, Bedford, Bell, Bigelow, Bonham, Brown, of Northampton, Brown, of Philadelphia, Clarke, of Indiana, Cleavinger, Coates, Crain, Crawford, Cummin, Curll, Darrah, Dillinger, Donagan, Doran, Earle, Fleming, Foulkrod, Fry, Fuller, Gamble, Gearhart, Gilmore, Grenell, Hastings, Hayhurst, Helffenstein, Hopkinson, Hyde, Ingersoll, Keim, Kennedy, Krebs, Magee, Mann, Martin, M'Cahen, Miller, Nevin, Overfield, Porter, of Northampton, Read, Ritter, Scheetz, Sellers, Seltzer, Shellito, Smith, of Columbia, Smyth, of Centre, Sterigere, Stickel, Sturdevant, Taggart, Weaver, Woodward—59.

So the committee determined that the main question should not now be taken.

Mr. INGERSOLL said, if it was the pleasure of the body to discuss this question, out of time and out of temper, he should endeavor to proceed as well as he could, in time, and, he would assure gentlemen, in perfect good temper. He thought it to be a question, in comparison with which, all the other questions, which we have had before, were of minor importance. He had a great deal more to say upon it, than he could possibly say in the hour which would be allotted to him ; and he must, therefore, not only abridge, but mutilate his argument.

Mr. I. here gave way, at the request of several gentlemen, to

Mr. COCHRAN, on whose motion the committee rose and reported progress.

The PRESIDENT having resumed the chair,

Mr. PORTET, of Northampton, moved a suspension of the rule, for the purpose of offering a resolution to rescind the resolution restricting members to one hour in debate.

Mr. INGERSOLL called for the yeas and nays on this motion, which were ordered, and were, yeas 39, nays 52, as follows :

YEAS—Messrs. Baldwin, Bell, Biddle, Carey, Chambers, Clarke, of Indiana, Coates, Cochran, Cope, Crain, Cummin, Curll, Denny, Dickey, Donagan. Doran, Dunlop, Fleming, Foulkrod, Gamble, Helffenstein, Houpt, Ingersoll, Jenks, Kennedy, Magee, Martin, M'Cahen, M'Dowell, M'Sherry, Meredith, Porter, of Lancaster, Porter, of Northampton, Royer, Scott, Serrill, Sterigere, Thomas, Woodward, Sergeant, *President*—39.

NAYS—Messrs. Banks, Barclay, Barndollar, Barnitz, Bedford, Bigelow, Bonham, Clarke, of Beaver, Clark, of Dauphin, Cline, Crawford, Darlington, Darrah, Dillinger, Earle, Fuller, Gearhart, Gilmore, Grenell, Harris, Hastings, Hayhurst, Hays, Hyde, Keim, Kerr, Krebs, Maclay, Mann, M'Call, Miller, Montgomery, Nevin, Overfield, Pollock, Reigart, Read, Ritter, Russell, Saeger, Scheetz, Sellers, Shellito, Smith, of Columbia, Smyth, of Centre, Snively, Sturdevant, Taggart, Weaver, Weidman—52.

So the convention refused to suspend the rule.

The convention then adjourned.

THURSDAY, DECEMBER 28, 1837.

The PRESIDENT laid before the convention a communication from the clerk of the commissioners of the county of Philadelphia, accompanied with the following statement presented in compliance with a resolution of the convention, adopted on the 22d instant.

STATEMENT,

Showing the annual cost of each of the State courts of justice, in the city and county of Philadelphia, for the four years prior to the first day of December, 1837, and the fees received out of the county funds, by the Attorney General, or his deputies, on the several criminal prosecutions therein, during that period of time.

For the year ending	Supreme court.	District court.	Court of Common Pleas	Oyer and terminer and Quarter sessions.	Mayor's court.	Recorder's court.	Fees received by the Attorney General.
November 30, 1834	$1,482 32	$6,876 18	$2,721 25	$10,165 18	$7,068 54		$1,615 50
" 1835	2,070 48	8,962 06	3,506 12	11,397 85	8,017 81		1,801 50
" 1836	2,891 40	11,750 97	4,526 76	11,910 39	9,128 19		1,593 00
" 1837	3,014 95	13,026 72	4,811 58	9,048 22	12,481 48	$8,051 12	2,301 50
	$9,459 21	$40,615 93	$15,565 71	$42,527 64	$37,596 02	$8,051 12	$7,311 50

NOTE.—The fees received by the Attorney General are included in the respective amounts charged to the different courts.
Attest—J. PLANKINTON, Clerk to County Commissioners.

COUNTY COMMISSIONER'S OFFICE, Philadelphia, December 28, 1837.

Mr. Doran, of Philadelphia county, moved that the communication be printed, which motion was decided in the negative.

The communication was then laid on the table.

Mr. Earle, of Philadelphia county, presented a petition from citizens of Philadelphia county, praying that the right of trial by jury may be extended to every human being.

Which was laid on the table.

Mr. Riter, of Piladelphia county, presented two memorials from Philadelphia county, praying that measures may be adopted so as effectually to prevent all amalgamation between the white and coloured population, so far as regards the government of the state.

Which was also laid on the table.

Mr. Porter, of Northampton, from the committee to whom was referred the letter of the auditor general, accompanied with documents relative to the affairs of the banks of this commonwealth, for the purpose of arranging the same for publication, made report:—

" That the abstract of the affairs of the banks in this commonwealth, on the first discount days in the months of January, May, June and November, of the current year, be printed entire, so arranged as to exhibit, at one view, the state of each bank on each of these days.

" That the abstracts of the affairs of the Bank of the United States, as furnished monthly since March last, in the recapitulating statement of each month, be printed in like manner. They, therefore, offer the following resolution, viz:—

" Resolved, That the said abstracts be printed according to the form herewith submittted, under the direction of the secretary."

The resolution was then taken up for consideration, read a second time, considered and agreed to.

Mr. Porter, of Northampton, moved, that there be printed five hundred extra copies of this communication, for the use of the convention.

Mr. Dickey called for the yeas and nays on this question, and they were ordered.

The question was than taken on the motion of Mr. Porter, and decided in the negative, as follows, viz:

Yeas—Messrs. Baldwin, Bell, Chambers, Cochran, Cope, Crain, Cunningham, Dillinger, Dunlop, Forward, Foulkrod, Grenell, Helffenstein, Houpt, Kennedy, Magee, M'Cahen, M'Sherry, Merrill, Overfield, Porter, of Lancaster, Porter, of Northampton, Reigart, Scheetz, Scott, Serrill, Smith, of Columbia, Stevens, Sergeant, *President—*28.

Nays—Messrs. Agnew, Ayres, Banks, Barclay, Barndollar, Bedford, Bigelow, Bonham, Carey, Clarke, of Beaver, Clark, of Dauphin, Clarke, of Indiana, Cleavinger, Cline, Craig, Crum, Cummin, Curll, Darlington, Darrah, Denny, Dickey, Dickerson, Donegan, Earle, Fleming, Fry, Fuller, Gamble, Gearhart, Gilmore, Harris, Hastings, Hayhurst, Hays, Henderson, of Dauphin, Hiester, Hopkinson, Ingersoll, Jenks, Keim, Kerr, Konigmacher, Krebs, Maclay, Mann, M'Call, Meredith, Merkel, Miller, Montgomery, Pennypacker, Purviance, Read, Riter, Ritter, Royer, Russell, Saeger, Sellers, Shellito, Smyth, of Centre, Sterigere, Stickel, Sturdevant, Taggart, Thomas, Todd, Weaver, Woodward, Young—73.

Mr. INGERSOLL, of Philadelphia county, submitted a motion as follows, viz:

" That the convention reconsider the vote of the 26th instant, on the second division of the resolution, in the words following, viz: " And that this convention will adjourn *sine die* on the second day of February next,"

Mr. DICKEY, of Beaver, called for the yeas and nays on this motion, and they were ordered.

Mr. INGERSOLL said it had been strongly doubted by very high authority, whether a resolution abridging a debate to an hour, is constitutional. He wanted all the attention of gentlemen to the seventh section of the ninth article of the present constitution, which runs thus:

" The printing presses shall be free to every person who undertakes to examine the proceedings of the legislature, or any branch of government: and no law shall ever be made to restrain the right thereof. The free communication of thoughts and opinions, is one of the invaluable rights of man; and every citizen may freely speak, write and print, on any subject being responsible for the abuse of that liberty," &c.

He had no idea, when he voted to fix the day of adjournment, of two facts: one, that fixing the day has little or no effect, because the majority can unsettle the descision at any time. This was a fact with which he was not precisely acquainted. The other fact was, that this extraordinary, and as he was inclined to think it, unconstitutional resolution, limiting the right of a speaker to address the convention, to one hour, which had been sprung upon us, would be the result of the adoption of the other resolution. He now moved the reconsideration of the vote, with a view to the reconsideration of the whole matter, in order that no injustice may be imposed on the rights of debate. He would refer gentlemen to the circumstances which occurred yesterday, which were not to be remembered with pleasure—not only because they took place in the presence of the general auditory, but because members of the legislature were present. The average of our ages he took to be about forty-five years; and it might naturally be supposed that we should be able to deliberate calmly and and efficiently, without any other check than the previous question. Deliberation was always more benefici 1 than action. Deliberation can tend to nothing but good, while action may be injurious. As fixing of the day of adjournment had produced the other resolution, and as a great question had been introduced last night, on which, although we are in an unquestionable minority, the magnanimity of our opponents should permit us to be heard, I trust, said Mr. I., that my motion will prevail, and that we shall hereafter profit by the experience of yesterday.

Mr. DICKEY, of Beaver, could not discover that there was any connexion between the two resolutions. He thought it would have been much the better plan to reconsider the resolution limiting the time of speaking to one hour. He had voted for that resolution, because he did believe that the gentleman from the county of Philadelphia desired to accelerate the termination of our business. Nothing had occured to convince him that there was any thing wrong in fixing the day of adjournment. He was willing to give full time for debate on the subject of corporations, which he regarded as an important one; and he had, in every instance, when it was asked, voted in favor of giving a speaker leave to continue his remarks beyond the hour.

He hoped the present motion would not prevail, as he did not see that there was any sufficient reason brought forward to justify its adoption.

He was anxious, as he had already said, that those gentlemen who had not spoken on the subject of corporations, should have an opportunity of doing so. And, whenever a motion had been made to permit a gentleman to proceed with his remarks, he had invariably voted in favor of the motion, as he would continue to do. He was in favor of rescinding so much of the rule as related to the committee of the whole. He hoped the motion to reconsider the resolution would not prevail.

Mr. REIGART, of Lancaster, hoped the motion to reconsider would not be agreed to. He thought the convention ought to go on with their business as fast as they possibly could, for two or three weeks longer, at least, and then they could be the better able to judge whether they could be able to adjourn on the 2d of February. The gentleman from the county of Philadelphia, (Mr. Ingersoll) has remarked, that the rule restricting debate was unconstitutional. What, he (Mr. R.) would ask, was the previous question, but an arbitrary rule? It cuts off all amendments, and all debate. It was like the rule to limit speeches to an hour; or the rule to prohibit a delegate from speaking more than twice on the same question, without leave. It was nothing more. The principle was the same as applicable to both. As well might the gentleman tell us that all the rules of this body were unconstitutional, because they were arbitrary. He was of opinion that no possible good could result from reconsidering the resolution at this time.

Mr. EARLE, of Philadelphia county, said he felt very greatly indebted to his colleage, (Mr. Ingersoll) for the instruction he had afforded the committee. It enabled him (Mr. E.) to solve a riddle that had greatly puzzled him for the last six weeks, and that was—to find out what was in order. According to the little book he now held in his hand, "every citizen may freely speak, write and print on any subject, being responsible for the abuse of that liberty." Yes, the constitution of Pennsylvania says, we may speak on any subject, and, therefore, any thing and every thing is in order. But inasmuch as this convention was not exactly acting under the constitution, and as there might be some doubt as to whether a gentleman ought to be allowed to speak as long as he pleased, and particularly as the previous question prevailed, and had been enforced both by his colleague and himself, the clause quoted by the gentleman (Mr. Ingersoll) was not applicable here. He hoped the motion to reconsider would not prevail. He had been opposed to fixing a day, but as that was done, he would not reconsider.

He was very sorry to hear the delegate from Beaver (Mr. Dickey) express his readiness to vote for the reconsideration of the rule which limits members to speak one hour only in committee of the whole. He was sorry to hear the declaration from the gentleman, because he (Mr. E.) went hand in hand with him, with regard to putting an end to debate. He thought the gentleman called for the previous question, in order to put an end to the debate on corporations. Surely the delegate could not be in favor of taking such a course as would inevitably protract the debate for four or six weeks longer? He (M. E.) hoped not.

How could the gentleman reconcile such a vote with the call for the previous question yesterday? He thought there were important amendments yet to be offered. He trusted that this debate would not be cut off, as it would doubtless be, if this rule limiting members was not reserved. He hoped it would not be rescinded—that this salutary rule would be preseved, for he could not believe it was the wish of gentlemen's constituents, that they should spend more than one hour each, and thus close their labors in six weeks. Indeed, the advocates of the motion submitted this morning, admitted that there was no possible hope of carrying it. He was determined to vote against every attempt that might be made to rescind the arbitrary rule, as it had been denominated. He regretted that it had become his duty to vote against allowing the gentleman from the city of Philadelphia (Mr. Chauncey) to proceed further with his remarks. But we had by melancholy experience found, that if one gentleman was allowed to speak for more than an hour, others must have the same privilege conceded to them. He, therefore, under all the circumstances of the case, felt himself bound to vote against the motion to reconsider.

Mr. PORTER, of Northampton, said, had he been present, he would have voted against the resolution fixing the day of adjournment, as well as against the adoption of the gag law, to prevent the delegates from speaking more than one hour. He, himself, occupied the floor three hours and a half on the subject of corporations, and he would not have cut off other gentlemen who wished to express their sentiments. He had not troubled the body with long speeches, and had only on two occasions exceeded an hour. He felt a strong repugnance to measure gentlemen's efforts by the hour. It was a well known fact, that some delegates here, possessed the faculty of saying as much in one hour, as others did in an hour and a half. He apprehended that the gentleman from the county of Philadelphia (Mr. Ingersoll) was right when he said that the resolution was a violation of the spirit, if not the letter of the constitution. On all subjects he wished to have light and knowledge, and the way to obtain it, was by a full and extended discussion. The convention had the power when it chose, to put an end to unnecessary debate.

What was the effect of the rule limiting members to one hour. Any gentleman could speak as often as he pleased in committee of the whole. And what was the result? Every member got up and spoke an hour, and afterwards obtained the floor again, and continued their arguments. If gentlemen were not allowed to finish their arguments, they would speak twice or thrice, instead of once. So that the convention had the speeches a little at one time, and a little another, instead of all at once. It was in vain to attempt to prevent members from expressing their sentiments. But, being detained in that way, they did not produce the same effect on the audience, as if spoken at one time. He had read an anecdote of two boys, who were ordered to sleep together in one bed, and one complained of the other that he did not get his half of the bed. The second said that he did get his half, when the other replied that he had no right to take his half in the middle, and leave him a quarter on each side. The great leader of reform, himself, had lately given a fair exemplication of the absurdity of the rule, by speaking a little now and a little then, instead of delivering his views *in extenso*—all was heads and tails—a perfect *olla podrida*.

Mr. BROWN, of Philadelphia county, said that his colleague (Mr. Earle) had alluded to the rule which prohibits a delegate from speaking more than twice.

[Here Mr. PORTER said—No sir, there is no such rule.]

Mr. BROWN, knew that an attempt had been made to adopt a rule of that kind. Perhaps, the gentleman from Northampton, (Mr. Porter) was correct in his statement. When the convention commenced its labors, his desire was to go into the consideration of whatever subject might be brought before it, and deliberate upon them as long as was absolutely necessary, leaving it to the good sense and discretion of the delegates to arrest the debate whenever it might be deemed proper. The convention had now, however, thought it expedient to check debate with a view to bring its labors to a close as speedily as possible. The gentleman from Beaver, (Mr. Dickey) must have been satisfied that gentlemen were anxious to come to a termination of their labors, and that the convention did not sit hours enough, or that there was too much speaking.

He regretted to hear the gentleman from Beaver, (Mr. Dickey) say that he was willing to rescind the rule as far as it related to the committee of the whole, as he was apprehensive that they could never get to second reading previous to the day fixed for adjournment.

He (Mr. Brown) would say that if it was the determination of the convention to adjourn on the 2d of February, he would vote that no delegate should speak more than once for one hour. And, he would go farther, and prevent a gentleman from speaking twice. From the assembling of the convention up to the present time, the conduct of certain members had been such as to cause him great pain. He would not make any personal allusions, lest he might be called to order, and no good would be answered by it. He came here with a firm determination to do his duty, and he trusted that he had fulfilled it. The fact was, there had been placed over the convention in the shape of rules, a sort of machinery, which had prevented him and others from introducing the amendments they desired. The people had not seen these things ; but with respect to his own motives he would leave the people to judge. He was well aware that it behooved him to speak cautiously, as he was now treading on unsafe ground. He would pledge himself that, in as much as the people could not see things in their proper colors, as they were managed here, he would, on some future occasion, shew them up in their proper light elsewhere. He had felt the influence which prevailed here, from the very commencement of the labors of the convention up to this moment. The convention had been four or five months deliberating on subjects—many of them, certainly, of the highest importance ; and doubtless, he had had his full share in the various discussions that had taken place. He did not mean to say that the object of gentlemen had been to bring the convention into discredit, nor to leave matters in a crude and indigested mass, in order that the people might reject the constitution. He for one, was in favor of rescinding the resolution fixing the day of adjournment, and going on deliberately and steadily until they had completed their labors, and then adjourn. He had rather stay there a year than not to make those amendments which the people desired.

Mr. FULLER of Fayette, said he was opposed to reconsidering the resolution to adjourn *sin ' die*. He had voted against the adoption of it, believing that it would be time enough to introduce such a resolution when the convention should have approached nearer to a termination of its labors. The convention, nevertheless, had thought proper to adopt it. And now, without waiting to see whether the convention could get through its labors by the time fixed for adjourning, a motion was made to reconsider the resolution. He was opposed to it for more reasons than one. In the first place, it appeared to him unbecoming the dignity of this body to vote for a resolution without being at all certain that the convention would be able to terminate its business by the day fixed. If our business was not disposed of, by the 2d of February, the resolution could be rescinded by the same majority that passed it. He could not at present, give his consent to the rescinding of the resolution. The question pending was one of the greatest importance, and he could not do any thing that would have the effect of preventing those delegates, who had not yet given their sentiments, from expressing them, when it was manifest there were several yet to speak.

He would put it to the gentleman from Beaver, (Mr. Dickey) to say when we would be able to get through our labors, if the the resolution was to be rescinded. He (Mr. F.) believed that every gentleman might so abridge his remarks as to be able to say all that he desired in the course of an hour. Every man, at least, could give his opinions. And, although party spirit might urge on many members of this body to pursue a course which was calculated to prevent other delegates from offering their opinions, or putting their views in the form of amendments to the constitution, yet it was not the less their duty to persevere. It was too true that a certain party in this convention labored under great disadvantages with respect to the amendments they desired to propose, on account of the rules of the body being brought to bear against them. They could not be brought forward in the form desired by their constituents. All that he (Mr. F.) desired, was to have their propositions met fairly, and if a majority chose to vote them down, still he would be satisfied that he had discharged his duty. He maintained that every amendment ought to be met fairly. The party spirit, and bank spirit might have induced the officers of this body to believe it to be their duty to evade questions which are not palatable to them. And this spirit might have reached even the President himself. He would, however, renew his efforts, and would offer such amendments as he conceived to be right and proper. He was, as he had already said, against rescinding the resolution, fixing the day of adjournment; because if it was withdrawn, another would, in all probability, be brought forward, and thus we should lose time by this course of proceeding. If the convention found, a short time before the 2d of February, that they could not get through by that date, they could rescind the resolution.

The gentleman from the county of Philadelphia, (Mr. Ingersoll) had expressed his belief that the resolution restricting delegates to speak, but an hour each, was unconstitutional. Now, he (Mr. F.) must say that such an impression was rather extraordinary. The "father of the convention" had spoken of the arbitrary character of the rules of this body. In his (Mr. F's.) humble judgment, if arbitrary rules were not in operation, we might give up all idea of making amendments to the constitution.

Mr. STERIGERE, of Motgomery, said some gentlemen seemed to think that they possessed rights which others had not. The delegate who had just taken his seat, had told the convention that he has a right to submit such propositions or amendments as he thought proper. He (Mr. S.) would ask whether, on the same principle, every other gentleman had not a right to give his reasons and opinions in regard to them.

[Here Mr. FULLER said—certainly he has.]

Mr. S. Then why did the delegate attempt to prevent arguments from being made? Why was he for suppressing discussion? The gentleman laid down a principle to which his practice was entirely opposed. He (Mr. S.) did not think the resolution respecting debate, unconstitutional. He maintained that this body had the power and the right to adopt such rules and regulations, as they deemed proper, for facilitating the despatch of their business. Our own legislature, and congress also, are guided by expediency in the adoption of their own rules, and are the sole judges of what is right and proper to aid them in the discharge of their duties. He was not to be intimidated by the threats of the gentleman from the county of Philadelphia, (Mr. Brown) who threatened to hold up.—

Mr. BROWN begged to explain. He had not alluded to the gentleman from Montgomery (Mr. Sterigere.) The gentleman never entered his mind.

Mr. STERIGERE: The gentleman spoke—

Mr. BROWN rose for the purpose of saying something—when

Mr. STERIGERE observed—If the gentlemen will let me go on—

The CHAIR said—The gentleman from the county of Philadelphia, rose to explain.

Mr. SRERIGERE: I do not object to his explaining, but he has no right to make the threat he did.

Mr. BROWN repeated his explanation—that he made no allusion to the gentleman.

Mr. STERIGERE said that he understood the gentleman as well as he did himself. He (Mr. S.) was among those whose votes the delegate threatened to expose here and elsewhere. The gentleman could not explain away the fact. He (Mr. S.) had voted by mistake, for the resolution to adjourn on the 2d of February, and did not correct his vote, because he thought the resolution would be reconsidered. He had always voted against restrictions on the freedom of debate, because they were productive of no good. Fixing the day of adjournment was of no use. He thought the convention would be able to get through with its business in a few weeks, and hence he would do nothing that was calculated to lead to unnecessary haste in despatching the business yet to be done. What, he asked, was the scene witnessed in congress just before closing their labors? Nothing but bustle and confusion—a complete bear garden. What was done at Harrisburg for the last few days before the convention adjourned to meet here? Why nothing but talking. And, what had been the effect of the rule adopted limiting members to speak one hour only? Confusion and a waste of time. Not one half of yesterday was taken up with profitable discussion, and the time was thrown away in considering trivial motions and calling for the yeas and nays. He was desirous that the convention should adjourn as soon as possible; but still, if found necessary, he should have no objection to remain as long as his duty required him to do. As he had before said, he was opposed to rescinding the resolution. If however, the convention could adjourn by the middle of January, he should be very much gratified: but, if they must sit till the 2d of February, he would with patience submit, as it was his duty to do.

Mr. DENNY of Allegheny, said that he had been struck with the remarks of the gentleman from the county of Philadelphia, (Mr. Brown) and the gentleman from Fayette, (Mr. Fuller) who had both complained that the rules of the convention had operated very much against those who came here to reform the constitution.

Mr. FULLER explained. He had not said that the rules interfered with his proposition, but that they had been manœuvred so as to evade and prevent the amendments from being offered in the form most desirable to his constituents.

Mr. DENNY: The gentleman did complain that the propositions which he thought it his imperative duty to submit, were evaded—were not met on account of the rules of the convention.

Mr. FULLER: He had said that it was owing to a sort of manœuvre by the majority of this body.

Mr. DENNY thought that this was a remark which called for an explanation, because it was reflecting not only on the convention itself, but also on the presiding officer. He begged to call the attention of gentlemen to another remark, which he made a note of, and at the moment it fell from the lips of the delegate. The gentleman said that the party spirit and the bank spirit might have reached the President himself. He (Mr. D.) was about to call the delegate to order—for it was grossly out of order. The gentleman spoke of party spirit and the bank spirit reaching the officers of the convention! What sort of language was that to go to the people of the state? It might do for the gentleman's constituents; but the people of this commonwealth knew who was the presiding officer of this convention, and would do justice to the spirit by which he was animated. They would not doubt but what he was guided by the most pure, honorable and impartial motives. He (Mr. D.) denied that there had been any evasion or infringment of the rules, and insisted that they had been fairly and impartially observed. The President of the convention had been sustained at all times. If the gentleman had any thing to say, either with regard to the conduct of the presiding officer or that of any other member of the convention, he had better make his charge here where members might be confronted face to face, than go home and do it. Did the gentleman suppose that the grave charge which he had made would be allowed to pass without contradiction ? No, he could not. The delegate from the county of Philadelphia, (Mr. Brown) had complained that the rules had operated as a kind of machinery to prevent him and others from getting in the amendments they wished, to reform the constitution. The gentleman surely was aware that a great many propositions had been offered as amendments, which in fact, were not amendments. Alterations do not always mean reform. Many attempts had been made to introduce amendments of the most vague, wild and visionary character. To have adopted them would have been to make a worse constitution than is possessed by any state in the Union. The gentleman might when he went home, go through his district, and tell his story—his grievances. He (Mr. D.) hoped that if the gentleman had any charges to make, that he would make them here, where they could and would be met. It was his duty to do so, and not return to his constituents and defame the character of this convention.

The debate was continued by Messrs. DENNY and FLEMING,

When Mr. HAYHURST rose, and said, that as he believed all the members were ready to vote, he would call for the previous question.

Which demand was seconded by the requisite number of delegates.

And on the question,

Shall the main question be now put ?

The yeas and nays were required by Mr. REIGART and Mr. SMYTH, of Centre, and are as follows, viz :

YEAS—Messrs. Agnew, Ayres, Banks, Barclay, Barndollar, Barnitz, Bedford, Bell, Bigelow, Bonham, Brown, of Northampton, Brown, of Philadelphia, Carey, Chambers, Chandler, of Philadelphia, Chauncey. Clarke, of Beaver, Clark, of Dauphin, Clarke, of Indiana, Cleavinger, Cline, Coates, Cochran, Cope, Cox, Craig, Crain, Crawford, Crum, Cummin, Cunningham, Curll, Darlington, Darrah, Denny, Dickey, Dickerson, Dillinger, Donogan, Doran, Farrelly, Forward, Fry, Fuller, Gamble, Gearhart, Gilmore, Grenell, Harris, Hastings, Hayhurst, Hays, Helffenstein, Henderson, of Dauphin, Heister, Houpt, Hyde, Jenks, Keim, Kennedy, Kerr, Konigmacher, Krebs, Mann, McCall, McDowell, Meredith, Merkel, Montgomery, Overfield, Pollock, Porter, of Lancaster, Porter, of Northampton, Purviance, Reigart, Riter, Ritter, Royer, Russell, Saeger, Scheetz, Scott, Sellers, Seltzer, Serrill, Shellito, Sill, Smith of Columbia, Smyth, of Centre, Snively, Sterigere, Stevens, Sturdevant, Taggart, Thomas, Todd, Weaver, Woodward, Sergeant, *President—*99.

NAYS—Messrs. Baldwin, Dunlop, Earle, Hopkinson, Ingersoll, Maclay, Magee, M'Cahen, McSherry, Merrill, Miller, Young—12.

So the convention determined that the main question should now be taken.

And on the question,

Will the convention agree to reconsider the said vote ?

The yeas and nays were required by Mr. MANN and Mr. SMYTH, of Centre, and are as follows, viz :

YEAS—Messrs. Ayres, Bigelow, Bonham, Brown, of Northampton, Brown, of Philadelphia, Clarke, of Indiana, Cline. Cochran, Crain, Crawford Cummin, Curll, Darrah, Donagan, Doran, Dunlop, Fleming, Foulkrod, Fry, Gamble, Hastings, Helffenstein, Hopkinson, Houpt, Ingersoll, Keim, Kennedy, Mann, M'Cahen, M'Dowell, Miller, Porter, of Northampton, Read, Riter, Sellers, Shellito, Sterigere, Stickel, Sturdevant, Taggart, Woodward—41.

NAYS—Messrs. Agnew, Baldwin, Banks, Barclay, Barndollar, Barnitz, Bedford, Bell, Biddle, Chambers, Chandler, of Philadelphia, Chauncey, Clarke, of Beaver, Clark, of Dauphin, Cleaving'r, Coates, Cope, Cox, Craig, Crum, Cunningham, Darlington, Denny, Dickey, Dickerson, Dillinger, Earle, Farrelly, Forward, Fuller, Gearhart, Gilmore, Grenell, Harris, Hayhurst, Hays, Henderson, of Dauphin, Hiester, Hyde, Jenks, Kerr, Konigmacher, Krebs, Maclay, Magee, M'Call, M'Sherry, Meredith, Merrill, Merkel, Montgomery, Overfield, Pennypacker, Pollock, Porter, of Lancaster, Purviance, Reigart, Ritter, Royer, Russell, Saeger, Scheetz, Seltzer, Serrill, Sill, Smyth, of Centre, Snively, Stevens, Thomas, Todd, Weaver, Weidman, Young, Sergeant, *President*—74.

So the motion to reconsider was not agreed to.

SEVENTH ARTICLE.

Agreeably to leave given

The convention again resolved itself into a committee of the whole, Mr REIGART in the chair, on the report of the committee, to whom was referred the seventh article of the constitution.

The question being on the motion of Mr. FULLER, of Fayette, to amend the amendment offered by Mr. READ, as modified by him, by adding to the end thereof, the words following, viz :

" No bank shall issue any bill, check, note or paper credit, of a less denomination than ten dollars."

Mr. INGERSOLL rose, and said :

I had before me a few notes, with some preface in relation to the prior question, but I will dispense with that, and proceed at once to the mere dry question of the right of repeal by enactment. I said last night, and I now repeat, that I deem this the greatest pending question of the day, in this country. I begin, by disclaiming all power in this convention to act upon the subject directly—I mean to say, that I know of no power, possessed by this body, to act upon this subject, except indirectly through the legislature ;—in other words, that the power which has been ascribed to a convention, to do that which it is a question whether the legislature can do, I altogether disown. I, for one, claim no such power. I claim in behalf of this body, the right, by organic institution, to act upon the legislature, and in that way we can get at the subject ; but I disown altogether, the power which has been attributed to this body, of direct action upon it.

In the next place—and as the gentleman to whom I am about to allude, is absent, and as he has been spoken of, in somewhat rough terms here, it is proper I should say, that I wish to be understood as speaking of him, not only in all delicacy, but in all kindness of feeling—in the next place, I dissent from the whole argument of Mr. Dallas' letter, and I took occasion in private conversation, to tell him that I did so. In the first place, I deny his concession of the contract ; and, in the second place, I disown his argument in relation to fraud. I deny that it is in the power of any collateral body of men to repeal an act of the legislature, on the ground of alleged corruption or fraud in those who voted for it I know of no such authority. And I believe that such a repeal is unauthorized and impracticable.

In the third place, I much question the doctrine of Mr. Dallas' letter, and of the resolution of the gentleman from Luzerne, (Mr. Woodward) as to the necessity of the restoration of the bonus. Upon this subject, I would say what I think. I doubt much whether a repealing law, either in justice or in any other respect, involves the necessity of returning what has been given in the form of a bonus. And there is no part of the recent message of the chief magistrate of this commonwealth, who I am glad to see has condescended to honor us with his presence to day, which I have read with so much pleasure, as the intimation it contains, that hereafter, the legislature of this state, should cease to take any bonus from banks, I believe that, if that principle be carried out, as I shall endeavor to develope it, it is of immense importance to the welfare of the people of this commonwealth.

In the fourth place, I disclaim altogether the unfortunate illustrations of Mr. Dallas' letter, as to the power of this convention—which he says are mere illustrations, but which I consider as arguments, and which have no doubt been used *pro* and *con* as arguments.

In the next place, I acknowledge the supremacy of the supreme court of the United States—or, in other words, I acknowledge the supremacy of the federal government, either through the agency of the supreme court of the United States, or otherwise, to review, and, if unconstitutional, to annul whatever we may do here. I mean to say, that there is no difference, in my opinion, between a legislative enactment and a constitutional ordinance, as has been asserted by gentlemen of very high authority. There is no difference in the superintending power of the federal government.

Let me be precisely understood on this subject. There are those who hear me, who will recollect, that there is a large and growing party in this country—Charles M'Kean was a member of it, and many distinguished men in the southern states—who deny the exclusive authority of the supreme court of the United States, to declare a law unconstitutional. I will not enter into that question; nor will I say what my opinion is. All I will say is, that I acknowledge the power of the judicial, or of some other branch of the federal government, to review and revoke the acts of this body in the same manner as it would review or revoke the acts of a legislature. And, in the next place, I beg to be understood as repudiating and deprecating every thing which, in the slightest degree, looks like a violation of property. I consider, without reserve, that no state can resume a grant, provided that grant be a grant of property.

He conceded, without reserve, the doctrine in the decision of the case of Fletcher and Peck, and he should accept of the opinion there given by Judge Marshall. He conceded, where the legislature of a state, made a grant of property, that it was not in the power of the legislature to resume that grant; and he wished to be understood, in all his argument, to found it on an effort to preserve property from the operation of certain special privileges, which always interferes with it. And lastly, for these were his premises, he repelled without hesitation, the concession of Mr. Dallas and Mr. Forward, that a future act of assembly cannot annul an act of assembly passed previously.

He believed this principle had been asserted by his friend on his left, (Judge Hopkinson) which gave it the weight of his authority. But he (Mr. I.) disclaimed it altogether, and it seemed to him that the argument of Judge Marshall, in the case of Fletcher and Peck, was irresistible, and not to be set aside by the assertions of gentlemen on this floor. It was imputed to two members on this floor, and two or three other gentlemen who were not members of this body, that they voted for the charter of the Bank of the United States from corrupt motives. He only introduced this for the sake of the argument. But granting that to be the fact, which has been disproved, he denied that in consequence thereof any judicial or collateral body could repeal that act, unless it could be shown that every man of the majority, who voted for it, or, at least, a sufficient number to carry it, had been so influenced.

He denied, that an act could be repealed in consequence of this corruption, and in support of his position, he would avouch the argument of the supreme court, in the case he had before alluded to. He avouched that argument as being irresistible and conclusive, that even though Mr. A. B. C. and D. may be proved to have voted from corrupt motives— you may place it in the most gross and offensive manner which you can, still he denied that that made the act a nullity. Because any two, three, or four members of the senate of Pennsylvania, voted for any particular measure from corrupt motives, that did not make the law which they voted upon a nullity. He denied and disclaimed all this matter and produced in support of his opinion, the argument of the supreme court in the case of Fletcher and Peck, as being altogether conclusive. There it is written in such manner that no gentleman can mistake it, and every gentleman who desires to consult that authority, has an opportunity of doing so.

Having disposed of these premises, he came to the main question which he intended to discuss. He denied entirely, that a bank charter was a contract, and he would pledge himself to show to the satisfaction of every dispassionate hearer, that this assertion was correct. He pledged himself further, to show that it never has been adjudged a contract, and that it seldom or never has been called a contract; but that all the common sense, all the moral philosophy, all the political law, and all the adjudication on the subject had determined it otherwise. It had been taken for granted by some, from the decision of the Dartmouth college case, which was a totally different kind of case, it being a private contract of an eleemosynary character, altogether different in all its circumstances. He acknowledged that one judge of the supreme court of the United States, whom he might be permitted to call his friend, and who, for twenty-five years, he had been on terms of intimacy with, had said that a bank charter was a contract; but he (Mr. I.) pledged himself to show to this body that, except the say so of this judge, for it was but his say so, as a judicial opinion had never been given on the subject, and it might be doing injustice to the judge alluded to, for him to introduce this opinion of his here, no judge, no legist, no moral philosopher, no philologist, had ever given an opinion that a bank charter was a contract. On the contrary, all the authorities were on the other side. He was not so sure, but what some of those who compile books, had this in their books, for there are books making every day by young lawyers, who have nothing else to do; who have but little experience, and who, the moment they find any thing said by some one, write it down as facts, and matter of authority ; and it may be, that in such compilations as these, some such assertion may be found. But here again, he demurred from their authority.

He wished gentlemen now to remember that he was merely speaking of a bank charter, and he did not wish to place all charters together on the same footing, as the gentleman from Allegheny had done in his letter. He wished to be understood as speaking of no other than a bank charter. He was speaking of that kind of an institution which makes a currency for the country, which makes a substitute for money. He was speaking of that and of nothing else ; and, he did not think that any man who will bring his mind to that single point, will see any very great reason for being shocked at the assertion he was about to submit to the consideration of the committee. He held in his hand the strictures upon a letter, published by himself, of some anonymous gentleman he did not know, but whose work was written in a very able and eloquent manner ; and accompanying it he found certain letters of the gentleman from Allegheny, (Mr. Forward) Mr. Dallas, Mr. Biddle, &c. And he wished to read a few lines from the letter of his friend from Allegheny, to show what he says on this subject. " It is conceded" (he says) " that the anulling of a charter is the destruction of contracts, by the annihilation of vested rights of property. The question, therefore, in its plain and naked terms, is just this—can a majority of the people appoint a body of delegates with the power to annul contracts and destroy vested private rights. I take the negative side of this question for the following reasons." Now, this was all very fully laid down, but the truth is, that he speaks of these vested rights, and annihilation of vested rights of property, apart from the question we were now discussing.

Mr. FORWARD said that the gentleman would find that he was there referring to the concessions of Mr. Dallas.

Mr. INGERSOLL. Mr. Dallas concedes the whole case. It was not necessary then for him to pursue this matter any farther as the argument of the gentleman is predicated on the concessions of Mr. Dallas. Mr. I. was speaking of a bank charter, and of nothing else, and he wished gentlemen to do him the justice to recollect that he had nothing else in view, but a bank charter. There was an obvious difference, too, between an ancient charter and a modern charter, and there was still as great a difference between the different kinds of modern charters. An ancient charter was a grant of liberty. It was separating a few men from the oppression of the then rulers. A modern charter is a grant of privileges. It is separating a few men from the general mass of the community, and conferring a portion of the liberty of the community upon them in the shape of special privileges. You must not, therefore, look upon ancient and modern charters in the same light, neither must you confound all modern charters. These charters are almost altogether peculiar to this country, and this was a matter which is almost always lost sight of. Did the learned gentleman from Erie, (Mr. Sill) who had told us so much about these corporations doing wonders, suppose that the wonders which had been worked in England were the offspring of corporations ? Mr. I. spoke not now of what the spirit of liberty and labor-saving machinery, had done ; but, does the gentleman from Erie suppose, that the canals, the rail roads and other improvements of England, were completed by the aid of corporate bodies? If so, the gentleman labors under a very great mistake. They are not made by incorporated companies. There are but very few of these companies incorporated in that country, and corporations such as we have in this country are altogether peculiar to this country. They were formerly the asylums of liberty, but now they have become the strong hold of property. He would here, however, disclaim all idea, even the most remote, of interfering with any man's property, real or personal. When he spoke of a bank charter, he spoke of it as a power conveyed to a certain number of individuals, or the same power might be conferred upon a single individual, to make a public currency, which is a substitute for money. Now, he would ask, in the first place, and it was a very curious question too, which he did not mean to concede, nor altogether to affirm. But, he would ask whether the power to make this species of grant was a legislative power at all? This was a very interesting and a very serious question. It had, to be sure, been always taken for granted, but he would ask, whether under the institutions of our state, when an individual was elected a member of the legislature, he is by that authority, for there is no express grant, empowered to give up to one or more individuals, a portion of the sovereignty of the people? He desired an answer to this question soberly and dispassionately. Looking into the nature and origin of things, he would ask what is the social compact? Most modern philosophers, and among them he might name Mr. Paley, as standing among the first of them— ascribe the origin of society either to parentage or force. The United States government was unquestionably a government of consent ; and, whether the state governments were the same is perhaps a question which it is hardly necessary to argue much about. But, sir, looking to the origin of society, let us inquire whether these powers, which are claimed, exist at all. If any American legislator was to answer him in the affirmative, it must be by a tacit commission, for there is no express grant to be found any where, which gives power to a member to grant these charters. He knew very well that a large proportion of those who were elected to the legislature, suppose they are elected to do any thing which is not morally wrong, and they believe that there is no limit to their authority. He, however, denied this altogether. The American legislator holds by a limited trust. He holds by none of that parliamentary immortality which exists in England. He asked gentlemen to turn their attention to the acquisition of power, and show him where it was to be found. He would refer gentlemen to the very able views of the gentleman from Erie, (Mr. Sill) on this subject. He bestowed a large portion of his argument in an effort to show that corporations were not a monopoly. Mr. I. did not say whether they were or whether they were not, but he took it for granted, and the argument of the gentleman went to show this, that if they were a monopoly, the legislature had no power to grant a monopoly ; and this was bringing the matter down to narrow grounds. Suppose a charter was not a monopoly. Suppose it was a perpetuity. He should like the lawyers of this house to tell him whether the legislature had a right to grant a perpetuity. Does not every lawyer know that a perpetuity is against the common law itself, and a judge sitting in our court, can uproot any kind of property received as a perpetuity ? A monopoly is questionable, but a perpetuity is unquestionable.

Now, the largest portion of stock which he held in any thing he held in perpetuity. He held as a stockholder stock in an institution which was perpetual. But, he questioned the right; he questioned the power of the legislature to confer any thing like a monopoly; and, he denied their power to grant any thing like a perpetuity. That the government of the United States has no power to grant charters is certain. We know that. We know that the Bank of the United States was sustained on a totally different principle. It was sustained on the ground of its being a fiscal agent of the government for a given end; but, we know very well that while the convention which framed the constitution of the United States was in session, an attempt was made to give the power to congress to confer charters, and that attempt totally failed, and was defeated. He was not now speaking of the United States Bank charter, but he was speaking of charters at large, and upon this subject he wished to be permitted to call the attention of the members of this body to the consitutions of our own state, from which a lesson of restriction was to be learned. In the constitution of 1776, chapter one, and section three and four, which is the bill of rights of that constitution, he found the following language:

" That the people of this state have the. sole, exclusive and inherent right of governing and regulating the internal police of the same. That all power being originally inherent in, and consequently derived from the people; therefore, all officers of government, whether legislative or executive, are their trustees and servants, and at all times accountable to them." And in chapter second, section nine, he found the following: " The members of the house of representatives, shall be chosen annually by ballot; they shall have power to choose their speaker and other officers; sit on their own adjournments; propose bills, and enact them into laws; judge of the election and qualifications of their own members; they may expel a member, but not a second time for the same cause; they may administer oaths or affirmations on examination of witnesses; redress grievances, impeach state criminals; and, *grant charters of incorporation.*"

The framers of that constitution deemed it indispensible that this power, which is a mere assumption of power on the part of the legislature under the present constitution, should be given in express terms, and they certainly considered that the legislature would not have had the power, if it had not been given to them in this way.

Again, in section ten, of the same chapter, the oath of the members was as follows: "I — do swear (or affirm) that as a member of this assembly, I will not propose or assent to any bill, vote or resolution, which shall appear to me injurious to the people, nor do or consent to any act or thing whatever, that shall have a tendency to lessen or abridge their rights and privileges, as declared in the constitution of this state; but will, in all things conduct myself. as a faithful, honest, representative and guardian of the people, according to the best of my judgment and abilities."

Upon the constitution of the United States then, and upon the constitution of 1776, he founded this argument, and when he founded it upon such authorities he thought he stood upon imprenigable ground. In the convention to form the constitution of the United States it was proposed to give this power to congress, and was refused. And, in the constitution of 1776, they had this right conferred upon them, but in the constitution of 1790, it was omitted. If this was an open question, then, (and we had not the experience of near fifty years in this state,) he was free to say, that he should declare that unless this power was conferred by a direct grant of the people, that it could not be assumed under any tacit authority, and for the simple reason, that no member of the legislature sits by any omnipotent power.

Let gentlemen never forget that in England, the parliament hold all power in their hands, and are the sovereigns. . Here, however, the representative has the constitution as his guide, and alone, and beyond, and superior to that, was the people themselves. They do not elect representatives for the purpose of doing any thing they pleased, which was not morally wrong. They do not elect them upon any such principles. The people look back to first principles and elect representatives to do that which is for the benefit of the mass of the people. The power to grant charters, and especially bank charters, was to say the least of it, a questionable power; it was a power which it was doubtful whether the people ever conferred upon their representatives. Sir, let us look into the present constitution of Pennsylvania, and see what can be drawn from it on this subject. He would beg leave to call the attention of gentlemen to the ninth article, first section, and there was to be found words that ought to have some meaning, and which any judge of a court in the state, would feel himself bound to give some meaning to. That first section was in the following words : "That all men are born equally free and independent, and have certain inherent and indefeasable rights, among which are those of enjoying and defending life and liberty ; of acquiring, possessing property and reputation, and of pursuing their own happiness."

This is not merely that all men possess inherent and equal rights, and that they shall enjoy personal liberty, but that they shall enjoy the right to property, and the right to transmit property. They are to have an equal right. Well, will any man pretend to say that the rights of individuals incorporated and unincorporated are equal? He again looks att he twenty-fourth clause of this same article ; "the legislature shall not grant any title of nobility or hereditary distinction, nor create any office, the appointment to which shall be for a longer term than good behaviour." Now, would any gentleman tell him that the stock which he held in a charter, which is perpetual, is not a hereditary distinction, by which he might enjoy the acquisition, possession and transmission of property, which those who did not hold in the same way, were deprived from enjoying? It seemed so to him at all events.

Well, sir, what is the civil law upon this subject from which we get many of our corporations ? Why, the civil law is that all the corporators are liable for the debts of the corporation. An inquiry on this subject, on the part of gentlemen, would be no less curious than profitable ; and, it was worth while to look into this matter, and see how these laws have been incorporated with our laws, for all the laws we have, are drawn from these fountains. Certain it is, that the legislature have the power to limit and regulate the issues of banks, and this was recommended to them in the governor's message; and, until he heard this called in question the other day by the highly respectable and learned judge on his left (Judge Hopkinson) he had never heard a doubt hinted as to the power of the legislature to make these regulations. It is a power which has been exercised by the legislature of every state in the Union at all times and under all circumstances, and never had he heard of a doubt being expressed in relation to it, until he heard it doubted by the gentleman from the city.

Why, sir, this was the postulate of the whole arguments of the gentleman from Beaver, who had, with a great deal of research gone, on to show us the progressive course of the legislature in placing restrictions upon banks. But, the learned judge had gone into an argument to show that we had no right to meddle with the ten dollar notes of the bank, and this gentleman was the first one he had ever heard doubt the right of the legislature to regulate the banks in this way. The first is, that the legislature to a certain extent have exercised this power, and that extent seemed to him to be such an extent as to settle the whole question. The first is, that the legists and modern philosophers, and all those who looked into the origin and source of things, would find it very difficult to reconcile these powers with reason.

But, the gentlemen from Northampton had introduced here one of the most despicable of characters, as proof upon this subject. The authority of Tom Paine, a man who was a weak politician, an infidel in religion, and a sot in old age; and, he was as weak and despicable authority as could be introduced on any subject whatever. By the subterfuges of this man, the gentleman attempts to prove and settle great political principles. Well, what does he say ? Why, he says, that a law incorporating a bank is not a law, but that it is an act; and, upon this miserable distinction does his whole case rest. It is an act of sale, but it is not a law. The legislature is not acting as a legislature, when they grant or sell bank charters; but, they are contracting for them, bargaining for them, and giving a *quid* for a *quo.*

This was the argument of Tom Paine, and he would leave it with this committee whether this was an argument which was to have any weight with them. It might with some of our legislators, and it might perhaps, with his friend from Allegheny. As the gentleman from Allegheny had written a letter on this subject, he wished to call the attention of the committee to a particular passage in that letter which related to this question, which was as follows :

" Can any one give a reason why the force of a contract should depend on the *numbers* that may constitute one of the parties to it—why the stronger party should be allowed to say one thing and mean another—should be permitted to keep or break its stipulations according as a majority may decide ? An individual claiming this privilege, would be set down as a knave. The obligation of a contract is a *moral* obligation, and therefore, just as binding upon governments and communities, represented by governments, as upon individuals. A contrary doctrine substitutes force in the place of right, and however disguised, is an attack upon liberty." Again he says, " The legislature which granted they bank charter, was clothed with limited powers ; but, to the extent of those powers, it represented the people and could bind them. It is for this reason, that the charter is constitutional. In other words, the power to grant it, was delegated by the people."

Here was an assumption which he thought the American people could not consent to, and to disprove which he would refer gentlemen to the same book of reports of the arguments of the court in the case of Fletcher and Peck. The powers of legislators are limited and must be limited, and when the gentleman from Allegheny assumes that a legislator can do any thing and every thing, he assumes what he cannot prove. But, he would now concede this power. As he had before disclaimed various principles, so would he now concede the power of the legislature to grant bank charters. In this last discussion he did not wish to involve himself in any metaphysical elements, but to address himself to the body in that simple manner that every body could understand him.

Well, as to the assumption of the gentleman, what is it ? The whole assumption is that a bank charter is a contract. Remember that this is an assumption and a mere assumption ; and, in what he was going to say, he intended no offence. But, how dare any man assume, as fact, what he cannot prove ? How dare any man assume that a bank charter was a contract, when it could not be found to be said so any where nor by any body, save the mere say so of a single individual ? How then dare any man to assume that which he ought to prove ?

I call upon them to prove it ; it is not for me to disprove it. I cast the burden of proof upon them ; let them shew what they assert to be true ; let them shew by reason, as well as by proof. Sir, they can not shew it either by the one or the other. The same authority which they have for it, concedes that a marriage is not a contract ; the legislature may divorce the parties, and the legislature has done so under most flagrant circumstances. They have taken the property of the wife, and given it to the husband. I need not—it is painful to me, even to refer to a recent transaction, which will suggest itself to the recollection of all who hear me. The legislature has, under circumstances of the most monstrous character, dissolved the marriage contract. They have taken private property— despoiled one party of it, and given it to the other.

The legislature, almost every day, reduces the salaries of those in office, unless it happens to be in the constitution, that they shall not do so. And, is it not a contract that when a man undertakes to do a piece of business, whatever it may be, for five hundred dollars, the legislature shall not interpose and say, we will give you only two hundred dollars ? There is no question, as a matter of salary. No one would oppose it. It is not, therefore, to be assumed—it is to be proved against these concessions, that this is a constitutional contract , that it is a contract, in view of these phrases of the constitution of this state, which uses the term " contract." It is not to be a common contract ; it is to be that which the constitution contemplates, and nothing else. There is, as I have said, an obvious distinction—a palpable classification.

Our young American lawyers, in certain treatises on this subject, for which I have no great respect, do not define any charter, that I know of.

They describe two; that is to say, a public charter, such as the charter of this city, or county, or of the overseers of the poor; and, secondly, a private charter, such as that of an insurance company, and for various other private purposes.

Some of my friends in this body, are chartered libertines on this particular subject; such as my friend from Franklin, (Mr. Dunlop) and from Northampton, (Mr. Porter.) It appears to me, that those who have *attended* to this question in some degree, have not ascertained their elements. I take it there is a private charter, such as the gentleman from Northampton (Mr. Porter) holds. It matters not whether it is granted to one or more individuals—that is a private charter. Then, there is a municipal charter, such as the charter of this city.

The CHAIR here announced, that the hour allowed by the rule, had expired.

Mr. WOODWARD rose and said :

Mr. Chairman, there seems to me to be an impression abroad, that this amendment conflicts with the resolution introduced at Harrisburg, by the gentleman from the city of Philadelphia, (Mr. Meredith) and adopted by a vote of this body. I will say a single word in reply to that suggestion. That resolution affirms, that a charter granted to a bank, is a contract, and that it can be avoided only in a certain mode. I had supposed that the legislature could avoid a charter, but this resolution affirms the contrary. If it be true, that a bank charter, is a contract, and can only be avoided in the way mentioned in this resolution, is it not competent for this convention, to introduce a provision into the constitution, giving to the legislature that power, which the resolution asserts the legislature does not at this time possess?

Mr. BELL rose to a point of order. He wished to inquire from the Chair, whether this was intended by the gentleman from Luzerne, (Mr. Woodward) as the continuation of the address, which was brought to an end yesterday, under the operation of the rule, limiting each delegate to the space of an hour?

The CHAIR said, it was not possible for him to say whether this was, or was not, intended as a continuation of that address. The gentleman from Luzerne had got the floor, according to the rules of order, and was entitled to it.

Mr. WOODWARD said, that he would very cheerfully answer the inquiry of the gentleman from Chester (Mr. Bell.)

Yesterday, said Mr. W., I submitted some observations to the committee, until I was called to order, under the operation of the new rule. I have now obtained the floor, and have, therefore, an opportunity to submit some additional remarks. I do not intend to recapitulate my observations of yesterday, I merely intend to offer some more in addition to them.

Mr. BELL said, he would then submit to the Chair, whether the gentleman from Luzerne was in order—whether he was not evading the rule?

The CHAIR said that, in the opinion of the chair, the gentleman from Luzerne (Mr. Woodward) was perfectly in order

Mr. BELL appealed from the decision.

And, the question thereon having been taken, the committee sustained the decision of the Chair.

Mr. WOODWARD,* took the floor, and made some remarks.

Mr. W. then gave way to Mr. M'CAHAN, on whose motion the committee rose, reported progress, and obtained leave to sit again.

The PRESIDENT, by leave, laid before the convention, a communication from the clerk of the commissioners of the county of Philadelphia—in compliance with a resolution adopted on the 22d instant—enclosing a statement, showing the annual cost of each of the state courts of justice in the city and county of Philadelphia, for the four years prior to the first day of December, 1837, and the fees received out of the county funds, by the attorney general or his deputies, on the several criminal prosecutions therein during that period of time.

A motion was made by Mr. DORAN,

That the said communication and statement be printed for the use of the delegates.

Which motion was disagreed to. And the communication and statement were ordered to lie on the table.

The convention then adjourned until half past three o'clock this after noon.

THURSDAY AFTERNOON. DECEMBER 28, 1837.

The Convention having assembled, and the question being—"Will the convention again resolve itself into a committee of the whole, on the report of the committee to whom was referred the seventh article of the constitution ?"

Mr. INGERSOLL asked for the yeas and nays on this question, and they were ordered accordingly.

The question was then taken, and decided in the affirmative, as follows, viz :

YEAS—Messrs. Ayres, Banks, Barclay, Bedford, Bigelow, Bonham, Brown of Northampton, Brown, of Philadelphia, Carey, Clarke, of Indiana. Cleavinger, Cline, Crain, Crawford, Cummin, Curll, Darrah, Denny, Dickey, Dillinger, Doran Fleming, Foulkrod, Fry, Fuller, Gamble, Gearhart, Gilmore, Hastings, Hayhurst, Helffenstein, Henderson, of Dauphin, Hiester, Hopkinson, Houpt, Hyde, Jenks, Keim, Kennedy, Krebs. Magee, Martin, M'Cahen, M'Dowell, M'Sherry, Merrill, Miller, Overfield, Porter, of Northampton, Purviance, Read, Riter, Ritter, Scheetz, Sellers, Seltzer, Serrill, Shellito, Smith, of Columbia, Smyth, of Centre, Sterigere, Stickel, Taggart, Weaver, Woodward—66.

----

*See Appendix.

NAYS—Messrs. Agnew, Barndollar, Biddle, Brown, of Lancaster, Chauncey, Clarke, of Beaver, Clark, of Dauphin, Cochran, Cope, Cox, Craig, Crum, Darlington, Dickerson, Farrelly. Harris, Hays, Kerr, Konigmacher, Martin, M'Call, Merkel, Montgomery, Pollock, Porter, of Lancaster, Reigart, Saeger, Scott, Young, Sergeant, *President*—30.

SEVENTH ARTICLE.

The Convention again resolved itself into a committee of the whole, Mr. REIGART in the chair, on the report of the committee to whom was refered the seventh article of the constitution.

The question being on the motion of Mr. WOODWARD to amend the amendment of Mr. READ, by adding to the end thereof the words following, viz :

" And the legislature may repeal, change or modify the charters of all banks heretofore iucorporated, or which may hereafter be incorporated in this commonwealth, whether the power to repeal, change or modify be reserved in such charter or not, : but when the legislature shall repeal the charter of any bank, or resume any of its corporate privileges, they shall provide adequate and sufficient compensation to the stockholders of such bank."

A quorum of members not being present, some delay took place, after which

Mr. WOODWARD* resumed the remarks he commenced on the last evening.

Mr. INGERSOLL rose and said, I have asserted Mr. Chairman, that it is absolute murder to an argument to mutitate in this way. And if it is not now the pleasure of this body to hear my argument out, I will renounce the intention of addressing it further on this subject.

Mr. PORTER of Northampton, rose and said : Mr. Chairman ; the issue presented by the resolution adopted on the 21st November last, as well as that presented by the amendment now submitted by the delegate from Luzerne, (Mr. Woodward) is a general abstract question. Has the legislature the right to repeal a charter granted to individuals for banking purposes, and if the right exists—would it be policy to exercise it ? This question I should like to hear discussed, without bringing other existing topics into the debate. In the whole course of the argument of that delegate, he has reference to one charter, the grant of which and the excitement produced in consequence, has no doubt led to the agitation of this subject.

The question is one of vast importance in principle and in its bearing upon the rights of the community and of the individual members of that community. If you establish the principle contended for it may involve in its consequences that title to every tract of land—to every house and lot—to every charter for a turnpike road—bridge—rail road—canal—church—school house,—college and academy in the country. Adopt the amendment now proposed and carry it out in its extent and you will give to your legislature, as whim, caprice, excitement or any thing else may move them, the power over every man's title and rights. This is a despotism to which I for one will never consent to submit.

---

* See Appendix.

So far from considering, with the esteemed delegate from Luzerne, that the adoption of the resolution of the 21st of November last, at Harrisburg, was a measure hostile to our institutions and fatal to the liberties of our country, I should dread the adoption of the amendment now proposed by him as calculated to produce those results.

Conceding for the sake of the argument to the Bank of the United States all power and influence attributed to it, and that it was unwise to have granted its charter, yet we must remember that what is law in relation to it, is law in relation to every other private corporation in the state, and to every foot of land held by every farmer, mechanic or other citizen of the commonwealth. I might assimilate the conduct of those, who, to remove what is esteemed a present evil, would give a vital stab to the security of our republican institutions, to that of the surgeon who would remove a wen from the patient's body, the inevitable consequence of which would be his death, when by leaving it undisturbed, his life would continue subject only to the inconvenience, and if you please the unsightliness of the protuberance, which a few years would remove without any other process.

I have deprecated as the greatest evil that can befal our country, the destruction of confidence in individual rights, and I solemnly believe that if our own liberties are destroyed, it will be by that means.

I deprecate, as destructive to the democratic party in this state and the Union, the fastening upon them of the charge that the democratic citizens as a party are willing to carry out the principles contained in the amendment now proposed; and I feel as well assured as I can be of any thing which time has not developed, that if this charge be credited, we shall be placed in the minority both in the state and Union—a result which no one would more seriously deplore than myself; but a result to which I feel we must prepare to submit, in consequence of departing from the path of duty and principle, should we make ourselves amenable to this charge.

The delegate from the county of Luzerne, in the argument which he has adduced, which is plausible, but in my judgment unsound, lays out of view all the judicial decisions on the subject. Why he has done so, he has not condescended to inform us. That delegate is a member of a learned and honorable profession, in which he stands deservedly high for his years, and gives rich promise of future usefulness—a profession which, permit me to say, requires its members to arrive at logical conclusions from given premises. A profession which teaches us to draw knowledge and information from the experience and learning and abilities of those who have gone before us. I am sorry to see one for whom I hope so much, rejecting the lights and aids by which alone the members of that profession can expect to arrive at great attainments in it. I know and respect his talents and his private worth, and I cannot but regret that one of so much promise, should put forth opinions which his own good sense, ere he has gone through the "*viginite annorum lucrabationse*"* necessary it is said to make a good lawyer, will compel him to recant. If this be not the case, then I am no prophet.

To the supreme court of the United States, as the court of the last resort belongs the decision of all questions involving the constitutionality of

* The lucrabations of twenty years.

legislative enactments. It being their province and their duty, under the
constitution and laws of the land. In making these decisions they do so
on points which come legitimately before them, and whatever may be my
own individual opinions, I am constrained to bow in submission to the law
of the land. In making these decisions the judges of your supreme court
are required gravely to consider and reflectively to decide the great and
important questions which come before them. We pay respect and defer-
ence, even if we do not admit their binding authority upon us, to the opinions of the learned and experienced, who fill the private walks of life.
How much more are we bound to yield up our own opinions upon legal
subjects, to the determination of the proper judicial tribunals. Any other
course would launch us upon the great ocean of doubt, confusion and uncer-
tainty without rudder, compass or chart. We should have no polar star of
principle to guide us on our way. Amid the gloom, darkness and confusion
of such a voyage, when tossed about by every wind, sailing to and fro without object and without end. What benefit would we derive from the cor-
ruscations of even the brightest genius, whose erratic course, like the
vivid lightning, illumines for the moment with a fitful glare to make the
horrors of our situation more appaling, or at best, like the *ignus fatuus*,
which only lights to allure, would entice us to ruin, and strand us on the
quicksands of error, or wreck us 'midst the breakers of destruction.   .

In saying that he would lay out of view, all judicial decisions in considering the question whether a charter of incorporation was a contract,
the delegate from Luzerne, added that he would test it by the common
sense of the community, and proceeded to ask whether the act incorporating the Bank of the United States, was not a law containing sections and
paragraphs and clauses just like any other law. This was a singular course
for a gentleman who is a lawyer to pursue in an argument. It is the first time
in my life that I ever heard of the common law of the land, and the common sense of the community differing. What is the common law, but
the embodied common sense of the community? The *lex n on scripta*.
The law which arises from time to time as circumstances call it into action.
That silent process of legislation going on from day to day, which from
the elastic nature of the common law, enables courts to give redress as
occasion calls for it. This is what I call the common sense of the community applied to legal matters, and by this test, I am willing to try the
questions proposed.

The circumstance of the act being in the form as to sections, and paragraphs of other laws, would not prevent it from constituting a contract.—
We must look to substance—The interest of the parties, not to form. Its
form however, is like that of every other act of incorporation for private
purposes. But it is said that it wants all the essential requisites of a con.
tract which is constituted by the terms " I will" and " I will not." Without stopping to inquire as to the accuracy of this definition, let us put a
case. Suppose one man says to another, " I will do so and so, if you will
do so and so," and the other party assents to the proposition and performs
his part of the terms. Is not this a contract to all intents and purposes,
and are not both parties bound ? If the legislature, who in this behalf are
the agents of the people, and act for them, say to a number of individuals,
if you will pay us so much money down and so much tax annually after.
wards, we will grant to you and your successors the right to carry on the

banking business for a given number of years, according to the terms and conditions contained in this instrument. If the individuals say they will do' this, and actually accept of the terms, and perform their part of the agreement, in what essential particular does this differ from an ordinary contract?

The state propose the terms. The company accept and comply with them. Where is the difference between this and a contract made between two individuals? If this be not a contract I am at a loss to conceive what will create one. It is in vain for gentlemen to argue against it. The delegate asks with great apparent triumph "where is the provision in your constitution that authorizes the legislature to make a contract?" I reply that it is one of the powers belonging to those exercising the sovereignty of every country. It was exercised under the constitution of 1776, which contained an express provision authorizing it. It is recognized in the 1st section of the 7th article of the existing constitution; the section . now under consideration. It is again recognized in the 1st section of the schedule annexed to the constitution in the following language : " all laws of this commonwealth in force at the time of making the said alterations and amendments in the said constitution, and not inconsistent therewith, and all rights, actions, prosecutions, *claims* and *contracts* as *well of individuals as of bodies corporate*, shall *continue* as if the said alteration and amendments had not been made." I think I have now turned the gentleman to the very provisions. But besides these clauses in the constitution, the constant current of legislation for nearly fifty years, and the decision of the supreme court of the United States, in Briscoe vs. the Bank of Kentucky, as well as that of Tennessee, in the case of Bell vs. the Bank of Nashville, recognize the power in the state legislature to create banking corporations, as well as all other corporations which are admitted to be private and consequently contracts.

I would like to know, and I will thank gentlemen who take these nice destinctions, to inform me if they can, wherein there is a difference or distinction to be drawn between a contract made by the people of a country through their constitutional agents, and a contract between individuals. If there be any difference, it should operate to bind the public as a contracting party the more firmly, because of the greater importance of the principle in preserving the public faith. An individual who intentionally failed in the performance of his contracts seldom obtains credit again, and there is generally no very high character for morality attached to those who wilfully refuse to perform their contracts. Would not an act which was wrong in an individual, be ten-fold more so in a community. I lay out of view all this *ad captandum* argument about " the sale of the rights and the farming out the liberties of the people, where the most money gets the most and best laws," &c; for all this presupposes, what I will never admit, corruption in the agents of the people and a dereliction of duty by them, which in effect is to brand the people themselves with incapacity for self government, and incompetency to choose honest and competent agents. To this conclusion, that part of the gentleman's argument necessarily leads.

It is said again, that the bank charter is not a contract, that there is no remedy for the violation of it. This is a mere gratuitous assertion, not supported by the law of the land. One hazarded without due reflection or examination. Let the Bank of the United States or any other corporation, violate the terms on which their charter was granted, and I will. vouch for it to find a remedy under the existing laws. If the gentleman will turn to the last act of assembly on the subject, passed on the —— day of —————, 1836, he will find that a general jurisdiction is given to the courts of this commonwealth, to exercise equity powers, in all cases of *corporations, partnerships and unincorporated associations.* This power is conferred on the supreme court and courts of common pleas, and I believe that independently of all this, there is a provision in the charter of the Bank of the United States, authorizing a proceeding by *scire facias*, on complaint made that the condition of its charter has been violated.

If gentlemen will look into the recent volumes of the New York chancery reports, they will find numerous instances of proceedings in equity against corporations, and the officers of corporations, and of the exercise of equity powers in relation to them. Let any set of directors, managers or trustees, mismanage their trust, and let their conduct be brought before a court having equity power, as our courts now have, and gentlemen will then see whether there is no remedy for breach, or violation by corporations, of the contracts contained in charters of incoporation.

My argument was, and my conviction is, that the members of the legislature are elected to perform *all* the functions that belong to legislators. That among these, is the power to grant charters of incorporation, as well for banking as for any other proper and necessary purposes. If they do so, and *they think* that the privileges conferred are worth a pecuniary compensation, to be appled in aid of the funds of the commonwealth, this is a matter of legislative discretion, which they are constitutionally competent to exercise, and if they improperly exercise it, they are answerable for their misconduct to their masters, the people, whose agents they are in the premises, and the contract and bargain they make, is between the people on the one side, and the corporations on the other.

I will not enter into any discussion as to the power of this convention to make a prospective provision on this subject. That it will have an undoubted right to do, and that I will join gentlemen in doing. I however, will never consent to destroy vested rights. This, had we power to do it, would be unloosing the bonds of society, and signing the death warrant of republican government. The attempt, too, would be perfectly nugatory were we to adopt the amendment proposed, for it would be declared null and void by the judicial tribunals of the country. The effect of urging these existing topics upon us, will only create distractions in the country and do no good. We have had too much of this—we find one party seizing on something which it is supposed will find favor with the people. Then the other party, fearing that their adversaries may gain something by it, take up the cry with equal zeal, and it is kept up until the whole community is worked up into fearful commotion. I fear if this thing does not cease, that the country will be ridden down with it yet. We have seen such things done heretofore, and I apprehend, we are now feeling the sad effects of these party divisions, distractions and excitement created to gratify the insatiated love of power and place, that seems to have taken hold of so many of our citizens.

Another position has been advanced by the delegate from Luzerne, that is, that a banking institution is a public, not a private corporation; and in support of this, he has referred to a remark made use of by Chief Justice Marshall, in deciding the case of Osborne vs. the Bank of the United States, reported in 9 Wheaton, 703. I ventured the assertion before, and I repeat it now, that such a point has never been decided in any court. It is true that Judge Marshall in the case alluded to, may have used the expressions quoted, *arguendo*, in relation to the late Bank of the United States, chartered by congress, when speaking of it as the fiscal agent of the government of the United States, and as to the illegality of a state taxing it; but there is no such decision of that or of any other court, as that banks are public corporations. And in the same book, 9 Wheaton at page 907, the case of the United States Bank, and the Planters' Bank of Georgia, the very reverse of the doctrine contended for, is decided, by the court, Judge Marshall delivering the opinion, in which he says: " 'The suit is against a corporation, and the judgment is to be satisfied by the property of the corporation, and not by that of the corporators. The state does not by becoming a corporator, identify itself with the corporation. *The Planters Bank of Georgia, is not the state of Georgia, although the state holds an interest in it. It is a sound principle, that when a government becomes a partner in a trading company, it divests itself, so far as concerns the transactions of that company, of its sovereign character, and takes that of a private citizen.*"

Again, they say in the same case, page 908. "The government of the Union held shares in the old Bank of the United States, but the privileges of the government were not imparted by that circumstance to the bank. The United States was not a party to suits brought by, or against, the bank, in the sense of the constitution. So with respect to the present bank." " 'The government by becoming a corporator, lays down its sovereignty, so far as respects the transactions of the corporation, and exercises no power or privilege which is not derived from the charter.''

I adduced some other authorities on this point, in my former remarks at Harrisburg, to show that banking corporations were private corporations. Judge Story in the Dartmouth College case says so. And I read to the same effect from Elementary Treatises. One by Angel and Ames on corporations. In referring to the quotations made from the elementary authors, the delegate from the county of Philadelphia, (Mr. Ingersoll) took occasion to speak very contemptuously of such works, as being written by *young lawyers* without experience, who write down as authority, whatever they find stated by any one, to make up a book, without ever inquiring into the matter themselves. I am not able to say how far Mr. Ames may be obnoxious to the charge of youth. Mr. Angel has been an author before the public for a number of years. I have been in the habit of citing them for perhaps twelve or fifteen years past, and his reputation has been that of a peculiarly accurate author on all the various subjects upon which he has written. What do they say on this subject? "In the popular meaning of the term, nearly every corporation is public, inasmuch as they are enacted for the public benefit; but yet, if the whole interest does not belong to government, or if the corporation is not created for the administration of political or municipal power, the corporation is private. *A bank, for instance, may be created by the government for its own uses, but if the stock is owned by private persons, it is a private corporation, although it is erected by the government, and its objects and operations partake of a public nature.*"

There was another person, from whose works I quoted a passage, who is certainly not a very *young man*, and who cannot be unknown, at least by reputation, to the delegate—James Kent, who has filled the highest judicial office both in law and equity in New York, and who, some years since, retired from the office of chancellor of that state, because he had attained the age of sixty years, the limit prescribed by their constitution. Since that period, he has been enlightening the people of this country, by giving them the result of his long and useful labors in the profession, for all which, we owe him a large debt of gratitude. What does Chancellor Kent say?—let us hear his own language : " A hospital created and endowed by the government, is a public and not a private corporation. *But a bank, whose stock is owned by private persons, is a private corporation,* though its objects and operations partake of a public nature. And though the government may have become a partner in the association, by sharing with the corporation in the stock."

We have here the decision of the supreme court of the United States in the cases of Briscoe vs. the Commonwealth Bank of Kentucky, and in the case of the United States Bank, vs. The Planters Bank of Georgia, as well as the opinions of Angel and Ames, and of Chancellor Kent, all direct to the point. And how can gentlemen stand up in this body, and contend that banking institutions are public, and not private corporations in the teeth of the unbroken current of authorities, from the wisest and best judges and jurists in the land.

In regard to this charge of youth and inexperience made against the writers of elementary treaties, so far as the same respects Messrs. Angel and Ames, I have only to say, that if no other gentlemen of my acquaintance, have any greater reason to regret the productions of their youthful pen, than those gentlemen have, they are exceedingly fortunate indeed.

In the case of the commonwealth, Arrison, *et. al.* our own Tilghman, in giving the opinion of the supreme court of Pennsylvania, (15 Sergeant and Rawle, 127,) lays down the law thus : " They (*banks*, turnpike, canal and bridge companies) are no further public, than as they have to do with great numbers of people. But if numbers alone is the criterion, it will often be difficult to distinguish public from private corporations." And in the case of Bonaparte, the Camden and Amboy rail road company, cited by the delegate from Luzerne, Judge Baldwin, says, (Baldw. Rep. 223.) " Private corporations are for *banks*, insurance, roads, canals, bridges, &c., where the stock is owned by individuals, but their use may be public."

The delegate from the county of Philadelphia, (Mr. Ingersoll) seems to think, that if the question be again brought before the supreme court of the United States, it will be decided differently, from the manner in which the judges of that court have heretofore laid down the law on the subject, as there has been a great change in the judges of that court. I would say to him as to this " Lay not that flattering unction to your soul." That court will, they must, adhere to the settled law of the land.

The present chief justice of the United States, one of the judges by whom the gentleman supposes this great change to be wrought, has already given his opinion on the subject. In an opinion given by him on the 5th of September, 1833, relative to the Camden and Amboy rail road company, he says: " It is now too well settled to be disputed, that a charter granted by a state, to a company incorporated to make a road or canal, where the funds for the work are provided by individuals, is a contract on the part of the state, and the public cannot by subsequent legislation, without the consent of the corporation, alter the terms of the charter."

This, sir, is the language of Roger B. Taney, the chief justice of the supreme court of the United States. I take it to be good authority, as proceeding from a distinguished jurist, although not chief justice at the time he gave the opinion, and because I find it to be in accordance with the law of the land. And my word for it, that distinguished judge will never jeopard the reputation he has acquired, as a lawyer, by maintaining a contrary doctrine.

The delegate from Luzerne, (Mr. Woodward) in his argument, endeavors to sustain the position he has assumed, by assimilating the resumption of a charter, to the case in which the private property of individuals, can be taken for public use. I admit the principle, that private property may be taken for public use, but I deny its application. The principle is this, if an individual owns ground, upon which it is necessary to make a *public improvement*, such as a road, canal, rail road bridge, or the like, the public has a right, where it makes the improvement itself, or by a corporation created for the purpose, where it chooses so to delegate the power, to take any land necessary to be occupied or used for the purpose, upon paying a proper compensation therefor. But the public has no right to take away any of his individual rights, except so far as those rights may be affected by taking away his property. It cannot take away the rights which subsist by virtue of the domestic relations of life; nor can you take from the United States Bank, or from any other bank chartered without the reservation of a power of repeal, the rights which have been granted to them, and for which they had paid a consideration. You may indeed take away their property *for public use*, as you may that of an individual, because the power to do so is part of the sovereignty remaining in the community, and is a reservation existing in every grant the proprietors, or the commonwealth made when they granted the soil. You cannot, however, take away incorporeal rights except so far as those rights may be affected by taking away corporeal rights for the public use. The public cannot take any thing from individuals for the purpose of *destroying it*. It has a right to take it for *public use*, not wantonly, or to trample it under foot. That any man's property may be taken for public use, it is true—but it does not follow that you can take away rights and franchises, which have been solemnly granted and paid for, nor even lands and buildings, if it be not for public use. That is a principle recognized by no law, and founded in no justice.

The delegate from the county of Philadelphia, (Mr. Ingersoll) speaking of some stock held by himself in a company, which has a perpetual charter, seemed to think that charter to be a violation of law. To be a perpetuity. I cannot see the force of the argument, unless we go at once to agrarianism or Fanny Wrightism, and carry out the principle that no man has a right to what his father has earned and left behind him at his death.—That land shall not descend from a man to his children.

We all know, that by our laws, a man may transmit his property to his heirs, devisees or assigns to all perputuity, if he does not tie up the course of that transmission to a particular course or line. This, the law, would not tolerate, as being contrary to its policy. It is not the meaning of the term perpetuity, as applied to real estate, that land shall not go in perpet. ual succession to a man and to his heirs and assigns ; but that it shall not go to them so tied up and restricted, that no one of the possessors shall have the control of it, to change its course by. alienation or otherwise. The stock held by a man in an incorporated company, no matter what be the duration of its charter, passes to his personal representatives at his decease, or is assignable and transferable by himself, in his life time, just as any other personal property he owns, and is liable to be taken in exe. cution for his debts. There is no perpetuity in the stock which he thus holds.

In some remarks made by me at Harrisburg, I took occasion to refer to the writings of Thomas Paine, and to quote largely, pertinent passages from his " Dissertation on Government." I admire the ingenuity with which the delegate from Philadelphia county, (Mr. Ingersoll) has avoided answering me. He says, that to sustain the distinction between the legis. ture acting as legislators in passing acts, which are appropriately denomi- nated laws, and acting as agents in making contracts and agreements with individuals, I relied on the " miserable sophism of the most despicable of human beings, who was weak in politics, an infidel in religion, and a sot in old age;" and adds, that he " cannot see whence he derived his celebrity."

Paine derived his celebrity from his political writings, perhaps as sound expositions of the principles of free government, as ever were written. I deny this charge of his weakness in politics. If ever there was a giant in politics, Thomas Paine was one. As to the two last charges against him—infidelity, and intemperance in his old age, I have no apology to offer for them or him. I spoke of him expressly as good authority in politics, but as a man to whom, upon religious subjects, I would never refer.

I do not, however, concur, as I have said already, with the delegate, in his estimate of Paine's strength and usefulness as a political writer. I have it from those who were actors in the revolution, and who were competent to judge, that Paine's writings had an immense influence, for good, among the people at large, in furthering the cause of American lib- erty. Ilis style was easy, natural, flowing and forcible. Its great recom. mendations were force, clearness and perspicuity. It carried conviction to the minds of those who perused his work, and I have heard more than one of the men of those days say, that he had contributed almost as much with his pen, as Washington did with his sword, towards the achievement of our independence. The gentleman may hold up his hands at this assertion, but I have my authority from the men of the revolution, who lived out their principles in their lives, and who, as well as myself, re.

gretted that Paine's subsequent vices and follies tarnished his just and well merited fame. If he had never written upon religious subjects, his name would have gone down to posterity, as one of the greatest benefactors of mankind. He is not, however, the only man whose folly in old age has deprived him of the merit due for the services of his earlier years.

I ask the delegate to point out the defects in Paine's politics. To answer, if he can, the arguments I have adduced from his works, and not to slide over or past them. To meet them manfully, by an argument of equal force, and not to attempt to get rid of that which he cannot answer, by calling it a sophism, and casting reproach upon its author.

I quoted thus largely from this work, because I found the ideas I wished to convey, there expressed with a force and clearness which, I should myself, in vain have attempted to reach by any language of my own. I will refer again to but two passages:

"All laws are acts, but all acts are not laws. Many of the acts of assembly are acts of negociation, and agency; that is, they are acts of contract and agreement on the part of the state, with certain persons therein recited. *An act of this kind, after it has passed the house, is of the nature of a deed or contract, signed, sealed and delivered, and subject to the same general laws and principles of justice, as all other deeds and contracts are; for in a transaction of this kind, the state stands as an individual, and can be known in no other character in a court of justice."*

"By "*laws*," as distinct from agency transactions or matters of negociation, are to be comprehended *all those public acts of the assembly or commonwealth, which have a universal operation, or apply themselves to every individual of the commonwealth.* Of this kind, are laws for the distribution and administration of justice, for the preservation of the peace, for the security of property, for raising the necessary revenues by just proportions," &c.

These, sir, are the general propositions, which carry the evidence of their truth on their front. They are undeniable. The rest of the quotations which I made, are but the elaboration or carrying out the argument *in extenso,* which is done with unequalled force and power.

The delegate from Montgomery, (Mr. Sterigere) has stated, that the legislature of Pennsylvania repealed the act incorporating the Bank of North America, and gives this as an evidence, that the legislature now possess the same power. Does the delegate recollect, that although the law was repealed, the bank denying the right of the legislature to repeal it, went on with its operations as if no such act had been passed? That the constitutionality of the repeal was a subject of discussion and agitation in the legislature, from the time of the repeal, in the fall of 1785, until the act reviving the charter of the bank was passed, in the spring of 1787, when the bank, to prevent the injury which the repeal had done to their credit abroad, compromised the matter, by taking a charter for fourteen years. This reviving act was a virtual acknowledgement, that the repeal was wrong.

But, the legislature then had all the power claimed for the British parliament, if they chose to exercise it; and there was then no constitutional barrier to the exercise of the power, as there is now ; for it is decided in the case of Owings vs. Speed, in 5 Wheaton, 420, that previous to the constitution of the United States going into effect, and where the state constitution contained no clause restraining them, the state legislatures had the right, in consequence of their sovereignty, to make laws operating upon the rights of property vested before that time.

The cases heretofore cited by me from the decisions of the supreme court of the United States, show that in law, there is no distinction between banking corporations and any other private corporations. In the Dartmouth College case, that court hold, that there is no distinction between a grant of land and a grant of corporate powers. The legislature, has the right to prescribe the manner in which the land of the state shall be sold and granted. So the right to confer corporate privileges, for banking purposes, as has been solemnly decided, exists in the community, which the legislature, as the agents of that community, may confer in the manner which they think best suited to promote the public good. Each is a grant and each is governed by precisely the same rules. The one is as solemn and irrevocable a contract as the other.

But, sir, I desire not to be misunderstood. I stated explicitly at Harrisburg, and I now repeat, that I believe public opinion does now call for the incorporation into the constitution, of a provision reserving in all future charters, the right to alter or modify them. Whenever such a provision is brought forward in proper shape, I shall concur in it heartily. And if no other delegate will offer it, I will. I, however, can never agree to cut loose the bonds which bind society together—to jeopard the property, and destroy the investments of our citizens, made on the public faith, simply because an act which I do not like has been passed, establishing a particular bank—an act which I think a majority of the people disapprove. I have heretofore said, and I now repeat, that I was opposed to the grant of the charter of the Bank of the United States, by the state legislature ; and were the question of its grant now to be decided, I should still be opposed to it.

But, sir, the remedy of the people is, if their representatives and agents have not done what they ought to have done, to be more careful thereafter in the persons they may select. Never, however, let the republic be subjected to the imputation of having acted in violation of public faith.

Mr. MEREDITH, rose and addressed the Chair.

[The remarks of Mr. MEREDITH, not having been returned in time for insertion in their proper place, will be given in the APPENDIX.]

Mr. MEREDITH here gave way to Mr. INGERSOLL, who moved that the committee now rise.

And on the question,

Will the committee of the whole agree to the motion?

The yeas and nays were required by Mr. CLARKE, of Beaver, and nineteen others, and are as follows, viz :

YEAS—Messrs. Ayres, Baldwin, Banks, Barnitz, Bell, Bigelow, Brown, of Lancaster, Carey, Chambers, Chandler, of Philadelphia, Chauncey, Clark, of Dauphin, Cline, Coates, Cochran, Cope, Cox, Craig, Crain, Cunningham, Darlington, Denny, Dickey,

Dickerson, Donagan, Farrelly, Forward, Foulkrod, Gamble, Gilmore, Hastings, Hays, Helffenstein, Henderson, of Dauphin, Hopkinson, Houpt, Ingersoll, Jenks, Konigmacher, Magee, Martin, M'Cahen, M'Call, M'Dowell, M'Sherry, Merrill, Pennypacker, Pollock, Porter, of Lancaster, Porter, of Northampton, Ritter, Russell, Scheetz, Scott, Seltzer, Serrill, Sill, Sterigere, Stevens, Weidman, Woodward, Young, Sergeant, *President*—63.

NAYS—Messrs. Agnew, Barclay, Barndollar, Bedford, Bonham, Brown, of Philadelphia, Clarke, of Beaver, Clarke, of Indiana Cleavinger, Crawford, Crum, Cummin, Darrah, Dillinger, Earle, Fleming, Fuller, Gearhart, Grenell, Harris, Hayhurst, Hiester, Hyde, Keim, Kennedy, Kerr, Krebs, Mann, Merkel, Miller, Montgomery, Purviance, Reigart, Royer, Saeger, Sellers, Shellito, Smith, of Columbia, Smyth, of Centre, Snively, Stickel, Thomas, Todd, Weaver—44.

So the question was determined in the affirmative.

And, thereupon, the committee rose, reported progress, and obtained leave to sit again; and,

The Convention adjourned.

———

FRIDAY, DECEMBER 29, 1837.

Mr. COPE, of Philadelphia, presented a memorial from citizens of Philadelphia county, praying that trial by jury may be granted in all cases where liberty is at stake.

Which was laid on the table.

Mr. CAREY, of Bucks, presented a memorial similar in its tone and character, from citizens of Bucks county.

Which was also laid on the table.

Mr. STURDEVANT, of Luzerne, submitted the following resolution, which was laid on the table for future consideration, viz:

" *Resolved*, That on and after Saturday next, when this convention adjourns, it will adjourn to meet at nine o'clock in the morning, and will continue in session until three o'clock in the afternoon."

Mr. EARLE submitted the following resolution, which was laid on the table for future consideration, viz:

" *Resolved*, That the report, No. 9, on future amendments to the constitution, be referred to a committee of the whole convention, and made the special order of the day for ———— next, and for each succeeding day, until the committee of the whole shall be discharged from the further consideration thereof."

Mr. HIESTER moved that the convention reconsider the following resolution, which was adopted on the 26th instant, viz:

" *Resolved*, That the rules of this convention be so changed, that it shall not be in order for any delegate to speak for more than one hour at any one time, except by the consent of two-thirds of the convention, or committee of the whole.

Mr. H. explained, that his object in making this motion, was so to amend the resolution, as that its effect would be to prevent gentlemen from speaking a second time. He considered the language of the resolution as bearing out the construction which had been put upon it by the Chair.

Mr. MANN, of Montgomery, moved the postponement of the motion for the present.

Mr. CHAMBERS, of Franklin, hoped the motion would be disposed of without postponement, and that the resolution would be reconsidered, not for the purpose of amendment, but in order that it might be rescinded altogether. When he had the floor, and this resolution was adopted, he forbore to make a single remark upon it. He believed that it was discreditable to this body. We stand low enough already, (said Mr. C.) and I should be sorry that we should do any thing to degrade us still lower in the estimation of the other states of the Union. There never was any instance before, in any political body, where such a limitation was imposed on the freedom of debate. If the debates are protracted, it ought not to be forgotten that the right of free discussion has been guarantied by the constitution, and that it is a most important right; and we ought to pause before we attempt to impose such limitation in this body, which is charged with the duty of constructing fundamental laws. We had seen this resolution in its operation, and had found that it does not answer the purpose of those who introduced it. It has been evaded, and will continue to be evaded. We had seen a gentleman address the convention for an hour, and resume his remarks after an interval of another hour. Some other gentlemen had been cut off in the middle of an argument. The presiding officer is compelled to keep a chronicle of time, to sit with a stop watch before him. If gentlemen would reflect, they would see that the operation of this resolution, is unworthy of this body, and that the resolution itself, is unfit to be among our rules.

Mr. REIGART, of Lancaster, said, it did not strike him that this rule had the effect of limiting the debate. It had been said that it was arbitrary in its operation, and tended to lower us in the estimation of the other states. The gentleman who made these statements, was a member of the committee on rules, and voted for the adoption of the rule, which sanctions the previous question, the effect of which, is to cut off a debate in a moment. Whenever we shall come out of committee of the whole, this rule will be, in a measure, inoperative. He admitted that it was rendered so at present, because a speaker could evade its spirit by continuing his speech at intervals, and if this practice were to be continued in committee of the whole, some remedy ought to be provided, either by rescinding, or amending the new rule.

Mr. BANKS, of Mifflin, expressed his regret that the rule had operated, so as to cut off the speeches of gentlemen, but it had been rendered necessary by the rule fixing the day of adjournment. The gentleman from Franklin, (Mr. Chambers) had not well weighed his words, when he cast reflections on the majority of the convention. They were as anxious to adjourn, as to hear speeches; and it would be impossible to adjourn on the 2d of February, if long speeches were to be permitted. He believed it would be well to have the work quietly done, and it would be better still, to have it well done. He was content to continue to act under this rule, although he was aware that evasions had taken place, and would again take place.

Mr. CLARKE, of Indiana, was against any postponement of this motion. Notwithstanding the resolution fixing the day of adjournment, which he had voted against, because we had to do a certain quantity of duty which was entrusted to us, he had voted against this resolution, and against the amendment. He was totally opposed to this abridgment of the right of speech. When we are in convention, a gentleman can only speak twice, without leave. This is a rule which prevails in all legislative bodies. The rule in courts of law, is, that a lawyer says all he intends to say, and afterwards, is at liberty to reply to the opposing lawyer. The rule gives an opportunity of rejoinder, and there stops. He knew there was no opportunity of delivering his sentiments in an hour; it could not be done. His argument was attacked by all. Could he make a reply in an hour? However bad the operation of the rule in the committee of the whole, it was still worse in convention. In committee of the whole, a member had the right to speak as often as was necessary; while in convention, he was restrained by the rules from speaking more than twice. This, therefore, is an unprecedented abridgment of the right of speech. He was sorry that those who were not in the habit of speaking, should think it proper to abridge the privilege of those who were. All the delegates are sent here for some purpose. Perhaps, said Mr. C., I was sent here for my talkative disposition; and if so, I am expected to talk. I am not one to strut and fret more than my hour. My gun soon expends all the ammunition I have. Why were we chafed the night before last, but through the operation of this rule. He was opposed to every attempt to curtail the freedom of debate.

Mr. HIESTER, of Lancaster, said, he had voted for fixing the day of adjournment, because he thought the convention had already sat longer than the people intended they should sit. There was entire unanimity on that point, out of the doors of this hall. What was expected to be done in six weeks, we have been engaged for months in doing. It was found to be impossible to get along without the adoption of some arbitrary rules. Under this rule, half a dozen persons could speak in one day; while, under the old practice, half a dozen speakers would take up a dozen days, and after that, the previous question could be called in to cut off every other person who desired to be heard. We had previously the previous question, and also another rule, which precluded all debate on questions of order. This was all necessary; and now we have this new rule, which is more democratic in its character than the previous question. He did not believe that we should get out of committee of the whole before the second of February, unless there was an end put to the practice of making long speeches. Any gentleman, he believed, could say what it was necessary for him to say, in one hour; and if he had not quite finished, there was no doubt that a majority would be willing that he should go on. This privilege had, to be sure, been denied in some cases; but it was because the committee was worried out, in consequence of the tediousness of an argument, three-fourths of which had no relevance to the subject. The time had come to bring the labors of the convention to a close. His constituents were anxious for the adjournment of this body.

He had letters daily on the subject, which told him that the people were becoming so excited by the long sitting of the convention, that they would not even look at the amendments, when they should have been made.

At the time, said Mr. H., I submitted this resolution, I did not antici- pate that it would have excited so much discussion. The matter is very plain to all of us; and I hope we shall come to the vote at once, one way or the other. I do not wish to protract the debate, but I desire it should be brought to a close as soon as posible.

Mr. M'SHERRY would inquire of the Chair, whether the motion to post- pone was in order, until the question on the motion to reconsider had been decided. The first motion was to reconsider, and the motion now, was to postpone the further consideration of that motion. Was the latter motion in order at this time?

The CHAIR said, that the motion to reconsider had been made and seconded; and it was the opinion of the Chair, that it was in order to move that the further consideration of that motion be postponed for the present.

Mr. BROWN, of Philadelphia county, said, he hoped the further con- sideration of the motion would be postponed, and that the rule would be made absolute.

We were told, said Mr. B., when we first met at Harrisburg, that the people of Pennsylvania, required certain amendments to be made to the constitution of 1790—which amendments they had well considered, and digested—and I, for one, came into this body, prepared to vote for those amendments. I am now prepared to vote for all such, and, however long we may remain in session, I shall not be ready to vote for any other. I believe that those amendments could have been carried just as well, and by about the same majority, on the first day on which we met, as they will be if we sit here for a year to come. What has been the course of our operations? We have been debating a proposition here, weeks upon weeks; and if any result at all has been arrived at, it has only been to confuse the minds of the members, and to impel them to bring the ques- tion to a vote, at all events, in order that they might get rid of it. The long debates which have taken place in committee, and in which I am aware that I have participated, has been the subject of complaint, and not the votes we have given. For my part, I am disposed to cut them short by all proper means. What has been the effect of these debates? A few gentlemen occupy the attention of the committee for two or three weeks, till the patience of the members were exhausted; whilst others, who might, probably, have said quite as much in a few words, have had no opportunity to speak at all. Thus it is, that the debates have tended to darken, rather than to enlighten our judgments. Such I believe to be the case at the present time—and such is the feeling entertained, in rela- tion to the question now before us. I believe there is a majority of the members who feel disposed to do something in regard to these corpora- tions; and yet the majority may be inclined to vote all such amendments down at this time, in order to get rid of the debate, and under a hope that on second reading, they may have an opportunity of getting them through. I think that one hour is time enough to speak to the question: though it is true, that if gentlemen, in the observations they may make, keep their eye, not to things here, but to the political aspect of matters out of doors, they may speak for a month. All sorts of personal reflections, and all kinds of political matters, have been considered in order. If we are to have the whole world to roam in, let us at least limit the time in which the journey is to be performed. If our rules are not of sufficient force to prohibit gentlemen altogether from roaming, let us at least say they shall roam only so long, if we cannot say how far. On second reading, every question will most probably have to be taken by yeas and nays, and we have agreed to adjourn finally on the second day of February. Where is the time to come from? I mean the time that will be indispensably necessary to get through with our actual business. The resolution to adjourn on the second day of February, was not thrown out by the gentleman from Beaver, (Mr. Dickey) as a "tub to the whale." No, sir, it was a serious position—introduced with a full intention to carry it out. I trust, therefore, that, considering the very short space of time which we have yet to remain together, and the many important matters which yet remain to be acted upon, we will keep ourselves steadily to the work which we have before us, and that we will not hereafter enter into long arguments which have no relation to the questions we are called upon to decide.

Mr. CLINE, of Bedford county, said he desired to make only one or two observations, in consequence of the votes which he had already given, and which he might hereafter feel himself compelled to give.

There can be no doubt, said Mr. C. that much precious time has been lost, by the long debates which we have recently had. There is a great complaint, both in and out of this body, that we have not proceeded exactly in the manner we ought to have done. There must be some cause for these complaints. Either we have not attended to our business as industriously as we ought to have done, or we have suffered our time to be frittered away in the discussion of irrelevant matters. I think we have attended here a sufficient number of hours every day ;—we have devoted about six hours daily, to the matters before us. The cause of complaint, then, can not be in the length of time, during which we are daily in session ; and, there must be some other reason. We must have fallen into some error, and I have attempted to ascertain what that error has been. I cannot attribute it to any thing else, than that there is a propensity in each member, to distinguish himself here, individually, by the speeches he may deliver. I do not say this in any disparagement ; it is a propensity which is common to all deliberative bodies.

It seems to me, however, that we have lost sight of our duties, as a body, and that we have been looking to our own situation and wishes. We have adopted a resolution to adjourn on a particular day. I cannot conceive with what appearance of propriety this body was able to bring itself to the adoption of that resolution. I cannot reconcile the proceeding to my mind. I was sent here by the people, whom I have the honor to represent, to perform a most important duty. I was to perform it to the best of my ability, upon proper consideration and reflection, and according to the best lights which experience might furnish, and yet I was called upon to say that that duty must, at all events, and under every hazard, be performed within a given space of time.   •

Sir, I will ask the members of this convention, are we to all appearances, nearer to the termination of our labors, than we were on the second day of May last? And, yet we have, by the adoption of this resolution, declared that we will adjourn on the second day of February—that is to say, in about four weeks from this time. But still that resolution has been adopted.

I was one of those who voted in favor of what has been designated " the gag law "—that is to say, the resolution limiting each delegate to one hour, in committee of the whole. I gave that vote with reluctance, and I felt desirous to take this occasion to explain why I voted in favor of the resolution, in order that my constituents may know the motives which have governed my conduct here. I am sorry, I was compelled to vote as I did ; but, I say, if we are to adjourn on the day fixed, it will be impossible for us to get through with our business, unless we impose upon ourselves some such restriction. How then is the end which we all had in view, when we voted for a definite day of adjournment—namely, the speedy termination of our labors—to be brought about? It must either be accomplished by a determination on our own part, to pay exclusive regard to the performance of the duties which we owe to our constituents as a convention assembled here to revise the constitution, or it must be accomplished by the more forcible measure of restricting the members in debate.

If gentlemen are willing now to rescind the resolution, fixing the second day of February, as the day of our final adjournment, I am willing, for my own part, to rescind the other resolution, throwing this obstacle, as we must all admit it does, in the way of the freedom of debate. But unless the former suggestion is adopted, I, for one, will not give my consent that all the time of this body shall be wasted in the discussion of one or two matters—probably irrelevant and unimportant ;—and, then, that we should jumble up all the rest, in one indiscriminate heap, and dispose of them, not less to our own dissatisfaction, than to the dissatisfaction and disappointment of our constituents.

We have propositions of every kind forced upon us, to which hitherto we have been compelled to give our attention. We were told, only so far back as yesterday, by the gentleman from the county of Philadelphia, (Mr. Ingersoll) that the gentlemen with whom he acted, in reference to matters which have so long occupied the attention of the committee, knew themselves to be in a minority in this body ; and, yet, with the knowledge of this fact, as they say, before them, they go on, urging their propositions upon us, with as much zeal, as if they had a fair prospect of success.

I have no desire to call in question the course of any gentleman here, but I do not think that this is correct. If there is not a reasonable chance that a proposition will succeed, let us not offer it; let us save every moment that we can; and, let us attend to our duties, not with reference to ourselves—to our individual wishes, feelings or objects—but, with the reference to the one single object which we should all have before us —to wit, the welfare of the people of this commonwealth.

Mr. President, I regret to have said so much ; yet, thus much I felt it necessary to say, in order to justify to my constituents, the course I have adopted here. •

Mr. HIESTER said, that rather than any further time should be consumed in this discussion, he would withdraw his motion.

So the motion to reconsider was withdrawn.

A motion was made by Mr. COPE, and read as follows, viz :

Resolved, That the President draw his warrant on the state treasurer, in favor of Samuel Sho·h, secretary, for two thousand dollars, to be accounted for in the settlement of his account.

And on motion,

The said resolution was read the second time, considered and adopted.

A motion was made by Mr. BEDFORD,

That the convention proceed to the second reading and consideration of the resolution, read on the 26th instant, in the words as follow, viz :

Resolved. That the following new rule be adopted, both in convention, and in committee of the whole, viz :

" That when any twenty delegates rise in their places, and move the question on any pending amendment, it shall be the duty of the presiding officer to take the vote of the body on sustaining such call, and if such call sha'l be sustained by a majority, the question shall be taken on such amendment, without further debate."

Which was agreed to—yeas, 50—nays, 47.

And the said resolution being under consideration,

A motion was made by Mr. DARLINGTON,

That the further consideration of the said resolution be postponed for the present.

In support of this motion, Mr. D. said, that he had submitted it, because only a few days ago, the matter had been partially discussed, and it had been found that the sentiments of the members were against it. If the discussion was allowed to proceed, he doubted whether it would be got rid of this morning. He hoped that the regular business of the body would not be farther delayed, in the discussion of propositions of this nature, at least at the present time. He did not see what good was to arise from a discussion on the resolution, and, from his knowledge of the sentiments of the members, he felt satisfied that the majority were opposed to it.

Mr. FULLER, of Fayette, said he hoped that the motion of the gentleman from Chester, (Mr. Darlington) to postpone the further consideration of the resolution, would not prevail ; although, he (Mr. F.) could not refrain from expressing the gratification he felt, in finding that that gentleman had changed his opinions within a very short period of time, in regard to the business of the convention. Heretofore, the gentleman had advocated speed in the transaction of business ; speed, at all events ; and, now he expressed a hope that the usual debate would not be interrupted by the discussion of this resolution.

What, said Mr. F., has been the usual debate for the last six weeks? I want light as much as any other gentleman, but I want to have it as speedily as possible. This resolution I think is well calculated to aid in bringing our labors to a more speedy termination.

It is well known that there is only one way, according to the rules of this body, by which a debate can be forcibly terminated; that is to say, by the application of the previous question; and, all amendments which may be pending at the time the demand for the previous question is seconded, are of necessity cut off. Many important questions may, in this manner, be passed over without any vote being taken upon them, and this is the great evil of which I complain, as resulting from the previous question; because, if a vote could be taken, it would often be very satisfactory to gentlemen, even, though, on that particular question, they might happen to be in a minority,

The previous question, however, is absolute in its application, and, as I have said, cuts off every thing. I do not think this is proper. I think it is desirable and right that some rule should be adopted, by which we may be enabled to have a vote upon all propositions for amendment which may be offered; and, it appears to me, that the resolution now before us, will effectually accomplish the object.

I hope, therefore, that the motion to postpone will not be agreed to, but that we shall have a direct vote taken on the resolution. It seems to me to be a preferable resolution to that limiting each delegate to an hour. I do not think that any proposition could have been offered, so well calculated as this, to bring our labors to a close, and to give general satisfaction on all sides of the house.

Mr. CHAMBERS said, that he hoped the postponement would not be agreed to, but that the resolution would be considered and finally rejected. The effect of the resolution, said Mr. C. will be, in my opinion, not to facilitate the business of the convention, but to embarrass it by a new rule.

The previous question was a rule which the majority of the house could at all times apply, for the purpose of expediting its business, or of taking any question when it was the disposition of the majority that it should be taken. But the effect of this new resolution, requiring that the vote shall be taken on any pending amendment, when any twenty delegates shall call for the question, will not be to bring the convention to a decision on the main question itself. The moment that the question, under this new rule, would be taken on the amendment, or on the amendment to the amendment, as the case may be, we should have new questions submitted and new votes taken, and so we might go on without end. The effect of it, in my opinion would be, to embarrass and delay our proceedings.

I hope, therefore, that we shall hold on to our rule as it now exists—that is to say, to the previous question—to which the majority may at any time have recourse. It is a parliamentary rule, and when the majority desire to expedite the business, they can do so through its instrumentality.

Mr. BELL, of Chester, said that he stood in rather a peculiar position, with reference to the various motions which had been made, with a view to expedite the business of the convention.

It is well known, said Mr. B., to all the members of this body that, until recently, I have opposed every motion or resolution, which had for its object, to precipitate our business to a conclusion. This I have done until my late visit home, and it may be remembered that I have incurred the rebuke in this particular of my venerable friend from the city of Philadelphia, (Mr. Hopkinson.) I was not, until recently, aware of the truth of the remark which has been made here, on more than one occasion—to wit, that this convention stood low in the estimation of the people. But, we have not yet heard the reason. Why is it, I would ask, that this convention is growing, as it were, into a monument, for scorn to point its slow unmoving finger at? I will tell gentlemen, it is because of the protracted and irrelevant debates which we have experienced here; and I now warn the friends of reform in this body that, if they do not take heed to their course, every salutary amendment which they may desire to adopt, will be merged in the unpopularity of the convention and that the people will look only to the expenditure of time and money, in the debates which take place here, and not to the amendments we may make to the constitution.

For this reason, I was in favor of the adoption of the resolution, by which each delegate was limited to the space of an hour. I acknowledge freely, that there is much inconvenience resulting from that resolution; but, it is still more inconvenient to the public, to be kept so long in suspense, awaiting the final action of this convention.

What is the proposition now before us? What is there in it to excite the alarm of gentlemen here? It is nothing more than a proposition to introduce the previous question in a new form. Is there any thing so terrible in this? We have been here debating amendment upon amendment, week after week. It is well known that on the bank question—decided the other day—members were ready to vote for three weeks before the vote was taken; and that, but for the operation of the previous question which would have prevented them from doing that which they were desirous of doing, the previous question would certainly have been applied. But what, I ask, is the proposition before us? Its object simply is to give us an opportunity to vote on all amendments which may be offered, and at any time when the question may be called for by a certain number of delegates. Where can be the objection to the adoption of such a rule? Is it not well calculated to expedite our business, and that, too, without detriment to any one? Will any gentleman say, after the many long months which we have spent in debate, that it is not desirable that our business should be expedited as much as it is possible for us to expedite it, without injury to the great objects for which we were called together?

The gentleman from Franklin, (Mr. Chambers) has told us that it is a rule which, if adopted, will retard, and not expedite the progress of our business. If he can convince me of that, I will go with him against it. But, until that time, and believing as I now do, that it will tend to bring our labors to a more speedy termination, I shall give my voice in favor of it.

Mr. Martin, of Philadelphia county, said, he sincerely hoped that this new resolution would not meet with any favor from the members of the convention. It appeared to him to be worse than the gag-law which had been recently adopted—he alluded to the resolution prohibiting the delegates from speaking for a longer period than one hour at a time. The resolution now under discussion gave absolute power to any twenty members to cut off all debate upon any proposition. It was, in fact, the previous question, yet its power was greater than that of the previous question. According to this rule, if adopted, no amendment could be offered which might not be choaked off without any discussion, if but twenty delegates were opposed to it, and chose to call for the question upon it. Was not this more than the resolution adopted lately, and with which so much fault had been found. As regards that resolution, said Mr. M., there is at least this advantage, that we can select from among us, for the purpose of expressing our sentiments, gentlemen who speak with great rapidity; as, for instance, the gentleman from the county of Philadelphia, (Mr. Brown) who speaks as much in one hour as I can speak in three.

But, as to the resolution now before us, there is no such hope. These time-saving machines have taken up nearly one-fifth of our time. I have, from the first, opposed them on that ground. This is another new machine of the same kind ; and, I regret that I am not prepared with a proper safety-valve for it.

Mr. BEDFORD begged leave explain. The gentleman from the county of Philadelphia, (Mr. Martin) seemed to overlook that fact that, although any twenty delegates might move the question on any pending amendment, still a majority of the whole body would be required to sustain the call.

Mr. MARTIN resumed. He could not see that the state of the case was altered in any material degree by the explanation of the gentleman from Luzerne, (Mr. Bedford) The question could be demanded by any twenty delegates rising in their places and sustaining the call. He (Mr. M.) did not like either the previous question, or this new patent machine which was intended to run at a rate, he could not tell how fast. He hoped it would be voted down ; and, that the disposition which had been lately manifested to gag the members of this house unconstitutionally— to close their lips by force—to smother the right of speech and to suppress the freedom of debate, would not be countenanced any longer. The constitution of Pennsylvania declared that every man should have the right to speak freely. This resolution would violate that right—it would gag every man. He had no hesitation in saying that it went further towards the suppression of the freedom of speech, than any proposition which he had ever known to be introduced into any deliberative body. He trusted that it never would receive the approbation of a majority of this body.

Mr. DARLINGTON, of Chester, then withdrew his motion to postpone.

Mr. HOPKINSON, of the city, said that although this was an incidental question, and did not relate to the business which we came here to do, but only as to the manner of doing that business, which, in his opinion, was one of great importance, yet it ought to claim the serious attention of the convention. He thought that all these attempts to abridge our labors by the introduction of new rules, or by imposing restraints on ourselves, were not only nugatory, but even worse—mischievous. Public bodies had been frequently in session in this city, and in various other parts of the United States, and had laid down certain rules for the governance of their proceedings. We should act wisely if we availed ourselves of their experience, instead of going further, and adopting rules, wholly unnecessary, and calculated only to delay rather than to facilitate the despatch of business. He did not entertain the slighest doubt that they would fail to prodnce the effect expected from them.

The gentleman from the county of Philadelphia, (Mr. Brown) had told the convention that the people had agreed upon all the amendments that were desired, and that they might have been disposed of in one week after we had been in session, had not the convention wasted its time in discussing resolutions which amounted to nothing. He was really astonished to hear such language on this floor. He would ask how that gentleman knew what were the opinions of the people of Pennsylvania? Let the gentleman state what were the amendment, they had agreed upon. He might know something of the opinions of the people of the south eastern portion of the state. He (Mr. Hopkinson) would venture to say that the gentleman did not know what were the opinions of one-third of the people of Moyamensing, the place of his own residence, on any one amendment.

Mr. BROWN, of Philadelphia county, explained that he had remarked that each member knew what his constituents required.

Mr. DUNLOP: (In an under tone.) I do not know what mine require.

Mr. HOPKINSON resumed.

The gentleman from the county of Philadelphia said that the amendments might have been disposed of in one week. He (Mr. H.) did not pretend to know more of the sentiments of the people than the gentleman did, but he thought that living as that gentleman did, and himself did in one corner of the state, that the gentleman could not possibly have such a general knowledge of the opinions of the people. He much doubted whether the gentleman could make out a list of one hundred individuals out of his own district, whose opinions he knew in reference to the amendments which were required to be made to the constitution, or he perhaps, might say, with whom he had any acquaintance. He made this remark, because what had been stated by the gentleman was an implied censure, not only upon himself, (Mr. Hopkinson) but every gentleman who dissented from the gentleman. He wished to know what the gentleman intended, when he addressed the convention, when sitting at Harrisburg, again and again, and for two, three or four hours at a time, on questions of far less importance than this. What was the object he had in view, and what was the necessity for speaking? The gentleman was certainly at liberty to judge for himself as to what were the opinions of the people in regard to the amendments which the people wished to be made to the constitution; but, he ought, at the same time, to be liberal enough to allow others to judge for themselves. He (Mr. H.) conceived that this was an entirely inopportune period to be introducing time-saving machinery. It was too late for that. The moment we came to questions of vital importance—questions requiring the most serious examination and discussion, we were at once to be told that we could not be allowed to speak more than one hour; and, thus we were cut off in various ways.

Need he remind gentlemen of the many hours that had been spent in debating questions of minor importance, and the number of days that . were consumed in discussing on what day the annual election should be held? And, now that we had arrived at the pith and marrow of our business, numerous attempts had been made during the last week, to curtail our labors, by imposing restraints upon our actions. Gentlemen would excuse him when he said that he saw more impatience manifested on their part to get home, than a desire to do the public business. He did not mean to impeach the conduct of any gentleman in particular; but, he wished every gentleman to examine the matter for himself, and explain how it happened that delegates were so quiescent— so patient during the debates that took place at Harrisburg, on many trifling questions, and now that we had reached those of a highly important character, they evinced so much impatience? What, he asked, had given rise to this feeling? We had adopted a rule that no member should speak more than an hour, and he desired to know what was to be the effect of it. He asked if any body had foreseen the disorder which had resulted from the adoption of this resolution? The day the resolution was brought up, a great deal of time had been consumed in discussing it, as there had been every morning since, and so there would be until we should get rid of this unwise and unjust course of proceeding. What else had we seen? We had seen an evasion of the rule, and really under the circumstances connected with it, he was not sorry for it. If gentlemen adopt an unwise rule, they must expect frivolous proceedings thereon. Well, after a gentleman had spoken an hour, and then not finished his speech, he avails himself of an interval of ten minutes (though he did not see why three minutes would not do as well) to resume and conclude his speech. He was aware that some gentlemen thought that by the adoption of this rule, the lawyers would be cut down, because, as he knew, the profession were liable to the charge of making long speeches. But, the fact was, that lawyers had very little temptation to make long speeches, except in the performance of their duty—to contribute their share of information, whatever it was, to the subject that might be under debate. He felt quite sure that if a question were to come up in relation to the farming interest, gentlemen unconnected with it, would be glad to hear what those had to say who had.

For his own part, he should not care what time was taken up—whether it was one hour, or more. We surely could not blame any gentleman for communicating information which we had not before in our possession. He trusted that we should not interrupt any gentleman, and prevent his imparting knowledge, which, perhaps, might be of the highest importance. As a lawyer, he put it to gentlemen, who did not belong to that profession, whether they would, on that account, deprive the lawyers here of an opportunity of throwing any light on this question, which was a new one, and of as great importance, at least, as any that had come before the convention for consideration.

The gentleman from Luzerne, (Mr. Woodward) who brought forward the proposition, was scarcely allowed time to express his views in relation to it, before he was obliged to suspend his remarks. Was there a gentleman present, but what desired to hear the delegate's observations, so that he might be able to vote intelligently on the subject? He certainly thought there was not.

The delegate from the county of Philadelphia, (Mr. Ingersoll) followed immediately after the gentleman from Luzerne, and had just reached the most interesting portion of his speech, when he was arrested by the Chairman, informing him that the hour had expired.

What, he asked, would the people of Pennsylvania think of such extra-ordinary proceedings as these. Here, was our Chairman obliged to watch the clock, instead of listening to the speeches, in order to check a gentle-man from proceeding with his remarks beyond the time allotted to each member to give his views on any subject that might be under considera-tion. And, then he was asked if he had given credit to the member for five or ten minutes, he had lost by being interrupted. This was a most miserable business, for such a body as this !

Experience, however, had fully illustrated the mischievous and evil effects of the rule. What, he inquired, were we about? We were dis-cussing a great constitutional question, partly on principle and partly on authority; and, he defied any gentleman, possessing the power of con-densation, to as great an extent as the delegate from the county of Phila-delphia, to speak, with any satisfaction to himself, or this body, all that he could desire to say to the convention, in the course of an hour.

He (Mr. Hopkinson) believed that he had not the character of being a long, or tedious speaker, and he found it impossible to express his senti-ments at any thing like the length he wished. Indeed, he defied any man to speak to any principle, or authority, in the time allowed each gentleman to address the body.

When he said "authority," he meant that authority only which this body was bound to respect, and must abide by. It had been very justly remarked, that this convention was as much bound to regard the federal rights and powers, in their proceedings, as was the legislature of Penn-sylvania, so as not to infringe or trespass on the constitution of the United States.

If, then, the legislature cannot pass any law, as this convention certainly cannot, in violation of the constitution of the Union, we do not possess authority to give them power, which we, ourselves, can-not exercise.

He would say that this was a question which peculiarly belonged to the profession of the law—the members of which were just as much qualified to give an opinion on it as were the farmers in reference to mat-ters of an agricultural character. What, then, he would ask, was the object which gentlemen had in view, in wishing to give their sentiments at large, on this important subject? It was, that they might convey to others, perhaps less acquainted with it, such information as was neces-sary to a thorough understanding of the great principles by which we should be governed, in deciding upon the important question before us. By regarding fundamental principles and high authorities, the members of this convention might not have to repent any of their acts, which otherwise they might have to do. Suppose that gentlemen here would not agree to listen to what was the opinion of the supreme court of the United States, on a highly important constitutional question, and which might prevent their falling into error, and that, in consequence of rejecting that information, they should so far commit themselves as to put in the constitution a provision which the supreme court should declare null and void. Would it not be a matter of very deep regret to them? Most undoubtedly it would. Let us not, then, longer impose upon ourselves a rule calculated to produce much mischief.

The gentleman from Lancaster had spoken of the previous question. Upon the subject of the "previous question," Mr. H. said, that he had never entertained but one opinion, and had always acted in conformity with it—that is, that it is a most despotic exercise of mere power by a majority, and most unjustly trampled upon the rights of a minority. I say, with the Grecian. "strike, but hear me." To refuse this right, is to violate the first principle of a free government, which is, that *all shall be heard,* after which the lesser shall submit to the judgment of the greater number—the minority to the majority.

On no other principle, except that of physical force, have ten men, or one hundred men, a right to control the opinions or action of one. Still, this power has the sanction of deliberative bodies in our country, as well as in that from which we have looked for precedents; and, he (Mr. H.) would not deny, that experience has shewn that circumstances may occur to justify it by necessity. It may be useful to prevent a greater abuse, although it is itself extremely liable to abuse, and is too frequently abused. It is a measure which should be resorted to only in extreme cases, to prevent some public evil or danger, and gentlemen have no right to use it—they greatly abuse their power, when they apply it without some urgent, public cause; and, merely, because they are weary of a protracted discussion, or anxious to get to their homes. It should never be used for reasons of personal convenience—or from an irritated temper. Much more unjust and reprehensible is it when this power is interposed as an expedient of legislative policy, to carry a favorite measure—to get a question taken at an auspicious moment—in the absence, or to the surprise of its opponents.

It cannot be honestly used; it is a violation of the rights of the members of the body and of the people they represent, when it is brought in to cut off a full and fair discussion of a public question—and, still worse, when the object is to prevent a *direct vote* upon such a question, and put it on one side, or smother it by this previous question.

Mr. H. said, he would state a case in which he would think this power might be properly used, and by this example, the convention might judge of the kind of necessity, which, in his opinion, would justify it. Suppose that in the last hours of a limited session of a public body, certain measures remained to be done, which were indispensable to the operations of the government—such as a necessary appropriation bill, and a member or members, should so far forget their duty, as to endeavor to defeat such a measure, and thereby embarrass the administration of the government, by speaking away the whole time that was left of the session, he would not hesitate to defeat such a design, by stopping the mouths of the offenders.

In such a case, the object and effect of the previous question, would be to prevent a great abuse—to avoid a great public evil ; in fact, to suppress a fraud.   He would go on a step further, if the public affairs—the public safety—the transaction of businesss, essential to the action of the government, required all the time that was left to the session, he would not suffer it to be consumed by speeches, although there might be no such design as he had stated, in those who were desirous to make them.

Mr. H. said, he would conclude his observations, by saying that it is better for us to be content with the rules we have—adopted for shortening the debates—and that it would have been well, if we had stopped before we had adopted that which limits the time which a member may occupy in a speech. The convention has the power, and they have not been slow to use it, to prevent any improper waste of their time, without resorting to these extraordinary regulations.

Mr. MERRILL, of Union, said, there appeared to be some mistake prevailing, as to the object of our meeting here. He thought that we had met for the purpose of consulting together, and giving our opinions and advice to the people, on the very important subjects now under the consideration of this convention.

It seemed, however, from what had fallen from the delegate from the county of Philadelphia, (Mr. Brown) that such was not the fact, in his opinion, at least.   He said that we came here as mere ministerial agents, to do the will of the people—to carry their wishes into effect.

Now, if that was really the case, he (Mr. M.) conceived that the sooner we went home to ascertain what are their wishes, the better—for there was most unquestionably, a great contrariety of opinion in respect to what the people desired. Gentlemen could not agree on that point. One delegate rose and stated that so and so, was the opinion of his constituents,—while another averred, that those he represented, entertained sentiments directly adverse.

He (Mr. M.) apprehended that this body had met to consult and to devise measures for carrying into effect, the united wishes of the people of the commonwealth of Pennsylvania, in regard to the amendments that should be made to the constitution. It had been said that the people are tired of watching our proceedings—that they are displeased and disgusted at our having been so long in session, and that they wished us to adjourn. There was, probably, some truth in these complaints ; and, it therefore behooved delegates to endeavor to act in such a manner as to preserve their own self-respect. He contended that it was the duty of gentlemen to give advice to the people of Pennsylvania, and to base their labors on the expressed will of the whole community. Action was required from this body, founded upon light and knowledge. But, were they to act in the dark ?—to jump to conclusions, at once, without giving to a subject, that thought and reflection, to which it was justly entitled ? Gentlemen had complained that the Chairman would not enforce the rule against members wandering from the subject immediately under discussion. Why, the fact was, the committee themselves would not permit him, and thus delegates had been allowed to proceed with their remarks, when entirely out of order. He repeated that that was the fault of the committee themselves, and not of the Chair. He trusted, that the rule limiting members to speak only a certain time, would be rescinded. There had been so much disorder growing out of the adoption of the rule in question, as to have consumed a great deal of the time of the convention, which might have been profitably spent, if gentlemen, instead of being arrested in the course of their remarks, had been allowed to proceed. If we would avail ourselves of the lesson of experience we had already taken, much time, he was sure, would be saved by it.

He could scarcely believe that any gentleman really thought that time was wasted in discussing the vital and important questions before this convention. We could not advise the people, without consulting among ourselves.

Suppose, a farmer to ask a lawyer his advice with respect to a title to his lands, does not the farmer wish him to take time in consultation? Undoubtedly he does. He would tell him to deliberated—not to speak previously—but to consult and take what time was necessary.

He (Mr. Merrill)cared not how long this convention deliberated—for deliberation could not be dispensed with. It was his settled determination to support every gentleman who was speaking to the subject before the Chair. No delegate ought to be called on to take his seat, at the very moment, perhaps, he was imparting valuable information. Proceeding in this extraordinary manner, was not preparing ourselves to give advice to the people. He thought that we ought to desist from making any further experiments. So long as this body had followed in the beaten track of those conventions that had heretofore been held, it had gone right. But, the moment it had departed therefrom, difficulties and unpleasantness occurred.

He thought that the gentleman from the county of Philadelphia, (Mr. Ingersoll) and the gentleman from Luzerne, (Mr. Woodward) had good cause to complain of their arguments being so cut up by interruptions.

Mr. DICKEY, of Beaver, moved the previous question; which was sustained.

The question next recurring was—"shall the main question be now put?"

Which was agreed to.

And the question then was on agreeing to the resolution.

Mr. BEDFORD, of Luzerne, asked for the yeas and nays; which being taken, the question was decided in the negative—yeas, 60; nays, 62.

YEAS—Messrs. Banks, Barclay, Bedford, Bell, Bigelow, Brown, of Northampton, Brown, of Philadelphia, Claike, of Indiana, Cleavinger, Cline, Crain, Crawford, Cummin, Curll, Darrah, Dillinger, Earle, Foulkrod, Fry, Fuller, Gamble, Gearhart, Gilmore, Grenell, Hastings, Hayhurst, Hiester, Hyde, Keim, Kennedy, Krebs, Lyons, Magee, Mann, M'Cahen, Merkel, Miller, Montgomery, Nevin, Overfield, Porter, of Northampton, Purviance, Reigart, Read, Riter, Ritter, Saeger, Scheetz, Sellers, Seltzer, Shellito, Smith, of Columbia, Smyth, of Centre, Sterigere, Stickel, Sturdevant, Taggart, Weaver, Weidman, Woodward—60.

NAYS—Messrs. Agnew, Ayres, Baldwin, Barndollar, Barnitz, Biddle, Bonham, Brown, of Lancaster Carey, Chambers, Chandler, of Philadelphia, Chauncey, Clarke, of Beaver, Clarke, of Dauphin, Coates, Cochran, Cope, Cox, Craig, Crum, Cunningham, Darlington, Denny, Dickey, Dickerson, Donagan, Doran, Dunlop, Farrelly, Fleming, Forward, Harris, Hays, Helffenstein, Henderson, of Dauphin, Hopkinson, Houpt, Ingersoll, Jenks, Kerr, Konigmacher, Maclay, Martin, M'Call, M'Dowell, M'Sherry, Meredith, Merrill, Pennypacker, Pollock, Porter, of Lancaster, Royer, Russell, Scott, Serrill, Sill, Snively, Stevens, Thomas, Todd, Young, Sergeant, *President*—62.

SEVENTH ARTICLE.

The CHAIR announced that, at the adjournment of the convention, last evening, the question pending was on the motion to grant leave to the committee to sit again—on which motion the yeas and nays had been ordered.

Mr. HIESTER, who had made that demand, rose and said that he would withdraw the same.

And, thereupon, the question having been taken on the ordinary motion, and leave having been granted:

The convention again resolved itself into a committee of the whole, Mr. REIGART in the chair, on the report of the committee, to whom was referred the seventh article of the constitution.

The amendment to the amendment being again under consideration.

[Mr. MEREDITH, here commenced and concluded his remarks, for which see APPENDIX.]

Mr. KONIGMACHER, of Lancaster, said:

Mr. Chairman, this subject has been decided at Harrisburg, and we have been discussing it in various shapes, ever since we came to this place. Many members who are anxious to express their views, have not yet had an opportunity. But this discussion has taken so wide a range, and consumed so much time, that it is evident that the committee is impatient to get the vote.

I had intended to give my views, relative to some unfounded charges made by members, but they have been so pointedly refuted, that I will forego that intention. I therefore, call the previous question.

Mr. M'CAHEN called for the yeas and nays on ordering the main question, which were ordered, and were yeas 60, nays 56, as follows:

YEAS—Messrs. Agnew, Ayres, Baldwin, Barndollar, Barnitz, Biddle, Brown, of Lancaster, Carey, Chambers, Chandler, of Phildadelphia, Clark, of Dauphin, Cleavinger, Cline, Coates, Cochran, Cope, Cox, Craig, Crum, Cunningham, Darlington, Denny, Dickey, Dickerson, Farrelly, Forward, Harris, Hays, Henderson, of Dauphin, Heister, Houpt, Jenks, Kerr, Konigmacher, Maclay M'Call, M'Dowell, M'Sherry Meredith, Merrill, Merkel, Montgomery, Pennypacker, Pollock, Porter, of Lancaster, Purviance, Reigart, Royer, Russell, Saeger, Scott, Serrill, Sill, Snively, Stevens, Thomas, Todd, Weidman, Young, Sergeant, *President*—60.

NAYS—Messrs. Banks, Barclay, Bedford, Bell, Bonham, Brown, of Northampger, Chauncey, Clarke, of Indiana, Crain, Crawford, Cummin, Curll Darrah, Dillinton, Donagan, Doran, Dunlop, Earle, Fleming, Foulkrod, Fry, Fuller, Gamble, Gearhart,

Gilmore, Grenell, Hastings, Hayhurst, Helffenstein, Hopkinson, Hyde, Keim, Kennedy, Krebs, Lyons, Magee, Mann, Martin, M'Cahen, Miller, Overfield, Porter, of Northampton, Read, Riter, Ritter, Scheetz, Sellers, Seltzer, Shellito, Smith, of Columbia, Smyth, of Centre, Sterigere, Stickel, Taggert, Weaver, Woodward—56.

So the main question was ordered to be now put.

The main question was on agreeing to the report of the committee, that it is inexpedient to make any amendment to the third section of the seventh article of the constitution.

Mr. BANKS called for the yeas and nays on the main question, which were ordered, and were yeas 64, nays 54, as follows :

YEAS—Messrs. Agnew, Ayres, Baldwin, Barndollar, Barnitz, Biddle, Brown, of Lancaster, Carey, Chambers, Chandler, of Philadelphia, Chauncoy, Clarke, of Beaver, Clark, of Dauphin, Cline, Coates, Cochran, Cope, Cox, Craig, Crum, Cunningham, Darlington, Denny, Dickey, Dickerson, Dunlop, Farrelly, Forward, Harris, Hays, Henderson, of Dauphin, Heister, Hopkinson, Houpt, Jenks, Kerr, Konigmacher, Maclay, M'Call, M'Dowell, M'Sherry, Meredith, Merkel, Montgomery, Pennypacker, Pollock, Porter, of Lancaster, Porter, of Northampton, Purviance, Reigart, Royer, Russell, Saeger, Scott, Serrill, Sill, Snively, Stevens, Thomas, Todd, Weidman, Young, Sergeant, *President*—64.

NAYS—Messrs. Banks, Barclay, Bedford, Bell, Bonham, Brown, of Northampton, Brown, of Philadelphia, Clarke, of Indiana, Cleavinger, Crain, Crawford, Cummin, Curll, Darrah, Dillinger, Donagan, Doran, Earle, Fleming, Foulkrod, Fry, Fuller, Gamble, Gearhart, Gilmore, Grenell, Hastings, Hayhurst, Helffenstein, Hyde, Keim, Kennedy, Krebs, Lyons, Magee, Mann, Martin, M'Cahen, Miller, Overfield, Read, Riter, Ritter, Scheetz, Sellers, Seltzer, Shellito, Smith, of Columbia, Smyth, of Centre, Sterigere, Stickel, Taggart, Weaver, Woodward—54.

So the report of the committee was agreed to.

Mr. EARLE rose to offer an amendment to the section.

The CHAIR said that it was not in order, inasmuch as the convention had adopted a resolution, declaring that when the vote should be taken on the then pending question, the convention should proceed to the second reading of the constitution.

Mr. EARLE appealed from this decision, on the ground that this resolution could not rescind an established rule of the convention.

The CHAIR stated that the resolution was not to be viewed as an alteration of a rule of the convention, but as merely applicable to this special purpose.

Mr. EARLE then withdrew his appeal ; and,

The committee rose, reported progress, and obtained leave to sit again ; and,

The Convention adjourned.

FRIDAY AFTERNOON, December 29, 1837.

The CHAIR announced that, agreeably to the resolution adopted by the Convention, all the reports and other propositions to amend the constitution would be considered as on second reading, and proceeded in accordingly.

A motion made was by Mr. PORTER of Northampton,

That the convention proceed to the consideration of the ninth article of the constitution as on second reading.

A motion was made by Mr. DICKEY,

To amend the said motion by striking out the words " the ninth article" and inserting in lieu thereof the words " the amendments to the first article of the constitution."

Mr. PORTER said, he would not unnecessarily consume the time of the convention, but he wished to say a single word in explanation of his reasons for the motion he had submitted. It was well known that there were certain amendments placing restrictions upon the legislature, which it had been the desire of many gentlemen to insert in some of those parts of the constitution which had been passed upon in committee, but which, as it was contended at the time, did not properly belong to any of those parts.

He was of opinion that those amendments did not belong to any other part of the constitution but to the ninth article. It was desirable that the convention should know in what place, in what order, and at what time these restrictions upon the legislature should be introduced; and, for that reason, should prefer, inasmuch as the convention had not entered at all into the consideration of the ninth article, that we should take it up now, in order to see where we should bring these amendments in.

Mr. STERIGERE submitted that the motion to amend the motion of the gentleman from Northampton, (Mr. Porter) was not in order, and could not therefore be entertained at this time.

After some conversation on the point of order,

The CHAIR decided that the amendment was not in order, and that the motion of the gentleman from Northampton was neither amendable, nor debateable.

And on the question,

Will the convention agree to the motion, that the convention proceed to the consideration of the ninth article of the constitution as on second reading?

The yeas and nays were required by Mr. DICKEY and Mr. CURLL, and are as follow, viz:

YEAS—Messrs. Bonham, Brown, of Northampton, Brown, of Philadelphia, Cline, Coates, Crain, Cummin, Dillinger, Doran, Earle, Fleming, Foulkrod, Fry, Hastings, Helffenstein, Houpt, Jenks, Kelm, Kennedy, Lyons, Mann, Martin, M'Cahen, M'Dowell, Nevin, Overfield, Porter, of Northampton, Read, Riter, Royer, Scheetz, Sellers, Serrill, Shellito, Sterigere, Taggart, Weaver, Young—38.

NAYS—Messrs. Agnew, Banks, Barndollar, Bedford, Bell, Biddle, Bigelow, B.own, of Lancaster, Carey, Chambers, Chandler. of Philadelphia, Chauncey, Clarke, of Beaver. Clarke, of Dauphin, Clark, of Indiana, Cleavenger, Cope, Cox, Craig, Crawford, Crum, Curll, Darlington, Darrah, Denny, Dickey, Dickerson, Donagan, Fuller, Gearhart, Gilmore, Hayhurst, Hays, Henderson of Dauphin, Hiester, Hopkinson, Hyde, Kerr, Konigmacher, Krebs, Maclay, Magee, M'Call, M'Sherry, Meredith, Merill, Merkel, Miller, Montgomery, Pennypacker, Pollock, Porter, of Lancaster, Purvaince, Ritter, Russell, Seager, Seltzer, Sill, Smith, of Columbia, Smyth, of Centre, Snively, Stevens, Stickel, Todd, Weidman, Woodward, and Sergeant, *President*—67.

So the motion was not agreed to.

A motion was then made by Mr. DICKEY,

That the convention proceed to the second reading and consideration of the amendments made to the first article of the constitution.

Mr. STEVENS hoped the gentleman from Beaver, (Mr. Dickey) would so extend his motion, as that the articles might be taken up in their order.

And Mr. DICKEY modified his amendment accordingly.

After some further consideration, the question was taken on the motion of Mr. Dickey, and was decided in the affirmative.

So the motion was agreed to.

The Secretary then proceeded to read the amendments to the first article of the constitution. A long debate followed on a point of order raised by Mr. EARLE, as to the order of proceeding.

When a motion was made by Mr. MEREDITH,

To postpone the further consideration of the first article, for the present, which motion was agreed to.

So the consideration of the same was postponed.

Mr. MEREDITH, of Philadelphia, on leave, offered the following resolution, which was read a first time :

Resolved, That on second reading, the Convention will consider the several articles of the constitution in their numerical order, and that the sections shall be read in the same order, and be considered and open for amendment : *Provided*, That when any section shall have been amended in committee of the whole, the section shall be read as amended.

Mr. M. moved to dispense with the rule which requires resolutions to lie on the table one day ; which was agreed to.

And the resolution was then read a second time.

Mr. STERIGERE, of Montgomery, moved to amend by striking out the words " amended in committee of the whole."

Mr. MEREDITH explained, that the effect of striking out the words in question, would be that the amendments made in committee of the whole would not be read.

Mr. STERIGERE then withdrew his amendment.

Mr. Brown, of Philadelphia county, moved an amendment and then withdrew it.

Mr. Bell, of Chester, moved that the convention do now adjourn.

The motion was negatived, and a division being demanded, there appeared—ayes 47, noes 49.

Mr. Cunningham of Mercer, moved to amend the resolution by striking out all after the word "resolved" and inserting "that when any article of the constitution shall be under consideration on second reading, the sections shall be read and considered in their numerical order, and sections to which amendments have been made in committee of the whole shall be read with the amendments."

Mr. Meredith accepted the modification.

On motion of Mr. Clarke of Indiana,

The Convention adjourned.

SATURDAY, December 30, 1837.

Mr. Konigmacher, of Lancaster, presented a memorial from citizens of Lancaster county, praying that the constitution may be so amended, as to provide that the civil rights, privileges, or capacities, of any citizen shall in no way be affected, diminished or enlarged, merely on account of his religious opinions; which was ordered to be laid on the table.

Mr. Lyons, of Delaware, presented two memorials from citizens of Delaware county, praying that no provision may be made for the further observance of the Sabbath, than that already provided by law; which was also laid on the table.

Mr. Cope, of Philadelphia, presented a memorial from citizens of Philadelphia county, praying that the right of trial by jury may be extended to every human being; which was also laid on the table.

Mr. Carey, of Bucks, presented a memorial of like import, from citizens of Bucks county; which was also laid on the table.

Mr. Sterigere, of Montgomery, presented two memorials from citizens of Bucks county, praying that the constitution may be so amended, as to prohibit negroes from the right of suffrage; which were also laid on the table.

Mr. Sellers, of Montgomery, presented a memorial from citizens of Montgomery county, praying that such measures may be adopted, as effectually to prevent all amalgamation between the white and coloured population, in regard to the government of this state; which were also laid on the table.

Mr. FOULKROD, of Philadelphia county, presented a memorial of like import, from citizens of Philadelphia county; which was also laid on the table.

A motion was made by Mr. BEDFORD, and read as follows, viz:

Resolved, That the following new rule be adopted by the convention, viz: " That when any twenty delegates rise in their places and move the question on any pending amendment, it shall be the duty of the presiding officer to take the vote of the body on sustaining such call; and if such call shall be sustained by a majority, the question shall be taken on such amendment without further debate.

This resolution was laid on the table for future consideration.

A motion was made by Mr. HIESTER, and read as follows, viz:

Resolved, That no corporation shall hereafter be created, until three months' public notice of the application for the same shall have been first given in the place where its establishment is desired, in such manner as shall be prescribed by law; nor shall any corporation possessing banking or discounting privileges, be continued for more than twenty years without renewal; neither shall any such corporation be created, continued or revived, that may not be modified, altered or repealed, by the concurrent action of two successive legislatures, but the commonwealth shall indemnify all losses and damages that may accrue to any corporation by such action; nor shall more than one act of incorporation be included in the same law.

This resolution was laid on the table for future consideration; and,

On motion of Mr. HIESTER, the resolution was ordered to be printed.

A motion was made by Mr. KONIGMACHER, and read as follows, viz:

Resolved, That when this convention adjourns, it will adjourn to meet on Tuesday morning, at half past nine o'clock.

A motion was made by Mr. KONIGMACHER,

That the convention proceed to the second reading and consideration of the said resolution.

And on the question,

Will the convention agree to the motion?

The yeas and nays were required by Mr. DARLINGTON and Mr. FULLER, and are as follows, viz:

YEAS—Messrs. Baldwin, Bell, Biddle, Brown, of Philadelphia, Carey, Chambers, Chandler, of Philadelphia, Chauncey, Clarke, of Indiana, Cline, Cochran, Cope, Cox, Craig, Crain, Cunningham, Curll, Donagan, Dunlop, Farrelly, Fleming, Forward, Foulkrod, Gamble, Hays, Henderson, of Dauphin, Hopkinson, Houpt, Jenks, Konigmacher, Lyons, Maclay, Martin, M'Cahen, McDowell, McSherry, Meredith, Pollock, Porter, of Lancaster, Porter, of Northampton, Read, Russell, Saeger, Scott, Sellers, Serrill, Stevens, Sturdevant, Taggart, Weaver, Sergeant, *President*—51.

NAYS—Messrs. Agnew, Banks, Barclay, Barndollar, Bedford, Bigelow, Bonham, Brown, of Lancaster, Clarke, of Beaver, Clark, of Dauphin, Cleavinger, Coates, Crawford, Crum, Cummin, Darlington, Darrah, Denny, Dickey, Dickerson, Dillinger, Donnell, Earle, Fry, Fuller, Gearhart, Gilmore, Grenell, Harris, Hastings, Hayhurst, Heister, Hyde, Keim, Kennedy, Kerr, Krebs, Magee, McCall, Merkel, Montgomery, Nevin, Pennypacker, Purviance, Ritter, Royer, Scheetz, Seltzer, Shellito, Smith, of Columbia, Smyth, of Centre, Snively, Sterigere, Stickel, Thomas, Todd, Woodward, Young—58.

So the question was determined in the negative.

A motion was made by Mr. EARLE, of Philadelphia county, and read as follows, viz:

Resolved, That the rules of this convention be amended by adding the following. "On second reading of the constitution, any new section or sections may be moved when the place is reached at which it is proposed to introduce such section or sections, and the previous question, if called and sustained, shall be upon such proposed new section or sections.

This resolution was laid on the table for future consideration.

A motion was made by Mr. STEVENS, and read as follows, viz :

Resolved, That no delegate shall be permitted to speak at one time, more than one hour and a half, without leave of the convention, and that the resolution restricting speeches to one hour, be rescinded.

This resolution was laid on the table for future consideration.

ORDER OF THE DAY.

The convention resumed the consideration of the resolution read on yesterday, as follows, viz :

Resolved, That on second reading, the convention will consider the several articles of the constitution, in their numerical order, and that the sections shall be read in the same order, and be considered and open for amendment: *Provided,* That when any section shall have been amended in committee of the whole, the section shall be read as amended.

The said resolution being under consideration,

A motion was made by Mr. CUNNINGHAM, of Mercer,

To amend the same by striking therefrom all after the word " Resolved," and inserting in lieu thereof the following, viz : "That when any article of the constitution shall be under consideration on second reading, the sections shall be read and considered in their numerical order, and sections to which amendments have been made in committee of the whole shall be read with the amendments."

The question being taken, the motion of Mr. CUNNINGHAM was agreed to.

Mr. EARLE, of Philadelphia county, moved to amend the resolution, by striking out all the words, after the word " Resolved," and inserting the words following, viz :

That the rules of this convention be amended, by adding the following: " On second reading of the constitution, any new section or sections may be moved when the place is reached at which it is proposed to introduce such section or sections, and the previous question, if called and sustained, shall be upon such proposed new section or sections."

Mr. CUNNINGHAM, of Mercer, suggested that, as this was a new rule, it must, under the rules, lie one day on the table, before it can come up for consideration. There were other reasons which induced him to object to the amendment. He had no objection to the first part of the proposition.

Mr. EARLE then said, he would decide the amendment. If the first part should be agreed to, the second would follow, as a matter of course.

Mr. MARTIN, of Philadelphia county, said he considered the amendment as entirely superfluous.

The PRESIDENT remarked, that the first part of the amendment was not merely superfluous, but would be found inconvenient in practice. On account of the words—" when the place is reached, at which it is proposed to introduce such section or sections "—it would impose on the Chair the obligation to point out the proper place.

Mr. M'SHERRY considered the resolution of the gentleman from the county of Philadelphia, as being wholly unnecessary. The proper course would be to take up the sections in their order. Then, after they were all passed upon, if any gentleman wished to offer a new section, he could do so, and it would be numbered according to its place. If this was not done, it would become necessary to change the numbers to all the sections following a new section.

Mr. HIESTER remarked, that notwithstanding all that had been said, with reference to changing our rules, he thought the better course would be to proceed according to the rules which we had. As our time was limited, he thought we had better do the most important work first. According to the rules which we have, we will proceed first to consider those amendments which were agreed to in committee of the whole, and he thought that that would occupy what time we have to spare between this and the day fixed for adjournment. If, however, we proceed in the course pointed out by this new rule, he would venture to predict that we will not have completed the first article, by the second of February. If we attempted to change our rules, he feared that we would get into a labyrinth of difficulties, from which it would be difficult to extricate ourselves.

Mr. STERIGERE thought the observations of the Chair were worthy of great consideration. He believed that the construction which the Chair put upon the rule was, that after the amendments agreed to in committee of the whole were passed upon, a new section might be introduced.

The CHAIR said, if the convention decide against the order, he would feel himself bound to receive new sections when presented : but, it would be for the convention to decide, whether the section should be inserted at such places. This, he believed, had been the uniform practice of the convention.

Mr. STERIGERE considered then, that this amendment was altogether useless, and worse than useless, and he hoped it would either be withdrawn or negatived.

Mr. AGNEW supposed that the gentleman from the county of Philadelphia, (Mr. Earle) considered that they were all asleep. The amendment now proposed, was nothing more than the substance of the resolution which the convention voted down on yesterday. The amendment would lead the convention into interminable difficulty. The effect of it would be just this, that every gentleman who had an amendment to move, no matter whether there was another person in the house who would vote for it, he would move it as a new section, and the house would be compelled to take a vote upon it.

In this manner would the convention be continually kept tak'ng votes upon questions which no person but the mover and seconder would vote for. For instance, we have had an amendment proposed in committee of the whole, in relation to a distribution of the powers of the government, and debated for a week and rejected.

Now, he did not suppose that such a proposition ought to be introduced again; but, if we adopt this new rule, every one of those propositions which have been rejected, will be again thrown upon us, and we will have to take a vote on each of them.

He considered that those amendments which have been made in committee of the whole, were of most importance, and that they ought to be first acted upon. He was, therefore, opposed to any alteration in the rules of the convention, more especially was he opposed to the one proposed by the gentleman from the county of Philadelphia.

Mr. EARLE said, that the objection of the gentleman from Beaver, (Mr. Agnew) had no weight in it, because a single member might just as well move an amendment as a section, and the convention would be compelled to take a vote upon it, unless the previous question was moved. But, it was considered entirely improper by the gentleman from Beaver, and others, and why? Why, sir, it was because they had a repugnance to taking a direct vote on certain questions. There has been a great repugnance by gentlemen in this convention, to having votes taken on many subjects, which the people have petitioned the body in relation to. There was a great repugnance to give votes on questions which are of the utmost importance to the people of this commonwealth. We have had petition after petition, to have something inserted in the constitution, in relation to religious liberty, test oaths, and the right of trial by jury; but the moment we reach that part of the constitution in which our constituents ask us to insert something on these subjects, that moment the gentleman from Beaver, and other gentlemen, vote to cut us off from all opportunity to make a motion, and get any thing inserted in the constitution on the subject.

Is the gentleman from Beaver unwilling to allow a vote to be taken on these important subjects, if the mover and seconder ask a vote to be taken? If questions are introduced, which no one but the mover and seconder will support, let them be voted down without discussion. That is by far the most expeditious mode of doing business, and an immense deal of time will be saved by it.

He had seen gentlemen here, voting to cut off their own speeches, for the purpose of preventing a vote being taken on a particular question. Afterwards, when they could not sustain themselves, they have turned round and denounced the rule which would not allow them to speak more than an honr. The rule he now proposed was not a new rule, but the president had marked out a course of proceeding, under the construction he had put upon the resolution pending, entirely contrary to the usage in the legislative body, and every where else. He had been assured that the legislative rule was directly the reverse of that which the President has declared to be his construction of this resolution.

·   Mr. E. was content to act under the legislative rules, and he wished that all the rules we had adopted were swept away, in order that we might take up the constitution, as a bill in the legislature. The construction, however, which the President had placed on the rules, was, that when section one is adopted, that no gentleman will have a right to move a new section, to be called section two, without asking leave of the convention to do so.

+ The PRESIDENT said, that the Chair ought to be very cautious about answering any question, in anticipation of a division which he might have to make on the subject. He must say, however, that the argument of the gentleman from the county, was founded on a total misapprehension of what the Chair had said. The opinion of the Chair was directly the reverse of what had been stated by the gentleman. The Chair had stated that he would receive any motion for a new section, at any time or place that it might be presented, and then it would be for the convention to decide, whether it would insert it at that place, and what number it would put to it, if it did so insert it; and, he was not aware of any rule in the legislature, or any where else, to the contrary of this.

Mr. EARLE still understood the Chair to say, that the convention would have to decide first, whether an amendment should be received in the shape of a new section.

The PRESIDENT replied, that he had said he would receive an amend. ment, proposing a new section, and afterwards it would be for the conven-'tion to decide whether or not it would insert it.

Mr. EARLE then withdrew his amendment.

Mr. DICKEY hoped the convention would not deviate from the rules already adopted. He agreed with the gentleman from Lancaster, that the amendments which had been adopted in committee of the whole, deserved the first consideration on second reading. If we had gone on yesterday with the first article, instead of proceeding to the discussion of rules of order, we might have passed upon several sections of the constitution by this time. Then, after we had got through with the amendments to the first article, the gentleman could have proposed any new section which he pleased. It appeared to him, that the rules already adopted, were amply sufficient. He, therefore, hoped that we would proceed immediately to the second reading of the constitution.

The question was then taken on the resolution as amended, and adopt-·ed.

Mr. BIDDLE then moved that the convention proceed to the second read-ing and consideration of the following resolution :

"*Resolved,* That not more than one hour in any day shall be devoted to the consid. eration of motions and resolution:."

Which motion was agreed to.

Mr. WOODWARD said, that with a view of preventing a discussion of questions of order, until the second of February, he would now move the previous question; which motion was seconded by eighteen members rising in their places ; and the main question was ordered to be put.

Mr. SMYTH, of Centre, here rose and referred the President to page 700 of the journal, where this resolution had been indefinitely postponed.

The CHAIR then decided the motion to be out of order, and the whole proceeding on the resolution fell.

Mr. BIDDLE then asked leave of the convention to introduce a resolution to the same effect; which motion was disagreed to—ayes, 44; noes, 32; not two-thirds in the affirmative.

ORDERS OF THE DAY.

The CHAIR then announced the orders of the day being the second reading of the first article of the constitution.

The first section was read, and no amendment being proposed thereto, it was passed over.

Mr. EARLE then moved the following new section to be numbered section two.

SECTION 2. The legislative power shall not extend to the granting or renewing of any special charter of incorporation, for a longer term than fifteen years; nor with power to own a capital exceeding one million of dollars, except by the concurrent act of two successive legislatures. The legislative power shall not extend to the granting of any charter of incorporation, without a reserved right of modification, and repeal by the concurrent act of the two successive legislatures, in such manner and on such conditions as such legislature may deem equitable and expedient.

Mr. DICKEY rose to a point of order. It struck him that it was not in order for the gentleman to offer this section without a postponement of the second section for the purpose of offering a new section.

The CHAIR decided the section to be in order.

Mr. STERIGERE considered the amendment to be in order. He would therefore move to postpone it, until the other sections were gone through with.

Mr. EARLE thereupon withdrew his amendment. The second section, as amended in committee of the whole, was then read as follows :

"SECTION 2. The representatives shall be chosen annually, by the citizens of the city of Philadelphia, and of each county respectively, on the *third* Tuesday of October."

Mr. SMYTH, of Centre, then moved to strike out the word "third" and insert the word "second," in order to restore it to the old constitution. He was induced to make this motion, because he found, after consulting freely with his constituents on the subject during the recess, that they were, he might say, unanimous in favor of the second Tuesday of October, in consequence of their being so long accustomed to that day, and because it did not interfere with their occupations any more that a later day would.

The CHAIR stated that this motion would not be in order, but the gentleman would accomplish his object by voting against the amendment of the committee of the whole.

Mr. READ then moved to strike out the words "third Tuesday of October," and insert "first Tuesday of November."

Mr. READ called for the yeas and nays on this motion, which were ordered.

Mr. STERIGERE submitted to the CHAIR, whether this motion was in order. It struck him thatt he question now should be. Will the convention agree to the amendment of the committee of the whole?

The CHAIR decided the motion to be in order, because it was an amendment to the amendment of the committee of the whole.

Mr. READ said that on this question he desired to have the yeas and nays because it was one of importance to his constituents. Some gentlemen had objected to this, to an amendment of this kind, because it would interfere with the sitting of courts in particular counties; but this, it seemed to him, was too small an objection, while we are proposing amendments to our fundamental law, to have any weight. How easy would it be for the legislature to accommodate the sitting of courts to any provision which we might make in the constitution on this subject. With regard to the propriety of the amendment itself, he agreed with gentlemen, that if we make no alteration, but that of a single week, it is not worth our while to alter it at all. At the time the existing constitution was adopted, the second Tuesday of October, might have been a convenient day, yet since that time large portions of the state has been settled and inhabited, where the climate is colder and the seasons later, which make it frequently very inconvenient for them to attend elections on the existing election day. It seemed to him, therefore, that there could be no substantial reason why those portions of the state which had colder climates and later seasons should not be accommodated by having the election put back, when it would be no disadvantage to any other portion of the state.

Beside this, the meeting of the legislature was to be put back some time, which would make it out of the question for the elections to interfere in any way with it. He hoped, therefore, that the convention would see the propriety of adopting this amendment.

Mr. CUNNINGHAM, of Mercer, said he was opposed to all amendments of the constitution in this particular. He thought that the time now fixed is the most convenient and the most suitable; and, he did not wish to do any thing which would break in upon the old habits of the people in this respect, especially as he did not see that any great benefit was to result from the change. It would be better to leave the constitution as it now is. His constituents had not asked him to use his efforts to procure any change of time, nor did he think that there was any difference of opinion on this point, in any part of the commonwealth. He, at least, had not heard a single complaint that the day of election was fixed at a wrong or inconvenient time. He thought it would be better that the convention should let alone these small and unimportant matters—for unimportant they were so far as any principle was involved—and that they should direct their attention to those great fundamental questions for the consideration of which they had been originally called together. He was opposed altogether to the contemplated change.

Mr. MARTIN, of Philadelphia county, said that he should not have made any objection to this amendment, if he had not been in a situation something similar to that of the gentlemen from Centre, (Mr. Smyth.) He (Mr. M.) had once entertained the opinion that to change the day of the general election might, in some respects, have a good effect; but, since he had talked the matter over with his constituents, he had altered his opinion. He was now of opinion that no advantage would be gained by an alteration in the day. He should, therefore, vote against the amendment of the gentleman from Susquehanna, (Mr. Read) and also against the amendment made in committee of the whole. He repeated that he adopted this course in consequence of the better know. ledge which he had recently obtained of the opinions and wishes of the people of his district on this particular point.

Mr. FLEMING, of Lycoming, said that he could not concur in the opinion which had been expressed by the gentleman from Mercer, (Mr. Cunningham) that this was a small or unimportant matter. He, Mr. F., did not regard it in that light. Nor did he agree exactly in the view which had been taken of this subject; by any gentleman who, up to this time, had expressed his opinion upon it.

It appears to me, said Mr. F., that this is really a matter of some im. portance to the people of Pennsylvania, and I will state briefly the reasons which lead me to that opinion. If it is important to the people— and who will deny that it is so, to live in harmony, peace and good fellowship with each other, then I should view the proposed amendment as being of considerable importance. I, for one, am willing at all times to extend the elective franchise and to let the people select their officers at all times; but, I do not want to have elections held every month in the year, and my reasons for opposing the multiplication of election days in this state, are these.

There is no general election held under the provisions of the constitution, but which must, in the nature, of things, produce more or less excitement; and, although it is well that the people should be on the watch-tower, and that they should keep a vigilant eye on their rights and liberties, yet, in the greater number of instances, the excitements which attend the elections do not, in my opinion, result in benefit to the people themselves.

I feel disposed, for my own part, to vote for the amendment of the gentleman from Susquehanna, (Mr. Read) in order to put it in the power of the legislature to fix the time of the election of state officers and of the electors of President and Vice President on the same day, if it should be thought proper so to do.

Under the act of congress, passed in the year 1792,—to be found in the laws of the United States—it is provided that the election for electors of President and Vice President of the United States, shall be held within thirty days preceding the first Wednesday in December. I have not yet heard any substantial reason assigned, why the election of state offi-cers should not take place on the same day on which we elect the electors of President and Vice President of the United States;—nor have I been able to discover that any evil could result from such an arrangment. Of one thing, however, I feel very certain—that is to say, that if the election of all these officers were to be held on the same day, it would be the means of preventing a great deal of confusion among our people; and, would have a strong tendency to keep down much of that excitement which is not at all times agreeable, and which it is the duty, no less than it should be the inclination, of every good citizen to keep down as much as possible. If it is necessary to aid the political advancement of any particular individual, that this inordinate political excitement should be kept up, year after year, I know nothing of it; it is a matter with which I am not conversant. But, it seems to me that, if the election of all these officers were to be held on the same day, it would be the means of saving a vast deal of ill-feeling among our citizens, and which is engendered, and sure to be engendered, by the multiplication of elections on different days. I say, therefore, put it in the power of the legislature to have the election for state officers, and for electors of President and Vice President of the United States, held on the same day, so as to have only one electioneering campaign in the commonwealth—and thus save a great deal of confusion, excitement, and ill-feeling, which will otherwise be found to exist among your citizens.

Mr. SHELLITO, of Crawford, said that he was in favor of the amendment to the constitution in this respect, because he thought that it would best answer the purposes and wishes of the people whom he represented. In conversation with his constituents upon this subject, he had learned that they would be well pleased that such a change should be made.

He could not forbear to express the surprise which he felt at hearing gentlemen who lived in towns, and who could reach the polls at any time and without any inconvenience, oppose this proposition for amendment. They should leave it to be decided by the farming majority of this body, since to those who lived in towns and cities, it was as easy to attend on one day as upon another.

But, as to the proposition that the two elections should be held on one and the same day, he would go heart and hand for it. He thought it would be a great benefit to our country that there should be only one general election day, on which all should turn out. He would fain hope that the change would be made.

Mr. SMYTH, of Centre, said that he did not agree with some gentlemen who had spoken on this subject, as to the propriety of holding so many elections in one day. The gentleman from Lycoming, (Mr. Fleming) had assigned as a reason why he should vote in favor of the change, that he was desirous to have the election for state officers and for electors of President and Vice President of the United States, held on the same day.

In recent conversation with my constituents, said Mr. S., I have laid this whole matter before them, and they were of opinion that it was not worth contending about. They, however, felt it to be more convenient to attend on the second Tuesday of October, the day prescribed by the existing constitution. They were, they said, accustomed to it and did not desire a change.

When this question was last under discussion in committee at Harrisburg, I advocated a change of the day under the idea that it would be acceptable to my constituents, and that it would suit their purposes better. In this, however, I have found that I was mistaken. I am also of opinion, that the excitement on election days, is sufficient at the present time, without increasing it by holding two elections on the same day; and, that the adoption of such a course would increase it, I have not a doubt. On further reflection, therefore, and on a better acquaintance with the opinions and wishes of my constituen:s, I think we should go back to the existing provision of the constitution.

Mr. CURLL, of Armstrong, said it would be remembered that this question had been discussed for the period of four days when last up at Harrisburg. For his own part he did not feel any anxiety in regard to changing the day of election. He always attended regularly at the polls on election day; he had never failed to attend at a general election for the last thirty years of his life. When the proposition was first brought up at Harrisburg, he had felt some inclination to go in favor of it, because he thought that some expense might be saved to the commonwealth by having the two elections held on the same day. But, after his return home during the recess, in conversation with his constituents, they appeared to be surprised that a great body like this should consume a space of four days in discussing so unimportant a change; and, although, when the question was taken at Harrisburg, he had voted more out of courtesy and with a view to favor some of the more northern members, than from any consideration affecting himself; still, as the matter now stood, and after the expression of the opinion of his constituents, which he had since that time received, he should feel it his duty to vote for a return to the old day.

Mr. CLARKE, of Indiana, said he could confirm the statement which had been made by his colleague, (Mr. Todd.) When the question was up at Harrisburg, he Mr. C., had voted in favor of a change of day; but since that time he had been at home and had had an opportunity of gathering the sense of his constituents. He found that the prevailing sentiment among them, was in favor of a return to the day fixed in the constitution of 1790. He could not, in any event, vote for the proposition of the gentleman from Susquehanna, (Mr. Read) because he thought that there was already sufficient excitement attending the elections, without increasing it by providing that the two elections should be held on the same day. He should, therefore, vote against it. But, his principal reason for the vote he should give against any change was, that his constituents would be better satisfied with a return to the old day.

Mr. DICKEY said, that when this question was up in committee, he had voted with the majority in favor of the third Tuesday in October; and the proposition, as had been stated by the gentleman from Armstrong, (Mr. Curll) was discussed at that time, for the long period of four days. During the progress of that discussion, gentlemen were very certain that they understood the views of their constituents, and that they represented those views correctly, though it now appears, from the statements of some of the gentlemen themselves, that they were mistaken in the course they had taken.

I trust, said Mr. D., that before the labors of this convention are brought to a close, a number of gentlemen may yet find that they have been mistaken on other and more important matters.

Mr. FORWARD said, that he had not risen with an intention to repeat the observations which he had felt it his duty to make at Harrisburg, on the subject of the change of the election day, or to the expediency of providing that the two elections should be held in one. The opinion which he then expressed, had not been, in any degree, impaired by subsequent information or reflection. He had taken an opportunity to converse with his constituents—not only with those residing in the city of Pittsburg, but with those also, residing in the county—and, so far as he was able to collect public opinion, in that portion of the state, it appeared to be universally opposed to the change. The second Tuesday in October, from long custom, had gained a sort of sanctity in the estimation of the people, and he could not see any sufficient reason why a change should be made.

He intended, therefore, to vote against the proposition of the gentleman from Susquehanna, (Mr. Read) and against the report of the committee of the whole, and in favor of a return to the provision of the old constitution.

Mr. CUMMIN, of Juniata, said he felt much surprise to find that gentlemen who came from the interior of the country, should be so ready to change their course on this question.

It is my opinion, said Mr. C., that to return to the day, fixed in the old constitution, is a step which cannot fail to meet the disapprobation of every farmer in the state. It is well known to all who hear me, that the second Tuesday in October, is one of the busiest seasons in the year, both as to bringing in grain and putting in seed. Upon that day, the people will not—cannot turn out. In my township, out of two hundred voters, upwards of seventy will remain at home, taking in their grain, and putting in seed. I know this to be the case ; whereas, if you change the day, it will give the people an opportunity of turning out to the polls en masse.

Allusion has been made, in several quarters, to the excitement which exists among the people on election days. I can tell gentlemen that it will be in vain for them to attempt to put it down. The more excitement there is in relation to the elections, the better it will be for the country, because it is the very means of bringing the citizens out to the discharge of their duty at the polls.

The election of state officers is an important election, but the election of electors for President and Vice President of the United States, is still more important. To go back to the provision of the old constitution, would be contrary to the sentiments and the wishes of all my constituents. I shall vote in favor of the first Tuesday in November, or the last in October, and I shall also vote in favor of holding the two elections on the same day. I believe there is no danger to be apprehended from the excitement which has been spoken of; I do not believe that that excitement will lead to any bloodshed, or to any improper conduct on the part of our citizens. Their interests require, not only that they should be as little away from home as possible, but that they should keep themselves out of trouble. It is a pleasing sight to see the people turn out en masse, to make their choice of the men by whom they would be represented. For these reasons, therefore, and believing that the change of day will have a beneficial tendency on the interests of the people, I shall vote in favor of the first Tuesday in November.

Mr. KERR, of Washington, said, it would be recollected that when the convention took a recess in July last, one of the principal reasons urged in favor of that step, was, that it would be advantageous to the interests of the members that they should return home, for a season, to attend to their private concerns. The same reason appeared to be assigned in favor of the present proposition. When this amendment was under consideration in committee of the whole at Harrisburg, he had voted in favor of a change of day, to the third Tuesday in October. This he had done, more with a view to get rid of other motions on the subject, than for any particular preference which he had for the day. When he returned home, he had talked to his constituents on this, as well as on many other matters having reference to the business of this body, and they appeared to smile at the idea of spending so much time on a point of this kind. They considered it unimportant. So far as he had understood their sentiments, they were opposed, generally, to a provision requiring the two elections to be held on the same day, especially if we had to choose all our county officers on the same day. But, as to the mere question of a change of the day, although they considered it unimportant, still, as they had been in the habit of going to the polls on the second Tuesday in October, they felt unwilling to make any change, and he felt satisfied that they would prefer that the day should be allowed to remain the same as it was.

He should, therefore, vote against the amendment of the gentleman from Susquehanna, (Mr. Read) and against the amendment adopted by the committee of the whole; and he should vote in favor of retaining the provision of the constitution of 1790.

Mr. BONHAM, of York county, said, that as he proposed to change his vote, and to give it differently from that which he had given in the committee of the whole at Harrisburg, on this question, it might be proper that he should briefly assign his reasons for so doing.

When the question was under discussion at Harrisburg, he was in favor of fixing a remoter day, in the season than that provided in the existing constitution, because he thought that a change would add to the convenience of most of the farmers in his section of the country. He had heard complaints of their not being able to get to the polls, on account of being engaged in seeding, and he had been under the impression that, by fixing a week or two later in the season, they would have got through with their labors, and thus have been able to attend to the performance of this most important duty. But, after the adjournment of the convention at Harrisburg, when he returned home, and inquired as to the effect of the change, which had been made in this provision of the constitution, he was told by his constituents that it was a matter of very little importance; but that, inasmuch as the second Tuesday in October had been the day upon which they had been accustomed to attend, for a series of years, they did not think it necessary that any alteration should be made in that particular. It was his intention, therefore, at the present time, to vote for a return to the existing provision of the constitution, as he believed that, by so doing, he would best meet the views and wishes of his constituents.

And the question was then taken on the motion of Mr. READ, to wit:

To amend the section, by striking therefrom, in the third line, the word "third," and inserting in lieu thereof, the word "first;" and by striking therefrom the word "October," and inserting in lieu thereof, the word "November."

On which said motion,

The yeas and nays were required by Mr. READ and Mr. DICKEY, and are as follows, viz:

YEAS.—Messrs. Cox, Cummin, Darrah, Earle, Fleming, Foulkrod, Fry, Gamble, Hastings, Magee, Mann, M'Cahen, Montgomery, Nevin, Purviance, Read, Shellito, Taggart, Weaver, Young—20.

NAYS.—Messrs. Agnew, Baldwin, Banks, Barclay, Barndollar, Bedford, Bell, Biddle, Bigelow, Bonham, Brown, of Lancaster, Brown, of Philadelphia, Carey, Chambers, Chandler, of Philadelphia, Chauncey, Clarke, of Beaver, Clark, of Dauphin, Clarke, of Indiana, Cleavinger, Cline, Coates, Cochran, Cope, Craig, Crain, Crawford, Crum, Cunningham, Curll, Denny, Dickey, Dickerson, Dillinger, Donagan, Donnell, Doran, Dunlop, Farrelly, Forward, Fuller, Gearhart, Gilmore, Grenell, Harris, Hayhurst, Hays, Helffenstein, Henderson, of Dauphin, Hiester, Houpt, Hyde, Jenks, Keim, Kennedy, Kerr, Konigmacher, Krebs, Lyons, Maclay, Martin, M'Call, M'Dowell, M'Sherry, Meredith, Merkel, Pennypacker, Pollock, Porter, of Lancaster, Ritter, Royer, Russell, Saeger, Scheetz, Scott, Seltzer, Serrill, Smith, of Columbia, Smyth, of Centre, Snively, Sterigere, Stevens, Stickel, Sturdevant, Thomas, Todd, Weidman, Woodward, Sergeant, *President*—89.

So the amendment was rejected.

A motion was then made by Mr. CUMMIN,

To amend the section in the third line, by inserting after the word "Tuesday," the words "and Wednesday."

Mr. C. said, that the reason which had induced him to offer this amendment, was, that the people in the country were so engaged in their business that they would not attend the polls, as they ought to do, on the day appointed; but if two days were given to them, they might almost make up the time they lost on the one hand, by the time they gained on the other, when time was of great importance to them.

I believe, said Mr. C., that the arguments which have been urged here by many gentlemen, in opposition to this change, are futile—that there is no force nor soundness in them. They say that the people are in favor of retaining the provision in the old constitution, because they have been habituated, for a number of years, to attend the polls on the second Tuesday of October.

Sir, this is a bad reason, and one which ought not to influence the minds of the members of this body, when it is considered that experience has shewn that the people will not turn out to discharge their duty at the polls, on the day now prescribed. Their bread, the staff of life, is at stake; they will not neglect it; nor is it to be expected that they should.

There is no man within the sound of my voice, who holds in greater respect than myself, the obligation which rests upon every good citizen, to present himself at the polls, and by his vote and example, to aid in the preservation of our liberties, and the free institutions under which it is our happy lot to live. But there are many important considerations on the other side, which we are not at liberty to disregard. If the gentlemen of the bar, and citizens from the cities, were not so numerous in this assembly as we know them to be, I have very little doubt that my amendment would be carried. I still entertain a hope that it may obtain the vote of a majority of the delegates. Let them reflect how hard a case this is for the farming community.

A neighbor, for instance, has some buck-wheat—a beautiful and precious grain—which it is much to be desired should be taken in. There is an appearance of snow, or the snow is falling upon it. It is the staff of life, and farmers will not leave their homes on that day to go to the polls, because, on that very day, they may be able to bring their labors to a close. Is it not wrong, thus to close the door upon them—to say that, because they will not turn out on a particular day, when, by turning out, their crops might be spoiled, however anxious they may be to vote, they shall not be allowed to do so ?

I am aware that gentlemen of the bar, and citizens of the cities, look upon these as small matters, but they are not so with us in the country.

[A suggestion was made, at this stage of his observations, in the ear of Mr. Cummin, by Mr. Stevens—but in so low a tone as not to reach the desk of the Stenographer. Mr. C., however, turned round and said aloud with great emphasis, though in a peculiarly good-natured tone of voice :]

Potatoes ! I will thank the gentlemen from Adams, (Mr. Stevens) to keep to his own country, without introducing mine. His country is as much a potatoe country as old Ireland ; and he need not, therefore, come whispering to an Irishmen about potatoes at such a time and in such a place as this. I think, however, that he is in favor of my motion, and I shall therefore take every thing he has to say in good part.

If his amendment should be adopted, he thought it would meet the wishes of the people generally, and particularly that portion of them which he represented. It was not the intention of those who sent delegates to this convention, that, after spending four or five months in debate, they should then fall back on the old constitution. Such a course of proceeding was ridiculous and absurd. It was nothing less than child's play. The convention put themselves in the condition of children, building houses with a pack of cards only to throw them down. They did one thing to-day for the purpose of undoing it to-morrow.

Mr. FRY, of Lehigh, had hoped the amendment of the gentleman from Susquehanna would be adopted. The amendment of the delegate from Juniata, (Mr. Cummin) would meet the wishes of the farmers of the state. He should vote for it. If there were more farmers and fewer lawyers and doctors in the convention, he entertained no doubt but that it would be adopted—as it was, however, he was afraid it would not prevail, though he hoped it might.

The amendment was negatived—ayes 9; noes not counted.

Mr. M'CAHEN, of Philadelphia county, moved to amend by striking out " third" and inserting " fourth."

Mr. M'C. asked for the yeas and nays, which being taken, the amendment was negatived—yeas 33 ; nays 77.

YEAS.—Messrs. Barndollar, Bedford, Carey, Cline, Cox, Crain, Cummin, Earle, Fleming, Foulkrod, Fry, Gamble, Hastings, Hiester, Jenks, Magee, Mann, M'Cahen, M'Dowell, Montgomery, Nevin, Purviance, Read, Russell, Scheetz, Shellito, Sterigere, Stevens, Stickel, Sturdevant, Taggart, Weaver, Young—33.

NAYS.—Messrs. Agnew, Baldwin, Banks, Barclay, Bell, Biddle, Bigelow, Bonham, Brown, of Lancaster, Brown, of Philadelphia, Chambers, Chandler, of Philadelphia, Chauncey, Clarke, of Beaver, Clark, of Dauphin, Clarke, of Indiana, Cleavinger, Coates, Cochran, Cope, Craig, Crawford, Crum, Cunningham, Curll, Darrah, Denny, Dickey, Dickerson, Dillinger, Donagan, Donnell, Doran, Dunlop, Farrelly, Forward, Fuller, Gearhart, Gilmore, Grenell, Harris, Hayhurst. Hays, Helffenstein, Henderson, of Dauphin, Hopkinson, Houpt, Hyde, Keim, Kennedy, Kerr, Konigmacher, Krebs, Lyons, Maclay, Martin, M'Call, M'Sherry, Meredith, Merkel, Pennypacker, Pollock, Porter, of Lancaster, Ritter, Royer, Saeger, Scott, Seltzer, Serrill, Smith, of Columbia, Smyth, of Centre, Snively, Thomas, Todd, Weidman, Woodward, Sergeant, *President*—77.

The question then recurred on agreeing to the amendment reported by the committee of the whole to the second section.

Mr. STERIGERE, of Montgomery, asked for the yeas and nays ; which being taken, the amendment was negatived—yeas 28 ; nays 80.

YEAS.—Messrs. Barndollar, Chambers, Cline, Crane, Cummin, Dunlop, Earle, Fleming, Foulkrod, Henderson, of Dauphin, Hiester, Jenks, Konigmacher, Mann, M'Cahen, M'Dowell, Merkel, Nevin, Purviance, Read, Russell, Scheetz, Shellito, Snively, Stevens, Stickel, Sturdevant, Weaver—28.

NAYS.—Messrs. Baldwin, Banks, Barclay, Bedford, Bell, Biddle, Bigelow, Bonham, Brown, of Lancaster, Brown, of Philadelphia, Carey, Chandler, of Philadelphia, Chauncey, Clarke, of Beaver, Clark, of Dauphin, Clarke, of Indiana, Cleavinger, Coates, Cochran, Cope, Cox, Craig, Crawford, Crum, Cunningham, Curll, Darrah, Denny, Dickey, Dickerson, Dillinger, Donagan, Donnell, Doran, Farrelly, Forward, Fry, Fuller, Gamble, Gearhart, Gilmore, Grenell, Harris, Hastings, Hayhurst, Hays, Helffenstein, Hopkinson, Houpt, Keim, Kennedy, Kerr, Krebs, Lyons, Maclay, Magee, Martin, M'Call, M'Sherry, Meredith, Montgomery, Pennypacker, Pollock, Porter, of Lancaster, Ritter, Royer, Saeger, Scott, Seltzer, Serrill, Smith, of Columbia, Smyth, of Centre, Sterigere, Taggart, Thomas, Todd, Weidman, Woodward, Young, Sergeant, *President*—80.

The convention next proceeded to consider the following section, as amended in, and reported from, the committee of the whole :

"SECTION 3. No person shall be a representative who shall not have attained the age of twenty-one years, and have been a citizen and inhabitant of the state three years next preceding his election, and the last year thereof an inhabitant of the city or county in which he shall be chosen, unless he shall have been absent on the public business of the United States, or of this state, or unless he shall have been previously a qualified elector in this state, in which case he shall be eligible upon one year's residence. No person residing within any city, town or borough, which shall be entitled to a separate representation, shall be elected a member of any county, nor shall any person residing without the limits of any such city, town or borough, be elected a member thereof."

Mr. SCOTT, of Philadelphia, had an objection to the amendment, because it was not sufficiently explicit. As the articles were now on second reading, it behooved gentlemen to be particularly careful to make every section as perfect as possible in every respect. The old constitution, then, it would be perceived by reading the first part of the section, required a residence of three years in the state, which would entitle the individual to be elected a representative in the lower branch of the legislature. The amendment reported by the committee permitted him to be so elected if he had resided in the state one year, "unless he shall have been absent on the public business of the United States, or of this state, or unless he shall have been previously a qualified elector in this state." A man might become a qualified elector in Pennsylvania by a residence of one year, according to the constitution as amended in committee of the whole. By living one year in the state, he shall be qualified for an elector. A man, thus qualified, might be absent from the state an indefinite period of time, and return and be qualified. In other words, a two years residence would give to him, who had been absent, one year, while, if he had remained at home, he would have had to wait three years, before he would have been eligible to the office of a representative. The committee had introduced some words in relation to the senate, to which he entertained some objection. The section required one individual to reside four years in the state of Pennsylvania, before he could be elected to fill a seat in that body; but, if he had been a qualified elector at any time, he was entitled. The man who had lived in Pennsylvania all his life, who had not been out of it, who had evinced an attachment to your soil, would not be eligible under four years; while here, perhaps, was a man, who came from another state, and remained a year, then went away, and again returned and staid another year, and yet became equally eligible with the other !

What, he asked, was the exception made to the old constitution as to absent men? It was a reasonable exception. If a man was absent, engaged on the business of the United States, or of this state, he did not lose his right to vote on returning, as would be the case, in numerous instances, if this section should be adopted in its present form. But according to the present section, we should permit an individual to expatriate himself to other lands—to abjure his own country from his affections—to select his own time to return to his country; and then, having passed one year among us, allow him, perhaps, to occupy the chair of the senate. Now, he apprehended that the framers of the constitution, when they inserted the provision, they did in that instrument, did so, because they deemed it necessary, that a man should give some proof of his attachment to the soil, before being permitted to enjoy all the rights and privileges of a citizen; and also, that he should make himself familiar with the institutions of Pennsylvania, and with the course of her legislation, and the manners, habits, wants and wishes of the people, before becoming a maker of laws. The objection he had urged to the section as amended in committee of the whole, was, in his opinion, a very strong one. An individual might go to Canada or Texas, or any where else, and reside there for a number of years, and become landholders, and afterwards return to this state, and after a single year's residence, participate in making our laws. He hoped the section would not be agreed to.

Mr. FARRELLY, of Crawford, moved to amend by striking out the words "a qualified elector" and inserting "eligible."

Mr. F., said, the adoption of this amendment would obviate the objection of the delegate from the city, (Mr. Scott.) It would be impossible for a man to become a representative, unless he had been a resident of the state for three years. If a man had been a resident, and then absented himself for some years, he would, on his return, have to reside one year before being entitled to the privileges of an elector. If there was a disposition in a man to return to his state, a preference should be given him over the foreigner. He thought the amendment should be adopted.

Mr. FLEMING, of Lycoming, was opposed not only to the amendment of the delegate from Crawford, (Mr. Farrelly) but also, to the section as it stood, though he was in favor of inserting in the constitution some general provision on the subject. The gentleman from the city, (Mr. Scott) had clearly shown the section to be objectionable. According to the terms of it, a man might go to England or any where else, take the oath of allegiance there, return to Pennsylvania, and vote for our public officers, although his property might be in some other country. .

I am fully satisfied, said Mr. F., that it never was the intention of the committee of the whole to make any such liberal provision in the constitution. The gentleman from Crawford, (Mr. Farrelly) proposes to strike out the words "a qualified elector" and to insert the word "eligible;" making it read " or unless he shall have been previously eligible in this state, in which case he shall be eligible upon one year's residence." There is much force in the course of reasoning of the gentleman from the city of Philadelphia, who has just taken his seat, (Mr. Scott.) Under the amendment proposed by the gentleman from Crawford, (Mr. Farrelly) and also, by the amendment made in committee of the whole, an individual may go and reside abroad for many years, and then may come back to the state of Pennsylvania, and, after one year's residence, get a seat in the legislature. It appears to me that the general provision, as it stands in the constitution of 1790. is altogether as broad and as liberal as can be found in the constitution of any other state in the Union. I am, therefore, opposed to the amendment as it stands, since the proposed amendment of the gentleman from Crawford, (Mr. Farrelly) and I am in favor of striking out the whole of the amendment as made in committee of the whole.

Mr. STEVENS said that he was in favor of the amendment. He could see nothing in the reasoning of the gentleman from Lycoming, (Mr. Fleming) which did not apply with equal force, to the existing provision in the constitution of 1790. If a man had become a citizen of Great Britain, during the last war, if he had left his country and gone to Canada or any other part of the world, and had taken the oath of allegiance to a foreign power—if his property was there—yet according to the provision of the present constitution, if he comes back to the state of Pennsylvania, and resides there for the period of three years, he will be eligible, just as much as the man who has been absent for a year, or for a few weeks only.

You may see, said Mr. S., how hard the case is in relation to our own citizens ; that is to say, where one of our citizens goes into a sister state, for a short time only, and, probably, only a few rods beyond the line, he loses his residence, and is put upon the same footing as the stranger coming into the commonwealth; and although, he may have a thorough understanding of all our institutions, and all our peculiar interests, still he is required to reside just as long as if he had come from a foreign country. This, I think, is extremely hard. And the possible case which has been put, of a man going among the pirates of Texas, is one of the evils which ought not to be suffered, to out-weigh the good that would be derived from an amendment of the present provision. It is wrong, and should be remedied. It was obviously an oversight on the part of the framers of the constitution of 1790.

I remember a case which occurred some time since, where a gentleman who had resided forty years in Franklin county, moved into the state of Maryland, and resided there for about a year—within a few rods of the line, and who, during the period of his absence, paid taxes on his property in the state of Pennsylvania. He returned to his native place, and was elected a member of our legislature. After the election had taken place, it was discovered that he had not resided long enough in the state, to make him eligible, according to the present provision of the constitution, and he was obliged to vacate his seat.

To my mind, it is unjust to say that one of our own citizens shall be required to reside as long as a stranger, before he can be made eligible; and the cases, on the other side, from which any injury could result, are so few and remote, that they ought not, in my judgment, to be taken into the account.

I hope, therefore, that the amendment made in committee of the whole, will stand; it was adopted with great unanimity, and I trust it will not be thus lightly rejected. I believe it ought to receive the sanction of this body.

Mr. EARLE said that he was not exactly pleased, either with the amendment which had been reported from the committee of the whole, or with that which had been proposed by the gentleman from Crawford, (Mr. Farrelly.)

I am not able, said Mr. E., to discover any sound or substantial reason why the citizens of any county in this state, should not be represented in the legislature, by any citizen or qualified voter, in whom they may choose to repose that confidence.

The provision contained in the section under consideration, appears to me to be an unnecessary, as well as an arbitrary and anti-democratic restriction.

For my own part, I think that the moment a citizen is entitled to vote, he ought at once, so far as residence is concerned, to be entitled to be a representative of the people, if the people choose to elect him. It is for the people to judge whether the individual is, or is not, sufficiently acquainted with their interests and their wants, to justify them in electing him as their representative—and the people, whose eyes are open to their own interests, will not fail to exercise the necessary precaution. You may find a citizen, for instance, who has a farm bordering on the line of the two states of Pennsylvania and Maryland—who may remove his house from one side of the line to the other. Is he not more fit to be a representative, than a stranger, or a man who has been abroad for a long period of time?

I am in favor, so far as residence in the state and payment of taxes are concerned, of making the qualifications of members of assembly precisely the same as those of voters. In reference to the senate, there may be a distinction, which may come up hereafter. It is probable, however, that I shall offer an amendment at a proper time.

Mr. AGNEW, of Beaver, said he was opposed to the amendment reported from the committee of the whole, and also, to the amendment thereto, proposed by the gentleman from Crawford. I am opposed to them, said Mr. A., on the broad ground, that the constitution is not intended to provide for every possible case, or contingency, that may arise in the course of events, and in the lapse of years. It is intended as an instrument, by which general principles may be laid down, and general rules may be prescribed. Beyond this it ought not to go, and when an attempt is made to meet particular cases, or to enter into elaborate details, we should not give it our countenance; for such is not the intent and object of any fundamental law.

The gentleman from Adams, (Mr. Stevens) has cited a case which he says is a hard case. But if it is so, what is the remedy? Is it to introduce into the constitution, a provision which gives rise to precisely the same kind of hard cases on the other side?—because such will be its effect, in throwing open the door to strangers and to persons unacquainted with our system of laws and our institutions. I admit, that the case which he has cited, seems to be hard; but I apprehend that we can not help that, inasmuch as it is our duty, as I have said, to lay down such general rules and principles, as we believe will produce the greatest amount of general good, without reference to individual cases.

The object of the constitution is not to restrict the people. It is simply a rule to direct themselves—and which is prescribed by themselves, and the object of which is to bring about the greatest amount of good. And gentlemen are quite wrong in saying, that this is a restriction on the people, or in regarding it in the light of an anti-democratic or arbitrary provision. Such, at least, is my view of the matter. Sir, it is no restriction; it has for its object, a benefit and not an injury.

What was the object intended to be accomplished by the insertion of this provision in the constitution of 1790? It was to secure, as members of the legislative body, such men only as were acquainted with the interests and the wants of the people whom they were to represent; so that his interests might be identified with the interests of the community. And, what do you now propose to do? Because a man lives on the other side of your state line, for a year, and thus loses his eligibility—and because this happens to be a hard case—you wish, by a new provision in the constitution, to throw the door wide open, and thus to admit, as eligible to the legislative body, men who have gone abroad, to Texas or elsewhere—and who have remained absent from their country long enough to have forgotten our system of policy—to have forgotten our system of legislation; or, in other words, men who have been long enough abroad to be among us exactly as strangers would be. The provision which you would now introduce, is neither more nor less than this. And is this, let me ask, consistent with the principles which this convention should adopt in the constitution, which are intended to promote the greatest good, and not to provide for particular cases? I think not. I hope that the provision in the constitution of 1790 will be suffered to remain as it is.

Mr. FORWARD said that he should vote in favor of the amendment of the gentleman from Crawford, (Mr. Farrelly) because he preferred it to that adopted by the committee of the whole. He did not exactly like the phraseology of the former, though that might be corrected at a future time.

The provision of the constitution of 1790, said Mr. F., requires " that no person shall be a representative who shall not have been a citizen and inhabitant of the state, three years next preceding his election." The amendment of the gentleman from Crawford, if I correctly understand its import, recognizes the principle, that where a person has been a resident for the period of three years, and has thereby become eligible—if he is absent from the state, he may on his return, re-acquire his eligibility, by a residence of one year. If my understanding of this amendment is correct, I prefer the principle of it, to that reported from the committee of the whole.

And, the question on the amendment of Mr. FARRELLY, was then taken, and decided in the affirmative ; ayes 53 ; noes 26.

So the amendment to the section, as reported from the committee of the whole, was agreed to.

The question then recurred on agreeing to the said section, as amended.

Mr. CLARKE, of Indiana, said, that when this question was up in committee of the whole, he had voted in favor of the amendment. But, as it appears that only one case of hardship has occurred within the long period of forty-seven years, I think it would be better to go back to the provision of the old constitution. If a man expatriates himself, of course he knows the consequences of his own conduct. There is, at all times, an abundance of good men and true, ready to enter the lists as the representatives of the people.

The gentleman from the county of Philadelphia, (Mr. Earle) seems to think it hard, that the citizens have not the right to make their own choice. This might probably be a good argument, if applied to a county officer, but does not bear on men elected to the legislature. I think it well that there should be a period of probation ; and for this reason, as well as for others which have suggested themselves to my mind, I shall vote against any amendment, and in favor of the retention of the provision in the constitution of 1790.

A motion was made by Mr. CLINE, of Bedford,

To amend the said section, by inserting in the eighth line, after the word " residence," the words " in the city or county in which he shall be chosen."

Mr. C. said, he had offered this amendment, because it appeared to him, that by the amendment adopted in committee of the whole, a person might go out of the state, having previously resided there for three years;

and after being absent for a long period of time, might come into a district only a day or two before the election took place ; or, in other words, a man might reside in Pittsburg, and by going to Philadelphia a day or two before the election took place might become eligible in Philadelphia. He did not suppose that this was the object of the convention.

Mr. Martin said, that he liked the amendment of the gentleman from Bedford, (Mr. Cline) and should himself have offered one of a similar tenor, if that gentleman had not anticipated him. It was no uncommon thing for gentlemen to do them the favor of coming from the city and remaining in the county, a few days before the election was held, for the purpose of being elected members of the legislature. I do not know, said Mr. M., whether this has been the case elsewhere. We have been subject to such interferences, and we are desirous to get rid of them for the time to come. The proposition of the gentleman from Bedford, in my opinion, points out the remedy. I shall, therefore, vote in favor of it, and hope it may succeed.

And, the question on the amendment of Mr. Cline, was then taken, and decided in the negative—ayes 35 ; noes, not counted.

So the amendment was rejected.

A motion was made by Mr. Curll,

That the convention do now adjourn ;

Which said motion was not agreed to.

A motion was then made by Mr. Hiester,

To amend the said section, by inserting in the seventh line, after the word "state," the words, "and shall heretofore have been a resident of one of the other states or territories of this Union."

Mr. Hiester said, that according to the view which he now took of the matter, he felt disposed to vote against the entire amendment of the committee of the whole ; but that, if it was to be retained at all, there certainly ought to be appended to it, such a provision as he had now proposed.

The gentleman from the city of Philadelphia, had pointed out the disadvantage which would result from the adoption of the amendment of the committee of the whole, under which persons, who choose to expatiate themselves—who went to Canada, or Texas, or any other part of the world—might return to this country, and, after a residence of one year, might become eligible. This he, Mr. H., did think was desirable ; and the amendment which he had proposed, would obviate all difficulty arising from this source. It would also obviate the difficulty and hardship arising out of such cases, as that which had been alluded to by the gentleman from Adams, (Mr. Stevens.)

Mr. Martin said, he did not feel exactly prepared to come to a vote at this time. Several ideas had been thrown out, which induced him to think that various alterations in this section might yet be required. He did not, therefore, wish to vote on this question, until he had examined its bearing further. He asked leave to make a motion.

Leave not having been granted,

Mr. M. said, as he could not make the motion which he desired, he would content himself with moving that the convention do now adjourn.

Which motion having been agreed to,

The Convention adjourned.

———

•

MONDAY, January 1, 1838

[Previous to the regular business, some discussion took place on a motion made by Mr. STERIGERE, of Montgomery, for a correction of the journal ; but as it was merely a question of phraseology, the motion was not agreed to.]

Mr. DARLINGTON, of Chester, presented a remonstrance from citizens of Chester county, against any change in the constitution making the right of citizenship and suffrage dependant upon the complexion of the individual.

Which was laid on the table.

Mr. THOMAS, of Chester, presented a remonstrance of like import, from citizens of Chester county.

Which was laid on the table.

Mr. PENNYPACKER, of Lancaster, presented a remonstrance of like import, from citizens of Lancaster.

Which was laid on the table.

Mr. COATES, of Lancaster, presented a memorial from citizens of Lancaster county, praying that constitutional provision may be made to prevent mobs.

Which was also laid on the table.

Mr. KEIM, of Berks, presented two memorials from citizens of Bucks county, praying that a clause may be inserted in the constitution, expressly providing that no one of the negro race be permitted to vote for any public office whatsoever.

Which were also laid on the table.

Mr. STERIGERE, of Montgomery, presented two memorials of like import, from the same county.

Which were also laid on the table.

Mr. STERIGERE presented a memorial from citizens of Lancaster county, praying that measures may be taken effectually to prevent all amalgamation between the white and coloured population, in regard to the government of this state.

Which was also laid on the table.

A motion was made by Mr. BIDDLE, and read as follows, viz:

Resolved, That not more than one hour in any day shall be appropriated to the consideration of petitions, motions and resolutions.

On motion of Mr. BIDDLE,

The rule prohibiting resolutions for changing the rules of the convention from being twice read in the same day, was dispensed with, and the said resolution was read the second time.

And being under consideration,

Mr. STERIGERE moved to amend the resolution by striking out the word "one" and substituting the words "half an," so as to read "half an hour."

Mr. BIDDLE accepted the amendment as a modification of the original resolution.

Mr. EARLE, of Philadelphia county, expressed his opinion that the operation of the resolution would be nugatory; and that this rule, if adopted, might be used injuriously by the minority. The majority could now control the action of the convention If this rule be adopted, it may have the effect of cutting off all resolutions. The usage in legislative bodies was, that the speaker might address the Chair on the subject of a resolution until the hour had expired; and thus, day after day, one speaker might consume the whole of the session, and prevent any resolution being brought forward before the time allowed by the rule, would, every day, have expired.

Mr. STERIGERE, of Montgomery, said the modest gentleman from the county had himself offered a resolution to restrict every one from speaking more than one hour, without his consent—or without the unanimous consent of this body, which was the same thing. What he has done, therefore, is a complete answer to what he says.

Mr. SMYTH, of Centre, was sorry that the mover of the resolution had adopted the amendment of the gentleman from Montgomery. He was willing to go for a restriction of the time to one hour. He would ask for the yeas and nays on the resolution.

Mr. M'DOWELL, of Bucks, hoped the amended resolution would carry. It would be still better to prohibit any one from offering any resolution until after the first of February. The discussion of resolutions and rules consumed one-third of our time. It seemed to be a part of the wisdom of this body to offer resolutions; and it was a worm thrown into the water to minnows—the moment a resolution is offered, every one jumps at it. Much of the time of the convention would be saved if we could exclude all resolutions for the next two weeks. In his opinion a quarter of an hour would be sufficient time to allow for their consideration.

Mr. BIDDLE replied that it had been his desire to put the resolution in the form which would be most acceptable. At the early stages of the session, it was necessary to allow a wide latitude for the introduction of resolutions. But there was no reason for giving such a range now. All, or almost all, the propositions which could be acted on, had now been offered. To obviate all objections, he would so far change the phraseology of the resolution as to make it read "That not more than one hour shall be appropriated to the consideration of petitions, motions and resolutions."

Mr. STEVENS, of Adams, asked if gentlemen were not involving themselves in some difficulty. Suppose a resolution should be introduced relative to the amendment of the constitution. We had nearly reached the end of the session. How is it to be discussed? Half a dozen of the amendments may not be disposed of, and it may be necessary to embrace all those which are required, and which cannot be reached, in a resolution to be afterwards passed upon. By the adoption of this rule, therefore, we may cut off some of the amendments. We still find numbers in a situation in which we must throw several amendments together, or we shall be compelled to leave some of them untouched.

Mr. FULLER, of Fayette, believed it might be found necessary, towards the close of the session, to occupy more than one hour in the consideration of resolutions. He moved that the further consideration of the resolution be postponed for the present.

Mr. DICKEY, of Beaver, remarked that if, towards the close of the session, it should be found necessary to occupy more than one hour, the rule might be suspended. It might become necessary sometimes to suspend the rule.

Mr. FULLER said if the resolution was adopted, it would be half-past ten o'clock before the house would proceed to business. An hour was long enough for the consideration of resolutions.

Mr. EARLE said the gentleman from Montgomery had a dozen times repeated the assertion that he (Mr. Earle) had spoken four hours and a half on a subject, and then voted in favor of limiting speeches to one hour in length. The gentleman had better have th,t assertion placarded on the wall, and at the door of the hall. But he omitted to state that he (Mr. E.) had previously voted for adjournment on the 2d of February, which would have been impossible without such a limitation. He hoped the gentleman would publish the statement which he had so often made. The gentleman's constituents would, doubtless, be willing to limit his speeches to half an hour. He was opposed to the resolution. The limitation had had the effect in congress to prevent action on resolutions. One member from the southern part of this state consumed the morning hour for fifteen days in a speech on a resolution.

Mr. STURDEVANT moved the previous question.

The motion was sustained, and the main question was ordered to be put.

And on the question,

Will the convention agree to the resolution?

The yeas and nays were required by Mr. FULLER and Mr. SMYTH, of Centre, and are as follow, viz:

YEAS—Messrs. Agnew, Baldwin, Banks, Barclay, Barndoller, Biddle, Bigelow, Bonham, Brown, of Lancaster, Brown, of Philadelphia, Carey, Chambers, Chandler, of Philadelphia, Chauncey, Clarke, of Beaver, Clark, of Dauphin, Clarke, of Indiana, Cleavinger, Cline, Coates, Cope, Cox, Craig, Crain, Crum, Darlington, Darrah, Denny, Dickey, Dillinger, Donnell, Farrelly, Forward, Gearhart, Gilmore, Hastings, Hayhurst, Hiester, High, Hyde, Kein, Kennedy, Kerr, Konigmacher, Krebs, Long, M'Call, M'Dowell, M'Sherry Merkel, Montgomery, Pennypacker, Pollock, Porter, of Lan.

caster, Purviance, Read, Ritter, Royer, Russell, Saeger, Scheetz, Scott, Seltzer, Smith, of Columbia, Snively, Sterigere, Stickel, Thomas, Todd, Weaver, Weidman, Sergeant, *President*—72.

NAYS.—Messrs. Bell, Crawford, Cummin, Cunningham, Curll, Donagan, Dunlop, Earle, Fleming, Foulkrod, Fry, Fuller, Gamble, Grenell, Harris, Houpt, Maclay, Magee, M'Cahen, Nevin, Porter, of Northampton, Shellito, Smyth, of Centre, Stevens, Sturdevant, Taggart, Woodward, Young—28.

So the question was determined in the affirmative.

A motion was made by Mr. FLEMING,

That when this convention adjourns, it will adjourn to meet again to-morrow morning at half-past nine o'clock.

And on the question,

Will the convention agree to the motion?

The yeas and nays were required by Mr. FULLER and Mr. FLEMING, and are as follow, viz:

YEAS.—Messrs. Baldwin, Banks, Barclay, Bell, Biddle, Bonham, Brown, of Philadelphia, Carey, Chambers, Chandler, of Philadelphia, Chauncey, Clark, of Dauphin, Clarke, of Indiana, Cline, Cope, Cox, Craig, Crain, Cummin, Cunningham, Curll, Denny, Dickerson, Donnell, Dunlop, Farrelly, Fleming, Forward, Foulkrod, Fry, Gamble, Gilmore, Hastings, Hyde, Keim, Kennedy, Konigmacher, Long, Maclay, Magee, Martin, M'Cahen, M'Dowell, M'Sherry, Meredith, Montgomery, Pollock, Porter, of Lancaster, Porter, of Northampton, Read, Russell, Scheetz, Scott, Shellito, Sterigere, Stevens, Sturdevant, Todd, Weaver, Weidman, Young, Sergeant, *President*—62.

NAYS.—Messrs. Agnew, Barndollar, Bigelow, Brown, of Lancaster, Clarke, of Beaver, Cleavinger, Crawford, Crum, Darlington, Darrah, Dickey, Dillinger, Donagan, Earle, Fuller, Gearhart, Grenell, Harris, Hayhurst, Kerr, Krebs, M'Call, Merkel, Nevin, Pennypacker, Purviance, Ritter, Royer, Saeger, Seltzer, Smith, of Columbia, Smyth, of Centre, Snively, Stickel, Taggart, Woodward—36.

So the question was determined in the affirmative.

A motion was made by Mr. PORTER, of Northampton,

That the convention do now adjourn.

Which was agreed to.

Adjourned until half past nine o'clock to-morrow morning.

TUESDAY, JANUARY 2, 1838.

Mr. FRY, of Lehigh, presented a memorial from citizens of Bucks county, praying that the constitution may be so amended as to prohibit negroes from the right of suffrage.

Which was laid on the table.

Mr. LONG, of Lancaster, presented a memorial of like import from citizens of Lancaster county.

Which was also laid on the table.

Mr. BIGELOW, of Westmoreland, presented a memorial of like import, from citizens of Westmoreland county.

Which was also laid on the table.

Mr. RITER, of Philadelphia county, presented a memorial of like import, from citizens of Philadelphia county.

Which was also laid on the table.

Mr. FORWARD, of Allegheny, having asked for the reading of one of these petitions, it was accordingly read.

Mr. F. then said, he had desired to know what was the specific object prayed for, under the name of amalgamation.   He hoped that the entry would be made on the journal in a proper manner, as these petitions seemed to look entirely to political effect.

The PRESIDENT replied, that the journal would be made up in the customary manner; and if it was not in conformity to the wish of the convention, it could be corrected to-morrow.

Mr. CAREY, of Bucks, presented a memorial from citizens of Philadelphia county, praying that no change may be made in the constitution, having a tendency to create distinctions in the rights and privileges of citizenship, based upon complexion.

Which was laid on the table.

Mr. DARLINGTON, of Chester, presented a memorial of like import, from citizens of Chester county.

Which was also laid on the table.

Mr. COATES, of Lancaster, presented a memorial of like import, from citizens of Lancaster county.

Which was also laid on the table.

Mr. BIDDLE, of Philadelphia, presented the memorial of " the association of friends, for advocating the cause of the slave, and improving the condition of the free people of colour," praying that the right of trial by jury, may be extended to every human being.

Which was also laid on the table.

A motion was made by Mr. HOPKINSON, of Philadelphia, and read as follows, viz :

Resolved, That a committee of ———— be appointed, to whom shall be referred the amendments made to the constitution on second reading, and whose duty it shall be to report, prepare, and engross them for a third reading.

And on motion,

The said resolution was read the second time.

Mr. HOPKINSON moved to make the committee consist of *five* members.

Mr. WOODWARD, of Luzerne, moved to make the number *three*.

Mr. WEIDMAN, of Lebanon, moved that the committee consist of *nine*.

The question being taken on the highest number, it was decided in the affirmative.

So the the committee was ordered to consist of nine members ; and,

Ordered, That Messrs. Hopkinson, Denny. Chambers, Cunningham, Clarke, of Indiana, Forward, Porter, of Northampton, Dickey, and Read, be a committee for the purposes therein expressed.

The question being on the resolution as amended, by the filling up of the blank,

Mr. DUNLOP, of Franklin, said he should like to hear some reason for the adoption of this resolution, which seemed to him to be calculated to retard the business.

Mr. HOPKINSON replied, that the reason was, simply, to prepare the amendments for engrossment, as we went along, and thus to accelerate the conclusion of our labors.

Mr. FORWARD, of Allegheny, thought it might be better to give the committee the power to change the phraseology of the amendments, where it should be found defective.

Mr. DICKEY, of Beaver said, that when once referred, it would not be in the power of the committee to alter the language of any of the amendments, without the authority of the convention. They could only report the amendments as they were, and the convention would be obliged to go into committee of the whole, to make any change of phraseology.

The resolution was then agreed to.

ORDERS OF THE DAY.

The convention resumed the second reading of the report of the committee, to whom was referred the first article of the constitution, as reported by the committee of the whole.

The question recurring,

Will the convention agree to amend the third section, by inserting in the seventh line, after the word " state," the words " and shall thereafter have been a resident of one of the other states, or territories of this Union ?"

It was determined in the negative.

And on the question,

Will the convention agree to the amendment of the committee of the whole as amended?

The yeas and nays were required by Mr. KREBS and Mr. BARCLAY, and' are as follows, viz:

YEAS.—Messrs. Brown, of Philadelphia, Chambers. Cline, Cox, Crain, Dunlop, Earle, Gamble, Krebs, Long, Magee, Mann, M'Cahen, M'Dowell, Montgomery, Porter, of Lancaster, Porter, of Northampton, Purviance, Riter, Russell, Scheetz, Sellers, Smyth, of Centre, Snively, Young—25.

NAYS—Messrs. Agnew, Baldwin, Banks, Barclay, Barndollar, Bell, Biddle, Bigelow, Bonham, Brown, of Lancaster, Brown, of Northampton, Carey, Chandler, of Philadelphia, Chauncey, Clarke, of Beaver, Clark, of Dauphin, Clarke, of Indiana, Cleavinger, Coates, Cochran, Cope, Craig, Crawford, Crum, Cummin, Curll, Darlington, Darrah, Dickey, Dickerson, Dillinger, Donagan, Fleming, Forward, Fry, Fuller, Gearhart, Gilmore, Grenell, Harris, Hastings, Hayhurst, Henderson, of Allegheny, Hiester, High, Hopkinson, Houpt, Hyde, Jenks, Keim, Kennedy, Kerr, Konigmacher, Maclay, M'Call, M'Sherry, Meredith, Merkel, Pollock, Read, Ritter, Royer, Saeger, Scott, Seltzer, Serrill, Shellito, Smith, of Columbia, Stickel, Sturdevant, Taggart, Thomas, Todd, Weaver, Weidman, Woodward, Sergeant, *President*—77.

So the question was determined in the negative.

Mr. MARTIN, of Philadelphia county, moved to amend the third section in the eighth line; after the words "no person residing," by inserting the words, "less than one year," so that the sentence would read thus:

"No person residing *less than one year* within any city, town or "borough, which shall be entitled to a separate representation, shall "be elected a member for any county, nor shall any person residing "without the limits of any such city, town, or borough, be elected a mem-"ber thereof."

In explanation of his motive, Mr. M. said, that some difficulty might arise, unless there was such an amendment, as there was some ambiguity in this section, as regards the city and county of Philadelphia. The city and county had a separate representation. It was not proper that a person, who was a resident of the county, should go into the city to be a candidate, or, *vice versa*, that a resident of the city should go into the county to be chosen. He wished to see the language of this section less ambiguous than it was in the third and fourth lines, which merely rendered it necessary that a person must have been "a citizen and inhabitant of the state, three years preceding his election, and *the last year thereof*, an inhabitant of the city or county in which he shall be chosen a representative," &c. He desired to have the language more clear.

Mr. AGNEW, of Beaver, said, he did not know if he rightly understood the amendment of the gentleman from Philadelphia county. If he did, he thought the gentleman must have overlooked the third and fourth lines of the section, which were very plain.

Mr. MARTIN repeated his explanation relative to the ambiguity of the third and fourth lines, by which persons residents in the county, could go into the city to be a candidate, and those from the county could go into the city.

Mr. MEREDITH, of Philadelphia, expressed his hope that the gentleman would withdraw his amendment. He did not see any ambiguity in the·

language of the third and fourth lines of the section.   The city, when this constitution was made, was in the county, and this clause was introduced to remove all ambiguity.   A residency could not be gained in the city by the residents of the county, so as to gain those rights which are vested in the body of the inhabitants of the city.   He did remember instances in which persons were elected in the county, who had not resided the previous year in the county.   The returns were laid before the senate, and, the only question was, if they had resided one year in the county ?   The amendment proposed by the gentleman, so far from reaching our object, would defeat it.

The clause would read—" no person residing less than one year within any city, town or borough," &c.   So that, by express implication, if he resided one year in the city, he would be eligible in the county.

He believed the clause, as it stood, was without any ambiguity whatever.   He trusted that his friend from the county of Philadelphia, (Mr. Martin) would withdraw his amendment, and let the constitution remain as it is, for he had never heard that there was any ambiguity in it.

Mr. MARTIN said, he would certainly take the advice of the gentleman, because he was not certain that the amendment would reach the evil.   No longer ago than last fall, a Mr. English, now an officer in the custom house, who had lived in the city only a few days before the election, removed into the county of Philadelphia, where he had made a few political speeches, and was, in consequence, elected to represent the county.   And, the year before, Mr. Peltz was also elected to represent the county of Philadelphia in the senate, although he had resided only three months in it.

[Here Mr. M'CAHEN made some explanation, in an under tone, the purport of which did not reach the reporter.]

Mr. MARTIN expressed himself satisfied with the accuracy of the delegates statement.   He, Mr. M., wished to bring the subject before the convention, in order that the ambiguity might be removed, if possible.

Mr. M'CAHEN, of Philadelphia county, would admit that there had been some difficulty in deciding before an election, whether persons residing in the city could represent the county ; unless they had resided in it.   It was to be recollected that a part of the city was in the county ; and hence, it had happened, when an election took place, that there was doubt as to which a man belonged.   He had no objection that a man, although a resident of the city, should represent the county, if competent to do so.   He would not vote for the amendment of his colleague, but would leave the people at liberty to elect a resident of the city, if they thought him best qualified.   He thought, however, it was indispensable, that the individual should be acquainted with those whom he represented, and that he should also be a representative of the policy of the state, to be a good representative.

He, Mr. M'C., could not see that the amendment was calculated to meet the expectations of his colleague or himself.   He could not agree with his colleague, when he said that the gentleman to whom he had alluded, (Mr.

English) was elected a representative to the legislature, merely because he had made a few political speeches. He, Mr. M'C., believed, that the gentleman was well known in the district, where he had long lived, and was popular and respected. The gentleman was thoroughly acquainted with their interests when elected; and he, Mr. M'C., did not believe the county of Philadelphia, had ever been better represented. One of the senators of the county, was now a resident of the city; he meant Dr. Burden.

Now, if that gentleman was not competent to represent the county when living in the city, it should be so declared by the constitution. He did not believe that the people of the county, would elect a gentleman from the city, if they were not satisfied that he was fit to represent them.

Mr. Martin here withdrew his amendment.

Mr. Earle, of Philadelphia county, moved to amend, by striking from the fourth line " city or county," and inserting the word " district," and inserting in the fourth line, after the word " in," the words " and for;" and by inserting after the word " chosen," the words " a representative;" and by striking from the section all after the word " state," in the fifth line.

Mr. E. [said he fully agreed with his colleague, (Mr. Martin) as to the necessity of an amendment. There should certainly be something explicit on the subject. According to the argument of his friend on the right, (Mr. M'Cahen) his constituents ought to be at liberty to select their representatives from whence they chose, in the state. But, by the construction put upon the constitution, the people of the county of Philadelphia, cannot elect a representative from the city, nor can the people of the city elect a representative from the county.

He, Mr. E., thought it highly necessary that an individual should reside one year in a district, before he should be deemed eligible to represent it. He was of opinion, that if the gentleman looked at the section, as he, Mr. E., would amend it, he would be satisfied that the alterations were desirable. They would considerably abridge the length of the section, by rendering all the latter part of it, after the fifth line, unnecessary. All ambiguity would be avoided, and the constitution made a reasonable length. He believed it to be well understood now, that the convention would not consent to give each county of the state a representative. What an absurdity would it be, to say that a representative shall live in the county he represents, when, perhaps, he may represent the three counties of M'Kean, Tioga, and Potter! He can only live in one county. In reference to the senate—the constitution provided that no person could be elected a senator, that had not resided the last year of four, in the district for which he might be elected. He was perfectly satisfied with the arrangement, that a representative of a city shall not represent a county, and *vice versa*.

Mr. Meredith, of Philadelphia, said that the amendment would leave the matter just where it was. The gentleman should bear in mind that the representative district was the city or county. The two words were synonimous. He, Mr. M., did not think it would make the section more intelligible ; and he thought that no man who read it carefully, would see any ambiguity about it. When the question was raised among the members of the two houses of the legislature, it was considered only a question of fact. The gentleman who was elected, had resided a year out of the city, and a year in the county. In the case, to which allusion had been made, no petitions were presented. One, was that of a gentleman who went into the county of Philadelphia to reside, and, in consequence of his seductive eloquence, the citizens thereof, elected him as one of their representatives.

He, Mr. M., supposed that the gentleman was so acceptable to the people generally, that they did not dispute about his election. There was no ambiguity connected with it. He saw no necessity for going into a correction of the phraseology, unless some purpose was to be answered. Having said thus much, and as we had but little time to spare, he would do what he had never done before, ask for the previous question.

Mr. M. withdrew the call.

Mr. Forward, of Allegheny, asked, whether a gentleman who resides three months in the city, was eligible for the county ?

Mr. Meredith should say that he was ineligible. The section reads, that an individual must be an inhabitant of the state three years, and the last year thereof, an inhabitant of the city or county, in which he shall be chosen. And, then we come to the inquiry—what is the county in which he is chosen ? The last clause, is to fix what is the residence, i. e. the last year of the three years.

Mr. Forward agreed with the gentleman from the city, as to the result. But, was it not better to put in plain words, what the gentleman, and every lawyer could arrive at by construction ? For, it was, after all, a matter of construction.

Mr. Meredith said, that his fear was, that, in attempting to remove doubts, which never existed, we might involve ourselves in greater difficulty. At Harrisburg, where the question was frequently up, he had not heard a doubt expressed. In that part of the state, from which the gentleman from Allegheny came, there was no distinct separation. And, in this part of it, he, Mr. M., had never heard of any difficulty.

Mr. M'Cahen regarded this as a very reasonable proposition, because, it expressed in plain words, where the representative shall be a resident of —where the qualification shall rest. He maintained that it was better to use plain, clear, and explicit language. Where there was the less, ambiguity—the slightest room for doubt, the objection ought to be removed, Where there was no difficulty as to the qualification—there would be none as to the selection of candidates.

But, in regard to the cases referred to, he would say, in reference to the gentleman who was elected, in 1835, to the legislature, that if his seat had been contested, he could not have retained it ; nor could the gentleman, who was elected in 1836, and who resided in the city, and not in the county ; and the county of Philadelphia would have been put to considerable expense. He could not see what objection could, reasonably, be made to putting the section in language more clear and unambiguous, and which would obviate difficulties in future. If the language was clear and explicit, the people would have no difficulty about the matter, and would take care to choose their candidates from their immediate residents. He hoped the determination to resist amendments, would not lead to the rejection of the present.

Mr. CHANDLER, of Philadelphia, said it appeared to him that the convention were about to violate the good old rule of "letting well enough alone." No proof had been given of any difficulties having arisen from a misconstruction of the constitution. They were attributable to inattention. With regard to the gentleman who was sent to the legislature in 1835, he could say that the gentleman in question had been a resident of the county of Philadelphia a sufficient time to entitle him to take his seat. He knew him, and understood all about the facts and circumstances connected with his election. It had been shown that both the gentlemen referred to, had been residents of the county the proper time. He thought the gentleman from the county, (Mr. Earle) had better let the matter stand as it did ; for, if any alteration was made, a new construction might be put on the section, and thus occasion many mistakes. It was now clearly understood that a gentleman elected from the city of Philadelphia, must have resided there one year before he could obtain the privilege of being one of its representatives. This being admitted—clearly understood, he saw no reason why any alteration of the constitution should be made to prevent any misunderstanding hereafter, when it was correctly understood now.

Mr. EARLE remarked that the gentleman from the city, (Mr. Chandler) had said he clearly understood the matter. He hoped however, that the gentleman would have some compassion on those poor mortals, whose perceptions were not so quick as his own, and who did not understand it. He (Mr. Earle) had been appealed to as a lawyer, to say whether the individuals alluded to were eligible or not. He had given it as his opinion that they were ineligible ; but others declared that they were eligible, and the matter was decided against him. If a man held a seat in the legislature, who had no right to it, was not that an evil? He apprehended it was. Was this constitution such a "matchless instrument" that it was not susceptible of improvement, and ought not to be touched? It appeared to him that nothing but a fixed determination not to alter the constitution could induce any gentleman to vote against such an amendment as this was. Not a single sound objection had been urged against it ; nor could there be any objection brought forward possessing the slightest shadow of plausibility. Both the delegates from the county of Philadelphia (Mr. Martin and Mr. M'Cahen) had stated that the two gentlemen elected to the legislature, had no right there. He would put it to delegates to say—whether it was not better that this convention should alter the section so as to prevent the recurrence of the like difficulties in future, than to leave it unamended, and give the legislature the trouble of deciding hereafter on the eligibility of the parties elected, after having spent months in discussion? Would gentlemen go so far as to say it was better not to anticipate the recurrence of such a state of things as had been described? He apprehended not. But, when gentlemen said that nothing of the sort had happened, they made the assertion in the face of notorious facts. He would ask the editorial gentleman, whose knowledge of language he respected, if he would be in favor of putting an article in ten lines, when it could be expressed in five? Now, he wanted to reduce the number of lines of the section from ten to five. He said he would modify his amendment, so as to dispense with the matter towards the close of the section, which he deemed entirely superfluous. Mr. E. was proceeding to state his modification, when

The PRESIDENT said it was not in order to strike out what was unaltered in the section; but he would put the question according to the rules.

Mr. EARLE said that he would appeal, because he regarded the decision of the President as contrary to the uniform practice of the convention. At Harrisburg it was entirely different. He contended that he had a right to offer an amendment to his amendment, in order to put it in the best and most perfect shape it was susceptible of. Mr. E. at the request of a delegate withdrew his appeal.

The PRESIDENT said it was out of order after asking an appeal, and making a speech, to withdraw it.

Mr. BROWN, of Philadelphia county, did not intend to follow the example of his colleague, who, by way of saving time, had made an appeal, spoken on it, and then withdrawn it. With regard to the section under consideration, and the propriety of amending it, he had a few words to say. The question resolved itself into a question of experience. We ought to look back in order to see whether it was necessary to provide for the future. Had the history of the past demonstrated the necessity of amending the section? In his opinion it had. The cases cited of two gentlemen being elected to represent the county of Philadelphia, who were not privileged to do so, went strongly to prove, if any thing could do, that an amendment ought to be made immediately to prevent a recurrence of the kind. As to leaving it to the legislature to declare, in the event of a contested election, who was and who was not eligible, we all knew that their decision would be in conformity with the political complexion of the body itself.

He recollected that not many years since, Mr. Benjamin W. Leigh, who ran as a candidate for the county of Henrico, (Va.) against another gentleman of opposite politics, was declared duly elected by the legislature, because they wanted his services. The next year, a Mr. Williams, who was a candidate, was declared ineligible, because they did not require his services. He maintained that if the seats of the two gentlemen sent from the county of Philadelphia, had been contested, the legislature would have decided the matter in accordance with their political character. The editorial gentleman, as he was called, had said that the question had been settled. He (Mr. B.) thought the gentleman could not point out a single instance of a gentleman being elected to the legislature, whom that body knew to be elected according to the meaning and intent of the constitution itself. He could not see what objection that gentleman, (Mr. Chandler) or any other, could have to rendering the language of the section clearer than it at present was—to prevent mistakes and the trouble which grew out of them. The eligibility of a man should depend upon fixed constitutional principles, and not on the political character of the legislature, to which he had been sent.

Mr. CHAUNCEY, of Philadelphia, had looked with great care at the section, and did not perceive any defect in it, nor had he ever heard a doubt as to the inaccuracy of the phraseology until now.   He could not conceive any reasonable ground there was for altering the section.   With regard to the latter part of the section, he would say that no language could be more appropriate to express the idea the framers of the constitution had in view.   He thought the amendment of the gentleman from the county of Philadelphia, (Mr. E.) would not attain the object of his wishes—that was, to make the section clearer, and which he supposes of doubtful construction.   He (Mr. Chauncey) did not think there was any such term in the constitution as a "representative district."   There was the term "senatorial district."   But, if the words "representative district" were to be inserted, they might give rise to a question as to what was meant by them.   The language of the section was perfectly clear—city and county are the only two places.   The amendment would introduce a new phrase ; and instead of removing doubt, would introduce one.

Mr. BROWN, of Philadelphia county, said that if a gentleman represented four or five counties, he could live in any one of them.   In his opinion "representative district" was the proper term.   He would tell the gentleman, (Mr. Chauncey) that the term "city and county," was ambiguous, because a gentleman did not represent either city or county.

Mr. DICKEY said the third section, as it stood, in connexion with the fourth, would answer all the purposes of the member.   We could not make it plainer than it now was, under the third and fourth sections. The lawyers in attempting to make it plainer, would only entangle it. Upon one year's residence in the state, a person who had been previously a qualified elector in the state, would be eligible.   That was the provision of the third section as it was reported.   The fourth section provides that no county hereafter erected shall be entitled to a separate representation, until an adequate number of taxable inhabitants shall be contained within it, to entitle them to one representative, agreeably to the established ratio.   He could not see that the amendment offered by the gentleman from the county, (Mr. Earle) was of any importance, and it would only serve to embarrass the motion, without at all improving it.   He was in favor of adhering as closely as possible to the form and phraseology of the old constitution, as far as was practicable, because its construction was well settled and well understood.   To encumber it with new and unmeaning provisions of doubtful utility and disputed construction would destroy the instrument.   He could anticipate no difficulty in the construction of the section as it stood.

Mr. M'CAHEN offered an amendment as a substitute for that moved by the gentleman from the county, (Mr. Earle.)   He proposed to insert the latter clause of the section, viz: the words following :

"Or unless he shall have been previously a qualified elector in this state, in which case he shall be eligible upon one year's residence.   No person residing within any city, town or borough, which shall be entitled to a separate representation, shall be elected a member for any county, nor shall any person residing without the limits of any such city, town or borough, be elected a member thereof," and to modify the section so as to provide, that "no person shall be a representative who shall not have attained the age of twenty one years, and have been a citizen and inhabitant of the state three years next preceding his election, and the last year thereof an inhabitant of the district for which he shall be chosen, unless he shall have been absent on the public business of the United States, or of this state."

Mr. EARLE accepted the amendment as a modification of his own.

Mr. M'CAHEN remarked that the proposition did not change the character of the constitution at all. It made no essential alteration, and would render the subject perfectly plain. He asked the yeas and nays on its adoption.

The question was taken on the adoption of the amendment, and it was decided in the affirmative, yeas 66, nays 40, as follow :

YEAS—Messrs. Banks, Barclay, Bell, Bigelow, Bonham, Brown, of Lancaster, Brown, of Northampton, Brown, of Philadelphia, Carey, Chambers, Clark, of Dauphin, Cline, Cox, Craig, Crawford, Cummin, Curll, Darrah, Dillinger, Donagan, Donnell, Dunlop, Earle, Fleming, Forward, Fry, Fuller, Gamble, Gearhart, Grenell, Hastings, Hayhurst, Helffenstein, High, Houpt, Hyde, Ingersoll, Jenks, Keim, Kennedy, Krebs, Lyons, Magee, Mann, Martin, M'Cahen, M'Dowell, Montgomery, Porter, of Northampton, Read, Riter, Ritter, Russell, Scheetz, Sellers, Serrill, Shellito, Smith, of Co'umbia, Smyth, of Centre, Snively, Sterigere, Stickel, Sturdevant, Taggart, Weaver, Woodward—66.

NAYS—Messrs. Agnew, Baldwin, Barndollar, Biddle, Chandler, of Philadelphia, Chauncey, Clarke, of Beaver, Clarke, of Indiana, Cleavinger, Cochran, Cope, Craig, Crum, Denny, Dickey, Dickerson, Gilmore, Harris, Henderson, of Allegheny, Hiester, Hopkinson, Kerr, Konigmacher, Long, Maclay, M'Call, M'Sherry, Meredith, Merkel, Pennypacker, Pollock, Porter, of Lancaster, Royer, Saeger, Scott, Seltzer, Todd, Weidman, Sergeant, *President*—40.

So the amendment was agreed to.

The question then being on the section as amended,

Mr. DICKEY, said he was opposed to the amendment. He could not see that it made any improvement on the old constitution. If the section as amended should be adopted, we must, he said, make a corresponding alteration of the seventh section. He did not see how that had been overlooked before. It had not been brought to the notice of the convention. The question had been hastily sprung upon us, and the object of the amendment had not been well explained. The committee of revision would see that the sections conformed with each other, and that the provision in regard to the choice of senators should correspond with those relating to the representatives. He was in hopes, however, that the section would be rejected, and that the old constitutional provisions on the subject would stand.

Mr. BROWN, of the county of Philadelphia, said it ought to be plainly shown that the language of the article was clear. If it was clear to others, it was not equally so to him. He was willing to make an alteration, if the principle could be carried out in clearer language. But unless it could be shown that the proposed language was plainer than that which the old constitution used, he should oppose the adoption of the section as amended. A district might contain more counties than one, and there may be representatives who do not represent any one county.

Mr. MEREDITH said he would ask the deliberate attention of the convention to what had been done, and to what it was proposed to do. He would put it to this body to say, after what had passed, whether it was not now apparent, that they should proceed with some deliberation and caution, in the adoption of amendments to the different sections of the constitution.

We have got along to this point in altering the section, without hearing all the objections that can be started to it. But, new objections spring up at every step.

The object too, is not, as is declared, to alter the character and meaning of the constitution, but to carry out its intentions in plainer language. After fixing upon a time for adjourning, and limiting ourselves to a single month for considering all the articles, we go on making verbal amendments, for the purpose of improving the language of the constitution, and we have no sooner adopted one amendment, than we find that we have fallen by it into some unforeseen difficulty. Every member may have verbal alterations to suggest, in regard to every section and clause that is adopted. There can be no end to the propositions of this kind, if the convention choose to consider and adopt them.

Now, sir, I will answer for it, that, if the majority of the convention will give their attention to verbal amendments, that a vast number of them will be offered, occupying our time to little purpose, and plunging us into many difficulties; and I will warrant that, by the second of February, you will not have got through with your chronological alterations.

What is the use of altering this section as proposed? I assert, that there was never a time when the legislature entertained the slightest doubt, as to the true construction of the third and fourth sections of the first article. To alter them for the purpose of rendering them plainer, is wholly unnecessary. There is no doubt as to the present laws on this subject, and why then should any alteration be made, not affecting the principle of the constitutional provisions on the subject? No one here has pretended that there has been any doubt on this subject. The case which had been referred to he was well acquainted with.

The right of a member to his seat was questioned, when he, Mr. M., was a member of the legislature, on the ground that he had not resided one year in the county for which he was elected. That he had resided in the district, was not disputed. The members required proof of the fact. But this proof was not made. He alleged that he had resided one year in the county, his country house being there. But it was maintained, that this was his occasional and not permanent residence. Will any alteration of the law prevent such question from arising? Every language has words enough for expressing the same idea in different forms.

There is not a clause in this whole instrument, which may not be expressed in various forms. But, by adopting other language, can you make the intention of the instrument any clearer? You provide a man shall reside one year in a city or county. Why provide that he shall reside in the district where he is elected? You say that if he resides in the city, he cannot be elected for the county. What is the district? Is not the county in the district? Is not the city in a county? You make this alteration to remove an ambiguity. Wherein does the alleged ambiguity consist ? Why provide that he shall reside in the district where he is elected ? In point of principle there is no difference, of importance, between the clause as it stood, and the amendment adopted. He should oppose the adoption of the clause as amended.

The people did not desire unnecessary alterations of this kind. In regard to the power of the people to elect representatives, he had no desire to restrict it. For his own part, he would be very willing that the people of Philadelphia should elect a resident of Crawford county, if they chose to do so. He objected to striking out the latter part of the section, which served to render the whole clear.

At present he would only add, to what he had said on this subject, that if the majority of the convention choose to go on making verbal alterations, they would see the second of February, before they had made much progress in their business.

Mr. AGNEW said, there was one view of this question, which struck him as important. In the eighth section, the word "district" is made use of. That section provides, that "no person shall be a senator who shall not have been a citizen and inhabitant of the state for four years next before his election, and the last year thereof, an inhabitant of the *district* for which he shall be chosen ; unless he shall have been absent on the public business of the United States or this state."

If the word district be used in regard to the senate, it will not answer to use the words "city and county," in relation to the representatives. Corresponding terms should be used in relation to both. The second section provides, that "representatives shall be chosen annually by the citizens of the city of Philadelphia, and of each *county* respectively."

It is necessary to look through all the provisions on the subject, and see how they conform with each other. Is it the wish of this convention, to attack and destroy the fundamental principle, on which this constitution is based? The most important principle of our fundamental law is, that of representation ; and the constitution, as I have shown, makes an essential difference between the mode of choosing representatives and senators.

The qualifications required for members of the two, are different ; and it is provided, that senators shall represent districts, while the representatives are chosen for counties. The principle of county representation, is not preserved in the senate. The framers of the constitution intended that the representatives should represent counties, and the senators districts. This intention had always been carried out from the beginning of our legislation, under the present constitution. The senators represent a mass of the people, without regard to the local divisions. The two bodies were intended to counterbalance and check each other, in order that the laws might not change as often as the popular will.

He trusted that, in all the alterations which might be made, the convention would keep in view the spirit and principles of the constitution, and the bearing of their alterations upon those principles. The constitution provides, that no county shall have a representative, until it have an adequate number of taxables ; but though each county have not a separate representation, it is still represented by a member of the assembly. That is the principle of the constitution, and it appears to me, that gentlemen have fallen into some error in regard to it, and instead of amending the clause, are rendering it ambiguous by alteration. It is very true, as the gentleman from the city, (Mr. Meredith) has remarked, that we ought not to consume our valuable time, in debating mere questions of phraseology. But the question now at issue, embraces, in my opinion, something more than one of mere phraseology. It vitally affects a leading principle of representation, as settled in the present constitution.

He would ask gentlemen, who go for reform, if they would encumber their favorite projects with questions of a merely verbal character. If no important object was to be gained by the alterations now proposed—and it was not pretended that there was—he hoped the section would not be adopted. It was more than a merely unnecessary alteration. It was founded on a mistaken principle. The representatives cannot be chosen as the representatives of *districts*, without destroying one of the essential distinctions of the constitution.

But, the third section, as amended, does provide, in effect, that a person may be elected as a representative, who has been a citizen and inhabitant of the state three years next preceding his election, and the last year thereof an inhabitant of the *district* for which he shall be chosen: and this provision is a clear contradiction of that principle of the constitution, which basis the representation of the lower house of the assembly on counties.

Mr. STERIGERE said, I voted for the amendment very reluctantly, because I thought the section was plain enough before. No difficulty has ever arisin in regard to the construction of this clause. The practice had been to consider the seat of a representative as vacant, until the fact of his residence was made out. It is the wish of every one, that we should not embarrass and encumber important amendments, with amendments of a merely verbal and unimportant character, such as I consider this to be. The new constitution should go to the people, with as few amendments as is consistent with necessary reforms and alterations. Only those alterations which affect principles, ought to be made. All others are unimportant, and will do harm, by embarrassing the subject, to say nothing of the time wasted in their consideration. Gentlemen look rather to what the old constitution is, than to the amendments which have been agreed upon in committee of the whole, and which are now before us for adoption. We must look to what amendments we have made in the various sections of the article, in order to judge of the conformity of the amendment with the other sections.

The argument of the gentleman from Beaver, (Mr. Agnew) is based upon the provisions of the old constitution, without reference to what was done in the committee of the whole. A proposition was made, in the committee of the whole, to give each county a representative, and it was rejected.

But, an amendment was adopted, giving a representative to certain counties in districts which were not separately entitled to representation. Thus, by the amendments, we have recognized the principle of representation by districts as well as by counties.

The argument of the gentleman from Beaver, therefore, applies to the constitution as it stands, but not to the constitution as amended in committee of the whole. Two or three counties may be united and repre-. sented. Their member is then the representative of a district, and not of a county.

The counties, in these cases, have not a separate representation. But the old constitution does not authorize representation, except by cities and counties. For this reason, it may be proper enough to alter the section, by introducing the word "district;" but though it may not be improper, yet still I consider it unimportant. I do not think that there could be, in any case, a difficulty as to the meaning of the provisions of the constitution.

I have risen now, to inquire what is the course which gentlemen intend to pursue on this subject. It appears to me that they begin at the wrong end—that they put the cart before the horse. The gentlemen who oppose the amended section, wish to restore and establish the old section. That will not be the effect of rejecting it.

The amendment cannot, therefore, have its intended effect. It appears to me that the effect of rejecting the amendment, must be to strike out the section entirely from the constitution. I would prefer the amended section, to the entire rejection of the whole section.

If a bill be amended, and the question on the engrossment of the bill as amended, be decided in the negative, there is an end of it. The whole bill is rejected. It appears to me that this will be the case with this sec- tion, if the section as amended be rejected. I would thank the President for the opinion of the Chair, on this subject, as it may affect the vote on the question of agreeing to the third section as amended.

The PRESIDENT said, the opinion of the Chair is, that the rejection of the reported section as amended, would restore the old constitution.

Mr. DICKEY had, he said, only one remark to make further upon this subject. By the old constitution, and also by the amendments reported from the committee of the whole, the senators are to be chosen from districts. If we take the third and fourth sections together, we find that together, they provide that the representatives shall represent localities. But the amendment will not hinder gerrymandering for representatives. Several counties could be thrown into one district. Nothing could prevent the legislature, if this section as amended, succeeded, from putting Berks, which was entitled to four representatives, into a district with another county. There was nothing in the fourth section, which could prevent gerrymandering, if the third section should be adopted, as amended.

Mr. CHAMBERS said he voted for the amendment, and he was still in favor of it. He was disposed to adhere to it, because there was an obvious necessity of omitting the latter part of the section, after the eighth line; and because, in his opinion, it expressed the meaning of the section with sufficient perspicuity. It is said that there are constitutional provisions in relation to representation, that render any amendment on the subject unnecessary and improper. Counties are represented. Is any town or borough entitled to a representative? No. The only representatives known to the constitution, are those from counties and cities. All that is said of towns and boroughs, is unmeaning, and ought not to have a place in the constitution.

To get rid of the latter part of the section as it stood, he voted for this amendment. All that part of the section was uncalled for. There is nothing to be apprehended from an attempt, by the legislature, to gerrymander the state, as the gentleman from Beaver supposes, because it is specially provided by the fourth section, that "each county shall have at least one representative." The apprehension of the gentleman from Beaver is wholly unfounded, and his argument does not apply to the facts of the case.

The second section, as well as the fourth, will prevent gerrymandering. It provides that representatives shall be chosen only by the citizens of Philadelphia, and of the several counties. As to the boroughs and towns, they cannot be represented as such. I am of opinion, that the amendment is important, and I shall vote for the section as amended.

Mr. Scott said, the suggestion of the gentleman from Beaver, was of sufficient importance, to entitle it to some consideration. His own objection to the amendment which we had adopted, was, that it left the section in some doubt as to its true character, and the principle which it was intended to carry into effect. In his opinion, if we adopted this amendment, we would adopt a new principle, in the constitution of this state, and a principle, too, of very deep interest and importance. We adopt the principle, if we agree to the section as amended, that the representatives in the lower house, may become representatives of districts, instead of counties, and which districts may be referred, altered, and gerrymandered, at any time, and from time to time, by the legislature. That principle, if once countenanced and authorized, would utterly destroy the true basis of our representation, as settled by the framers of the present excellent and well guarded constitution. Now, the present constitution recognizes but one species of districts, and these are senatorial districts. You do not find in the constitution any provision for representative districts. But if you adopt the section as amended, you will provide that, in the lower house of the assembly, the districts, and not counties, shall be represented. Then, there will be no check on the formation of districts. If we must have the amendment, let us adopt some check. But if the amended section should be adopted, simply as it stands, we give the legislature the power to regulate the whole subject, as they please, without any restrictions. They may put Allegheny, Erie and Monroe, all together in one representative district, if they please. Then, sir, what will be the result? It will be the same here as in Massachusetts, where the term gerrymander originated. We may be assured of this.

Political parties, in times of high party excitement, will avail themselves of the opportunity afforded by such a provision, to cut up the state into districts, so as to maintain their ascendency in the lower house. The operation of gerrymandering is performed by uniting several of the most remote counties together, so as to form a political district, with a majority in favor of the party represented, by a majority of the legislature framing the act.

In Massachusetts, the shape of the districts, thus carved out, was published, and so curious a figure did they make, that some persons gave it a name after the party, which made it. Hence the term gerrymanders. The map which was published, exhibited a most absurd figure, something. like a horse's head, and a fish's tail. The result was, that the party which thus divided the state, was driven from office at the following election, and the districts were formed geographically, instead of politically. Mr. S. was opposed, he said, to introducing the system of districting the state, for the purpose of electing representatives. The present constitution had wisely provided that the counties should be represented in the lower house. There, local divisions and interests were represented, while the senate represented masses of population, without reference to small localities. This system he was not disposed to alter. The old constitution says, sir, that "the representatives shall be chosen annually, by the citizens of the city of Philadelphia, and of *each county respectively.*" There is not a word in this constitution, that has not a distinct meaning. Every word of the instrument was adopted upon full and careful deliberation. This clause went to provide that each county should have a distinct and separate representative. A subsequent clause tells us when a new county, thereafter created, should become entitled to a separate representation. My belief is that, in adopting the amendment to the third section, we have departed from the wise and wholesome principle of representation, which lies at the bottom of the present constitution. The people of Pennsylvania are not, in my opinion, prepared for this. They will feel, if you adopt it, that they have lost one of their most important rights—the right of separate and distinct county representation. Conceiving, sir, the principle of representation, by counties, to be extremely important; conceiving that it was intended to answer great and wise purposes; conceiving that no county can be so well represented as by one of its residents, and that one county and its local interests are lost in a district, I cannot vote for the section as amended. The result of the proposed innovating amendment to the constitution would be, that, from one county, in any particular district, three or four representatives might be taken, and that the other three or four counties might not have any representative at all. This would be not only directly hostile to the spirit of the present constitution, but it would be directly contrary to the decisions made by this body in committee of the whole, whenever the question was presented. Such a result was not contemplated by the gentlemen from the county, (Mr. Earle and Mr. M'-Cahen) when they proposed the amendment.

We are now, sir, on the second reading of the amendments, and I trust we shall not hastily adopt principles which we deliberately rejected in committee of the whole. I do not think it possible to form an instrument, that will be as acceptable to me as the present constitution. But I do desire, that the amendments which we may send forth, shall be sent in a state of as much perfection as possible. I cannot vote for an imperfect and mischievous amendment, in order to secure the vote of the people, against the whole instrument. It is our duty to adopt the best system we can, and leave it to the people to choose between that and the old constitution. Believing that the principle of this amendment is a bad and dangerous one, I shall vote against it.

Mr. STERIGERE. I propose, before the word "district," in the section as amended, to insert the words, "*county, city, or.*"

The CHAIR stated, that these words had been stricken out.

Mr. KERR said, he was in favor of the amendments to the constitution, as they had been adopted in the committee of the whole, and opposed to the section as amended.

Mr. STERIGERE wished, he said, to have the question taken on the amendment, which he had offered.

The CHAIR stated, that the question was on the adoption of the section as amended, and the words " city, county, or," proposed by the gentleman from Montgomery to be inserted, had been stricken out. The motion of the gentleman was not in order.

Mr. KERR said, it was certainly not in order to insert words which had been stricken out. He should, at all events, go against the amendment. He was in favor, of amending the constitution, where amendment was necessary, but not where it was unnecessary. The people would consider this as an unnecessary amendment. He was surprised that an amendment should be insisted upon, when there was scarcely a person to be found, who considered that the amendment was necessary in order to render the section intelligible.

Two delegates, in the convention, say that the provisions of the section, as reported, are not sufficiently plain, and they are in favor of the amendment, in order to render the constitution, in this respect, more intelligible. But, others think the meaning of the section sufficiently plain without the amendment. We are called upon, then, to alter the section, because. forsooth, two members say they cannot understand it. Now, that is not a sufficient reason, in my view, for the adoption of the amendment, and I shall vote against the adoption of the section as amended.

Mr. BIDDLE said, the question was not now in precisely the same form, in which it was, when the amendment of the gentleman from the county, (Mr. Earle) commanded so large a vote. The objections so forcibly urged against the amendment adopted, would not be at all removed by the insertion of the words proposed by the gentleman from Montgomery, (Mr. Sterigere.) The word district, to which exception had been taken, would still remain, and would convey the same meaning, and confer upon the legislature the same power in regard to the system of representatives. He could add nothing to the beauty of the argument of his colleague, (Mr. Scott.) What was the inducement, he would ask, to change the principle of county representation, as established by the old constitution? Must the whole state be involved in difficulty, because, by possibility, a citizen of the city of Philadelphia, may be elected as a representative of the county of Philadelphia? The question is a local one. What is the great evil complained of? Is it, that the voice of the people is destroyed? No. The qualifications of a candidate will be as well known to the people of the county, as if he resided in the county, instead of the city. There might be an evil in electing a person residing in a distant part of the state. The people might not have a sufficient knowledge of his character. But where is the evil of electing a person residing in the very place with the citizens who are the electors? This evil, which was, at most, of a very partial and circumscribed character, was the only one that was alleged as the reason for changing the constitution in this important particular.

Was this an evil, he would ask, which would justify any important change in the constitution? Shall this section of the constitution, which has done its duty for fifty years, be now changed, merely because some persons may perchance, have been elected to represent the people of the county, whose technical residence was in the city? Let us make those changes only which are important, and not seek to make alterations, which are unnecessary, if not mischievious. He doubted whether any evil had been felt from the operation of this section. It was no evil that the representatives, chosen by the people, should be allowed to retain their seats as such. The more we look to the subject, the greater appears the mischief that must result from a change. It would lead to a political subdivision of the state into districts, to suit the parties temporarily in power. The change contemplated is full of difficulty. Who can tell what new questions may spring up under the proposed change of words? Let us abide by those words, which have stood the test of time and criticism, and there will be no difficulty.

Mr. FULLER said, he had voted for the amendment to this section, when it was proposed by the gentleman from the county, (Mr. Earle.) He believed that a part of the section, which had been stricken out, was mere surplusage, and that the form given to the section by the amendment, was made more clear and simple, than that of the section as it stood. He thought the old constitution a little ambiguous on this subject, and from the statements of gentlemen here, it appeared that some difficulty had occurred in understanding it. To avoid difficulty, in determining whether a member of the legislature had been duly elected, he thought the proposed amendment very proper and reasonable.

He was, for this reason, induced to vote for the amendment, and, though not a verbal critic, he did think that the phraseology of the section was improved by it. The principal objection now urged to the amendment, is, that it will lead to gerrymandering. If it should have that tendency, I admit that it would be improper to adopt it. But there is no danger that it will have any such effect. I am at a loss to conceive upon what good ground such an apprehension is founded. Every one knows, and must admit, that the constitution gives a representative to each county. Is there any thing in this amendment, which contradicts or invalidates that provision? Nothing at all. It leaves the constitution where it was in respect to the county representation. It does not enlarge the powers of the legislature, in any way, but rather restricts it. It prevents the legislature from giving a seat to an individual who is not duly qualified to hold it. It removes all doubt and ambiguity from the whole provision, making it plain who can be returned as a representative. The qualifications of residence are made intelligible, and put beyond question by the amendment. That is all that it is designed to do, and that is the only effect that it can have. To say, that it will enable the legislature to subdivide the state into districts for political purposes, and to destroy county representation, is altogether idle. There are many clauses in the constitution, particularly, that in the second section of the first article, which will prevent the legislature from doing any think like it. That article says, in so many words, that each county shall elect a representative. It is not proposed to do away with that salutary and wise provision, but rather to explain and secure it. Under the present system, Mifflin and Juniata counties were united, and if I thought the amendment would extend the license to gerrymander counties, I would not support it. I shall vote for the section as amended, because, it cuts off what appears to me to be unnecessary. But, I hope amendments will not be passed for the purpose of delaying the business of the convention. Such a course, at this late stage of the session, would be extremely embarrassing to the objects of the convention. All the amendments that may be offered, will, I hope, be proposed in the expectation that they will prove beneficial, and that they will be adopted by the convention. Should vexatious amendments be passed and debated, it is quite certain that we cannot conclude our labors by the second of February.

Mr. DICKEY said that Mifflin and Juniata were not entitled to a separate representation under the present constitution. He had only risen to make this explanation, in reply to the gentlemen from Fayette.

Mr. BELL said there was much cogency in the argument of the gentleman from the city of Philadelphia, (Mr. Scott.) If that argument was correct, the amendment ought, without doubt, to be rejected. We are told by some, that the amendment is only verbal and that it is not worth our time, at this late day, to debate phrenological amendments; others again, say that the amendment subverts a vital principle of the constitution, and deprives the counties of their separate, local representation.

The introduction of the word district is said to effect all this. But, how is this proved? It does not appear to be the necessary effect of that word as used in the amendment. The amendment does not obliterate all the provisions of the constitution, which guaranty a separate representation for each county. The idea of a county representation is not done away with by it. Representatives must still continue to be chosen annually, under the constitution as it stands, from the city of Philadelphia and each county respectively. In every instance where a county has a sufficient number of taxable inhabitants, the legislature will be compelled to give it a separate representation. "Each county," says the fourth section of the first article of the constitution, "shall have, at least, one representative; but, no county, hereafter erected, shall be entitled to a separate representation, until a sufficient number of taxable inhabitants shall be contained within it, to entitle them to one representative, agreeably to the ratio which shall then be established." Here is the rule, and here is the single exception to the rule. The amendment does not do away with the rule, but it only provides for and explains the exception to the rule. Until counties become entitled to a separate representation, under this constitutional rule, they must have a district representation, by being united together. The amendment means nothing more, and can effect nothing more.

If there was nothing in the succeding part of the constitution, on this subject, then the argument of the gentleman from the city would be well founded. The old constitution gave one representative to each county, then in existence, but declared that no county thereafter to be erected should be entitled to a separate representation, unless it have a sufficient number of taxable inhabitants to entitle it to such, agreeably to the ratio established by the legislature.

Again : if it were true that the word district superseded entirely the idea that counties should form districts, then again there might be some force in the gentleman's argument. But, when this section is taken in connexion with the succeeding one, his argument falls to the ground ; because there it is declared that every county shall form a separate representative district.

But, sir, have we not within the limits of Pennsylvania, districts entitled to one or more representatives in the house of representatives, which is composed of neither city nor county, but of both connected ? Yes, we have now a representative district, composed of both city and county. He referred to the county of Allegheny and the city of Pittsburg, yet no one ever thought of raising objections to that. There was nothing in the argument of the gentleman, therefore, in relation to city and county. When a state of things arose which made it necessary to unite city and county, in this way, he apprehended that there could be no constitutional objection raised against it, and no one had ever raised an objection to it. Here then was an answer to the argument of the gentleman from the city, (Mr. Scott) in relation to the city and county. The city and county of Lancaster, also formed a representative district, and who had ever raised a constitutional objection against it? But, says the gentleman from the city, the legislature have trespassed upon the constitution in consenting to form two or more counties into one representative election district ; in other words, the legislature must not unite two counties for the purpose of electing a representative to the legislature of the state. Well, sir, does not the fourth section of the constitution provide for this ? And from the time of the formation of the constitution down to the present day, there has never been any inconvenience experienced from it. The fourth section of the old constitution, says that "each county shall have at least one representative ; but, no county hereafter erected, shall be entitled to a separate representation, until a sufficient number of taxable inhabitants shall be contained within it, to entitle them to one representative," &c.

Now, sir, what is the meaning of the word separate, in this place ? Did any body contemplate such a state of things, that you could not unite several of these new and small counties together, for the purpose of allowing them a voice in your legislative halls ? Why, the argument of the gentleman would tend directly to disfranchise a portion of the people of Pennsylvania. Sir, you would have taxation without representation, a thing odious to the people of Pennsylvania, and to the whole people of these United States. You would have the counties along the northern frontier of our state, cut off from any voice in the councils of the commonwealth, and you would compel them to remain so until they obtained a sufficient number of inhabitants to entitle each one to a representative. The framers of the constitution, in the opinion of Mr. B., never contemplated any such thing as this. Their intention, he had no doubt, was to allow the union of all such counties as were not entitled to a separate representative, in order that they might have some voice in the legislature, and if necessary, to make up a representative district out of a city and a county, excepting the city and county of Philadelphia. He had deemed it proper to say this much in reply to the remarks of the gentleman from the city.

Mr. Scott said that the gentleman from Chester and himself agreed perfectly with reference to the second section. The delegate from the county of Chester, takes up the argument that the second section of the existing article of the constitution has, in it an affirmation of the principle of county representation, and here the gentleman and myself agree.   It does affirm strongly that principle. The gentleman then goes on to say that with the second section before us, we must understand the words "representative district," to mean counties. Now, if we are to understand the term representative district, as synonymous with that of county, why was it that the word county was struck out and the word representative district inserted ? If representative district means county, let us adhere to the language in the second section, and retain the word county, which is the established and well understood language of the constitution. When you use the word county in the third and fourth sections of the constitution, and then drop them when you come to the third and fourth sections, the irresistible conclusion will be that you meant something else. When you use one sign for one signification in one place, and change that sign afterward, the conclusion is that you changed the signification with the sign. This, it seemed to him, must be the conclusion of every lawyer and of every layman in the commonwealth, who examined the subject closely. His argument, was not that he considered it unconstitutional for the new counties, not having a sufficient number of inhabitants to entitle it to separate representation, to be united together to give them a representative, but he thought it rather trenching upon the constitution, to unite those new counties with one of the old counties, for the purposes of representation.

The gentleman from Chester, with a view of refuting his argument, had resorted to a supposed analogy between the union of cities and counties, as, for instance, Lancaster and Pittsburg; but, he could tell the gentleman that that analogy did not hold good, because these cities never had been separated by the constitution from the counties in which they were situated. The city of Philadelphia being the only city which had been separated by the constitution. Neither did the argument in relation to the temporary disfranchisement of the citizens of these counties have much weight. It might be that a new county would not have any voice in your legislative hall ; but, that would be but for a short time, and no great inconvenience could be experienced from it. But, it was their own act if they placed themselves in this situation. Counties would not be struck off unless the inhabitants of the county petitioned for it, and if they did so, and knew that this would be their fate, it would be a matter of their own choosing. But, the very argument of the gentleman shows the impropriety of making this change. He is a lawyer and has made it his business to study constitutional law, as well as myself, and he is just as likely to be right as myself, yet if we cannot agree, and must necessarily dispute about the matter, how would it be with those who come to decide on this matter hereafter ? If we find gentlemen here, at the very outset, disagreeing so much in the terms proposed to be employed, how would it be with all those who came to decide on this matter ? The very discussion which we have had here, and the difference of opinion which seems to be entertained on this subject shows the impropriety of adopting such a proposition in our constitution. The language of a constitution ought to be of the most close and perspicuous nature, and none ought ever to be introduced into such an instrument that was not of this character. When you have determined that a certain principle should be inserted into the fundamental law, that principle should be inserted in language that could not be misunderstood. If we cannot agree in relation to this language, how will your judges of courts and the whole people of the commonwealth, agree in relation to it ? This, it seemed to him, was a very strong reason why the amendment ought not to be adopted.

Mr. EARLE wished to correct the gentleman, for he feared that his zeal had led him to misconstrue this amendment. The gentleman's whole argument was founded on a misunderstanding of the amendment, and he did not yet understand it, and this seemed to be the case with the other members from the city.

Now, he (Mr. E.) attributed this to two things ; first, that by opposing the amendment, they gave the citizens of the city of Philadelphia a privilege which the citizens of the county had not ; and secondly, that they opposed it because they were opposed to all amendments in the constitution. Now, we know that the county of Philadelphia has been represented by a man right out of the heart of the city, and his seat was not contested in the legislature, because it was known that it was in vain to do so. It was well known that a gentleman going from the city into the county of Philadelphia obtained a privilege which a gentleman going from the county into the city did not. Therefore, he wished this amendment to be adopted, so that all might be upon an equality. The county members are ready to give us this equality, but the gentlemen from the city, because it is contrary to their interest, are not willing to give it to us. The motive for this, he could only attribute to the zeal of gentlemen to prevent all reform.

Well, sir, the gentleman from Beaver, (Mr. Dickey) has talked a great deal about gerrymandering and all that sort of thing. Now, the gentleman has had an opportunity of voting on a proposition which would prevent all gerrymandering, and how did his vote there stand ? The record would show it. He will have a chance again to vote to prevent this state from being gerrymandered, and let us see how his vote will then stand. Let him then come up and vote against all gerrymandering. The fact is, that this state has been gerrymandered for twenty years past, and he desired to see this evil remedied. When the proposition came up to remedy it, he hoped that the gentleman from Beaver and the gentlemen from the city would vote for it.

But, the gentleman says that we may cut a county in two. So we may now for aught he knew ; but, as we have seen the evil which has sprung up from the prevalence of party spirit, let gentlemen come forward now and vote to prevent every thing of this kind, by inserting proper provisions in the constitution on this subject. Gentlemen have said a great deal about the term " representative district" in this section, but he would beg leave to inform them that there was no such term in it ; the terms are "the district of which he shall be chosen a representative." He hoped the amendment of the gentleman from Montgomery would not be agreed to, because it would be bringing us back to where we started from. Mr. E. considered it entirely improper that a representative should be elected from one county, when he resided in another; yet this was in effect the case in the county of Philadelphia. He trusted that this amendment would be adopted, and that those opposed to reform would not attempt to tire out the friends of reform by bringing up opposition to those propositions. He attributed this to the zeal of gentlemen to prevent all reform, and not to improper motives; but he hoped they would refrain from making efforts of this kind in future.

Mr. DICKEY would not have said a word, had it not been for some remarks which fell from the gentleman from the county of Philadelphia, who had just taken his seat. It was because he (Mr. D.) was a reformer, and was anxious that only such amendments as the people had asked for, should be adopted, that he opposed those useless amendments submitted by many gentlemen, which the people never would adopt. It was strange that gentlemen should have passed over this section, on first reading, without proposing amendments to it, if there were any needed which were so very important. Where were these men, who now profess to be such advocates of reform at that time? and why were there any complaints when those, who were the real advocates of reform, resisted those trifling amendments offered by the gentleman from the county of Philadelphia, which can be of no service to the people at large? He anticipated, too, that if these amendments were not cut off in the start, that we would be harrassed with amendment after amendment, of the same description, coming from the same source, which would perplex the real reformers and prevent them from obtaining those reforms which the people desire, and which we are anxious to obtain.

Mr. BIDDLE hoped and trusted that he never would impute unworthy motives to any one, and he felt here in common with all his colleagues, that he would have no occasion to defend either himself or them against any such imputation. It is said that our motive for opposing this measure, is because gentlemen in the city of Philadelphia, desire to represent the county as well as the city of Philadelphia? Was there a representative of this body who contended for such a right, or who contended that any such right did exist? Have we not all equal rights under the existing constitution, and do we claim under the existing constitution such a right as this? How then, can gentlemen assert that a motive exists with regard to the matter now before us. It was said too by the gentleman from the county, that it was useless to carry their complaints to the legislature, because there was no chance there of contesting the seat of a member.

Now, he (Mr. B.) had a higher opinion of the integrity of that party who were almost always in the majority in the legislature, than to think that they would not do justice to any portion of the people of Pennsylvania who might carry any matter before them. He had too high an opinion of that political party to think for a moment that injustice would have been done the citizens of the county of Philadelphia, if they had carried their contested election case before that body. He believed, if the case alluded to, had been carried before the legislature, that that body would have acted with the most perfect integrity. He thought the experience of the past legislation of Pennsylvania, would not justify the suspicion that they would have acted otherwise. They would then, doubtless, have acted on the most correct principles, as they would on every other occasion which might arise. He had risen merely for the purpose of saying that there had been nothing in the conduct of those with whom he had acted on this occasion, to justify the imputation which had been cast upon us.

Mr. MEREDITH rose merely to make a few words of explanation in relation to a remark which had fallen from the gentleman from the county of Philadelphia. The gentleman had said that it was useless to contest the seat of Mr. English in the legislature of the state, because in consequence of party, injustice would not be done to the people.

Now, the gentleman who made this assertion, could not have understood the laws of the commonwealth in relation to the subject of contested elections. When a question of contested election comes up before either house, it does not come up as a party question. We have, on this subject, that which the United States, government has not. We have a copy of the Grenville act which it was found to be necessary to adopt in England on this very subject, and which gave such general satisfaction there.

In congress we see that they are too apt to be led by their political predilections on subjects of this kind, because of the constitution of the body ; but, that was not the case in the legislature of Pennsylvania. There, when a case of contested election comes up, there is a committee raised to take charge of the subject, and decide upon it. This committee is balloted for, and struck as a jury to decide the question ; and, he had never heard a single individual before complain that injustice had ever been done in this way. The framers of that law provided for all cases, and it is ample for the purpose, and he defied any man to point to an instance in which a contested election was not decided to the entire satisfaction of all parties concerned. This committee sit as a jury upon the whole matter, and it is decided by them upon the merits of the case without the least regard to party ; and he was astonished to hear any gentleman cast this imputation upon the legislature of his state. The fact was however, that the gentleman himself did not believe this charge. It was, impossible that he could believe it. With relation to the proposed amendment, it was merely changing a section in the old constitution from what was perfectly intelligible to every body, for one, that to say the least of it, was very ambiguous and liable to misconstruction. He believed the whole question to be a mere question as to the phraseology of the section, and the old section was more perfect by far than the proposed modification.

Mr. STERIGERE also believed that the proposed amendment was more ambiguous than the old section. To strike out the word county and insert district, certainly would lead to misconstruction in some cases, and besides this, it might lead to the difficulty suggested by the gentleman from Beaver, of forming a district out of two counties which were not adjoining each other. He had merely risen to call the attention of the convention to the amendment submitted by himself, which he thought, if gentlemen examined, they would find to be such a proposition as they ought to adopt ; and, if the other proposition was adopted, he thought this one was perfectly consistent with it, and such a one as ought to be attached to it.

Mr. DARLINGTON moved that the convention now adjourn. Lost.

The question was then taken on Mr. STERIGERE's amendment, when it was disagreed to.

The question was then taken on the third section as amended, when it was adopted, yeas 68, nays 42, as follows :

YEAS—Messrs. Banks, Barclay, Bell, Bigelow, Bonham, Brown, of Lancaster, Brown, of Northampton, Brown, of Philadelphia, Carey, Chambers, Clarke, of Indiana, Cline, Cox, Crain, Crawford, Cummin, Curll, Darrah, Dillinger, Donagan, Donnell, Doran, Earle, Fleming, Forward, Foulkrod, Fry, Fuller, Gamble, Gearhart, Grenell, Hastings, Hayhurst, Helffenstein, High, Houpt, Hyde, Ingersoll, Jenks, Keim, Kennedy, Krebs, Lyons, Magee, Mann, Martin, M'Cahen, M'Dowell, Montgomery, Porter, of Northampton, Purviance, Read, Riter, Ritter, Russell, Scheetz, Sellers, Serrill, Shellito, Smith, of Columbia, Smyth, of Centre, Snively, Sterigere, Stickel, Sturdevant, Taggert, Weaver, Woodward—68.

NAYS—Messrs. Agnew, Baldwin, Barndollar, Biddle, Chandler, of Philadelphia, Chauncey, Clarke, of Beaver. Clark, of Dauphin, Cleavinger, Cochran, Cope, Craig, Crum, Darlington, Denny, Dickey, Dickerson, Dunlop, Gilmore, Harris, Hiester, Hopkinson, Kerr, Konigmacher, Long, Maclay, M'Call, M'Sherry, Meredith, Merkel, Pennypacker, Pollock, Porter, of Lancaster, Royer, Saeger, Scott, Seltzer, Todd, Weidman, Young, Sergeant, *President*—42.

The convention then adjourned.

TUESDAY AFTERNOON, JANUARY 2, 1838.

FIRST ARTICLE.

The convention renewed the consideration of the report of the committee, on the first article, upon its second reading.

The question being on agreeing to that part of the report which relates to the fourth section ; it was read as follows :

" SECTION 4.—Within three years after the first meeting of the general assembly, and within every subsequent term of seven years, an enumeration of the taxable inhabitants shall be made, in such manner as shall be directed by law. The number of representatives shall, at the several periods of making such enumeration, be fixed by the legislature, and apportioned among the city of Philadelphia, and the several counties, according to the number of taxable inhabitants in each; and shall never be less than sixty, nor more than one hundred.   Each county shall have at least one representative; but no county hereafter created, shall be entitled to a separate representation, until a sufficient number of taxable inhabitants shall be contained within it, to entitle them to one representative; agreeably to the ratio which shall then be established."

Mr. READ moved to amend the section, by striking out the words, " within three years after the first meeting of the general assembly," in the second line, and inserting the words, " during the first session of the legislature, after the adoption of the constitution."

Mr. R. said, this amendment was absolutely necessary, in order to make this section correspond with the seventh section of the first article.   In order to effect the objects of the seventh section, it would be necessary to have a districting, immediately after the adoption of the constitution.

Mr. DARLINGTON hoped, he said, that the amendment would not be agreed to.   It was another effort to require a new enumeration of the taxable inhabitants, immediately after the adoption of the constitution, which proposition had been rejected.

Mr. READ said, it was not in order to refer to what had passed in committee of the whole.

Mr. DARLINGTON said, an attempt was made in the committee of the whole, to procure a new enumeration of the taxable inhabitants, in 1839, and it failed.   The committee did not sustain the proposition.   The amendment now offered by the gentleman from Susquehanna, is designed to effect the same object.   I am at a loss to see any reason for a new enumeration at that time.

The gentleman from Susquehanna complained, on a former occasion, that the state had been districted in an unsatisfactory manner, and he therefore wishes to shorten the period for a new enumeration.   I doubt the propriety of making general rules, for the remedy of temporary evils. There is no adequate reason, in favor of another enumeration, before the regular one in 1842.   I do hope, the amendment will be promptly rejected.

Mr. READ said, he must call the gentleman to order, for referring to what had been done in committee of the whole.

Mr. SCOTT could see nothing, he said, in the seventh article referred to by the gentleman from Susquehanna, (Mr. Read) to render the amendment necessary.   The senators from each district were each to be elected for two years, and no district is entitled to elect more than four senators. It will be necessary to make a new distribution of the senatorial districts, before the end of three years, after the adoption of the constitution; but, it would be unnecessary to make a new enumeration of the taxable inhabitants for this purpose.   In like manner, as to the representatives, the legislature would apportion them, after fixing their number, among the several counties, according to the last enumeration of taxable inhabitants.   The effect of the amendment would be to produce a total change in the distribution of members of the lower house.   He did not say whether it would be right or wrong, but he would bring the fact to the convention, that the county of Philadelphia would be greatly the gainer by the new enumeration, as its population had greatly increased. It would be the gainer by one or two representatives.

He hoped the effect of the amendment would be duly considered, before the vote was taken upon it. The amendment of the gentleman would force a new enumeration, and the distribution of members of the lower house, would be made in conformity with it. The amendment, it should also be recollected, was not necessary for the purpose of carrying out the provisions of the seventh section.

Mr. READ rose to ask the yeas and nays on the amendment to the amendment; and, while up, he would, he said, remark that it has already been decided, that the present district system is wrong. The seventh section fixes that matter, and, as the convention have decided that the districting system is wrong, there is great propriety in making it conform with the principles which the convention deem to be right.

Mr. DICKEY hoped, he said, that the amendment would be adopted. He believed it to be necessary, in order to carry out the provisions of the seventh section, and also to secure a just and equal representation to different parts of the state. It was true, that the amendment was offered in committee of the whole, and rejected; but, he hoped the convention would now give it a favorable consideration.

He thought he should be able to shew to the convention, that the new enumeration and distribution, now proposed, was necessary, in order to secure justice to all the inhabitants of the commonwealth. Every portion of the people were entitled to an equal representation, and under the present apportionment, they had not got it.

In 1835-6, the last enumeration and apportionment took place, and the apportionment and the representations were not fairly distributed, according to the number of taxable inhabitants. He would draw the attention of the committee to some particulars on this subject. It would be found by reference to facts, that a part of his district had great injustice done to it, by the apportionment. He would ask members to turn their attention to the facts.

One district, with fourteen thousand seven hundred and seven taxables, was allowed only five representatives in both houses—three in the lower house and two in the senate; while Philadelphia, with fourteen thousand and seven taxables, had nine representatives—seven in the lower house, and two in the senate. Great injustice was done, in this manner, to several counties.

Mr. READ, of Susquehanna, moved to amend, by striking out "three years," and inserting "one year."

Mr. FORWARD, of Allegheny, said he understood this amendment went to anticipate the regular period for making the enumeration.

Mr. READ replied that it did not, inasmuch as there had not yet been any time fixed under this constitution.

Mr. FORWARD did not look at the matter in that light. His understanding was, that the enumeration would go on, as though the constitution was not amended at all. Now, taking it for granted, that the amendment was to answer a mere temporary purpose, he could not see what necessity there was for putting it in the constitution.

Mr. BELL, of Chester, said if he recollected rightly, this very question was discussed in committee of the whole, while the convention was sitting at Harrisburg. During the discussion, gentlemen went into an inquiry as to whether the amendments ought to be submitted to the people as a whole, or separately. He believed it was decided that they should be submitted as a whole. The simple duty of this convention was to propose and frame for the people of Pennsylvania, certain amendments. The question, then, which gentlemen had to decide was, whether they would make any alteration in the fourth section, relating to the enumeration of the taxable inhabitants of the commonwealth—whether they should anticipate the time set forth in the constitution, for making the enumeration ?

The constitution of 1790, confers on the legislature of Pennsylvania, the power of directing when, and the mode and manner in which, the enumeration shall be made. It leaves, also, to them the power of fixing the number of representatives and apportioning them. Notwithstanding the enumeration had been constitutionally made, yet there had been some complaint made of injustice having been done. He did not know whether it was well or ill founded. But, he presumed, that as the enumerations had been made under the authority of the legislature, they had done their duty, and taken care to have the enumerations carefully and accurately made.

What was the object of the amendment of the gentleman from Susquehanna, (Mr. Read) ? It was, as the gentleman from Allegheny (Mr. Forward) said, a mere temporary arrangement in an organic instrument. It was simply to do—what? Why, to induce the legislature to apportion the representatives at an earlier period than had heretofore been done. It was not pretended that the enumeration had been made at a time when it ought not to have been made. Neither was it pretended that the enumeration had not been correctly made : at least, he had not heard any thing which went to prove that such was the fact. But, it had been said by some gentlemen that the representatives of the people had abandoned their duty, and gone beyond the powers entrusted to them. Now, if this was the case, then, undoubtedly, the people ought to be apprised of it, and the delinquents should be properly punished.

He would ask, however, if the mode pointed out by the gentleman from Susquehanna, was the proper one ? Was this the time, and the course adopted by the delegate, the proper one, to effect the object he had in view ? The purpose of the gentleman was to obtain—what? Why, merely a repeal of an act of the legislature of the commonwealth of Pennsylvania.

This convention was convened to make amendments to the existing constitution. At the commencement of its labors, he and many other gentlemen, came to a settled determination to vote for no alteration of the instrument which should involve a departure from established principles. If the delegate from Susquehanna, or any other gentleman, would say that the proposition did not look to the introduction of a new principle—that it was not to be temporary, but was brought forward in order to correct some evil—to remove some defects, he (Mr. Bell) would vote for it most cheerfully. But, he could not, consistently with his former declarations, give his consent to a change which was merely temporary.

Mr. FLEMING, of Lycoming, remarked that he should be very glad if he could agree with his friend on the right, (Mr. Bell) and do his constituents justice at the same time; and he could not vote for any amendment, unless it embodied some degree of principle, which he considered this did. We had been told that it relieved us only from a mere temporary evil. Why, was it possible that any body would object to it on that account?

For his own part, if it would relieve the people from an evil but for one month, he would not talk about its being temporary. He would maintain that if there was any thing wrong in regard to the ratio of representation, or as to its practical effects, it was the duty of this body to remove it, and that immediately.

What! a temporary evil, and within the power of this body to remove —a body, assembled for that and other purposes, of that character—why then should it not be removed? Why should it be suffered to exist upon the statute book of the commonwealth, even for a short time? Why ought it to be borne with, because it would last only a month or so, and would then pass away?

Surely, this was not a proper course of conduct to pursue. Here was a convention met to amend the constitution—to repair the fundamental laws of the state of Pennsylvania, and when a glaring wrong was staring them in the face—which they saw with their eyes open, and which every member on this floor knew to be a gross violation of the rights of the people, under which they were suffering—why, then, he would ask, should they get up here and say, the evil would soon pass off, and therefore they would not introduce a remedy? Why should the evil not be corrected? He was not disposed to find fault with those who had made the present standard of representation, or those who had said how many representatives there should be from each district. However, he was not disposed to take things as a matter of course, as the gentleman from Chester did. His belief was, that the people of Pennsylvania could procure, in a reasonable time, a fair representation.

He did not rise, now, for the purpose of reiterating the arguments heretofore advanced; but, he gave notice, that whenever the subject should come up, he would have something to say.

He had seen and felt the effects of the present apportionment bill, which one of his colleagues (Mr. Smyth) had so aptly described. "The city of Philadelphia," (continued Mr. F.) "now sends two senators to the legislature, for her fourteen thousand taxables, and seven representatives. No other part of the state has an equal representation, for the same number of taxables of all the districts, representative and senatorial in the commonwealth.

Perhaps his immediate constituents had as much reason to complain as any other. The number of taxables required by the apportionment bill of 1835-6, to elect a senator, is nine thousand two hundred and fifty-six, the district which he had the honor to represent had at the last enumera-

tion of taxables, thirteen thousand and thirty-four. Add to this the taxables
of Clearfield county, forming a representative district with Lycoming, to
wit: thirteen hundred and ninety-five, which together, is fourteen thousand four hundred and twenty-nine, for which we now have four representatives and one senator; whereas, the city of Philadelphia, for fourteen
thousand four hundred and nineteen taxables, now has seven representatives in the lower house, and two senators, giving the city a majority of
three in the lower house and one senator over the twelfth district, and
that upon a less number of taxables. These are facts taken from the
record, and are indisputable; and yet we are told that is all right, and
that every portion of the state is as fairly represented in numbers under
the apportionment of 1835-6 as at any former period.

Not wishing, sir, to have a number of apportionment bills incorporated
into the remarks I feel compelled to make upon this subject, I will, sir,
ask the members of this body to compare, for themselves, the bill already
referred to, with that of any former apportionment bill, for the purpose of
making an honest comparison; and if they will take the trouble, the conclusion will be irresistible that gross injustice has been done in the last
apportionment. Why, then, should you procrastinate and postpone the
time when the people shall again be fairly represented? Is there any
other grand conservative scheme to be effected against the wishes of the
whole people, which makes it necessary to resist the effort now made to
do them justice?

Sir, if the existing provision for the apportionment of representatives is
subject to the evil, and can be construed to mean any thing to suit the
selfish dispositions of the designing, it is time it was stricken from the
charter of our liberties. At a former period of our labors, (said Mr. F.) when
he had given his views at greater length and advocated a different standard of representation with a view of doing justice to the sparsely populated counties, his efforts were then unavailing. And, as his individual
sentiments on this important subject were well known, it was unnecessary that he should now re-state them.

Those living in the north-western part of Pennsylvania had felt the
effects of the present system of representation, and particularly of the last
apportionment; and if their fellow citizens, living in the eastern counties,
and holding the power of the government, persisted in refusing to do
them what he conceived to be mere justice, they must, as good patriots
and good citizens, peaceably submit to what they must ever consider an
unreasonable and unjust exercise of power by the many over the few.

Mr. DICKEY, of Beaver, said the object of the gentleman from Susquehanna, (Mr. Read) must be apparent. The contemplated new bill to be
introduced in 1838-39 would not effect the purposes of that gentleman,
and the gentleman from Lycoming, (Mr. Fleming) as also those avowed
by the delegate from Centre, (Mr. Smith.) Now suppose the enumeration to be made in 1838-39, and the legislature to be of the same politics,
and governed by the same principles as the legislature of 1835-36, and
the amendment of the delegate from Susquehanna to be adopted, the gentleman from Lycoming would not obtain the object of his wishes. He
would assert that the apportionment bill of 1835-36 was perfectly fair in
its operation, and the people had been better represented under it than

any other. But, adopt the amendment of the gentleman from Susquehanna—make a mere temporary provision, as the gentleman from Allegheny said, what security had the gentleman from Lycoming, that the bill of 1835-36 would be altered to meet the principles of that of 1838-39?

Mr. FLEMING said he could only say as he had always said, that he hoped there would be honest men in the legislature, and that, consequently the apportionment bill made under the constitution of 1838 would be an equitable apportionment of the people of Pennsylvania.

Mr. READ would be glad to learn from the gentleman from Chester, (Mr. Bell), when and where it was decided that the amendments we should agree upon, would be submitted to the people as a whole? His recollection on the subject was quite the reverse of that of the delegate. He, Mr. R., well remembered the debate, and that no decision was made by the convention. The general impression, however, which prevailed was, that the constitution, as amended, would have to be submitted as a unit. With respect to the amendment now pending, both the gentleman from Chester and the gentleman from Allegheny, Mr. (Forward) were mistaken in supposing that it contained no principle. He would refer delegates to the tenth section, by which the time of meeting of the legislature had been changed from December to January, and would then ask them whether it was necessary to make the other section accord with it? He should say, that most unquestionably it was. The convention had decided that it was wrong in principle to have more than two senators to represent any one district; and yet the gentleman from Chester objected to carry the principle into effect until the expiration of four or five years, because the evil under which we were at present laboring was temporary? He, Mr. R., denied the charge that the amendment had been introduced for political effect. He cared not what might be the political character of the legislature. He was quite certain that no legislature—no matter what might be their politics, or the party to which they belonged—would ever again pass a bill so unjust, so iniquitous as was the bill of 1835-36. Had not the delegate from Centre (Mr. Smyth) shown that the comparatively small population of Philadelphia were entitled by the present unfair and iniquitous apportionment bill to nine members in both houses of the legislature of Pennsylvania, and that counties, possessing an equal population, were entitled to only five or six? He (Mr. Read) had proposed, the amendment because he thought it a very proper one; because, too he believed it would relieve the people from acknowledged wrong. He would repeat what he had said, that the bill was unfair and iniquitous in its provisions. It was perfectly immaterial to him what might be the character of a subsequent legislature, for he could not bring his mind to believe that they would be so recreant to their duty as to pass a bill of the character of the last.

Mr. DENNY, of Allegheny, said the gentleman from Susquehanna seemed to have settled upon the apportionment bill as one of the main grounds of attack. The convention had not yet adopted any proposition which made it necessary to change the septennial enumeration of the inhabitants, or taxables of, the different counties of the state. Although we had not reached the proposition, yet we were called on now in anticipation of a change of the kind being adopted by the convention, to adopt the amendment of the delegate from Susquehanna. Now, that was not the proper ground on which the convention ought to stake their action. They must act on the merits of the proposition itself, and not act in *futuro.*

The argument of the gentleman from Lycoming, (Mr. Fleming) as well as of the gentleman from Susquehanna, seemed to be based on the attainment of some special amendment; and this body, which had been convened for the purpose of considering what amendments ought to be made to the constitution, were to enter into a review of the labors of the legislative bodies of Pennsylvania! Now, that was not one of the logiti mate objects for which the convention met. The legislature had been arraigned, if it had not been—to use the language of the delegate from Lycoming—found guilty of fraudulent conduct. Why, the members of the legislature were amenable to their constituents—to the people of the state, if they acted improperly. It was not the province of this body to administer correction to them. To undertake to do so, was to assume a power not conferred on the convention. As he had just said, the legis. lature was answerable to the people.

He had no reason to find fault with the apportionment bill. But, it, appeared to him, judging from the tone of the argument of the gentleman from Lycoming, that this movement in relation to the taxables of the state, had its origin in political feeling, more than in any thing else. Did the legislature, he would ask, act constitutionally? Were they vested with power to divide the state into districts, as they have done? Did they act with open doors—within the hearing of every one? Certainly they did. Why, it was most extraordinary, that under such a state of circumstances as these, the legislature should be charged with fraud. If he (Mr. Denny) were a stranger, just entering this hall, and had heard the representation that had been made as to the conduct of the legislature, he should think that we had fallen on calamitous times, when an honest and faithful set of men could not be had to represent the people! If the legislature was corrupt and frau-lulent, what must be the character of their constituents? He apprehended that the legislature of Pennsylvania was governed by as pure motives as any other in the Union. These charges against the legislature implied a reflection on the good sense and intelli. gence of the community.

I entertain no apprehension (continued Mr. Denny) that any legislature will be so reckless, as to pass such an outrageous bill, as has been suggested as the consequence of this amendment.

This convention had never adopted an amendment requiring any change to be made in the mode of distributing the representatives.— We were called upon, in anticipation of a change, to direct a new enumeration. We ought to act upon the merits of the proposition before us, and not upon the supposition that some amendment may, here. after be adopted, that will render necessary the proposed provision. The convention was appealed to, to correct what was alleged to be inju. dicious legislation.

It has been alleged that the legislature, some years ago, made an unjust apportionment, and we are called upon to correct it. He doubted whether it was proper for us to interfere in the matter. We did not come here to take the legislation of the state into our hands. While we were correcting one alleged evil, we might fall into error of equal magnitude. He did not think it incumbent upon us to direct a new enumeration before the regular period, in order to correct any error in the present apportionment of representation. No. If the legislature have erred, they are amenable to the people and to their constituents. We are not to correct them. If we undertook to supervise legislative acts, we should usurp powers which were not conferred upon us, and did not belong to this body. We must leave it to the people to remedy the error of ordinary legislation. They have it in their power to do it, and to us they look only for the establishment of fundamental laws, for the direction and limitation of the government. He, himself, had no reason to find fault with the last enumeration of taxables.

The objection to it, urged by the gentleman from Susquehanna, was political, more than anything else. His object is to produce an impression out of doors, for political effect. Why does he talk of fraud on the part of the legislature? Where is the fraud of their proceedings in relation to this matter? It was very surprising that the gentleman would indulge himself in such inconsistencies and invectives, against the freely chosen representatives of the people. If a stranger were to come into the hall, and hear his charges of corruption, he would be induced to suppose that the people of Pennsylvania, must be very corrupt—that, in fact, there was no purity in the state, either in public or private affairs. If the legislature be so corrupt and fraudulent a body, what must their constituents be? Every one must take it for granted, that a people who have the free choice of their representatives once a year, will choose those whom they consider as fairly representing their character and wishes. To abuse the legislature, is to cast censure on the people who compose that body, and who elect it. If we expect to be properly treated ourselves, we must treat the legislature and the people with becoming respect.

I am disposed to vote against the proposition of the gentleman from Susquehanna, (Mr. Read) because I consider it wholly unnecessary and improper for this body to interfere with the ordinary and regular enumeration of taxables.

Mr. PORTER, of Northampton, said, that in referring to an entire list of the taxables of Pennsylvania, on which the present representation was founded, he found that the whole number of taxables in the state, was 394,000. The ratio was established accordingly. He was not disposed to censure the legislature for the distribution they made of representatives and senators, but he was of opinion that it was made very unfairly in regard to some counties.

It had been said, that where counties lost their due weight in the senatorial representation, it was made up to them in their number of representatives in the lower house. But this was not, in every instance, the case. It was not the case in Lycoming and Centre. I apprehend that every political party, when it has the ascendency, will so make the apportionment of representatives, that their opponents shall not get the advantage of them.

The democratic party took care of that; but they did not go quite so far as did the legislature of 1835–6, when that body made the present apportionment. Northampton and Lehigh, with thirteen thousand taxables, had one senator, while Philadelphia, with 14.419 taxables, had two senators. But it must be recollected, that Northampton and Lehigh were on one side, and Philadelphia on the other. If the legislature had committed an error, he thought it no more than just and proper, that the people should be allowed an opportunity to correct it, if they chose.

His friend from Philadelphia, (Mr. Scott) had alluded to the practice of gerrymandering, under the administration of Mr. Gerry, in Massachusetts. The practice was resorted to by the state administration in order to preserve the ascendency of the party which supported it, but they got served very much as some other parties had been in similar cases :—the people took the matter up, and defeated the scheme, and the administration together. The result produced, was, as was the case with the Philadelphia enumeration, very different from what was intended. Several counties had great injustice done to them by the last apportionment. He was of opinion, that less regard was paid to the number of taxables in the several counties, in the last apportionment, than in any previous once. He had not wished to make this a political question, but, as others had done so, they were welcome to all they could get by it.

Centre county was a democratic county, and it lost a thousand taxables in the apportionment. The Lycoming and Clearfield district, with 13,003 taxables, lost 3000 in the distribution. If these things did not require correction in the constitution, he did not know what did. The party to which I belong is in a minority here, but I do not doubt that, on the other side, there is honesty enough to see justice done in this matter. It was idle to make a political question of what may be done by any party. It was all a false idea, to take up such a subject as one for party contest. It was disparaging to the character of Pennsylvania, to permit injustice to be done in the distribution of representatives, for the sake of any party consideration. I wish to make no political question of the matter, but as other gentlemen have done it, I ask them if they have not honesty enough in their party, to permit what is known to be a gross injustice to be corrected.

Mr. CHANDLER, of the city of Philadelphia, merely rose, he said, to make a single remark. It had been often asserted that Philadelphia had not a due number of taxables for her number of representatives, but he believed she had more. Fourteen thousand, he believed to be far short of the number of taxables in the city of Philadelphia. It was very true that this and all other questions here, ought to be treated on higher grounds than those of party merely, and I am glad (he said) by our party it has not been treated as a party question.

Mr. DICKEY said, the apportionment made by the legislature of 1835-6 was one of the best and fairest ever made in Pennsylvania. Of that fact he had no doubt, and it could be proved on comparison with apportionments previously made. In regard to the number of taxables, that apportionment left a smaller aggregate of fractions, than any previous apportionment.

Mr. MARTIN was a little surprised to hear the gentleman from Beaver, (Mr. Dickey) talking about this apportionment bill, which had rendered such universal dissatisfaction, being the fairest and most honest apportionment which was ever made in Pennsylvania.

Now he, Mr. M., would say nothing about the senatorial districts, as they had been noticed already by other gentlemen; but he would call the attention of the convention to a couple of the representative districts. He would turn the attention of gentlemen to the condition of the city and county of Philadelphia, and ask them if that was the fairest thing that could be? In the county of Philadelphia, with twenty-five thousand taxables, and something over, we have eight representatives; while, in the city of Philadelphia, with fourteen thousand four hundred taxables, they have seven representatives. This was the kind of justice which was done by this act, which was the fairest and most equal apportionment bill which we have ever had in Pennsylvania. By this state of affairs, it was plain to be seen that it required three thousand and a fraction in the county of Philadelphia, to entitle them to a representative; while, in the city, it only required two thousand and a fraction to a representative. If this was one of the fairest and most honest things which we have ever had in Pennsylvania, he wished to be excused from having any more such honest laws as this. He hoped the gentleman from Beaver, would not again attempt to show the honesty and fairness of that law, which had been almost universally condemned.

Mr. Banks could not see what the evil deeds of the legislature could have to do with the amendment which we propose here to make to the constitution. It was necessary for us to ascertain what acts of the legislature were democratic, and what acts were anti-democratic, what acts were proper, and what were improper, in order to come to correct conclusions in relation to those amendments. These things had nothing to do with the question, and he hoped the deliberations of this body would not be distracted with them.

The gentleman from Allegheny, had admitted that there was something wrong in the last apportionment act. Then, if that was the case, was it not right that the people should have the privilege of correcting the errors, whatever they might be. If there had been no fraud practised, nothing erroneous in the apportionment law, and every thing done was proper and right, why, the people will see it, and will carry out their apportionments on the basis laid down by the legislature of 1835-6; and if that apportionment was wrong, was it not right, that the people should have an opportunity of correcting that error? Ought not the people to ascertain the truth, and act accordingly? Was it not right that the people should have the whole matter submitted to them, so that they might act on the subject?

It seemed to him, however, that these vexed political questions, ought not to be introduced into this convention, because they can have no good result, and nothing good can flow from them. If the people have a right to govern themselves, let them have an opportunity to decide on this question, and they will decide it correctly. Give them the privilege of approving or disapproving of this principle, and they will decide upon it correctly, and determine whether the act of the legislature was wrong, without our disputing and quarrelling here in relation to it.

Mr. Scott believed with the gentleman from Mifflin, that the debate on this question had taken an improper course, and that this convention ought not, a second time, to get up an exciting discussion upon this subject. Nevertheless, as the discussion had taken this range, he wished to mention a circumstance in relation to it, in which he himself was an actor.

It is universally admitted, that the enumeration of taxable inhabitants of the city and county of Philadelphia, made at the last assessment, was erroneous. The county commissioners made a mistake in the making of the enumeration, and, consequently, the enumeration was rejected by the legislature, as being incorrect. He, Mr. S., was then a member of the legislature. being elected to fill a vacancy, which had occurred in the city representation, by the death of a member. He was there, when the apportionment bill alluded to, passed; and in relation to Philadelphia city, he wished to state this fact. He did, in his place, so soon as it was ascertained that the enumeration of the city was incorrect, introduce a proposition, for the purpose of giving the city of Philadelphia an opportunity of making a new enumeration by the proper officers, before that bill was passed, and that proposition stands upon the records of that house to this day, where every man could see it, who desired to do so. He introduced that proposition, and begged and entreated the house, on behalf of the city he represented, that the privilege should be granted to them, of making a new enumeration. The opportunity, however, was denied to him by that house, and the members from the county of Philadelphia, from what cause he knew not, did not second him in that effort, and did not bring forward a proposition to give the county a similar privilege. He presumed they thought they were pursuing the proper course; but he, for the city he represented, considered that he ought to do every thing in his power, to obtain for them justice and right. This was, however, denied to the city, and he would ask, with what sense of propriety, gentlemen could say, that that city was unduly and unfairly represented? If they had been listened to by the legislature, they would have had a fair enumeration by proper officers, and would have been willing to stand by that, whatever it might be.

His colleague (Mr. Meredith) knew what he was now stating, to be correct. He would, therefore, say to this convention, that the city of Philadelphia, through her representatives, asked of the state of Pennsylvania permission to make an enumeration, which would not be susceptible of a doubt, and the assembled representatives of the people of Pennsylvania denied her that privilege; therefore, he trusted no man here would be heard to say that she had more than she was entitled to.

It had been asserted here, by the gentleman from Susquehanna, that the seventh section of this article, makes it necessary that a new enumeration should be made. If that argument was founded in truth, it was a very good argument; but how was it with regard to that section? The seventh section reads in this way—"The senators shall be chosen in districts, to be formed by the legislature, each district containing such a number of taxable inhabitants as shall be entitled to elect not more than two senators," &c.

Well, sir, adhere to this section, and does it require a new enumeration to be made? He apprehended not. It reduces the senators to two, and will require a new organization of the districts, but it will not require a new enumeration to be made. But if the object be to have a new enumeration, and a new representation in pursuance of that new enumeration, you must go farther, and order new elections based upon that enumeration. If there has been any injustice done any where, and you make a new enumeration, and stop there, that will not cure the injustice. It will not remedy the evil. Then you must go further, and, having made a new enumeration, you must also proceed to hold new elections under that new enumeration. Then if you do this, you deprive those who hold seats for the remainder of their term, which is an objection that you have endeavored to remedy in another section. You have already provided in the ninth section, that the present senators shall continue in office until the expiration of their term, and then follows this provision, that senators are to be elected for three years. Now, however, if we are to have a new enumeration, and a new election of senators in the course of eighteen months or two years ; if this be the object of gentlemen, it furnishes an additional reason for voting against the amendment now pending. The whole argument of the gentleman from Susquehanna, and the gentleman from Lycoming, falls to the ground, if this is their object. If we are to have an election of new senators, the schedule is the place to insert that provision. But he apprehended, there was a long foresight wrapped up in this proposition, and he apprehended, before we got through, that it would be discovered that there was some other object sought than that which was avowed. But if it was the case, that gentlemen desired to have new elections, and remove those who now held seats in the senate, that there would be but very little gained by it. He would inquire of gentlemen, whether they had reflected upon the time which it would take to effect this object? When will these amendments be submitted to the people ?

Here we are now, at the beginning of the year 1838. If we give the people six or eight months to deliberate on the amendments which we may propose it will be the fall of 1838, before the constitution will be passed upon by the people. Then a return must be made, and a law will have to be passed at the session of 1839–40, for making your new enumeration and by the time that return is made, and the state districted, it will be 1841, before you will get your new election. So that if it be the object to remove the old senators, you will gain but one year, because their terms will all expire in the year 1842. He would submit to this convention, even if that were the object of gentlemen, whether it would be worth while going to all this expense and trouble, for what would be gained to them by it. He trusted, therefore, that the amendment would not be agreed to.

Mr. STERIGERE thought it was time to desist going into political discussions in this body, if it was the intention to do any thing by the day of adjournment.

He was about calling the gentleman from Allegheny (Mr. Denny) to order, a short time ago, when he was denouncing those who denounced this apportionment bill, as a political measure, because that gentleman, on several occasions, had denounced the officers of the general government, for acts similar to this ; but, on reflection, he thought it was best to let him go on, so that he might show his own inconsistency. So far as the apportionment act of 1835–6 was concerned, he was disposed to let it rest, and not go back to rake it up afresh. He thought those who had a hand in passing that law, should be spared the mortification, which they must feel in defending it, for it was such a measure as no man could defend successfully.

Some may think that it was right, but a much larger portion think it was wrong, and they never can be convinced that it was right. But he was disposed to view this matter as if it was right, and as if every thing in that law was fair and proper, for the sake of getting a vote on this proposition.

Then he would ask gentlemen, in case that apportionment was fair and right, and proper, what argument was that against the amendment submitted by the gentleman from Susquehanna. Could any man oppose this proposition on that ground? He apprehended not. He would place his vote on the footing that that apportionment was strictly honest, right and proper, and then what had he to support him?

Let gentlemen turn back and see the course pursued on former occasions, in relation to this matter. Under the constitution of 1776, an enumeration was required to be made in the year 1778, within two years from the adoption of the constitution.

When the constitution of 1790 was adopted, an enumeration was required to be made within three years from its adoption, which was a short period.

Now, these two precedents are not binding on us, but they are deserving of some consideration. Why should we, under the constitution which we are framing, not require an enumeration of taxables to be made within a reasonable time? and why should we put it off longer than it was put off, on former occasions?

The increase of population in 1776, was slow to what it was in 1790; and the increase in 1790, was slow to what it now is and this circumstance should induce us to fix upon as early a day as possible. The organization of our districts and the enumeration of the inhabitants thereof, certainly should go together.

The objection urged by the gentleman from the city, (Mr. Scott) in relation to the amendment of the ninth section, is not well founded; and he apprehended, if the gentleman examined that section, he would find it conforming very much to the section of the constitution of 1790. As to the change in senators, they were made to come in as usual, one-third every year, but provision was made that the old senators should serve out their full term. He was opposed to having those senators who were elected for a term of four years, removed while their term lasted, and this section made provision for this difficulty.

He thought then, taking into consideration the precedents which we have had from former conventions, that we ought to determine upon having a new enumeration made within a reasonable time. We have a right to carry out the will and wishes of the public, in this respect; and he had no doubt but it was the desire of the people, that a new enumeration should be had.

As to the remarks of the gentleman from the city, in relation to a long foresight, and concealed motives, being at the bottom of this matter, he took it that it was all imagination, because we have a provision in the succeeding sections, which guards against any thing of this kind. He hoped, therefore, that the amendment of the gentleman from Susquehanna might be adopted.

Mr. COMMIN moved to strike out three years and insert one year. He regretted, he said, that there had been so much heat manifested in this discussion. The subject was one that ought to be discussed without blood or heat. Violence and warmth did not become this grave and deliberate body upon any question much less upon a question like this, which demands so much of cool consideration. It was a matter of regret with him that the interests of party had been mentioned at all, in connexion with the subject. It was, he believed, the object of every one in this body, to do justice to all. He could not believe otherwise of this body, collectively or individually.

But, if all that was said, in regard to the injustice done under the last apportionment, was true—and there appeared to be no doubt of it—there was no one who could say that flagrant injustice had not been done by the last apportionment to the people of this state, in some portions of the country. The impolicy of supposing such injustice to pass by uncorrected, must be manifest to all.

The very basis of our government, and of all republican governments, was true, fair, just, honest, and free representation. When this failed, the republican system was done away with—destroyed. The government which might be founded upon the ruins of equal representation, could not be republican—whatever politicians may choose to call it. The vital principle of free representation, was equality. Without that it could not be free. If any wrong was done under the last apportionment, the sooner it was righted, the better. It ought not to remain for a day, to disgrace and deface our statute book.

He could not see that it was the interest of any party to adhere, obstinately, to a system founded on error and manifest injustice. It could not subserve the interest of any party, obstinately to adhere to the errors which it might commit, especially when they were, like this, of a nature to unite the sense of mankind, generally, as to their injustice. It was useless to deny, and, indeed, it had not been denied, that the last apportionment was unequal. It could meet the interest of no party, to defend it and adhere to it. It was evident, from facts which had been adduced, that injustice had been done. There were five counties in which gross injustice had been done. Huntingdon, Mifflin, Union, Juniata, and Perry—these five counties elect two senators only. To elect these two senators, the people are gathered from a compass of two hundred and fifty miles. The city of Philadelphia, which lies within a small compass, also elects two senators. But, this far extended district, which elected only two senators, contained nearly eighteen thousand taxables, while the city of Philadelphia had but fourteen thousand. What a vast difference there was here, in number—a difference of nearly four thousand!

One district, with the greater number of inhabitants, is three hundred miles long, and two hundred and fifty broad; while the other lies within a narrow compass. But, the details were unimportant. If we were assured and certain that there is any thing wrong in the apportionment made by the legislature, in 1835–6, we should correct it. The wrong ought to be righted. We can certainly make a provision by which the error can be corrected. if the people wish to correct it ; and, surely, we can trust them to decide for themselves, whether the acts of the legislature require correction or not.

It has been said here, that the people would amend the error in their next elections ; that they would choose those who were to represent them, and cause any legislative error to be remedied. But, some years would pass before the next enumeration and apportionment, and as the representatives and senators must be distributed in conformity with the new constitution, there ought now to be a new enumeration. The new apportionment would then be made fairly and equally, if the people wished it, no matter what party might be in power ; and without a new enumeration, there could not be a fair and equal distribution of representatives. Many amendments were offered here, with a view to destroy the constitution—and to prevent its acceptability with the people, but this was not of that character, and he hoped it would be adopted. It could not be considered as a vexatious or a trivial amendment. It was a proposition of interest and importance, or it would not have elicited so warm an opposition.

The amendment provides, that there shall be an enumeration within one year, so that equal justice could be done to all.* The last apportionment brought together counties which were strangers to each other, and wide apart. Counties which were separated by mountains, were put together in the same district.

This was a fact, and as it was a grievance, it ought to be remedied. There was no fair and honest man, but would say, that the distance was too long, and that it ought to be shortened. There was no doubt about this.

In conversation with gentlemen of all parties here, this was readily admitted. The voters had to come from a most inconvenient distance to attend the elections, and so wide was the district, that they could not all of them have that intimate and positive knowledge of the persons to be voted for, that was at all times desirable.

Why should such a change, as was now proposed, be resisted on mere party grounds? Parties can have no interest in continuing such a state of things. One party may be in ascendency to-day, and avail itself of the unfairness and inequality of representation ; but after a while, the tables will be turned, and the minority becomes the majority. The party that rules one year, may not rule next year ; and the minority of one year becomes the majority of the year following. No party, therefore, can be interested in keeping up this state of things. All parties stand on an equal footing in respect to the subject of representation. A wound inflicted upon that sacred feature of our system, must be felt as a wound by men of all parties—by majorities and by minorities. Parties must look to the interest of the whole body of the people, or they cannot long stand by the aid of the people. Private and local interests cannot be brought into consideration on this subject. This was, in fine, the last topic in the world, that could be availed of to carry into legislative halls, what ought not to be there—party, private, personal, and local considerations and interests.

If members of this body were disposed to do what was fair and honest, if they were disposed to allow a fair and equal representation to all the different sections of the state, and all its inhabitants, they would not place the counties embraced in the same district, one hundred and fifty miles apart. Let us lay aside every consideration but what concerns equal and exact justice to all, and if we do that, we shall, without doubt, pass the amendment.

Mr. BROWN, of the county of Philadelphia, said, that one might suppose, from the warmth of the gentleman from the city, (Mr. Scott) that he had made an appeal to this body, for justice to Philadelphia, and that justice had been refused. If any injustice had been done, the error ought to be corrected. But, how far was this from the fact? Philadelaphia, so far from being deprived of her proper and just number of representatives, had more than she was actually entitled to from her number of taxables. She was entitled to no more than five members. The county of Philadelphia had many more taxables. But what was the fact? The city of Philadelphia had seven representatives, and the county eight. Is that honest and fair? No one can consider it so.

There was no gentleman here so ingenious and eloquent, as to be able to make it appear fair and equitable. The gentleman from the city says that he made an appeal, and the legislature would not heed it. But the delegates from the county are the friends of the city of Philadelphia, and it would be wrong to blame them for not seconding the appeal.

Mr. SCOTT here said that the gentleman must not understand him as censuring the delegates of the county of Philadelphia. They had no right to control the matter. The opportunity was refused to us, as to correct our enumeration. That was what he had complained of, and still complained of. He respected the rights of the county of Philadelphia, as much as he did those of the city of Philadelphia. All he wanted for one, he wanted for both. For both he asked a fair and just representation.

Mr. BROWN said, there was no doubt that the county of Philadelphia was unfairly dealt with, in the last apportionment, by the legislature. After all had been done to alter the enumeration, the legislature could not much reduce the original number of taxables, as first enumerated. The county had twenty-five thousand taxables, while the city of Philadelphia had but fourteen thousand. But the legislature, in the apportionment, gave seven representatives to the city of Philadelphia, and only eight to the county.

Now, he would ask, if seven to eight, was the fair and just proportion between fourteen thousand and twenty-five thousand? The county of Philadelphia was robbed and defrauded of her just rights, by that apportionment, and he, for one, was in favor of restoring them to her. If the legislature, by an unjust apportionment, defrauded any county or district of their due representation, it was undoubtedly our duty to right the wrong thus done.

We are called upon by the highest principle of right and justice, to give back to the counties, which have been defrauded, all that they are entitled to, when, in thus doing, we commit no injury to any other county.

He maintained that we had now an opportunity to remedy this crying injustice, without in any way, impairing, or invading the just rights of other counties and districts. He did not suppose that any one here would be willing to keep back from any portion of the people of Pennsylvania, their just rights. To suppose any such gross injustice, would be a slander, and a reproach upon this intelligent and respectable body. It must be presumed, that it is the wish of all here, to do what is just and right, in regard to every section of the commonwealth, in the important matter of representation.

The facts that he had referred to, were undoubted and undisputed, then why should there be any opposition to the proposed remedy ?

The gentleman from the city, tells us that we must not make any amendments, on the second reading of the articles, which have passed through the committee of the whole. But, if the committee of the whole were not prepared to act on the subject, if they avoided it on account of the agitation they supposed its discussion would create, he trusted that the convention would not be afraid to look it in the face, and meet it fully and fairly, as becomes the representatives of a free and intelligent and honest community.

It must be recollected, that when we were in committee, the county of Philadelphia was the standing subject of attack, and its members had to come into this body, armed to the teeth, to resist the most outrageous and wanton assaults. If the subject of the representation of that county was then kept back, in order to avoid agitation, there is no reason why it should not be presented and acted upon now.

That county had been defrauded of its rights, and it was the duty of its members to demand and insist upon redress—full and adequate redress. He trusted that there was honesty and disinterestedness enough in this body to afford it.

Mr. MEREDITH said, he thought it quite too late for the convention to employ its time upon a subject of ordinary legislation. The subject had been repeatedly brought before this body, and there had been always manifested an indisposition to interfere with it. This was from a general and strong conviction that by our interference, we should commit as many errors, and do as much injustice as we remedied; and also, from the belief that we had nothing to do with a subject of ordinary and regular legislation.

This body met in May last, and here in January, we are still talking on the subject of the last apportionment. Instead of going on with our business, and endeavoring to complete it by the 2d day of February, we are still disputing about an enumeration of taxables made three years ago, and which, in process of time, must be renewed and rectified by ordinary legislation.

The regular enumeration of taxables, will take place in 1842, and we cannot, by any amendment, cause one to be made before 1839. Was it worth our while to delay and embarrass our business, by an attempt to anticipate, for a short time, the regular course of legislative action on this subject? Of all the difficult, laborious, and perplexing subjects, that occupy the attention of our legislature, this one of enumerating the taxables, and apportioning the representation, is the most so. It occupies a large portion of their session, in which it is attended to, and after the greatest effort to do justice to all, with a sincere desire to make a fair and equal apportionment, they can but approximate to what is just and equal. Absolute equality is not attainable. Some districts must have fractions left, which are unrepresented.

He believed that the legislature generally, in making the apportionment, were actuated by a desire to do what was best. He would ask whether the representatives from the county of Philadelphia were doing justice to their constituents, and promoting their interests, by disturbing this body perpetually with this subject?

Mr. BROWN: I will settle that matter with my constituents.

Mr. MEREDITH continued. Was it not enough, he asked, that the city of Philadelphia should have to encounter the hostility of the county commissioners? Was it not enough, that the county, illegally appointing its own men, should attempt to do injustice to the city? Was it not enough, that they should make an enumeration, which every inhabitant of the city could prove to be wrong? Was it not enough that the county should report a list of taxables, which every one repudiated as incorrect and fraudulent, and which a majority of the legislature refused to recognize? Should the county, after all this, endeavor to keep up a perpetual agitation of the subject, and even in this body, which has nothing to do with it?

The city of Philadelphia, applied for a lawful and fair enumeration, and the legislature did what they thought best in settling the matter. The county was dissatisfied with the course taken by the legislature, preferring of course, its own illegal and unfair enumeration, as a basis of the apportionment. He deprecated the perpetual agitation of the subject here. We could not correct the procedure before 1839, and in 1842 the legislature would order a new enumeration, and make a new apportionment. In the mean time, it was not worth our while to bring up the subject for agitation here.

Mr. WOODWARD said, it was now manifest that, unless the difficulties between the city and county of Philadelphia could be settled somewhere else than here, the convention would not be able to adjourn before 1842. Under that conviction, he should demand the previous question.

At the request of some gentlemen, Mr. WOODWARD withdrew the motion for the previous question.

Mr. DICKEY renewed it, and the motion was seconded.

Mr. READ moved an adjournment. Lost.

Mr. STERIGERE said, that there was nothing on which the previous question could be put.

The CHAIR stated that the previous question would cut off the amendment of the gentleman from Susquehanna, (Mr. Read.) The main question would be on agreeing to the report of the committee, in regard to the fourth section of the first article.

Mr. M'CAHEN moved an adjournment. Lost.

Mr. M'CAHEN asked the yeas and nays, on ordering the main question to be put.

YEAS—Messrs. Agnew, Baldwin, Barndollar, Bell, Biddle, Brown, of Lancaster, Carey, Chambers, Chandler, of Philadelphia, Chauncey, Clarke, of Beaver, Clark, of Dauphin, Cline, Coates, Cochran, Cope, Cox, Crum, Darlington, Denny, Dickey, Dickerson, Dunlop, Forward, Gearhart, Harris, Hayhurst, Hays, Hiester, Houpt, Jenks, Kerr, Konigmacher, Long, Maclay, M'Call, M'Dowell, M'Sherry, Meredith, Merkel, Montgomery, Pollock, Purviance, Royer, Russell, Saeger, Scott, Seltzer, Serrill, Smith, of Columbia, Snively, Sturdevant, Thomas, Todd, Wiedman, Woodward, Sergeant, *President*—57.

NAYS—Messrs. Banks, Barclay, Bigelow, Bonham, Brown, of Northampton, Brown, of Philadelphia, Clarke, of Indiana, Cleavinger, Crain, Crawford, Cummin, Curll, Darrah, Dillinger, Donagan, Donnell, Earle, Fleming, Foulkrod, Fuller, Gamble, Gilmore, Grenell, Hastings, High, Hopkinson, Hyde, Keim, Kennedy, Krebs, Lyons, Magee, Mann, Martin, M'Cahen, Porter, of Northampton, Read, Riter, Ritter, Scheetz, Sellers, Shellito, Smyth, of Centre, Sterigere, Stickel, Young, —46.

So the question was determined in the affirmative.

The question then being,

Will the convention agree to the report of the committee of the whole, so far as relates to the said fourth section ?

The yeas and nays were required by Mr. EARLE and Mr. HOPKINSON, and were as follow, viz:

YEAS—Messrs. Agnew, Baldwin, Barndollar, Bell, Biddle, Brown, of Lancaster, Carey, Chambers, Chandler, of Philadelphia, Chauncey, Clarke, of Beaver, Clark, of Dauphin, Cline, Coates, Cochran, Cope, Cox, Crum, Darlington, Denny, Dickey, Dickerson, Dunlop, Forward, Gearhart, Harris, Hayhurst, Hays, Heister, Hopkinson, Houpt, Jenks, Kerr, Konigmacher, Long, Maclay, M'Call, M'Dowell, M'Sherry, Meredith, Merkel, Montgomery, Pollock, Purviance, Royer, Russell, Saeger, Scott, Seltzer, Serrill, Smith, of Columbia, Snively, Sturdevant, Thomas, Todd, Weidman, Young, Sergeant, *President*—58.

NAYS—Messrs. Banks, Barclay, Bigelow, Bonham, Brown, of Northampton, Brown, of Philadelphia, Clarke, of Indiana, Cleavinger, Crain, Crawford, Cummin, Curll, Darrah, Dillinger, Donagan, Donnell, Earle, Fleming, Foulkrod, Fuller, Gamble, Gilmore, Grenell, Hastings, High, Hyde, Keim, Kennedy, Krebs, Lyons, Magee, Mann, Martin, M'Cahen, Porter, of Northampton, Read, Ritter, Scheetz, Sellers, Shellito, Smyth, of Centre, Sterigere, Stickel, Woodward—44.

So the question was determined in the affirmative.

On motion of Mr. HASTINGS,

The convention then adjourned.

WEDNESDAY, January 3, 1838.

The President laid before the Convention the returns of the election for a senatorial delegate to represent the district composed of the counties of Venango, Warren, Jefferson, M'Kean, Potter and Tioga, in the Convention, certifying the election of Hiram Payne, in the place of Orlo J. Hamlin, resigned.

Mr. Mann, of Montgomery, presented a memerial from citizens of Montgomery county, praying that measures may be taken effectually to prevent all amalgamation between the white and coloured population, in regard to the government of the state.

Which was laid on the table.

Mr. Mann, presented a memorial of like import, from citizens of Bucks county;

Which was also laid on the table.

Mr. Sellers, of Montgomery, presented a memorial of like import, from citizens of Montgomery county.

Which was also laid on the table.

Mr. Sellers, presented a memorial of like import, from citizens of Bucks county.

Which was also laid on the table.

Mr. Bonham, of York, presented a memorial of like import, from citizens of York county.

Which was also laid on the table.

Mr. Biddle, of Philadelphia, presented a memorial from citizens of the county of Philadelphia, praying that no change may be made in the existing constitution, having a tendency to create distinctions in the rights and privileges of citizenship, based upon complexion.

Which was also laid on the table.

Mr. Coates, of Lancaster, presented a memorial of like import, from citizens of Lancaster county.

Which was also laid on the table.

Mr. Carey, of Bucks, presented a memorial of like import, from citizens of Bucks county.

Which was also laid on the table.

Mr. Earle, of Philadelphia county, presented a memorial of like import, from citizens of Philadelphia county.

Which was also laid on the table.

Mr. Thomas, of Chester, presented a memorial of like import, from citizens of Chester county.

Which was also laid on the table.

Mr. Meredith, of Philadelphia, presented a memorial from citizens of Philadelphia county, praying that the clause in the constitution which gives the qualifications of voters, should be amended by inserting the word "white," so as to confine the right of suffrage exclusively to that class of citizens.

The petition being read,

Mr. Sterigere, of Montgomery, moved that the petition be printed.

Mr. Hiester, of Lancaster, opposed the motion, and asked for the yeas and nays on the question.

Mr. Meredith, characterized the document as argumentative and worthy of being perused and circulated.

Mr. Cox, of Somerset, objected to the printing, on account of the expense.

Mr. Hiester, opposed it because he considered it a bad precedent.

Mr. Forward, of Allegheny, expressed his hope that the petition would be printed, in order that the members might be in possession of the whole of the argument brought forward in favor of restriction, and the abridgment of the liberties of any portion of our citizens. He felt some curiosity to see the argument, and to be in possession of it.

Mr. Brown, of Philadelphia county, said, that if the gentleman from Allegheny would wait until the question came up, he should have the argument, not in favor of the restriction of any existing rights, but to show that the rights to which that gentleman had reference, were rights not guarantied by the constitution.

Mr. Porter, of Northampton, was in favor of printing the petition. He had no desire to go into an argument on the subject at this time; but he should vote for the insertion of the word "white," whenever the question should come up.

Mr. Cochran, of Lancaster, asked for the reading of the resolution adopted by the convention, requiring a vote of two-thirds to authorize the printing of a petition.

The resolution was accordingly read by the secretary.

Mr. Earle, of Philadelphia county, expressed his hope that the printing of this document would be sanctioned by the requisite majority of two-thirds, because it was the first argument which had been presented on the subject, and ought to receive deliberate consideration at the hands of the convention.

Mr. Fuller, of Fayette, stated that he was opposed to the printing of the petition, although he was in favor of obtaining all the information which could be obtained on the subject. All memorialists were entitled to equal favor, and if this were printed, other gentlemen presenting other petitions which they may deem it important to have printed, will demand the same privilege, and who can tell what will be the amount of printing required to be done ? He hoped the motion to print would not be agreed to. Any gentleman who desired to look on the petition for the purpose of informing himself of its purport, could do so by going to the secretary's desk.

The question was then taken on the motion to print, and decided in the affirmative, as follows, viz :

YEAS—Messrs. Agnew, Baldwin, Barclay, Bell, Biddle, Bigelow, Bonham, Brown, of Lancaster, Brown, of Northampton, Brown, of Philadephia, Carey, Chambers, Chandler, of Philadephia, Chauncey, Clark, of Dauphin, Carke, of Indiana, Cline, Coates, Cochran, Cope, Crain, Crawford, Crum, Cummin, Cunningham, Curll, Darlington, Denny, Dickey, Donagan, Donnell, Doran, Earle, Fleming, Forward, Grenell, Hays, High, Houpt, Hyde, Ingersoll, Keim, Kennedy, Kerr, Krebs, Long, Lyons, Maclay, Magee, Mann, Martin, M'Dowell, M'Shery, Mered th, Montgomery, Pennypacker, Poll ck, Porter, of Lancaster, Porter, of No thampton, Read, Rit er, Royer, Russell, Saeger, Scheetz, Scott, Sel ers, Serrill, Shellito, Sill, Smyth, of Centre, Snively, Sterigere, Stickel, Thomas, Todd, Woodward, Sergeant, *President*—78.

NAYS—Messrs. Banks, Barndollar, Cleaving r, Cox, Darrah, Dickerson, Dillinger, Dun'op, Fry, Fuller, Gearhart, Gilmore, Hayhurst, Hi ster, Hopkinson, Jenks, Konigmacher, M'Call, Merkel, Se tzer, Smith, of Columbia, Sturdevant, Weaver, Young—24.

Mr. KONIGMACHER, called up for the second reading and consideration of the following resolution heretofore offered by him :

Resolved, That twenty copies of the Debat s and Journal of this Convention in the Engl sh language, and the like num'er in the German la guag', be deposited in the State Library ; thirty copies each be d posited in the office of the Se re a y of he Commonwealth, to be dis ribut d among the heads of the State d partme.ts; one copy each be d posited in the prothonota y's and commiss one s' office of th s ve al c untics in the co nm nwea th ; that each of the secre aries and stenograph cis of this Con vent on receive one c py each ; the balance to be d stribut d in qual nu ber of copies among the members of this Convention, to be by them placed in such pub.ic libraries lyceums and other places as they may deem beneficial and proper.

Which was agreed to.

The resolution being under consideration,

Mr. KONIGMACHER modified it so as to read as follows :

Resolved, That the Debates and Journal of this Convention, ordered to be printed in the Engl sh and German language, be distributed in the following manner, to wit :

	COPIES,
To the members of the Convention, one copy each,	133
To the three members who have resigned, one copy each,	3
To the State library,	20
To the prothonotary's and commissioners' office of each county, fifty-three counties, one copy each,	106
To the secretaries of the Convention, one copy each,	4
To the sergeant-at arms and door keepers, one copy each,	4
To the stenographers, one copy,	5
To printers of Journal and Debates, one,	2
To the Congressional Library,	5
To Governor and heads of departments,	6
seven copies to each member of Convention,	931

The balance to be deposited in the office of the Secretary of State.

Mr. STERIGERE moved to refer the resolution to a select committee of seven members, which motion was agreed to. And,

Ordered, That Messrs. Konigmacher, Sterigere, M'Sherry, Fry, Agnew, M'Dowell, Cleavinger, Russell, and Smith of Columbia, be the committee for the purposes expressed in the resolution.

FIRST ARTICLE.

The Convention then resumed the consideration of the report of the committee on the first article of the constitution, and the 5th section was read as follows :

SECTION 5. The senators shall be chosen for three years, by the citizens of Philadelphia, and of the several counties, at the same time, in the same manner, and at the same place, where they shall vote for representatives.

Mr. EARLE moved to amend the section by substituting for it the following as section fifth, leaving section fifth to be adopted as section sixth.

"Not more than three counties shall be united to form a representative district. No two counties shall be so united unless one of them shall contain less than one-half of the average representative ratio of taxable population. And no three counties shall be so united, unless two of them combined shall contain less than one-half of the representative ratio aforesaid."

Mr. DICKEY, said the motion was not in order.

M. EARLE said, he hoped the motion would be received and adopted. He thought it a very proper and necessary amendment, and the form of offering it was quite immaterial. He had intended to offer it previously to the adoption of the last section, after the debate which we had upon the subject of gerrymandering, but he then found no opportunity. The present rules of proceeding greatly embarrassed the business, for, if we voted in the negative on a question, then the effect of the rules was to make a new law ; but if the majority voted in the affirmative, then there was no new law. He offered this amendment for the purpose of preventing the practice of gerrymandering. He hoped there would be no objection to the motion. It was put off at the suggestion of several gentlemen till the second reading, which we were told was the proper time for offering such amendments. But the motion was lost in committee, by only two votes. This amendment was rather different in form from the former one. Its object was to reserve a fair and equal representation. He would ask if any gentleman here was not concerned in suppressing, by a fundamental law, the gross partiality and injustice that had been practised in districting representatives and senators by the legislature. Every political party being desirous of maintaining its power, is strongly tempted so to make the apportionment, as to favor its own interests. That had been exemplified by the legislature on many occasions. The legislature of 1835-6, as had been shown here had done much injustice in this way. The amendment if adopted would effectually prevent the practice in future. It would give the people security in their rights, and confidence in the legislature. Under the present system, they cannot feel safe. At every new appointment, they have to run a gauntlet through the parties in the legislature. If the predominent party in the legislature be favorable to a particular district, they may be secure of an adequate representation; but the politics of a district or county differ from those of their legislative masters, they must expect to lose a portion of their fair and proper representation.

He would ask whether there was a single person here who doubted or desired this? Was there a member on this floor, who was not convinced, in his judgment, that there had been gross partiality practised by the legislature, in making the apportionment of representatives? The gentlemen who offered the amendment, had not undertaken to prove that there was not fraud and partiality in the last apportionment. They did not deny it; nor was it denied, that the partiality evinced by the legislature was of a political character. They took care of their own political interests, giving an undue and uniform proportion of representatives and senators to those counties and districts that were of their own party. If these facts be not denied nor disproved, what reason will be offered for preventing the practice in future? The operation of the amendment will be equally fair towards all parties. It cannot, like the amendment offered yesterday by the gentleman from Susquehanna, (Mr. Read) be considered as militating against the interests of the party by which the last apportionment was made. Mr. E. was himself in favor of some enumeration of taxables, and a new apportionment to be made at an early day. The earliest day in which we could cause a new apportionment to be made, was in 1839, and he was in favor of the amendment offered by the gentleman from Susquehanna, providing that the same enumeration should be ordered by the legislature at their first session after the adoption of the new constitution. But that amendment failed. It was evaded by the usual means of resorting to the previous question. But no good and sufficient argument was offered against the principle of that amendment. The object of this amendment was similar, but it did not provide for a new enumeration. It did not look to a remedy for present evils. It left them to be cured in process of time, by ordinary legislation. It only proposed to guard against the recurrence of those legislative frauds upon the people.

The member from Philadelphia city, who yesterday opposed a motion similar to this, proved conclusively that great abuses have been practised in the distribution of representatives. He contended that there had not been a fair enumeration of the taxables in the city of Philadelphia, and the city called upon the legislature for a remedy. They, he says, refused to approve it. Was not this a proof that an evil existed which must be remedied by a provision like that now offered? That body also refused to do justice to the county of Philadelphia. Will not the gentleman from the city; go with the members of the county, after the county has suffered so much from the frauds of the legislature, in preventing those abuses hereafter? The members from the county, have been charged with a disposition to do injustice to the city of Philadelphia.

Mr. MEREDITH rose to order. He did not desire to see the city and the county brought again into collision. There had been too much of that. He trusted that the gentlemen from the county, would not press their local quarrels perpetually. They had been the constant theme of discussion here, since the first meeting of this body. The gentleman's propo-

sition does not involve the subject, and any allusion to it is irrelevant.

The CHAIR decided that the remarks of the gentleman from the county
were irrelevant, and that they referred to what was said in debate on
another subject.

Mr. EARLE, resumed. It would be rather difficult, he said, for the
Chair to pronounce what was the bearing and application of his remarks,
until he had heard them out. There is no amendment offered to prevent
abuses in the apportionment of representation by the legislature, and I
am endeavoring to show that abuses have existed in past time, and do still
exist. Hence. I mean to infer that it is the duty of this body to avail
themselves of this opportunity to prevent the recurrence of these corrupt
practices. I would ask, whether it is not in order for me to prove that
it is proper to adopt a provision to prevent injustice in this matter? Am
I in order to prove that injustice has been done in past time ?

The CHAIR. It is not in order for the gentleman to address questions
to the chair.

Mr. EARLE. Then I will take it for granted that I can proceed in my
argument, and show that the proposed amendment is necessary in order
to prevent the gross abuses heretofore practised by the legislature in apportioning the representation. In the first place, it is admitted that injustice
can be done by the legislature in this matter; and, if it was in order, I
would prove that great injustice was done to the county of Philadelphia,
in the last apportionment. But, as that is out of order. I will content
myself with asserting what cannot be denied nor disproved, that the legislature, at various times, in different apportionments, and more especially
in the last apportionment, has been guilty of political partiality and favoritism. But I will not speak further of the apportionments that have been
made, and will confine my remarks to the formation of districts. In regard to the arrangement of the districts, I will say that there is not an
individual here, who will maintain that injustice has not been done in that
matter ; and, further, sir, there is not a man here who will not say, that
there will be hereafter great injustice done in the same manner, unless we
adopt some provision to prevent it.

The legislature will always be divided into parties, and so will the people be. The party which, at the time, has the ascendency in the legislature, will take care of its own interests in the apportionment, unless, by
some fundamental law, they shall be prevented from exercising any partiality. He was about to refer to what had been said, in the debate yesterday upon the practice of gerrymandering, but, as he was fearful, that it
would not be considered in order, he would omit that remark—merely
saying that there appeared to be a general opinion here against the adoption
of the practice in this state. But it has been and will be practised in this
state. It is a practice that has often disgraced this and other states ; and
there is every reason to believe, that it will be continued in this state,
unless we devise and adopt effectual means to prevent it. The question
is a practical one. It addresses itself to the convenience of every one, as
a question of practical honesty. Is it fair and right, under our institutions
that one district should have a fuller representation, in proportion to its
population, than another district? Are they not equally entitled to be

represented ?   Ought the political complexion of the state, for a year or more, to be determined by the legislature, and settled by means of a legislative fraud on some of the counties and districts ?   Are the constituents of any gentleman here, so averse to justice, so indifferent to the character and welfare of the commonwealth, as to wish to perpetuate so disgraceful and mischievous a practice ?

He did not charge injustice more upon one party than another. He assumed that, whatever had been our first experience, all parties would avail themselves of the practice of gerrymandering, and partial apportionment, for the sake of procuring them power. The amendment, therefore, addressed itself to the mutual interests of all parties, and to the regard which all parties ought to cherish for the honor of the state. He asked every man of patriotic and just sentiments, in this body, to unite with him in forming and adopting some check to this disgraceful and injurious practice. No one could regard such iniquity with indifference, and he trusted that all would be willing to prevent it. He was not tenacious of the particular form he had given to his amendment. He would support any amendment, which would effect the object in view. Could all the Philadelphia lawyers in this body, form a rule which would effectually secure free and fair representation in the legislature ? There was nothing in the problem that could puzzle them. They would find it very easy, if they would undertake it. It would, however, puzzle their ingenuity to show that such a rule was unnecessary or inexpedient.

If any gentleman here would bring forward a better provision than this, or any provision effecting the same objects, he would cheerfully support it ; and if, contrary to his expectation, the convention should reject the proposition, to amend the constitution in this respect, he would then offer a resolution for the appointment of a committee of the two parties, to inquire whether it be not practicable, in some mode, to do away with this outrage and disgrace, of forming districts, and apportioning representation for party purposes. He believed that the amendment which he now proposed, would effect the object which all must desire ; if not, let some other be offered. Let the ingenuity of gentlemen be exercise upon the subject and some other adequate amendment will be offered in lieu of this, if this will not do. But let us take a stand, here in the constitution, against legislative frauds upon the representation of the people. If the representation be not equal, there is no guaranty for any other right. A minority may rule the state, contrary to the principle of our institutions.

If we would always trust the legislature, there would be no need of a written constitution. It is because, that we cannot repose unlimited power with safety, even in the hands of the people's representatives, that we are obliged to have recourse to constitutional guaranties. We must set up a barrier against legislative encroachments on popular rights, and there is no way in which the legislature can inflict a deeper wound on the public rights and interests, than by an unfair and partial apportionment of representation. Parties will often act under excitement, and some party or other, will have a temporary ascendency in the legislature, and will shape the districts, and apportion the representatives so as to promote their political interests, regardless of that justice and equality which ought to characterize the representation of the state in the legislature. Districts will be carried out by the parties in the legislature, so as to suit their party interests, unless we put it out of their power by the adoption of some such provision as this. That the people of the commonwealth will give their hearty approbation to such a provision, there could be no question. The people are always disposed to what is just, and they have a lively sense of the honor of their state government, as well as of its just and fair administration.

To the people, the amendment would be particularly acceptable, for it proposes to guaranty to them, what is dearest to them of all their rights and privileges, a free and equal representation. Some gentleman here had said, that the convention had nothing to do with this subject, and that we were not sent here to interfere with the legislature. If we were not sent here for the purpose of guarding the rights of the people, the more effectively from legislative usurpations and abuses, he was at a loss to know what we were sent for. If we did not consider such a subject as this, as within our powers and privileges, he was at a loss to know what we were to do here. If we were to do anything, besides talking and adjourning, this was one of the subjects upon which we should act. But he was aware, that some gentlemen here openly avowed the opinions that nothing ought to be done—that the constitution needs no amendment, and ought to remain as it is.

To such gentlemen, he did not address his arguments in favor of this proposition, because it would be useless; but even these would not undertake to dispute the propriety of controlling the action of the legislature in this particular.

The amendment will secure the small counties in their rights. A small county, if its members exceed half of the ratio, will, under this amendment, be entitled to one representative. It provides, that not more than three counties shall be united in any one representative district, and no two shall be so united, unless one of them shall contain less than one-half of the average ratio of taxable population. The remaining provision is, that no three counties shall be united in one district, unless two of them combined, shall contain less than one-half of the representative ratio. These provisions will prevent the legislature from placing more than two counties in any one district. The ultimate effect of this amendment, would be to give each county a representative, as soon as its number of taxables exceeded the half of the ratio, it would become entitled to a representative. Every county, in the end, would become entitled to a separate representative, and this was a great desideratum.

We have not yet brought our system of representation to that degree of perfection, of which it is capable. But he hoped, we soon should be able to do it. The principle had been adopted in impeachments of representing fractions, and it had been found to work very well. No complaint was made of its operation, and it rendered the representation more equal, than it could be made in any other way. The fractions in Massachusetts were represented precisely according to the strength of each county. Some counties or rather townships, send a representative one year out of three. Something of the same sort would do well if adopted here. It enables us to approximate more nearly to exact justice in distributing the representatives, than we could in any other mode. He offered this amendment, to see if there was any disposition to repress a practice which had been universally censured by men of all parties, and which it was acknowledged had prevailed to some considerable extent in this state.

The only question is, whether it is in the power of the convention to apply a remedy? He could have no doubt of this. It came as fairly within the scope of our powers, as any other subject of whatever nature. The evil was admitted. The power of the convention to check it, by the adoption of a constitutional provision, was unquestioned; and he submitted whether the amendment which he proposed would not answer the end in view.

Mr. STERIGERE said, he was opposed to considering new sections, till we have disposed of the old ones. He moved to postpone the consideration of the amendment, until we had acted upon the section as reported from the committee of the whole.

Mr. EARLE hoped, he said, that this motion would not prevail. He hoped the gentleman would withdraw the motion, as there was no other proper place for the amendment than this.

The motion to postpone was rejected.

The question being on the amendment.

Mr. EARLE demanded the yeas and nays, and the question was taken and decided in the affirmative, yeas 59; nays 47, as follows:

YEAS—Messrs. Banks, Barclay, Barndollar, Bell, Bigelow, Bonham, Brown, of Northampton, Brown, of Philadelphia, Clarke, of Indiana Cleavinger, Cline, Crain, Crawford, Crum, Cummin, Curll, Darrah, Dil inger, Donagan, Donnell, Doran, Earle, Fleming, Forward, Fry, Fuller, Gearhart, Gilmore, Grenell, Hayhurst, Helffenstein, Hiester, High, Houpt, Ingersoll Keim, Kennedy, Krebs, Lyons, Magee, Mann, Martin, M'Cahen, M'Dowell, Montgomery, Read, Ritter, Ritter, Russell, Scheetz, Sellers, Shellito, Smith, of Columbia, Smyth, of Centre, Stickel, Sturdevant, Weaver, Woodward, Young—59.

NAYS—Messrs. Agnew, Baldwin, Biddle, Brown, of Lancaster, Carey, Chambers, Chandler, of Philadelphia, Chauncey, Clarke, of Beaver, Clark, of Dauphin, Cochran, Cope, Craig, Cunningham, Darlington, Denny, Dickey, Dickerson, Dunlop, Harris, Hays, Hopkinson, Hyde, Jenks, Kerr, Konigmacher, Long, Maclay, M'Call, M'-Sherry, Meredith, Merkel, Pennypacker, Pollock, Porter, of Lancaster, Purviance, Royer, Saeger, Scott, Seltzer, Serrill, Sill, Snively, Thomas, Todd, Weidman, Sergeant, *President*—47.

So the question was determined in the affirmative.

The convention then proceeded to the consideration of the following section, reported from the committee of the whole.

SECTION 5. The senators shall be chosen for three years by the citizens of Philadelphia and of the several counties at the same time, in the same manner, and at the same places where they shall vote for representatives.

Mr. DARRAGH, of Berks, moved to strike out "three" and insert "two," and asked for the yeas and nays.

Mr. DUNLOP, of Franklin, wished the gentleman from Berks would assign the reasons, why he desired to make so important an alteration in the section.

Mr. Doran, of Philadelphia county, said, that the subject had been fully discussed in committee of the whole at Harrisburg. It was well known that senators had frequently violated their pledges, and the people, in consequence, had become very dissatisfied with them. He was desirous that they should be elected for as short a time as possible, so that they might be brought more within the reach of their constituents. It was under this feeling and impression that the proposition was made at Harrisburg. His opinion was, that senators should be elected for a shorter period than three or four years.

Mr. Forward, of Allegheny, said, that the argument of the delegate from the county of Philadelphia, fell short of its conclusion. The delegate ought to say one year.

He (Mr. F.) apprehended that the reason for requiring a term longer than one year for senators was, in order that we might have men who knew something of the affairs and legislation of the commonwealth. He did not know that it was either wise or politic to be always following the caprice of popular opinion. These fluctuations in the gales of popular opinion, should sometimes be withstood. For his own part, he would vote to retain the existing term, and against the amendment.

Mr. Doran observed that his argument applied only to senators, and not to representatives. If he had intended it to apply to representatives, he would have said, that they should be elected for three, six, or nine months. But, looking to the members of the senate, as having the control of the action of the lower house, he entertained the opinion that they ought to be elected for the shortest possible time. He could not concur with the delegate from Allegheny, that popular gales ought to be withstood.

He (Mr. D.) considered that every member was bound to obey the voice of the people; and if he was against that, he was opposed to the republican principle, on which rests the security of our free and happy government.

Mr. Shellito, of Crawford, said, that he rose for the purpose of saying a word or two on the subject. He would show that eight states of the Union have adopted the principle in their constitutions, of electing two senators for a term of one year. The names of those states are Maine, New Hampshire, Massachusetts, Rhode Island, Connecticut, New Jersey, North Carolina and Georgia. The states of Ohio and Tennessee, elect two senators each for a term of two years. He would examine and see how the principle had worked. We ought not to enter upon wild experiments. Experience was the best school in which a man could be taught. His reverend friend from Philadelphia, (Mr. Hopkinson) in the course of his argument a few days since, remarked that Pennsylvania had owed her prosperity to her excellent constitution and her wise laws. He (Mr. S.) fully agreed with him, Pennsylvania is like Tyre of old, seated on the sea, and the gentleman said, she was teeming with treasure, and every thing calculated to make a people happy. He would call the gentlemen's attention to the condition of Ohio. Ohio had not the advantage of situation that this state possessed. It was quite inland, and only the other day was a howling wilderness, in which the foot of the white man had never trodden. Now, as she had advanced in population, wealth nd prosperity, with a rapidity five times as great as that of Pennsylvania, the consequence necessarily followed, from the learned judge's argument, that her constitution must be five times better than that of Pennsylvania. Her senatorial term was two years, as he had already stated, and no complaint had ever been made as to its being too short.

Then, why, he (Mr. S.) asked, should we not adopt what had been beneficial there, or in other states? He concluded that two years was long enough, and that no senator ought to hold his seat against the will and wishes of his constituents. When a member no longer entertained the same views and sentiments as his constituents, it was high time he resigned his seat, went home, and let them choose one who would be more acceptable to them.

We ought to follow the example of other great states of the Union—the empire state among the number, and give to the people of Pennsylvania, a constitution as free as their's, and equally as congenial to the people's wishes. The experiment of short terms had been tried, and proved successful. Why, then, should we not venture to follow in the footsteps of other states—when this experiment was staring us in the face? He would conclude by saying that he hoped the amendment would be adopted, as a term of two years was quite long enough, and placed the senator within the reach of the people.

Mr. Agnew, of Beaver, would say a few words on the subject, because it was important, and had not been fully discussed in committee of the whole.

He believed that only two gentlemen had spoken—the gentleman from Union, and the gentleman from the county of Philadelphia. Those who went for a change of the senatorial term, based their arguments in favor of it, on the ground that a senator was bound to represent the will of the people. In doing so, he verily believed they departed from the principles on which our government was framed. It was necessary to be borne in mind, that under the constitution of 1776, there was but one body of representatives, and it formed the legislature. But, the constitution of 1790, effected a change in this feature of the government, by the introduction of a senate, to operate as a check on the house of representatives, and *vice versa*.

By this arrangement, hasty and injudicious legislation would be prevented. The senate differed from the other branch, in many of its essential features. The members of that body were fewer in number, and elected for four years, and were selected from among those men in the community, who were of mature age, and had had much experience in public life. The senate might be regarded, rather as an advising body, than one exercising a checking power. It differed from the house in this respect, that the senators represent districts, and not counties, as do the members.

They, therefore, do not represent local interests, but look to the welfare of the whole community. The body being entirely differently constituted, was calculated to prevent those changes in the laws of the state, which sometimes took place. Laws should be changed as seldom as possible. Frequent alterations in a system of policy, are injudicious, and seriously affect the best interests of the community, and therefore they should be avoided.

The senate requires more experience than the house. to enable them to act on the subjects which must necessarily come before them. They were in the habit of acting on principles which looked only to the common good, and on opinions long formed, confirmed by experience. He ventured to say, that there was not a member of this body, who could draw up a charter for a railroad, without referring to a precedent. Gentlemen made a great mistake, in desiring to reduce the senatorial term, for by doing so, they destroyed that balance of power which was vested in the senate, by the constitution, for good and sufficient reasons.

What, he asked, was the senate of the commonwealth of Pennsylvania? It was the high court of impeachment—a court, before which every officer in the state, might be tried for political offences. It possessed even higher authority than that of the supreme court itself, or any tribunal in Pennsylvania.

Now, he would ask, whether that body, which could displace the officers of the government, ought to be subjected to the wild caprice of every popular gale which might blow over the state?

He repeated, that the change contemplated, greatly tended to destroy that balance of power in the government, which was deemed essential to its preservation, when the constitution of 1790 was adopted. The proportion of voters in the commonwealth, was about one to five of the whole population. And, of those voters, one-sixth, or thereabouts, remain at home, and do not attend the polls. So that the elections are, in fact, managed by about one-sixth, or perhaps one-eleventh of the power of the senate.

This was the principle on which the change was asked, and which went to degrade the constitution of the state. The actual majority of the people was made subservient to the minority. One-eleventh part only of the people of Pennsylvania was to govern! Now, that was democratic. The framers of the constitution never imagined when they divided the government into several departments, for the purpose of making each responsible, and the senate a check on the other branch of the legislature, to prevent hasty and injudicious legislation, that an attempt would hereafter be made to get rid of a fundamental principle, which keeps the power of the government in the hands of the many, instead of the few. By reducing the senatorial term, the power of the government was transferred to the minority, from the majority.

For his own part, he was free to declare, that he could not consent to give his vote for any alteration of the constitution, that diminished the term. He was for adhering to the constitution of 1790, in this respect, at least. The character of the senate, when sitting as a court of impeachment, was very important, and ought to be well considered, by the convention, before they gave their votes on the amendment now proposed. When we reflected that the judicial department of the government might be prostrated at the feet of the legislative branch, it was all-important that we should keep the senate on the same footing as at present, to prevent its being destroyed by the fluctuations of the popular will.

He recollected that when the convention was at Harrisburg, the gentleman from the county of Philadelphia, (Mr. Doran) attempted to introduce an amendment, having in view the same object as the one now pending. And, it was admitted at the time, by those who favored it, that it was very important the two legislative branches of the government should not be suffered to interfere with each other. And yet, here was an amendment, the direct tendency of which was to produce that consequence. If we desired to preserve the constitution, we must do it by adhering to those practical checks, which render it so efficient and valuable to those who have the happiness to live under it. It was not enough to say that the legislature shall exercise legislative power; the executive, executive power, &c.; but it was absolutely necessary to provide that noone branch shall interfere with another. The moment the barriers which separate the several departments of the government were broken down, that moment a very important change would be wrought in its character. He would, therefore, advise gentlemen to be careful how they vote on this amendment.

Mr. BONHAM. of York, said that he was sorry this amendment had been introduced. When the convention re-assembled in October, he was glad to hear there was a general understanding as to the amendments which had been agreed upon. And, with regard to the amendment, limiting the term of senators to three years, he had supposed it met the approbation of the body.

He regretted, however, to find that he was mistaken, and that some gentlemen were in favor of still further reducing the length of the term—from three years to two. He felt certain that the senatorial term, as agreed on in committee of the whole, would meet the entire approbation of his constituents, and he trusted that the convention would agree to it. He could not vote for the amendment of the gentleman from Berks, (Mr. Darragh) because he was satisfied with that which had been adopted in committee of the whole. As they had spent so much time in committee, they ought to get on with the rest of the business as quickly as possible, and thus endeavor to allay the excitement which prevailed out of doors, on account of the protracted sittings of this body. He did not believe that a single vote would be changed by continuing the discussion.

Mr. DARLINGTON, of Chester, said he did not know that he could add any thing to the remarks of the gentleman from York, as to the impropriety of the amendment. He had risen mainly to express his dissent from the gentleman, as to the people being satisfied with the amendment, adopted in committee of the whole, changing the senatorial term, from four years to three. As far as he (Mr. D.) had any knowledge of the sentiments of his constituents, he was convinced that the alteration of the term, had given very great dissatisfaction to them.

He would vote not only against the amendment under consideration, but against every other, that went to reduce the senatorial term ; and, when the proper time should arrive, he would give his vote for the old constitution.

The vote being taken, the amendment to the amendment was negatived —yeas, 32; nays, 72; as follows:

YEAS—Messrs. Banks, Brown, of Northampton, Brown, of Philadelphia, Cummin, Darrah, Dillinger, Donagan, Doran, Dunlop, Earle, Fuller, Gearhart, Gilmore, Hayhurst, Helffenstein, High, Keim, Kennedy, Krebs, Martin, M'Cahen, Read, Riter, Ritter, Scheetz, Selcers, Shellito, Smith, of Columbia, Smyth, of Center, Sickel, Weaver, Woodward—32.

NAYS—Messrs. Agnew, Baldwin, Barclay, Barndollar, Bell, Biddle, Bigelow, Bonham, Brown, of Lancaster, Carey, Chambers, Chandler, of Philadelphia, Chauncey, Clarke, of Beaver, Clarke, of Dauphin, Clarke, of Indiana, Clevinger, Cline, Coates, Cochran, Cope, Cox, Craig, Crain, Crawford, Crum, Cunningham, Curll, Darlington, Denny, Dickey, Dickerson, Fleming, Forward, Fry, Grenell, Harris, Hays, Hiester, Hopkinson, Houpt, Hyde, Ingersoll, Jenks, Kerr, Konigmacher, Long, Macay, Mann, M'Call, M'Dowell, M'Sherry, Meredith, Merkel, Montgomery, Pennypacker, Pollock, Porter, of Lancaster, Purviance, Royer, Russell, Sager, Scott, Seltzer, Sill, Snively, Sterigere, Sturdevant, Todd, Weidman, Young, Sergeant, President—72.

The question then being on agreeing to the amendment to the fifth section, as reported from the committee of the whole, making the term of senatorial service three years, instead of four,

Mr. DICKEY called for the yeas and nays, and they were as follow, viz :

YEAS—Messrs. Banks, Barclay, Bell, Bigelow, Bonham, Brown, of Northampton, Brown, of Philadelphia, Clarke, of Beaver, Clark, of Indiana, Clevenger, Crain, Crawford, Cummin, Curll, Darrah, Dillinger, Donagan, Donnell, Doran, Earle, Fleming, Fry, Fuller, Gearhart, Gilmore, Grenell, Hayhurst, Helffenstein, High, Houpt, Hyde, Ingersoll, Keim, Kennedy, Krebs, Magee, Mann, Martin, M'Cahen, Montgomery, Purviance, Read, Riter, Ritter, Scheetz, Sellers, Seltzer, Shellito, Smith, of Columbia, Smyth, of Centre, Sterigere, Sickel, Sturdevant, Weaver, Woodward—55.

NAYS—Messrs. Agnew, Baldwin, Barndollar, Biddle, Brown, of Lancaster, Carey, Chambers, Chandler, of Philadelphia, Chauncey, Clark, of Dauphin, Cline, Coates, Cochran, Cope, Cox, Craig, Crum, Cunningham, Darlington, Denny, Dickey, Dickerson, Dunlop, Forward, Harris, Hays, Hiester, Hopkinson, Jenks, Kerr, Konigmacher, Long, Maclay, M'Call, M'Dowell, M'Sherry, Meredith, Merkel, Pennypacker, Pollock, Porter, of Lancaster, Royer, Russell, Seager, Scott, Sennill, Sill, Snively, Thomas, Todd, Weidman, Young, Sergeant, President—53.

So the question was determined in the affirmative.

The PRESIDENT stated the question to be on the section, as amended.

Mr. BIDDLE asked the yeas and nays upon it.

Mr. FORWARD rose and said, he felt much solicitude about this question. It was a question upon agreeing to the section, as now amended, and this assumes a higher importance, in consequence of its connexion with some other parts of the constitution, decided upon by the committee of the whole.

It has been decided in the committee of the whole, that the President shall appoint certain executive, and other officers, by and with the advice and consent of the senate. This alteration gives a dignity and importance to the senatorial functions, which they did not before possess ; and, it furnishes a very strong reason in favor of continuing the term of senatorial service, as it stands in the present constitution. It constitutes a strong reason for enlarging, rather than abridging, that term of service. He should exceedingly regret it, if this body should not recede from the course taken by them on this subject. An abridgment of the senatorial term would be inconsistent with the character of the additional duties and responsibilities imposed upon the senate. If they were to take part with the governor, in the exercise of his power, and especially in the power of making appointments to office, it was a strong reason, in his opinion, for lengthening their term of service to five years, instead of abridging it to three years.

The true republican principle of representation, requires obedience on the part of the representative, to the wishes of those whose interests are to be affected by their votes.

But, shall a man, coming from Crawford county, be bound to promote the wishes of the people of Philadelphia county? Or, shall a man, representing a western county, know or care any thing about the wishes or interests of the eastern counties?

But, a general law affects the interests, not of any one part of the state, but of the whole. On what principle could it be said, that a representative should obey those who elect him, instead of regarding the interests and rights of those who are to be affected by his acts?

This consideration, shewed the necessity of having in the legislature, one branch which is independent of local interests, and which shall consult, not local, but general welfare in their acts. When the lower house is made up of representatives, elected annually, and representing counties, it was of high importance that the senate should possess greater permanency, in order to form a check against hasty or partial action by the house.

It was all-important, therefore, that the senators, in order properly to discharge their functions, should remain long enough to become well acquainted with the interests of every part of the state, which interests are to be affected by their votes. These interests are complicated, and cannot be immediately comprehended and understood. A senator must have some experience, and time to acquire it. The population of this state is now a million and a half, and, in process of time, it may be ten millions— it may be as large as that of England—and is the term of four years too long to give a man an opportunity to become acquainted with the various interests of every part of such an empire? How is a senator to know the wishes and interests of those, in different parts of the state, who are to receive from his hands, the laws which govern them, and the high executive officers who are to carry the laws into effect? He cannot know them by intuition, and a complete knowledge of them is necessary to the competent discharge of his duties. We were to gain nothing, gentlemen might be assured, by this abridgment of the senatorial term of service. It would give the legislature of this state, a capricious and unsettled character. Confidence would be wanting in it.

Mr. READ here interrupted the gentleman from Allegheny, upon a point of order. He said the gentleman was discussing a section which had been disposed of, and finally agreed to.

The PRESIDENT stated the question to be on the section, as amended.

Mr. READ appealed from this decision, and supported the appeal at some length.

The PRESIDENT stated the case.

Mr. MEREDITH supported the decision of the President.

The PRESIDENT decided that it was now too late for an appeal to be entered.

Mr. READ appealed from that decision, and asked for the yeas and nays upon it.

Mr. STERIGERE regretted, he said, that the appeal had not been received, because it could never, in his opinion, be too late, before the question was taken.

Mr. MEREDITH expressed the hope that the appeal would not be sustained, and went into an argument to shew that the decision of the Chair was correct, and ought to stand.

Mr. BROWN, of the county of Philadelphia, said he considered that the vote on the section had been taken and seconded.

Mr. MEREDITH remarked, that the question now was, whether the appeal was taken in time?

Mr. BROWN called for the reading of the minutes.

Mr. BIDDLE said, the journal was of no authority until it was corrected.

Mr. BROWN maintained that when the gentleman from Susquehanna found that the gentleman from Allegheny was debating a question that had been settled, it was in order for him to appeal.

[A considerable discussion ensued on this question of order, occupying nearly an hour.]

The question was then taken: " Will the convention sustain the appeal?"

The yeas and nays were required by Mr. FULLER and Mr. FORWARD, and were as follow :

YEAS—Messrs. Bigelow, Brown, of Northampton. Brown, of Philadelphia, Clarke of Indiana, Crain, Crawford, Cummin, Curll, Darah, Dillinger, Donigan, Donnell, Dunlop, Earle, Fleming, Fry, Fuller, Gamble, Gearhart, Grenell, Hastings, Hayhurst, Helffenstein, Hiester, High, Houpt, Hyde, Ingersoll, Keim, Kennedy, Lyons, Magee, Mann, M'Cahen, Montgomey, Read, Ritter, Scheetz, Sellers, Shellito, Smith, of Columbia, Smyth, of Centre, Sterigere, Stickel, Taggart, Weaver, Woodward—47.

NAYS—Messrs. Agnew, Baldwin, Banks, Barclay, Barndollar, Bell, Biddle, Bonham, Brown, of Lancaster, Carey, Chambers, Chandler, of Philadelphia, Chauncey, Clarke, of Beaver, Clark, of Dauphin. Coates, Cochran, Cope, Cox, Craig, Crum, Cunningham. Darlington, Denny, Dickey, Dickerson, Forward, Harris, Hays, Hopkinson, Jenks, Kerr, Konigmacher, Krebs, Long, Maclay, Martin, M'Dowell, M'Sherry, Meredith, Merkel, Pennypacker, Pollock, Porter, of Lancaster, Porter, of Northampton, Purviance, Royer, Russell, Seager, Scott, Seltzer, Serrill, Sill, Snively, Sturdevant, Thomas, Todd, Weidman, Young, Sergeant, *President*—60.

So the question was determined in the negative.

Mr. FORWARD resumed the floor, but yielded it to Mr. DARLINGTON, on whose motion,

The convention took the usual recess.

WEDNESDAY AFTERNOON, January 3, 1838.

ORDER OF THE DAY.

The convention resumed the consideration of the report of the committee on the first article, and the question being on agreeing to the fifth section as amended,

Mr. Forward resumed his remarks on the subject:

When the question arose, he had not intended himself to take any part in its discussion, and he was not now, he said, prepared fully to consider it in all its bearing. He had hoped that some other member, better prepared than himself, would give it his attention. He thought that so grave and important a question ought not to be taken in silence. Few questions had been submitted to us, of more interest than this proposed reduction of the senatorial term, and it derived additional importance from the changes already made in other parts of the constitution, by which the senate had been clothed with new powers, in co-operation with the governor. The reduction of the senatorial term of service, as proposed by the section before us, after that body had been clothed with new powers, did appear to him, to be a very extraordinary and ill-considered measure. After what we had done, in relation to the powers of the senate, it was certainly important to give that body the advantage of experience, by allowing to it as long a term as was consistent with their due responsibility to their constituents. We now reduce the term, after adding a very strong reason for lengthening it.

I do feel, sir, said Mr. F., very anxious on this subject. I should much deplore any abridgment of the present term of four years, which I consider as being quite as short as is consistent with that experience which is necessary to a proper discharge of the important trusts of that body. I may urge these views in vain, and it may be considered that I give them undue importance, but I trust, that every candid man will well weigh these arguments before he gives his vote upon the question. A due regard for the public interests, and the reputation of this body for enlightened wisdom, will induce every one here, I trust, to consider this question maturely before he gives his final vote upon it. Why is it that we have divided the legislative branch of the government into two branches? Why should we not have a single branch, reflecting the popular will alone? Why should we have a senate, constituted differently from the house, elected for a longer term, of greater age, and fewer numbers? Why not have one branch alone, embodying the popular will? Why not have one house, annually elected, as is the legislative body. What want we more than the popular will for the time being? Would not the cardinal purpose of carrying out the will of the people, be better effected by one branch, than by the addition of the senate to it, as a check? Why constitute the senate as a barrier against the popular will? The reason is, that the popular will is often governed by sudden impulses, and violent passions, and that we wish so to contrive the legislative department as to prevent hasty action from such causes, and to represent the sober and settled sentiments, and wishes of the body of the people. The object of creating a senate, as a check upon the action of the more popular branch of the government, is to cause due knowledge and consideration of a subject, before final legislative action upon it. It is to insure a careful and deliberate course of legislative action. For the same reason, before the act of the legislature shall finally become a law, and be binding upon the whole people as such, the assent of the governor to it, is also required. Hurried legislation is, in this way, prevented. Has the experience of this state, and of this country, demonstrated that no such checks are necessary upon legislative action? Have the two independent branches of the legislature, elected for different terms, been found inconvenient, and inconsistent with the objects of free government? Does our experience shew that the senate is unnecessary? Can any reason be given, for dispensing with the senate, or for so modifying its character, as to render it more similar to the popular branch? I apprehend not. Every reason that we can advert to, goes to this point—that the term of senatorial service, ought to be lengthened, instead of abridged. That is the lesson of wisdom and experience on this subject. All experience of representative legislation, goes to shew that there should be two branches of the legislature, and that one of them should hold office for a longer term than the other; that one of them should be so much more permanent than the other, as to be independent of that sudden influence and violent excitement which not unfrequently sweeps over the public mind. What is the business of the legislature of Pennsylvania? It is vast in amount, and various in character. The acts of each session, form large volumes. The legislature of Pennsylvania, at each session, transacts three or four times as much business as congress, though they have not more private bills than in congress. The public acts of the Pennsylvania legislature, at each session, make four or five hundred pages. What are all these subjects of legislation? They embrace a vast variety of topics. Sectional and general interests are involved in them. The system of jurisprudence forms one subject of legislation. The subject of incorporations is another. Rail roads and canals form another. Who can calculate the extent of business growing out of the subject of internal improvement? Will one session. put a man in possession of all the information, requisite to intelligent action on all these intricate and varied subjects? Are all these vast and complicated interests to be comprehended at a glance? Is no knowledge, no experience, no study necessary, to enable a legislator to understand them?

What has been the chief cause of complaint, in regard to our legislature? Has it not been inconsiderate legislation? Have not the errors of the legislature grown out of want of experience? Will any one tell me that no study is necessary to a sufficient knowledge of all these vast interests? Let me ask every one here, whether one or two sessions put him in possession of adequate experience for the discharge of legislative duties? What is a new member able to do at his first session? Let me ask every one this question. I was a member for one session, and am free to say, that I found myself wholly incompetent for a proper discharge of my duties, in relation to the great variety of new topics presented for my consideration and decision.

On certain great and leading questions, it is 'true that every one is ready and prepared to act; but on general subjects, no one can say that an unexperienced member can act intelligently. No one ever entered upon a discharge of his duty as a legislator, without feeling his insufficiency for the task, on account of his necessarily limited experience upon the subjects presented to him. A service of three, four, five, or six sessions, is necessary to qualify one to attend, in a proper manner, to the business of legislation, vast and varied as it is. The subject of internal improvement, and the complicated local interests involved in many questions, render such experience and knowledge necessary to a member of the legislature. I ask for the senate, a term of four years, which the present constitution gives to that body. That term, in my opinion, is short enough. I am confident, that the term of four years is necessary, in the case of ordinary individuals,—I speak not of prodigies—to fit a man to discharge his duties as a senator.

Suppose a man to be elected as a senator from Crawford county. Is he to legislate for Crawford alone? Is he not, also, to legislate for Berks. and for Philadelphia? And must he not have some knowledge beyond the concerns of his own county or district? In order to qualify himself for his duty, in relation to the important interests which will be affected by his votes, he has every thing to begin to learn. Many and clashing local questions are to be settled by him. He must act, not in reference to his own county, but to the general interests of the state. He must look to the general interests, and then settle the local questions, in a manner not inconsistent with them, and yet do justice to every part of the commonwealth.

This is no very easy matter. It requires much labor, and much experience to become sufficiently well versed in these subjects. The legislative business of this state, in nine cases out of ten, involves local interests, but the action of the legislature affects every part of the commonwealth. Legislation is a matter of practical business in Pennsylvania, and business knowledge, and business experience, are requisite for legislation here.

Am I to be told, then, that all this knowledge and experience are to be acquired in a day? Sir, I put it to you, to say whether two or three years' experience are adequate to qualify a man to discharge these laborious and complicated duties? What I contend for, is, that the legislative body of the country, should have that experience, which will secure to it, enlightened action, and that they should be able to approach every subject with a full knowledge of all its important bearings on local and general interests. I ask for the senate of Pennsylvania, not independence of the popular will, but I ask for them that experience which can only be gained by a lengthened term of service. This is what I want; and, sir, the business of the legislature of Pennsylvania is vastly increasing in amount every year. Why is it that the number of legislative acts is every year increased, instead of diminished? It will be so for a length of time. because local interests of importance are to be attended to, and the number of questions growing out of local interests, must, necessarily, increase with our population, and with the extent of our internal improvement system.

I stated, this morning, that the importance of this question, had, in my opinion, been greatly enhanced, by the determination which the convention has made to unite the senate with the governor, in the discharge of some of his most important executive functions. For the reason that we had thus enlarged the sphere of their responsibilities, their term of service ought, in my opinion, to be lengthened, rather than abridged. If he recollected right, the strongest arguments urged in favor of dividing the appointing power between the governor and the senate, were based upon the permanent character of the senate, which would enable it to withstand executive influence, and prevent the fluctuations of executive will, reflected in appointments to office. This consideration was urged upon us by those who wished to give the senate a negative upon all the appointments of the governor. The senate of Pennsylvania are to be created into a high court of justice. They are to sit in judgment upon official and individual character. They are to decide whether individuals nominated for public office are proper and fit men to be appointed. The senate is also the tribunal to try impeachments. Are the people of each district to instruct their senators how to vote upon nominations and impeachments? Is it not, on the other hand, desirable to remove the senate, as far as possible, from the influence of all popular feeling in such matters? There may be occasions when it is necessary for the public interest that the senate should disregard the popular will. To disregard entirely, the indications of popular sentiment is impossible. But, if a senator is to act on all subjects, in accordance with the popular will at home on all these subjects; if he is to be influenced in all his acts by a regard for the will of his local constituents at the time, and not by his own judgment, then may we dispense with the senate altogether, and put the whole legislative power of the state into the hands of a single branch, instead of two branches. But, it is argued that the senate must be more immediately responsible to the people—brought nearer to them, in order that the people may have a guaranty that they will carry out their wishes; and it is said that if their term of service is continued as long as at present, they will be less mindful of the will of their constituents than if the term should be reduced to two or three years. He could see no reason for such an apprehension. A just and proper degree of responsibility is already amply secured under the present constitution ; and the curtailment of the term will only tend to impair the efficiency of the body, by depriving it of its most valuable members at the time when their experience has been gained by three years' service. Senators will be desirous of a re-election, and ambitious of popular favor and distinction, and there are ties which secure their proper responsibility to the people, more than the abridgment of their term of service.

But a word as to this matter of obeying the will of constituents. He desired gentlemen to look into the acts of assembly, and see what they consist of. What will they find there? nothing but acts concerning local interests. A member from one county has to legislate for fifty-three other counties. Must he, on all these questions, consult the wishes of his own constituents? What a chaos of confusion would such a doctrine, if carried into practice, bring us into! In at least nineteen cases out of twenty, each member of the legislature must, after all, act for himself, according to the lights of his own experience and judgment, without any instruction from his immediate constituents. Obedience to the will of his constituents on these subjects is absurd to speak of. His constitu.

ents know nothing of the subjects, and the senator must act from his own knowledge, and according to his own judgment. His constituents cannot instruct him in regard to the local interests of the several counties. He cannot represent the popular will in reference to those interests . and, in acting for himself, his course ought to be such as to promote the interests of the commonwealth. Hence, a due degree of experience is absolutely necessary to enable him to discharge his duties. Were he to obey any local instructions, in such matters, he would be made the instrument of doing much wrong, and from ignorance and inexperience he may also do the same wrong.

Another consideration in regard to the right of popular instruction is, that a representative in Pennsylvania represents the whole state, and, by his acts, bind the whole body of the people of the commonwealth. Every man is bound by the acts of the legislature, because, as a member of the community, he tacitly assents to the constitution and laws of the state. I am bound by every act of the legislature, because, on the theory of government, I tacitly assent to be bound by the laws which may be made by the majority of the representatives of the people. Each member of the legislature, therefore, binds the whole people when he votes for a bill which becomes a law. A man from Allegheny county binds the people of Centre county as much as he binds his own constituents, by every law which he passes with his vote. Each representative, therefore, represents and binds the whole people, so far as making laws for the whole may be concerned. It follows, then, that a representative cannot be bound to do injustice and wrong to the whole state, for the sake of pleasing or accommodating the people of his own precinct, by whose votes he was elected. Am I, as a representative from Allegheny, bound to do injustice to the whole people of the commonwealth, because it may suit the caprice or the temporary interests of the people of Allegheny? Does the right of instruction, as thus considered, rest upon any proper principle? Can the wishes of a small number of people form a good reason for doing injustice to the whole. The senator or representative who acts on such a principle as this, is guilty of inexcusable violation of his trust; for, on the theory of our government, he must consult the interests of all those whose interests are to be affected by his vote.

On some great leading questions of policy, I admit that a representative may be excusable for governing his course according to the sentiments of his immediate constituents, but no man is bound to consult the wishes of his constituents in regard to general questions affecting local interests. Before looking to any instructions from his constituents, the representative is bound to study the interests which will be affected by his vote, and he is inexcusable for doing injustice in local legislation.

Is it desirable that there should be, in the legislature, that amount of knowledge and independence of mind that are requisite to carry out the principles of government? Must there be a concurrence of popular will in every act of the assembly? Can no senator act on any subject except in conformity with the will of his own immediate constituents? How then can the interests of the commonwealth be properly guarded and promoted? How can the independence of a senator be secured for a single year? What has been the experience of Pennsylvania in regard to this subject? Has it not been that most of the legislation has been inconsiderate, from want of experience and proper independence? It is also true that some good acts have passed, which could not have passed, had the senate been elected for three years instead of four years. It is very fashionable to talk of obedience to the popular will. But let me bring gentlemen to the point and ask them why, if they wish the popular will to be obeyed in all cases and at all times, they do not abolish the senate and construct a legislature with a single popular branch, annually or semi-annually elected? This would bring the law-making power nearer to the people, and enable them to carry out their will promptly and thoroughly. The refusal of gentlemen to give up the checks on legislation is a surrender of their argument. Free governments are over-turned by stormy, changing, and popular legislation. If popular feeling be admitted too far into legislation, it will destroy free government, and open the way for despotic rule. Are our checks, which the framers of the present constitution adopted against the influence of popular feeling in legislation, too great? I doubt whether they can be considered by any one as too great. The experience of the state does not shew that they have been too great. I certainly desire that the popular will may be known, and that it may be carried out, but that it may be checked in its excesses.

I might, Mr. President, dwell much longer on this subject, and go into it much more fully, but not wishing to trouble the convention further, at this time, I conclude by expressing an earnest hope that the attention of members will be given to the subject, and that it may be fully considered before it shall be finally decided upon.

Mr. PORTER, of Northampton, said he was one of those who were of opinion that the amendment proposed by the committee of the whole, ought to be adopted. Upon the subject of the proper length of the sena-torial term of service he had reflected, before he came into this body, and the result of all his reflections had been to confirm him in the idea that the present term of service was too long. Here were two great objects in view in the construction of a legislature with two branches. The popu-lar branch was intended to represent the immediate wishes of the people, and the senate was constituted for the purpose of preventing vascillating, hasty and inconsiderate legislation, and for giving effect to the *deliberate* opinions and wishes of the people. It was to be taken for granted that the object of both bodies was the same, though they were differently constituted. This object, under our form of government, was to express and carry out the deliberate will of the people. Representa-tives were not bound by every ebullition of popular feeling, arising from impulse and sudden excitement—not from reason; but the people had a right to govern by their *deliberate will.* The legislature was so consti-tuted as to exclude all sudden and capricious influence and to express the sober and deliberate sense of the community. The representatives in one branch bring the voice of the people into immediate action, while the senate checks any hasty and improper procedure. To prevent govern-ment from becoming oppressive to the people it had been found necessary that those entrusted with power should be required frequently to account to the people for its exercise. Frequent elections were the only means.

of preserving our institutions from the grasp of ambition and corruption. Though power does not always and necessarily corrupt, yet it has a tendency to corruption. It was necessary that the agents of the people should frequently be required to lay down the power which has been delegated to them to be regranted to them, if found worthy, or conferred on others more deserving. That principle must be kept in view in all representation under our government.

In regard to the senate, the question is, whether they ought to be elected to serve three years or four years? His mind had been brought to the conclusion that three years is the proper term. He loved symmetry and uniformity in the construction of government. The senate ought to be in keeping with the character of our other institutions, and if on a term of service so long as four years, while that of all executive officers was less, he could see no reason nor propriety.

In relation to the constitution of the United States, he thought that two years for the representatives, and six for the senators was very proper, when he took into consideration the immense territory of the Union. We had heretofore fixed the term of our representatives at one year, and that of the senators at four years. If we preserved the same proportion which the constitution of the United States has established, our senatorial term would be three years instead of four. The term of four years for senatorial service was, he believed, as long as that which any one of the states had adopted, and perhaps longer. He could see no reason why the senators should hold office longer than the governor and other executive officers of the commonwealth.

The governor is elected for three years, and makes his appointments to hold during his pleasure. That has been the rule; yet as the duration of his office was but three years, that may be said to be the extent and duration of office in the commonwealth, except those of a judicial character—except the senatorial.

Now, I will admit that the senate is to act as a balance wheel in the government; but you must not carry the principle too far, that is, to remove the senate so far from popular responsibility, that they may obstruct the legitimate operation, of the government, or you will spoil the symmetry of the whole, and your legislature will fail to answer the object of expressing the will of the people. If the senate become stubborn and restive, you destroy the harmony of the whole system. It is said that experience in legislation is of great value. So it is very often. I will admit that experience in legislation is necessary. But when I grant this, I say you must never lose sight of the rule, that at a periodical term they must return their power to the people. And, in looking after one, take care that you do not lose sight of the other. In avoiding Sylla beware of Charybdes.

It is said that there is a vast increase in the legislation of your commonwealth. This is granted. But this affords no reason why your senators should have a longer term than the governor, nor more than three times as long as the representatives. Let us be warned by more than one instance in the history of our own country, that senators may sometimes set the people at defiance. If an increase in legislation requires that there should be a longer term for the senate, why not for the popular branch?

It is said, however, that there should be more permanence given to the senate, because there has been a controlling power conferred on it, in another part of the constitution, over the executive, in making appointments. I am not one of those who are for making a distinction between the senators and governor, as to the durat on of their term of service. It is said, you have taken away from the governor a great deal of his patronage. This may be, or it may not. What have you left to him? The appointment of the judicial officers, and the inspectors of the city and county of Philadelphia.

I am not one of those who think that this body is not disposed to burden the senate with too much power. I think they should have nothing to do except with legitimate legislation. But, can any good reason be assigned, why the senate, which acts on nominations, should have a longer duration than the power which makes the appointment—the governor? He is elected for three years.

Again: with regard to the power of impeachment. I do not know that a man would be any more or less qualified to discharge the duty of a judge of a high court of impeachment, because elected for three years only instead of four. The qualification must rest with the man, and not depend at all on the period for which he is elected. And, therefore, I cannot see any force in the objections, urged with such great zeal, by the gentleman from Allegheny, (Mr. Forward) against reducing the senatorial term from four to three years. I see as clearly, and with as much force, as the gentleman from Allegheny, the necessity of having two branches. I think that the permanent and steady character which should always characterize legislation, will be sufficiently preserved by a senate, the members of which, shall be elected for three years. One-third going out annually, so that at least two years will have gone by before the majority of those who enact a law, will be succeeded by new senators. In this I also see the government of the commonwealth harmonious in all its parts, as are the departments of the general government. I desire, also, to carry out the wishes of the people—the wishes of the people of Northampton county, who sent me here, who I know desire the proposed reduction in the senatorial term.

Mr. Woodward, of Luzerne, said, he rose to call the attention of the convention to the question before it. The fifth section had been reported by the committee of the whole, with an amendment changing the senatorial term, from four to three years. This morning, the report was again taken up, and it was decided, by a clear majority, on a call of yeas and nays, that the convention would agree to the same.

The question now pending, was on agreeing to the section as amended; that was, whether the fifth section, as amended, should be retained in the constitution of Pennsylvania, or expunged, stricken out, dispensed with? That was the question to be decided. It was not, whether the senatorial period should be four or three years. That was settled by a vote this morning; and, therefore, any argument from the gentleman from Allegheny, or any other delegate, on that point, was entirely behind the record. He would repeat, the question was settled, and was no longer open. The question before the convention now, was, whether the fifth section should be retained in the constitution, or not? That section provides, that

PENNSYLVANIA CONVENTION, 1837.

" 'The legislative power of this commonwealth shall be vested in a general assembly, which shall consist of a senate and house of representatives.' "

Now, he was in favor of it, because he believed it to be the wisest distribution of the power of the commonwealth that could possibly be devised.

The great and radical defect of the constitution of 1776, consisted in the representatives of the people being assembled in one body instead of two. He thought that the division of representatives, into two branches, instead of meeting as one branch only, was a wise and salutary improvement on the constitution of 1776, and indispensable to the liberties of the people.

The whole argument against the section, was only an argument against the distribution of legislative power. And, to part with the section, was to reject the principle of distribution of power between the house of representatives and the senate. Was not this a sufficient reason why the convention should adopt the section? Yet, they were asked to reject it. He would inquire of delegates if they were prepared to give up this salutary distribution of power between the two departments?

But, if the question was to be discussed as to the senatorial term of service, after it had been decided, then let us ask why four years are better than three, and what it is that renders three years an unsafe term, and four a safe one?

The delegate from Allegheny had asked what was the reason gentlemen preferred three years? Now, he, Mr. W., would ask that gentleman, why *he* was in favor of four years; and why four years were essentially better than three? And, why was it that the people of Pennsylvania, through their representatives in convention, could not change the senatorial term of service, from four years to three, without changing the foundations of our republic? Was it a question of such vast magnitude? Was it a question involving such serious consequences? He did not think so.

It was said that four years were necessary to qualify a man for the duties of his station—that he must have experience—that he was not prepared to legislate in regard to the great interests of Pennsylvania, until he shall have had experience. But, he would ask, would not three years give him experience? What was to be said in regard to a four years' term?

If the argument was so strong in favor of four years, as it was assumed to be ; if the reason given was unanswerable why the term should not be changed from four years to three, then the argument was equally unanswerable that the term ought to be increased beyond four years ; for a man would have more experience in eight years, than four, and still more in twenty.

This train of reasoning amounted, virtually, to an argument in favor of a life tenure, and against all limitations. And, it would be very natural, after having obtained that, to take one step further, and agree that the senators shall not only be elected for life, but that the office shall hereafter be hereditary—that the eldest son shall fill it after his father, although he may happen to be a fool. Now, this argument resulted in what he had stated, when carried out.

Was this convention, he asked, prepared to go for such a principle? Was it consistent with the power that was given to the house of representatives and the senate? No; he trusted not. That power was given to those bodies as a trust, to be exercised with care and discretion. And the more frequently that power returned to the people, having a due regard to the permanency of our institutions, the more safe those institutions would be.

We set out with the principle, said Mr. W., that the people are capable of self-government; but the only mode in which they can govern themselves, is to leave them to choose their own rulers. Let them choose those who shall make their laws and administer them. But, you violate the principle of self government, unless you also allow to the people opportunities, at reasonable periods, to change as well as choose their rulers. And, the argument against the three years' term, goes to this, and would be just as satisfactory in favor of eight, ten, or twenty years, as it is in favor of four.

I believe three years to be too long a term. I voted for two years prior to the adoption of that amendment. At the end of two years we would oblige a senator to go home and account to his constituents for what he had done. And, if he had served them faithfully, they might, perhaps, re-elect him.

I think two years just long enough, and because he preferred the shortest period—he preferred three years to four. I would not vote to make the senatorial term the same as the representative; because I am of opinion, that it should be somewhat longer.

He, Mr. W., contended, that a provision which limited the term of senators to two years only, was both wise and salutary, as it gave an opportunity to the people to change their legislators when they thought proper. He admitted that in both branches of the legislature, the members ought to be men distinguished for intelligence, integrity and caution, in order to represent the great interests of the commonwealth of Pennsylvania.

But, he would submit to the gentleman from Allegheny, and to every gentleman who had had as much experience in legislation, whether the old time-worn, hackneyed and broken down politician, was the most honest and faithful legislator? Does experience in the arts, too often the *tricks* of legislation, eminently qualify a man for a faithful performance of his duties as a representative of the plain republicans of Pennsylvania? He greatly doubted it.

He ventured to say, that Pennsylvania would be quite as well represented—her interests as faithfully watched over, and as wisely promoted by men drawn "fresh from the ranks of the people." During the first winter, before a man became contaminated, he would do his duty. The longer he remained at Harrisburg the more had he to learn, and he was not quite sure that all he learns there was favorable to an honest discharge of duty.

He, Mr. W., was sure the people would be as faithfully represented by the farmers, mechanics, lawyers and merchants, newly elected, as by those longer in service, and whatever would be lost on the score of experience would be more than compensated by the devotion to business, which always characterizes the conduct of fresh agents.

Suppose the question to be submitted to the people of this commonwealth, would they not rather trust their interests to men annually responsible to them, than to those who are responsible only once in four years. He had no doubt of it, and he could not doubt, therefore, that a senatorial term of three years would be more acceptable to them than any longer term.

When it was proposed to make judges in some way responsible to the popular will, we were told with vehemence, that it would be dangerous and perhaps ruinous, to subject *them*, in any degree, to such an influence.

But, is there any thing in the senatorial office, so peculiar and sacred, that the people may not touch it. What is the senator but a mere servant of his constituents? And, if a servant, let him be held to a strict and frequent responsibility, and let him be discharged, when, for any reason, he is no longer fit for service.

It had been said, that the senate might become a court of impeachment. It is true it may, but what does this prove against the three years tenure? If an upright and fearless discharge of his duties, in this capacity as well as every other, be the thing desired by a senator, experience affords as much reason to expect it from senators recently elected, as from those who have been long in service—with prejudices deeply fixed, and political alliances extensively formed.

But, if gentlemen are afraid to trust the impeaching power to the senate, let them modify it so as to limit the sentence to mere removal from office. My opinion is, that the impeaching power should extend no farther, however the senate may be constituted, and with such a limitation, this power, now idle and inoperative in your constitution, might become useful and efficacious.

He asked again, whether there were any peculiar duties pertaining to the senatorial office, which made it imprudent to reduce the tenure to three years? He had heard of none, nor as yet, had any satisfactory reason been shown him for preferring four to three.

Mr. President, the gentleman from Allegheny, (Mr. Forward) says that hasty and injudicious legislation is checked by our permanent senates. Is this so, sir? It is the first time that I ever heard of it. On the contrary, I believe that there has been no check in the senate or elsewhere, on injudicious legislation. Every year's experience shows us, that our legislature is far too hasty and inconsiderate, and that local feelings have too much influence upon it. The evil of partial legislation has become a crying one in this state.

The gentleman's senatorial check was all this time in full operation, and what influence had it exerted? None at all. It had been found to be neither a more independent, a more considerate, or more wise and prudent body than the lower house. The senate must be responsible for its full share of all the hasty and improper acts, that have passed our legislature.

It was only last year that the governor of this commonwealth was constrained to veto an important internal improvement bill, on the ground that it squandered the people's money on local objects. Does the senate interpose a solitary check to partial and inconsiderate legislation? No. As to the matter of yielding to the caprices of the people, the senate had not shown itself any more independent than the other branch of the legislature.

I hardly know what is meant by the caprice of the people operating on the legislation of the state. We were told that we must beware of the caprices of the people upon the senate, though they act upon only one-third of that body at a time. Gentlemen may call it caprice, if they will; but the popular will or popular caprice, if so they choose to call it, will prevail, and ought to prevail as long as the people are free. The people have a right to self-government, and they have the right to change their opinions as often as they please on any subject in relation to their own affairs.

It may be true that the gale of popular passion shall blow this year one way, and the next year the other, but this is no reason why representatives should not obey the will of their constituents. They are *representatives* of the popular will, and if they are honest and faithful they will give it effect. I hold that the people have a right to change their opinions, their measures, and their agents. That is a right which we are bound to respect; and we must recognize it, and put its spirit into the provisions of the constitution.

The committee of the whole agreed to the proposed reduction of the senatorial term, from four years to three years, without much opposition. The debates in this body, show that no one thought it necessary to stand up and warn us of the danger of reducing the term to three years. It was agreed to without calling the yeas and nays. This day the amendment was again agreed to, and now, at this late stage of the question, it for the first time meets with opposition. An attempt is now made to deprive the people of this very small concession, made to popular power by reducing the term of the senators to three years, a term quite as long as that of any other officer of the government, except the judicial officers, and three times as long as that of the representatives of the other house. Until he should hear some further reason assigned for rejecting the amendment of the committee of the whole, he should continue to give it his support, as he had done heretofore.

Mr. MEREDITH said he was opposed to the reduction of the term proposed and preferred the original section of the constitution as it stood; but, he would not hazard the loss of the whole of the original section of the constitution, by rejecting this section. There had been repeated decisions in this body that the rejection of an amendment proposed by a committee would restore the original section of the constitution; but, he believed it was now held otherwise in regard to the amendments made by the committee of the whole. Before the vote was taken on this question he wished to ask the Chair what would be the effect of rejecting the section as amended by the committee of the whole,—whether it would be to restore the old constitution, leaving four years as the senatorial term, or whether it would defeat the whole section altogether? He wished himself to come back to the constitution of 1790. Before the vote was taken he should ask the Chair whether this would be the effect of rejecting the amendment. He was at a loss to know why three years had been fixed upon as the proper term of senatorial service. The convention had more than once refused to adopt the term of two years. It was plain that gentlemen were not voting on the principle that the shortest term was the best. They had refused to go below three years, and yet had divided against four years. Now, he wanted to know why four years was too long a term, and two years too short a term? Why was the term of three years the precise term which was best? It had been argued that it was necessary to bring the senate nearer to the people. But, if there was any thing in short terms that would make them more obedient to the wishes of the people, why not reduce the term to two years or to one year? He knew that the doctrine was, that a representative should never speak or act, except according to the wishes of his constituents, and that no man should be trusted to discharge his duty to his constituents, unless he was tied and bound and subjected to punishment for disobedience to their will. He was aware that this doctrine was gaining ground, and he thought it a very mischievous one. The principle endeavored to be established was, that there is no security for the exercise of power conferred upon a representative, but the power of the people to interpose their instructions. All sense of duty to the country, and all sense of individual character, were to be thrown aside and to go for naught. Fear is held up as the only principle upon which a representative can act faithfully in the discharge of his public duties. No principle of public duty is allowed to have existence or operation at all. But, if these doctrines were correct, then the term of two years was too long, and one year or six months, ought to be substituted. The effect of the argument against four years, and in favor of short terms, was to show that free governments could not exist, there not being patriotism and public virtue enough among the representatives of the people for the security of their fidelity. When a sense of public duty ceased to control the acts of men in power, no other principle of action could be found that would make a proper and safe substitute for it. If we find that all confidence is betrayed upon the first opportunity that may be offered, and that every one takes power with the purpose of betraying the trust reposed in him as soon as he can get an opportunity, then it is not worth our while to choose representatives at all.

It appeared from the votes which had been taken, and from the views which had been expressed in the convention that a majority of this body was in favor of allowing a longer term for the senators than for the representatives. If they believed it proper and necessary that the senatorial term of service should be longer than that of the other body, then the only question was what should be the proportion between the two terms? He submitted that all the considerations which would render proper the term of three years for senatorial terms would be equally good in relation to term of four years. The latter term had the advantage of having been tried, with success, for forty years, and the people were accustomed to it, and had never complained of it. What is the reason for the general belief in this body, that the senators should be elected for a longer term than the representatives? Is it not that the senators, in the opinion of all, ought to have greater experience, more legislative wisdom, and more knowledge of local interests and of general interests, and that upon them also devolves duties of grave importance as a tribunal for trying impeachments, in regard to which the popular feeling ought to have no influence? There are other weighty considerations which have impressed the people of this state with the propriety of rendering the senate a more permanent body than the lower house. They intended the senate to operate, as a check upon the violation of private property and the rights of minorities, in times of high party excitement. They looked upon it as a barrier against the encroachments of popular demagogues, and the only means by which, in times of high political excitement, they could prevent the whole state from being prostrated at the foot of one party.

But, sir, (said Mr. Mereidith,) we are challenged to show why the exact term of four years was adopted by the framers of the present constitution. There is no doubt that they had weighty reasons for it. The house of representatives was to be chosen for one year, and the governor for three: then why, it is asked, should the senate be elected for four years? The men of that day, who formed the constitution, had not opened their eyes to the ideal and sophistical doctrine, now so prevalent, that a representative would only be secured in his fidelity by being subjected to the fear of immediate removal, unless he obeyed the wishes of the people upon all questions in relation to his trust; nor, did they intend that the senate, which was instituted as a check upon injudicious and partial legislation, and as a high court for the trial of impeachments, should be so immediately responsible to the people for all their acts. They were alive to the interests of the commonwealth and looked to its future political condition, in every principle which they adopted. They saw that the state was then divided into parties, and that parties, in relation to which the people would take sides, must always exist, and that the minorities, in times of excitement, might be trampled upon. They instituted the senate, therefore, with the longer term of four years, as a check upon party tyranny. These, sir, are the reasons why the wise framers of the constitution of 1790, provided that the senatorial term of service should be four years.

But, gentlemen have, throughout this argument, assumed that the senate was chosen, as a body, for four years, in like manner as the executive is chosen for three years. Their argument has been founded upon this view; but, it is entirely erroneous and incorrect. The senate is not chosen for four years as a body, though the term of service of each senator is four years. They are so divided into classes, that only one-fourth of them are four years removed from the people. One-fourth of them go out of office every year, and one-half every two years, and three-fourths in three years. One-fourth are elected every year; and, thus the body is always necessarily deeply imbued with the popular feeling of the day, whatever it may be. It would be impossible, therefore, for the senate long to withstand the current of public sentiment; while, at the same time, they might check legislation founded upon temporary and casual excitement.

The senate does not sit there as a body elected for four years. Three-fourths of them sit there for three years, and one-half of them only for

two years.   How then could it be said that the senate was a body elected
for four years, when one-fourth of the senators were made responsible to
the people every year ?   Was it not a fact that three-fourths of the senators
held their offices for but three years, and one-half for less than two years
from any given time ?   Then, why, was it that all this excitement and dis-
turbance was got up in relation to one-fourth of the senate ?   This was the
theory of this matter.   Then, as to its political effects.   He might appeal
to many gentlemen around him, as to political experience, in relation to
that body.   What has been the state of the senate with regard to political
parties, for the last twenty-five years, and he need not say, that we
have had warm political excitements in that time ?   He might state here,
he believed without fear of contradiction, that during the greater portion
of that time, the senate was made up of about twenty members, belonging to one political party, and eight to another.   Well, that being the
case, let what political excitement would come upon the people, and the
senate would remain firm and unchanged.   If the people were carried
away, in the frenzy of their zeal, in relation to any matter, the senate
remain firm and would act as a check upon them ; because even if th
whole of the senators elected in one year, were elected by that party,
that would only make sixteen, while there would be seventeen of the
other party.   This, he presumed, was taken into view by the framers of
the constitution, so that the government might be kept steady and not be
carried away by popular excitements.   They also took care on the other
hand, by regular rotation of the senators, that the senate should not be a
body elected for four years, which would have been objectionable to the
people, if it had been the case.   In fact, this matter seemed to be so
handsomely checked, and balanced, that he took it, there was very great
danger, in disturbing it in any way whatever.

These sages, in their wisdom, took care not to vary from republican
principles ; while, at the same time, they guarded against popular excitements changing the whole of the departments of government in one year,
your governor, your house of representatives and your senate.   This
was the manner in which the framers of the constitution of 1790 reasoned,
and he would ask gentlemen, whether this kind of reasoning did not
apply with all its force at the present day ?   In fact, it seemed to him,
that it ought, if any thing. to apply with greater force.   He would now
call the attention of the convention to the state of the case, if this amendment, electing senators for three years, prevailed.   If you elect senators
for three years, one-third will be elected annually.   He would then
take the majority, as he had stated it before, say there were twenty-five of
the dominant party, and eight of the other party.   Then, in case of a
popular excitement, at a governor's election, which would carry the whole
of the one-third to be elected that year, it would reduce the former dominant party to seventeen, while the other party would have nineteen in
your senate.   Thus would you have the whole government of the state
changed in a single year.   You would have a new government ; a new
house of representatives, and a new senate.   Thus, then, you would
have as complete a revolution in your government, as though your senators were elected for the same term with your representatives.   The
whole government might be changed by these means in a single year, and
this was the very thing which the framers of the constitution of 1790,

were anxious to guard against. It was admitted on all hands, that some longer term was required for senators than for representatives, for the purpose of having something like stability in the government, but he thought he had shown clearly that three years was no guard in this way, as the senate might be carried away by a popular excitement in a single year, just as well as though they were elected for the same time with the representatives. We know that the people will come back to correct principles, if they are carried away for a season, and this four years senate is the very institution which is to hold the goverment steady during popular excitements, and prevent the torch from being thrown into the temple of liberty, in the madness of excited party feeling. An election, however, of one-third of the senators annually, with a term of three years to serve, will in nine cases out of ten, fail to produce the result which was guarded against by the framers of the constitution of 1790. In nine cases out of ten, the senate will be carried away in a single year, and for all political purposes, you might as well have them elected for a single year. He would not stop to inquire any thing about the senators of the United States, and congress, because their acts do not come home so directly to the bosoms of the people, as those of our own senators. They act upon matters of national concern; and he would not stop to inquire why they should be more or less responsible to the people than those who sit under their immediate eye; but, he would say that there was this difference between the house of representatives of the United States and our senate that has not been referred to. It was that the members of the house of representatives of the United States were all elected for the same term : they all holding for two years, whereas in the senate of Pennsylvania, you have from any given time, one-fourth of its members holding for one year, one-fourth for two years, one-fourth for three years, and but one-fourth of them holding their offices, for four years. Then the whole of this contest is in relation to one-fourth of the senate being removed four years from the people. Now, he begged gentlemen who had voted on this question, as he apprehended there was no one here who was not anxious that the best interests of the people should be consulted, to weigh this matter well, and ask themselves whether they were willing that a time should come, when all our rights, liberties and interests might be prostrated at a single blow, by a successful party, at a single election ? He begged those who were the friends of popular government, as all were here, to reflect and consider that there might be times when the people would be led astray by the violence of party, and to preserve those safeguards for them which were provided by the framers of the constitution of 1790. He begged those who were in favor of giving the people time to consider and reflect after a warm party contest, to reflect that by adhering to this amendment they destroy the whole of that doctrine; because they put it in the power of the people at a single election to change the senate as well as the house of representatives.

Let the question go to the real people who are seldom seen or heard from, but at the ballot box, and his word for it, they would pronounce this a dangerous doctrine, and would ask that they might be protected from sudden mutations of party, and feverish excitement, which might carry away the governmnnt, and destroy the rights, privileges and interests of the people at a single blow, and lay the axe at the root of the tree of liberty.

Mr. CRUM moved the previous question, which was seconded by eighteen members, and the main question was ordered to be put.

Mr. AGNEW called for the yeas and nays on the main question—which was on agreeing to the section as amended in committee of the whole—which were ordered, and were, yeas 59; nays 54; as follow:

YEAS—Messrs. Banks, Barclay, Bell, Bigelow, Bonham, Brown, of Northampton, Brown, of Philadelphia, Clarke, of Indiana, Cleavinger, Crain, Crawford, Cummin, Curll, Darrah, Dillinger, Donagan, Donnell, Doran, Earle, Fry, Fuller, Gearhart, Gilmore, Grenell, Hastings, Hayhurst, Helffenstein, High, Houpt, Hyde, Ingersoll, Keim, Kennedy, Krebs, Lyons, Magee, Mann, Martin, M'Cahen, Miller, Montgomery, Porter, of Northampton, Purviance, Read, Riter, Ritter, Sheetz, Sellers, Seltzer, Shellito, Smith, of Columbia, Smyth, of Centre, Sterigere, Stickel, Sturdevant, Taggart, Weaver, White, Woodward—59.

NAYS—Messrs. Agnew, Baldwin, Barndollar, Biddle, Brown, of Lancaster, Carey, Chambers, Chandler, of Philadelphia, Chauncey, Clark, of Dauphin, Cline, Coates, Cochran, Cope, Cox, Craig, Crum, Cunningham, Darlington, Denny, Dickey, Dickerson, Dunlop, Farrelly, Forward, Harris, Hays, Henderson, of Allegheny, Heister, Hopkinson, Jenks, Kerr, Konigmacher, Long, Maclay, M'Cull, M'Sherry, Meredith, Merkel, Pennypacker, Pollock, Porter, of Lancaster, Royer, Russell, Saeger, Scott, Serrill, Sill, Snively, Thomas, Todd, Weidman, Young, Sergeant, *President*—54.

So the section as amended was adopted.

The convention then adjourned.

THURSDAY, JANUARY 4, 1838.

Mr. DARLINGTON, of Chester, presented a memorial from citizens of Chester county, praying that no change may be made in the constitution, having a tendency to create distinctions in the rights and privileges of citizenship based upon completion.

Which was laid on the table.

Mr. PORTER, of Northampton, presented the memorial of twenty three citizens of Berks county, constituting the grand jury of the said county at the present court of quarter sessions, praying that the convention do adjourn forthwith, *sine die.*

Mr. MEREDITH, of Philadelphia, (the petitions having been read) expressed his hope that this petition would not be received.

Mr. KEIM, of Berks, hoped the petition would be received, and that it would be printed. He had been told long ago of a great revolution of sentiment which had taken place in his county—of an avalanche which was to descend, in all its destructive power, upon those for whom it was intended. After all, it turns out to be only a rivulet—the inundation of a mountain stream. He was not about to receive instructions from any source, but the democracy of the county, let it express itself as it might, whether it was a stage coach or steam boat opinions.

Mr. WOODWARD, of Luzerne, hoped that the gentleman from North. ampton would withdraw this memorial, as the President of the convention, and other gentlemen had determined to do in the case of a scandalous petition which had been sent to the convention.

Mr. MEREDITH also coincided in this wish that the memorial might be withheld.

Mr. PORTER replied, that he had no personal acquaintance with any of the gentlemen whose names were appended to the memorial. He was assured that they were respectable; and, finding nothing disrespectful in the language of the document, he had done, as in consultation was thought best. He had supposed, that he was in duty bound to present the memo. rial, and he had only performed his duty. Had there been any thing disrespectful in its language, he would have hesitated. He could say nothing, as he knew nothing of the gentlemen whose names were affixed. They might constitute a packed jury or any thing else, for aught he could tell to the contrary.

Mr. COX, of Somerset, said that although he was generally opposed to the printing of memorials, he was disposed to vote for this motion. There was nothing disrespectful, and nothing offensive to truth in this memorial. The gentleman who presented it, thought that the petitioners told the truth, no doubt. The bank question had been sprung on us, with which, in fact, we had nothing to do. Because these gentlemen had, as freemen of Pennsylvania, told the truth, surely the gentleman from Berks, would not charge gentlemen who were his constituents, with being a packed jury.

Mr. KEIM replied, that he had not charged the gentlemen who signed the memorial with being a packed jury. He would say, in reply to the gentleman from Somerset, that the political friends of that gentleman held the best offices in the county.

Mr COX, was delighted to hear that the sheriff and commissioners of the county were on his (Mr. C's) side, while the majority of the county was on the other side.

Mr. KEIM dissented from the statement of the gentleman from So. merset.

Mr. COX. Then the sheriff and commissioners were on the other side, and who was it, in that case, who packed the jury? He hoped there were more of the constituents of the gentleman from Berks, who were of the same stamp as the signers of the memorial.

Mr. COCHRAN, of Lancaster, called for the previous question, and the call was sustained by the number required by the rule to second the call.

Mr. PORTER rose to express his willingness to withdraw the memorial, but the universal cry from all sides of the convention was in the nega- tive.

The question being,

Shall the main question be now put?

The yeas and nays were required by Mr. DICKEY and Mr. MANN, and are as follow, viz :

YEAS—Messrs. Baldwin, Banks, Barclay, Bigelow, Bonham, Brown, of Lancaster, Brown, of Northampton, Brown, of Philadelphia, Chambers, Clarke, of Beaver, Clark, of Dauphin, Clarke, of Indiana, Cleavinger, Cline, Cochran, Cope, Crain, Crawford, Crum, Cummin, Cunningham, Curll, Darlington, Darrah, Denny, Dickerson, Dillinger, Donagan, Donnell, Farrelly, Forward, Foulkrod, Fry, Fuller, Gamble, Gearhart, Gilmore, Grenell, Harris, Hastings, Hayhurst, High, Hyde, Keim, Kennedy, Kerr, Konigmacher, Krebs, Long, Maclay, Magee, Mann, M'Call, M'Sherry, Merkel, Miller, Montgomery, Pennypacker, Porter, of Lancaster, Porter, of Northampton, Read, Riter, Ritter, Russell, Saeger, Scheetz,, Seltzer, Serrill, Shellito, Smith, of Columbia, Smyth, of Centre, Sterigere, Stickel, Sturdevant, Taggart, Weaver, Woodward—77.

NAYS—Messrs. Agnew, Barndollar, Bell, Biddle, Chandler, of Philadelphia, Chauncey, Coates, Cox, Craig, Dickey, Earle, Fleming, Hays, Henderson, of Allegheny, Hiester, Hopkinson, Houpt, Ingersoll, Jenks, Martin, M'Dowell, Meredith, Pollock, Purviance, Royer, Scott, Sill, Snively, Todd, Young, Sergeant, President—31.

So the question was determined in the affirmative.

And on the question.

Will the convention agree to the motion, viz :   That the said memorial be printed?

The yeas and nays were required by Mr. KEIM and Mr. MACLAY, and are as follow, viz :

YEAS—Messrs. Biddle, Chauncey. Clarke, of Beaver, Clark, of Dauphin, Coates, Cope, Cox, Crum, Darrah, Denny, Dickey, Dickerson, Dillinger, Donagan, Foulkrod, Harris, Hastings, Hays, Heister, Jenks, Keim, Kerr, Konigmacher, Long, Maclay, McCall, McSherry, Pennypacker, Ritter, Royer, Saeger, Scott, Seltzer, Weaver, Young, Sergeant, President—36.

NAYS—Messrs. Agnew, Baldwin, Banks, Barclay, Barndollar, Bell, Bigelow, Bonham, Brown, of Nothampton, Chambers, Chandler, of Philadelphia, Clarke, of Indiana, Cleavinger, Cline, Cochran, Craig, Crain, Crawford, Cummin, Cunningham, Curll. Darlington, Donnell, Farrelly, Fleming, Forward, Fry, Fuller, Gamble, Gearhart, Gilmore, Grenell, Hayhurst, Helffenstein, Henderson, of Allegheny, High, Hopkinson, Houpt, Hyde, Ingersoll, Kennedy, Krebs, Magee, Mann, Martin, Mc-Dowell, Meredith, Merkel, Miller, Montgomery, Pollock, Porter, of Northampton, Purviance, Read, Riter, Russell, Scheetz, Serrill, Sill, Smith, of Columbia, Smyth, of Centre, Snively, Sterigere, Stickel, Sturdevant, Taggart, Todd, Woodward—68.

So the question was determined in the negative.

Mr. READ moved that the petition be not received.

The CHAIR was of opinion, the petition having been received and a vote taken upon it, that the motion was not now in order.

Mr. PURVIANCE then moved that the petition be rejected.

Mr. HIESTER, thought it was too late to receive this motion, after the petition had been received, debated, and a vote taken upon it. Certainly, to his mind, it appeared that a motion to reject the petition was not now in order.

The CHAIR decided, however, that the motion to reject, was in time, because the opportunity was not before given for the body to express an opinion upon this matter.

Mr. MARTIN said, as this petition had claimed the consideration of the convention for some time, he thought it was time now to get rid of it. He believed the right of petition to be a sacred right, when properly exercised, but when there was a disposition to turn the right of petition into ridicule by any set of persons, who professed to exercise the sacred right of petition, he conceived that it ought to receive the stamp of disapprobation of the body. He therefore moved to throw the petition under the table.

The CHAIR did not consider that this motion was in order, as there was another motion pending.

Mr. PURVIANCE said, it was not often that he troubled the convention with motions of this description, but on this occasion, he felt constrained to make the motion which he did, and as that motion was somewhat out of the ordinary course, and was somewhat of an extraordinary character, he would beg leave to explain the reason, in a few words, why he made it. The petition purports to be a petition from the grand inquest of the county of Berks, and it undertakes to dictate to this body, what shall be its future action in reference to its adjournment. Now, he should like to know by what authority the grand inquest of the county of Berks, or of any other county, should undertake a duty of this kind. Why, he had always understood, that the duties of a grand inquest, was to inquire and make presentments under oath, of matters belonging alone to the county in which they resided.

Mr. PORTER explained, that they had not signed this petition in the character of jurors, but in their character as citizens.

Mr. PURVIANCE asked if they had not their endorsement on the back of the petition, as from the grand inquest of the county of Berks! Then this grand inquest undertakes to say, that we have gone beyond our duties, and that we should adjourn *sine die*. Now he should like to know from whence they derive their power to interfere with the business of this or any other legislative body. In his little knowledge of the laws of the country, he had always supposed that the jurisdiction of the grand inquest of any particular county, was not only confined to matters within that county, but that it was limited to criminal matters, and he had yet to learn that this convention had committed any offences against the laws of the country; or, that it has committed any penal offences. If the petition came from citizens of Berks county, he did not know that he would have any objection to receive it; but when it came from a body of men, in a public capacity, which had no right to send a petition here, he thought it ought to be rejected.

Mr. DICKEY regretted that the gentleman from Butler should have conceived it to be his duty to move the rejection of this petition, which certainly was not disrespectful in its terms. The document was not a presentment of the grand jury of Berks county, but it was a petition of the citizens of Berks county presented to this convention, couched in respectful language, asking it to terminate its session at once, and assigning reasons for this request.

Mr. D. had supposed that it was the province, alone, of southern gentlemen to object to the right of petition, and move their rejection whenever they did not suit their views; and he regretted, that in the halls of a convention of the people of Pennsylvania any such motion should be made. He sincerely regretted, that in a body of this kind an attempt should be made to reject the petition of any portion of our citizens, which was couched in respectful language.

Why, sir, this petition states nothing but the truth, and nothing but what has been asserted in this hall over and over again. He had looked into this petition which was represented as coming from the grand inquest of the county of Berks. The petition set out by saying "we the undersigned inhabitants of the county of Berks—(not the grand inquest of the county of Berks)—respectfully represent that your honorable body has been in session since the second of May last, with an interval from July to October, at an expense of one thousand dollars a day." Well, sir, is not this the truth? Have not certain members of this convention, time and again asserted that the expenses of the convention were a thousand dollars a day? Has not a single speech on this floor cost the people of Pennsylvania two thousand dollars, and he would ask the people of the state, whether that speech was worth two thousand dollars to them?

The facts, therefore, set forth in the petition are true, and being true, are respectful to the body. The petitioners further set forth, that they have reason to believe that a great majority of the people of the state, have been long since convinced that no salutary amendments to the constitution, such as will meet their approbation, will be made. Well, has not this been reiterated over and over again on this floor, and can that be looked upon as disrespectful to the convention? He was of opinion, that from the course this convention had been pursuing ever since May last, that those salutary amendments which the people had called for, would not be made. Why, then, should this petition be rejected, when it but told us the truth? The petitioners further state, that the convention has been discussing political and party matters, entirely foreign from the purposes for which they were met. Well, was not this, again, the truth; and had it not been reiterated over and over again on this floor? This had been asserted by many members on former occasions on this floor, and it could not be looked upon as disrespectful to the body.

Mr. EARLE rose to ask whether it was in order to refer to former debates on matters not now before the convention?

The CHAIR considered the gentleman from Beaver in order.

Mr. DICKEY resumed. It was notorious that this convention had been engaged a greater portion of its time in the discussion of questions with which it had nothing to do, and in relation to which the people had never asked an amendment. These questions with which we have nothing to do, this convention has been debating week after week, and we have reason to expect that no salutary amendments to the constitution will be made.

The CHAIR here interrupted the gentleman by announcing that the hour had arrived for proceeding to the orders of the day.

The convention proceeded to the consideration of the sixth section of the first article. The sixth section having been read and no amendment proposed, it was passed over by the convention.

The convention then took up the seventh section, as amended in committee of the whole, as follows:

"SECTION 7. The senators shall be chosen in districts, to be formed by the legislature, each district containing such a number of taxable inhabitants, as shall be entitled to elect not more than TWO senators : *Unless a single city or county shall at any time be entitled to more than two senators ;* when a district shall be composed of two or more counties, they shall be adjoining ; neither the city of Philadelphia, nor any county shall be divided in forming a district."

Mr. STERIGERE then moved to strike out the words "not more than two senators" and insert "one senator," and strike out the word "two" where it occurs in the fifth line. This motion, he would state, was made in committee of the whole, and came near passing there. Not, however, being fully discussed, and fully understood, it failed. He introduced it upon the ground that every district for the election of senators, or any other officers of government, ought to be as small as possible.

No matter what might be its political effect, so far as he was concerned, he would go for it. He was in favor of an arrangement of congressional districts, to make them as small as possible ; and upon the same principle, he was in favor of making all the other districts as small as possible. By having small districts, the people were made better acquainted with their representatives, and the representatives knew better the will and wishes of their constituents, than they could do if they were separated from them, as they were frequently in large districts. It would also prevent counties being cut up for political effect; and in every point of view in which he looked at it, it was better to have small than large districts. If there could be any sound objections urged against this amendment, however, he should like to hear them.

Mr. BELL said, it struck him that one great objection to the amendment was this. It so happened now, that one county frequently holds such a proportion to another, that one has more than sufficient to entitle her to a representative, while the other has not a sufficient number to be entitled to one, without being united to the larger county. For instance, the county of Chester, had taxable inhabitants enough to entitle her to one senator, and she had a large fraction over. While Delaware had not a sufficient number of taxable inhabitants to entitle her to one. Then, by uniting these counties, they were entitled to two senators Whereas, if you divided them, they would either be entitled to but one between them, or else you must deprive them of a representative on the large fraction, and the other of any influence in the halls of the senate. If you adopt the amendment of the gentleman from Montgomery, you must either throw away the very large fraction in Chester, or deprive the county of a senator; either of which would be very unjust. If it would not operate in this way, he should be as much in favor of small districts, as the gentleman from Montgomery ; but as it was, he took it, that the amendment of the gentleman would do manifest injustice to many counties.

Mr. FLEMING thought that the instance referred to by the gentleman from Chester, was not an insuperable objection to the amendment of the gentleman from Montgomery. In that case, Chester would be entitled to one senator, and have a large fraction over. Delaware county would have a senator given her on a number of taxables, which was larger than the fraction in Chester. Thus would the senators be given to the largest fractions, and no injustice would be done.

Mr. BELL felt satisfied, that from the injustice which would be done the counties he had alluded to, that the amendment ought not to be adopted. It might be the same case with regard to many other counties. The county of Chester had 11,600 taxables, while the county of Delaware only had 3,900. Then, by uniting these counties, you gave them two senators ; but if you divided them, you must either not give Delaware any senator at all, or you must give her a senator, and throw away a fraction in Chester, almost as large as the whole number of taxables in Delaware county. This taken in either way, would be doing injustice.

The argument of the gentleman from Lycoming, was, that the small counties would have the largest fractions, and would be, therefore, entitled to senators on these fractions. This might be so, or it might not be so, and it was just as likely not to be so, as to be so. You will find that the ratio increases faster in large than in small counties ; therefore, the large counties would be most likely, always, to have more than their proportion of senators. He had pointed to the injustice which would be done in Delaware county, and such might be the case in other counties. He hoped, therefore, that the amendment would not be agreed to.

Mr. READ would make but a single remark, to draw the attention of the gentleman from Montgomery to the effect of his amendment. The effect of that amendment would be to disfranchise twenty-three of the small counties in this state in the senate of the state. We have fifty-three counties now, and we know not how many more we will have, and but thirty-three senators. Then, if you take off two senators for the city of Philadelphia, and three for the county, the consequence will be that in all time to come you will have at least twenty-three of the small counties of the state, which will be entitled to no representatives in your senate. Should the number of counties increase, of course the number of disfranchised counties will increase. It seemed to him that the argument in relation to the matter, ought to induce the gentleman from Montgomery to withdraw his amendment.

Mr. STERIGERE said, if the amendment which he had submitted, would have the effect which the gentleman from Susquehanna apprehended it would be would withdraw it, but it would not have any such effect. The gentleman has told us that if the amendment was agreed to, that there would be a great many counties disfranchised. Now, he would rather the gentleman had shown this to be the fact, than that he should merely have made the assertion.   He had gone over all the counties, and he did not find the fact to be as stated by the gentleman, and of course he could not take that gentleman's word for it.   He had made an enumeration, and by it he found that acting on this principle, an apportionment could have been made much more equal than the one that was then made. He spoke of the counties in reference to each other, and without any regard to political effect, for he had laid that entirely out of view, in a question of this kind.

Mr. STERIGERE then read to the convention the following statement, which he had prepared to show the operation of his amendment.

At the last apportionment the senatorial ratio was about 9,000 taxables. Single districts could have been formed as follows :

			giving	senator, and a surplus of / deficiency	
1st	Adams and Franklin counties,	12,100 taxables	1	surplus of	2,500
2d	Allegheny,	18,700 "	2	deficiency	5,500
3d	Armstrong, Indiana and Clearfield,	9,100 "	1	"	500
4th	Bucks,	11,700 "	1	surplus	2,100
5th	Berks,	10,400 "	1	"	800
6th	Chester,	11,700 "	1	"	2,100
7th	Union, Mifflin and Juniata,	8,800 "	1	deficiency	800
8th	...er,	16,800 "	2	"	2,600
9th	Montgomery and ...e,	13,200 "	1	surplus	3,600
10th	Northampton and Monroe,	9,200 "	1	deficiency	400
11th	Philadelphia city,	18,400 "	2	"	800
12th	Philadelphia county,	30,000 "	3	surplus	1,200
13th	Washington,	8,500 "	1	deficiency	1,100
14th	Westmoreland,	8,200 "	1	"	1,400
15th	York,	9,600 "	1	"	000
16th	Bedford, Somerset and Cambria,	10,200 "	1	surplus	600
17th	Fayette and ...ne,	9,400 "	1	deficiency	200
18th	Beaver and Butler,	9,600 "	1	"	000
19th	...ld,	9,000 "	1	deficiency	600
9h	Centre and Huntingdon,	10,800 "	1	surplus	1,200
21st	Mer and Venango,	8,200 "	1	deficiency	1,400
22d	...d and Erie,	11,200 "	1	surplus	1,600
23d	Jefferson, Warren, M'Kean, Potter, Tioga and Lycoming,	10,400 "	1	"	800
24th	Bradford and Susquehanna,	8,300 "	1	deficiency	1,300
25th	...n and Lebanon,	9,900 "	1	surplus	300
26th	...gh and Schuylkill,	10,000 "	1	"	400
27th	Columbia and ...ld,	8,800 "	1	deficiency	800
28th	...ne, Pike and Wayne,	9,100 "	1	"	500
			38		

The taxables and fractions are stated in round numbers. The fractions are less than in the apportionment made, and politically balance each other very nearly.

He took it that by this system there would have been a much fairer distribution than under the present apportionment. The fractions would have been smaller, and not a single county or district would have been disfranchised. The gentleman from Chester had made great objection to this amendment, because it might disfranchise Delaware county. Now did the gentleman not know that under the present system, two Senators might be given to Chester, and Delaware be deprived of any ? Under the present apportionment bill, Chester, Delaware and Montgomery are put together, and the consequence of it is, that the district extends over some fifty or sixty miles, and the constituents of the senators know no more about them than if they resided in some of the extreme western counties of the state. This was a matter that ought to be prevented, and it was the intention of this amendment to prevent it. It must be apparent to every man that men can better represent the will of their constituents, when they reside among them, and know from their own knowledge the wants and wishes of those constituents. There could not be a doubt in the mind of any man, but that members who represented small districts were better able to represent their constituents truly, than where their district was scattered over some sixty or seventy miles of territory.

Mr. STERIGERE then called for the yeas and nays, upon his amendment; which were ordered, and were yeas 16, nays 90, as follow :

YEAS—Messrs. Banks, Clarke, of Indiana, Crum, Earle, Fleming, Grenell, Harris, Hastings, Houpt, Hyde, Ingersoll, Magee, Mann, Scheetz, Smyth, of Centre, Sterigere—16.

NAYS—Messrs. Agnew, Baldwin, Barclay, Barndollar, Bell, Biddle, Bigelow, Bonham, Brown, of Lancaster, Brown, of Northampton, Carey, Chambers, Chandler, of Philadelphia, Chauncey, Clarke, of Beaver, Clark, of Dauphin, Cleavinger, Cline, Coates, Cochran, Cope, Cox, Craig, Crane, Crawford, Cummin, Cunningham, Curll, Darlington, Darrah, Denny, Dickey, Dickerson, Dillinger, Donagan, Dunlop, Farrelly, Forward, Foulkrod, Fry, Fuller, Gamble, Gearhart, Gilmore, Hayhurst, Hays, Helffenstein, Henderson. of Allegheny, Hiester, High, Hopkinson, Jenks, Keim, Kennedy, Kerr, Konigmacher, Krebs, Maclay, M'Cohen, M'Call, M'Dowell, M'Sherry, Meredith, Merkel, Miller, Montgomery, Pennypacker, Pollock, Porter, of Lancaster, Porter, of Northampton, PurvLance, Read, Riter, Ritter, Russell, Saeger, Scott, Seltzer, Serrill, Shellito, Sill, Smith, of Columbia, Snively, Sturdevant, Taggart, Todd, Weaver, Weidman, Woodward, Sergeant, *President*—90.

The question then being on the amendment, reported from the committee of the whole,

Mr. DUNLOP moved to amend the section by striking out the words, " unless a single city or county shall, at any time, be entitled to more than two senators."

Mr. DUNLOP said, he would not long trespass upon the time of the convention, in expressing his views of this subject, inasmuch as he had spoken in relation to it heretofore, while the convention was at Harrisburg. It was with great difficulty, in fact, that he could bring his mind to a discussion of the subject at all. The operation of the section would be to throw the legislative power, and a large portion of the executive power, so far as the senate is hereafter to constitute a portion of the executive power, into the hands of some small localities in the state, while the larger and more sparsely peopled sections would have but little right in the senate. He wished to see the senatorial representation based more upon territory, and spread about more among the people.

It would be unnecessary for him to say that a thinly settled and extensive territory could not be so well represented by one man, as a small district, or a city.   One individual can be better acquainted with the interests of a city, lying within the compass of the sound of a bell, than with a district comprehending many counties, and a great extent of territory.   Territory, combined with population, ought to form the basis of representation in the senate.   Unless this was done, a small locality would rule a large portion of the state.   But should not the local interests of every part of the state have more representation?   Should a single locality, by means of a dense population, be enabled to control the local interests of large portions of the state ?   Was not the advantage given to the densely peopled districts in the lower house, sufficient?   Population had its full weight in the lower house ; and in the senate, some other principles ought to be considered in settling the basis of representation.   One-sixth of the senate is now elected by the city and county of Philadelphia.   What a vast advantage does this fact give to its interest over the country interests ?   What an ascendancy, for good or for evil, does this give to the small and densely peopled county, which thus holds the balance in the senate?   This same district, it must also be recollected, sends an army of representatives into the lower house, where in general, their vote, when united on local questions, must control the decision of every question.

He submitted whether it was the policy of a free commonwealth, thus to put it in the power of one or two single and very small sections to control all the rest.   Could not the influence of the city and county representation, prevent any other portion of the state from advancing in the career of commercial prosperity ?   Could it not be so used as to repress the industry, enterprize, and improvement of rival sections, or sections that, in time, might enter into competition with them ?   Could they not so shape the legislature of the state, particularly in regard to internal improvements, or make every section of the state tributary to them alone, although it might be the true and permanent interest of the state, that a portion of its trade should take a different direction ?   It seemed to him to be worthy the consideration of the people of the state, and of this body as representing them, on this important occasion, whether there ought not to be some restriction on popular representation in one branch of the legislature.   Ought not the number of senatorial representatives from each district, to be so restricted, as to distribute the whole number of senators more generally throughout the various sections of the state?   This is an important question for our inquiry, and consideration.   This constitution is to fix the basis of representation for many years, and at a very critical period of our career, and it is vastly important, especially when we are continuing our system of internal improvement, that the interests of sections, territorial interests should be consulted.   We must provide for the interests of the millions whose destines are to be shaped by this constitution.

An additional reason was now presented for the policy which he urged.   We had enlarged the powers of the senate, and the local interests and feelings which may get the ascendancy in that body hereafter, will rule the commonwealth.   The new powers conferred on the senate, was, in his opinion, an additional and strong reason in favor of restricting the number of senatorial representatives to be elected from each district.   If we did not do it, we gave, in effect, the whole power of the common-wealth into the hands of small localities.

It would not be said that there was no reason for an apprehension that the local interest and feeling of the populous districts would control their action in the legislature.   Experience had taught us a lesson on this subject ; and if that had been silent, every one knew too much of the nature of mankind, to suppose that, in all time hereafter, the advantages given by the constitution to localities, would never be used to the preju-dice of other local interests.

The city and county of Philadelphia, with their twenty votes, have always exerted a most powerful and prejudicial influence against the interests of other sections of the commonwealth.   He would not now enter into any particulars.   He was satisfied, indeed, with resting upon the principle which he had stated, without appealing to past experience. Every gentleman here, he presumed, fully comprehended the subject, and it was unnecessary for him to dwell and dilate upon it.   The subject had been brought to our notice heretofore, and he begged gentlemen now to give it their candid attention.

He asked gentlemen to consider whether the senate, especially since new powers were to be conferred upon it, ought not to be put upon some other basis, than mere population alone, and whether the number of sena-tors to be elected by each district, ought not to be further restricted?

Under the federal constitution, the principle for which he contended, had been fully recognized.   In the senate of the United States, population is not represented, but the sovereignties of the several states.   Thus, Delaware, with but two thousand one hundred and twenty square miles, is entitled to her two senators, while Virginia, with sixty-four thousand square miles, is entitled to no more.

So, a state with but seventy-six thousand inhabitants, has the sam number of senators, with a state, whose population exceeds a million and a half.

There had been some interesting occasions, when the votes of the city and county of Philadelphia had been thrown, in a solid body, against the interests of other sections ; and, in the nature of things, it must continue to be the case, hereafter.   But, this was a subject of former altercation which he did not wish to renew.

In a former conversation upon it, his ursine friend from the city of Philadelphia, (Mr. Meredith) was brought out.   He would not press the subject further, but he hoped that gentlemen would take it into serious consideration.

Mr. BIDDLE expressed his regret, that any attempt should be made in this body to revive the long-forgotten prejudices between the city and the country.

The time was, he said, when these prejudices existed between the city of Philadelphia, and the distant counties of the state, but they had yielded to the more frequent and easy communications which our system of internal improvements had established.   The utmost confidence and good feeling now existed between the most distant parts of the state, and he hoped nothing would ever occur that could interrupt their harmony. All the prejudices which the remarks of the gentleman from Franklin were calculated to revive and foster, had passed away, and he trusted that the attempts made again to excite them would fail.

The reasons given by the gentleman, for a territorial representation in the senate, were none of them sound or conclusive. No other basis than that of taxable population could be fair and equal, or politic, in this state, in reference to the interests of every section of it. The true interest of no section could be promoted by depriving other sections of their full share of representation, in proportion to their taxable population.

The argument which the gentleman attempted to derive from the constitution of the United States senate, was altogether inconclusive. The reason for equal state representation in the United States senate, could not apply to this commonwealth. There was no analogy between the national senate and the state senate. The object and character of the two bodies were very different.

The federal constitution was the result of a compromise between independent sovereignties. In the senate, those state sovereignties were represented as equals, by an equal number of senators, without regard to territory or population; while, in the house of representatives, the people of the states, according to their numbers, were represented. But, here it is not so. The counties in this state did not assume to be sovereign and distinct communities. They were neither so in fact nor in feeling, and there was, therefore, no reason for a distinct territorial representation in either branch of the legislature.

He hoped that the people of all the counties considered themselves as brothers of the same family, and as citizens of one great and powerful state. If there was any one principle that was dear to the freemen of this state, it was that taxation and representation should go together. That principle has always been maintained, and acted upon in this state, and can never be departed from, without an abandonment of our republican form of government.

This was not the first time, as the gentleman from Franklin had suggested, that an attempt had been made here, to exasperate the people of the state against the city and county of Philadelphia. But, the attempt was reprobated heretofore by almost every one, and he trusted that would be the same case now.

Mr. AGNEW said, he agreed with the gentleman from Philadelphia, who had just spoken, that the prejudices between the city and country had, in a great measure, died away. But, in relation to this subject, I find myself, said he, conservative and cannot go with my friend from Philadelphia, who, in this matter, advocates what I conceive to be in effect, a change of the constitution.

The gentleman from Philadelphia, in this matter, is a reformer, while I adhere to the constitution. I believe we are about making a change in the whole construction of the senate, which is inconsistent with the general spirit of the constitution. I call the gentleman's attention to the circumstances under which this clause was introduced in the constitution.

It was supposed that it would prevent gerrymandering—Philadelphia county had now three senators, and, in a few years, it was supposed that the city of Philadelphia would have three.

The change is this. We are about giving a district a greater vote, in proportion to its population, than the old constitution gave. The reading of the old constitution is, that " the senators shall be chosen in districts, each district containing such a number of taxable inhabitants, as shall be entitled to elect not more than four senators. When a district shall be composed of two or more counties, they shall be adjoining. Neither the city of Philadelphia, nor any county, shall be divided in forming a district."

Thus, four senators was the greatest number of senators which any one district could elect, and that no county, nor the city of Philadelphia, could be divided. The time may come, when the population of the city and county of Philadelphia, may entitle them to six or eight senators each, if they continue in their present career of prosperity and improvement, as I trust they will do.

But, it must be admitted, that to give such a predominance to one district, would be contrary to the spirit and genius of our constitution. The difference between the amendment and the old constitution, is this. Under the existing provisions, the county of Philadelphia cannot be divided, and can never elect more than four senators. The same is the case with the city of Philadelphia. But, according to the amendment of the section, the county and the city may be entitled, severally, to elect more than four senators, if their population shall, at any time, entitle them to more.

Under this amendment, therefore, the city and county may, and probably will, in the course of time, have each six or eight senators. The old constitution, for wise purposes, imposed a restriction upon the number of senatorial representatives from each district, and that restriction we now propose to do away with.

He agreed with the gentleman from the city of Philadelphia, that taxation and representation ought to go together. But, he was of opinion, that representation should be so formed, that the interest of localities should never be too great. The object of the old constitution is to prevent the senate from being under the influence of mere localities. No one can question the wisdom of this principle, which the framers of the constitution adopted. Time would prove its wisdom and its consistency with the objects of free government. Particular sections would be tempted by a commanding influence to depress the interests of other parts of the state, for their own local advantage.

The senate was not, therefore, designed to represent localities, but the people of the commonwealth at large. The whole constitution of the senate shews that mere numbers and localities were not looked to in forming it. If it was only intended to represent people, according to taxable numbers, why should there be any difference between the qualifications required for election to the senate, and those required for the other house? The age made necessary for election to the senate, the small number of the body, and their longer term of service, shewed that the senate was intended to be a differently constituted body from the house of representatives, and that it was designed for other purposes, than the mere representation of numbers, according to taxable population.

The amendment adopted, would overturn one of the conservative principles of the constitution, and he trusted, therefore, that the proposition of the gentleman from Franklin, (Mr. Dunlop) to strike out the clause which permits a district to elect as many senators as her population may entitle her to, would be sustained.

He apprehended that those who voted at Harrisburg for this innovation upon the constitution, did not see its full bearing and operation. It could not have been understood, when it was agreed to, that its effect would be to remove all restriction from the number of senators to be elected from each district, and to permit each district to elect as many senators as her population may entitle her to.

There is nothing now in the constitution—this section being adopted—to prevent the throwing into the senate, the whole weight of local population and interest. Surely, gentlemen could not be prepared to assent to this, after a full and deliberate view of its consequences. The old constitution is infinitely preferable, in regard to the good of the whole state, to the new provision.

The old constitution, I prefer, because it so forms the senate, that it will represent the state at large, and all its interests. A senator frequently represents two or three counties. Does he look only to the one from which he comes? He must look to the interests of the district from which he is elected, and to the interests of the state at large. What is the case with the representatives? The representatives scarcely look beyond their own county, to see what may come before them. They decide upon every question, in reference to the interests of their own respective counties. The representative is expected, by his constituents, to look more closely to their local interests, than their senator. From the senate, they do not require exclusive attention to local interests and concerns.

The public impression is, that the senate is intended to represent the state at large, and that their views and actions, are not to be confined to local feelings and interests. That was the object of the senate, as formed by the present constitution. But, under the amendment adopted, a particular locality may have a dozen or twenty senators, or a majority of the whole number.

He would earnestly ask gentlemen to look to the effect of this principle. The constitution limits the number of senators from each county to four, and the city cannot have more than four senators. But, if this section, as now amended, pass, the number which they may have, is without limit. He possessed no hostile feeling against the city and county of Philadelphia, and he wished to excite no prejudices against them. He was proud, and justly so, as every Pennsylvanian was, of the noble and beautiful city of Philadelphia. But, when we were about to organize the government of the state, he could not consent to surrender the interests of the state at large, to the hazards of local legislation. He must look, as the framers of the constitution of 1790 did, to the interests of the whole people, and every part of the state.

I object to the section as it now stands, because it gives too much influence to localities in legislation.

Mr. BIDDLE wished, he said, to say a few words in reply to some of the suggestions of the gentleman from Beaver, and it was with pain, that he found that gentleman among those who were in favor of restricting the number of representatives from any section of the state. The gentleman calls me a reformer, because he says I am in favor of the section, as amended, which, as he supposes, makes a change in the spirit of the constitution. But, the gentleman is under a mistake as to the object and spirit of the clause in the old constitution which he read. The old constitution provided, that no district should have more than four senators ; but, that was done in 1790, when the population of Philadelphia was only thirty thousand. The meaning of that constitution, in relation to this matter, was nothing more than this :—that a less number than thirty thousand people should not elect a number of senators exceeding four. But, now the population of the city exceeds a hundred thousand, and am I to be told I advocate a principle inconsistent with the constitution of 1790, and that I am a reformer. because I am not willing to limit the city and county of Philadelphia each, to two senators ?

Mr. AGNEW remarked that he had not applied to the gentleman from Philadelphia, the term reformer, as a term of reproach.

Mr. BIDDLE said, the term was used in application to me, and with the inference that I was inconsistent with my professions ; and I refer to it now, for the purpose of vindicating my consistency. I know the kind feelings of the gentleman, and that he did not use the term as a reproach ; but that is its effect, so far as it imputes to me any inconsistency. What is now proposed ? It is, that after 1839, the number of senators from each district, shall be restricted to two, whatever may be the population of the district. This restriction will take from the county of Philadelphia one senator immediately, and it will deprive the city of Philadelphia of the just and fair representation in the senate, to which, after some years, it will become entitled. Should the city and county increase in commerce and population, they may each become entitled hereafter, to more than three or more than four senators, and who can say that it is inconsistent with the spirit of the constitution, that they shall have them ? The old constitution does not warrant the supposition, that it was intended by its framers to restrict any district to a less number of senators than its taxable population entitled it to. It looked to the number of inhabitants in the city of Philadelphia, and the several counties at that day, and provided, in effect, that for thirty thousand inhabitants, not more than four senators should be elected.

But the amendment proposed by the gentleman from Franklin, and advocated by the gentleman from Beaver, would limit the city and the county, with over half a million of inhabitants each, to two senators. Whether it was the gentleman from Beaver or himself that was the reformer in this case, he would submit to the convention, after this statement. But what is the reason for this projected reform in the senatorial representation ?

The gentleman from Beaver says that the constitution intended to form the senate differently from the house, and designed that the senate should represent territorial interests, and the interests of the state at large, while the people were more immediately represented in the lower house. The gentleman's doctrine, in my opinion, is anti-republican, and it sets aside some of the leading principles of a free representative government—principles which have always been recognized and established in this state. The introduction of the principle, that territory shall be represented instead of population, in either branch of the legislature, will, indeed, be an innovation upon the constitution. Shall mere soil be represented? Shall each district elect a number of senators in proportion to the number of acres which it may contain? Shall square miles be made the basis of senatorial representation, instead of taxable population, which the powers of the old constitution intended it to be? To the extent that this principle of territorial representation shall be established, will the people of the state be disfranchised. The senate of Pennsylvania is as much a branch of the legislature representing the people of the commonwealth, as the house of representatives. The senate represents the people as directly as the house does. A longer term of service was allowed to the senate, and greater age was required for its members, in order to secure it against party influence, to which the house, from its constitution, is more subject. There was no argument in this fact, in favor of a territorial representation. The qualifications required for the members of the senate, so far as they differed from those of the other house, were not of a territorial character. There was nothing in them indicating that the senators, any less than the representatives, were to look to the interests of the constituents who elected them; and certainly we could find nothing in the constitution of the body which justified the supposition that they were not designed as direct representatives of the people of the state.

The gentleman from Beaver had furnished us, therefore, with no argument against the section as it stands, except the potent one that, under it, in the course of time, the city and the county of Philadelphia, may become entitled, in virtue of their taxable population, to a dozen representatives. This argument was certainly addressed to those local prejudices and interests which the gentleman from Beaver so much deprecated, and which he was so very anxious to guard against in the construction of the legislature. Should the population of the city and county ever arrive at that point which will entitle them to eight or ten, or even twelve senators, they ought to have them; and, if the principles of republican government should prevail, they will have them. Should the population of any county increase to so disproportionate an extent, that county will be entitled to be represented in the senate accordingly. It was not the city and county of Philadelphia alone, to which the principle would apply. But Berks or Allegheny, if they increased greatly and rapidly, as he hoped and believed they would, would also become entitled to an increased representation in the senate. But, it was probable, after all, that the population of every part of the state would increase at a rate, very nearly equal, and that when the thirty-three senators came to be apportioned among the several districts, no one district, of whatever population, would take a very large share in the whole representation. The disparity in favor of any one district, would never be so great as the gentleman from Beaver seemed to apprehend. A disproportionate increase of any one district, in reference to the rest, was not likely to happen in this state. The tide of population was constantly flowing in upon, and filling every part of, the state. In a few years the population of the central and western portions of the state, would be greatly increased. Land now unproductive, would be settled, and brought under culture. The mineral regions of the state, were to become sources of vast wealth, supporting an immense and thriving popu. lation in the interior of the state. The resources of the interior, were to be rapidly developed through the facilities afforded by our system of internal improvement, and they would fill it with an industrious and enter. prising population. There was no probability, therefore, of any such great disproportion, as the gentleman had indicated, between the popula. tion of Philadelphia city or county, and any other part of the state. But whatever might be the result of the increase of population upon the rela. tive population of the several senatorial districts, he trusted that the prin. ciple that taxation and representation must go together, would never be lost sight of, nor departed from. He trusted that no one would, at this late day, seriously advocate a proposition to abandon that important and vital principle.

Mr. Dunlop said, he had called the attention of the convention to this new feature in the constitution, which the section as amended would intro. duce, and he hoped that every one would give his serious attention to it. He harbored no prejudices against the city and county of Philadelphia. He disclaimed the imputation of any hostility to their interests, as the motive of his proposition in this case. His proposition had regard to the permanent interests of the whole commonwealth. Philadelphia he viewed as a gem in the coronet of the state, and he would be the last man in the state, who would seek to impair its beauty and lustre. He had received too much of the kindness and hospitality of its citizens, for many years, to entertain any feelings of antipathy or of prejudice, in regard to her. He felt as deep an interest in all that concerned the true interest and glory of Philadelphia, as any one of its citizens. He had been the advo. cate of those interests on all occasions, and he had voted for every propo. sition in the state legislature which contemplated the improvement of the city, or would contribute to adorn or enrich it. There was never one proposition of that kind presented to him, that he did not vote for. But, if we pass this clause, it would be a subject of deep regret to our constitu. ents. By the present constitution, each district is entitled to elect not more than four senators. But by the alteration proposed, we give each district the right to elect an unlimited number, according to its taxable pop. ulation. The result must be, that the city and county of Philadelphia will obtain, at some future apportionment, a large portion of the whole number of senators, and thereby be enabled to control the legislation of the state for local purposes. He did not yet believe that this change was designed by the convention. He doubted whether the effect of the amendment agreed to, was seen. It could not be the deliberate sense of the conven. tion that a district should be entitled to elect an unlimited number of sen. ators. The old framers thought fit to limit the number which each district could elect to four; and could we undertake to say that there should be no limit?

The county of Philadelphia now elected three members to the senate, and he would venture to say that, at the next apportionment, the city of Philadelphia would also have three. The present constitution would never suffer the number from each, to exceed four, but we say that it shall be illimitable. We know that population in the city and county of Philadelphia, increases much faster than in the west, or in the central counties.

If it continue to increase in the same ratio as heretofore, it will become entitled, before many years, to elect one-third of the whole senate, under the new rule now sought to be introduced. He thought it highly impolitic thus to increase local power and influence in the senate, especially at the time when we were about conferring upon that body increased power and authority. He did not feel the slightest desire to curtail the just influence of any county in the state ; but every member must have felt the force and power of the solid phalanx of ten or fifteen votes in the lower house, for the city and county of Philadelphia, when arrayed, as they often were, against the interests of other portions of the state, and in support of their own local interests. It would be easy to imagine the effect of giving the entire control of one branch of the legislature to a local interest. It would necessarily end, in rendering the legislature of the state subservient to local interests.

He need instance the York railroad, the Franklin railroad, and the Susquehanna canal, against each of which improvements was the united voice of the city and county of Philadelphia. The delegation from both the city and county voted against the bills. Whether they did right or wrong was a matter of investigation, and wholly unnecessary for him to go into at this time. He knew that gentlemen from all parts of the state felt the effect and the influence of those votes.

And, it was with the greatest difficulty that he and his colleague—able as that gentleman was—with his, Mr. D.'s little aid, were able to get the bill passed, incorporating a company to construct a railroad from Chambersburg to the Potomac. The city and county of Philadelphia were totally opposed to it, because they supposed it would affect their pecu. niary interest, inasmuch as it would enable the southern border of Pennsylvania—which had not then received one single dollar from the legislature for improvements—to open a market to Baltimore. Although they did not ask that the expense of the road should be defrayed out of the public treasury, they had previously been denied the privilege of making a road, by two votes, to meet the Baltimore and Ohio railroad.

He, Mr. D. would have been glad if Philadelphia could have participated in the benefit of the improvement, but as Baltimore was so much nearer to the southern counties, they very naturally wished to send their produce to the nearest market. He believed that the delegation from the city and county of Philadelphia did not, on the occasion to which he adverted, represent the feelings and interests of the people of the commonwealth of Pennsylvania.

He would ask if it was right, that any one consolidated district in a country, should exercise all its influence and interest, against the remaining ? We all know that Paris might be identified with all France; and we all know, too, that that city had governed the whole country, containing a population of thirty millions. The population of the city and county, might, before any great length of time, become so great as to represent one-third or one-fourth of the state. Why, he asked, should the convention open the door to a fourth of the representation from that quarter ?

He would say, that if we are to give power to the senate—all parts of the commonwealth should be represented there, and too great a preponderance should not be given to one portion of the state over another. Although he loved societies, he loved truth more, and although he loved Philadelphia, he loved the commonwealth more. He looked to the good of the whole state.

The convention must either take the amendment which he had offered, or vote down the whole section. One or the other must be done. Serious as the subject was, he would be willing to restrict the senators in any one district, to two.

It did not follow, that in the representation of a government, it should be based on the enumeration of its inhabitants. If a different plan was better, and by which the whole interests of the community would be represented, it ought to be adopted. The subject was one deserving of the serious consideration of the convention.

Mr. PORTER, of Northampton, said he should never be able to bring his mind to support any provision which was calculated to do injustice to any portion of the commonwealth. It was quite probable that the effect of the amendment adopted in committee of the whole, might be to give the city and county of Philadelphia, a maximum of representation, according to their population; and that before any great lapse of time. And why, he asked, should it not be so?

There was a settled principle in our government, and that was, that representation shall be in proportion to population. That principle must be carried out in the house of representatives, as well as in the senate, or else we shall depart from the principle advocated from the commencement of the government, to the present day.

Now, suppose the result which the delegate from the county of Franklin, (Mr. Dunlop) has suggested, should actually take place, and that the population of the city and county of Philadelphia should increase farther than any other portion of the commonwealth. Is that any reason why they should not have equal rights with the people of the rest of the state?

He, Mr. P. however, conceived that the gentleman from Franklin would find himself entirely mistaken in his supposition. He believed there would shortly be a great change and increase in the population, in certain districts of Pennsylvania, such as the most sanguine advocate of internal improvements, never dreamt of.

As our mineral wealth becomes more fully developed, we should have our Manchester, Liverpool, and Birmingham springing up here, with as great rapidity as they have arisen in Great Britain. There are yet vast improvements in machinery to be made, and new adaptations of that already in use. All of which, will tend to people districts adopted for manufacturing.

His friend from Lycoming, (Mr. Fleming) suggested that animal magnetism would probably produce a great change. He would leave that subject to the delegate, as it did not enter into his, Mr. P.'s argument. He did not like to resort to any new fangled process, in philosophy, politics, or mechanics.

He had supposed representation was based upon population. He had always understood so in the school of politics in which he had been educated.

Now, why he would ask, should we depart from it? Why, if one part of the state should become more populous than another, should we depart from the common principle of the government, and adopt territory as the basis of representation? He had heard nothing like an argument—nothing to convince him of the soundness and propriety of adopting such a course. The moment we attempted to depart from the present principle—that of population—we should get into error, and great injustice would be done at every step of our progress.

He would not enter into any discussion, with regard to any peculiar feelings which might be entertained by the city or county of Philadelphia. He was not at all aware that the city and county had always gone together in solid phalanx. On the contrary, indeed, he supposed them to be opposed to each other. They often exhibited the scene of the Kilkenny cats, eating each other up.

But, sir, who carried into effect the internal improvements of your state, by furnishing the necessary funds? Why, the city of Philadelphia. And, in what instance had she been backward in contributing her aid, to promote the interests of the commonwealth? He had no particular attachment to the city of brotherly love; he was not a native of it, though he had resided here twenty odd years since, for some five years or so, and was in the habit of visiting it occasionlly. Yet he felt disposed to do Philadelphia justice.

It was true that the representatives from the city had endeavored, and very naturally, to get the products of the state brought to Philadelphia, by so pointing and directing the great avenues of the state, and there was nothing unnatural in this.

He trusted that delegates would not allow a jealousy of the interest of Philadelphia, to operate on their minds, and prompt them to do her injustice. Ought the fact, that she attends to her own interest, to prejudice us? Surely not. It was natural enough that delegates should look to the interests of their constituents, rather than to those of other gentlemen coming from another part of the state. If there were any who did not, then he must confess that he had never met with any such disinterested patriots. As far as his information went, he believed that every district had endeavored to get all they could for themselves, and none had fared better than Beaver.

The gentleman from Franklin, (Mr. Dunlop) in the course of his speech, found fault with his friends from the city of Philadelphia, for not aiding him in regard to the York railroad.

Mr. Dunlop explained: He did not say his friends. Had they been present, they would have lent their aid. It was another delegation.

Mr. Porter. The delegate said that he entertained no hostility to Philadelphia, yet it might be supposed he did, from the whole scope of his speech. He, Mr. P. heard very different language at the recent opening of the Cumberland Valley railroad, in the county of Franklin, when it was his good fortune to be at Chambersburg. It was said, on that occasion, that the people there were very much indebted to the members from the city of Philadelphia, for the assistance they had given the delegates from Franklin, in procuring the passage of the bill. He had heard no other language used than that of well deserved praise, bestowed on the city of brotherly love. " God preserve me from my friends," exclaimed Mr. P. " of my enemies I can take care myself."

Mr. P. did not think there was much danger to be apprehended of the city and county of Philadelphia, having more representatives than the number to which they were entitled. The whole of the rest of the state are generally careful to prevent any thing of the kind. When they had no more than what would be their just proportion, based on the principle of population, he should not object to the number, no matter how great it might be.

The old constitution contained a provision, that there should not be more than four senators to represent one district, so that the city and county of Philadelphia would never be entitled to more than four senators, whatever might be the population. The provision now introduced was, that there shall not be more than two senators, unless the number of taxable inhabitants in any city or county, shall, at any time, be such as to entitle it to elect more than that number.

Now, that provision was inserted for the purpose of carrying out the principle of representation, based on population. And, in his opinion, that was a correct principle. Many of the various conventions that had been held in different parts of the Union, had discussed the question as to what ought to be the principle upon which representation should be based.

Some states had decided and adopted the principle, that property ought to be the basis. In Virginia, and some other states, territory was regarded as the principle.

He, Mr. P. regarded it as an anti-republican basis, because counties were represented, and not the people. His principle was this: that the poorest man in the community, was entitled to equal rights with the richest, and that any given number of inhabitants in a given portion of territory, were entitled to the same rights and privileges as every other portion in the commonwealth.

He knew not, why three representatives for the county of Northampton should be equal to five for the city and county of Philadelphia, and until the gentleman, (Mr. Dunlop) could convince him to the contrary, or give some reason why a different rule should be adopted, at the expense of the city and county of Philadelphia, he, Mr. P. could not advocate any other basis for representation, than taxable population.

Mr. FLEMING, of Lycoming, said that he did not rise for the purpose of reiterating the argument heretofore advanced by him, on the subject of representation. He did not recollect that he had the pleasure of hearing his friend from Northampton, (Mr. Porter) at that time. But, if that gentleman would have the goodness to refer to the published debates of this body, he would there find the numerous reasons recorded, which had influenced his, Mr. F.'s mind on this subject.

It would be well if gentlemen from the country would go hand in hand, in order to protect themselves against the wrongs which might be done them by the action of this convention. The members neither from the city nor the county needed the aid of delegates from the country ; they were abundantly able to protect themselves. He had, at all times, since he became a member of the convention, seen that the members from the city and county of Philadelphia, were amply able, and exceedingly willing, to protect themselves. He had not discovered that it was necessary to make use of any kind of sophistry and argument for the purpose of aiding those delegates. They were many in number, and possessed both learning and talents, while the delegates from the country, were few in number, in proportion to the number of constituents they represented.

He maintained, then, that it was necessary to concentrate the forces of the country members, in order to be placed on something like a footing with those from the city and county of Philadelphia, and to take care of their rights and interests.

With respect to taking population as the basis upon which to send senators to the legislature, his opinion was, that it was neither an honest, an equal, nor a fair one. He conceived that it required no great ingenuity to foresee that if we were to be governed by population, or by the list of taxables, in the election of senators—in a few years hence, many counties in the interior of the state, might as well not elect any senators at all. What, he asked, did it amount to?

If we were to give to the city and county of Philadelphia, and the densely populated counties along the Delaware, senators in proportion to their population, what good could a man do who represented three or more counties ? He would ask, if there was any interest in the interior of the country which they could influence, or promote by their votes ? Unquestionably not.

He would remark, that he did not make these observations, because he entertained any prejudices against the city and county of Philadelphia. Nor would he stand up and say, that he liked either better than any other place. He was, however, in common with the rest of the community, devoted to the interests of the city and county. But, still he did not wish that day to arrive when the whole of the representation should be thrown into their hands.

Now, he would ask, if the principle which he advocated, was entirely new ? Were not the states of this Union as well represented by territory, as by population? Were the states represented in the general government by population? Unquestionably not. Each state, when admitted into the Union, was entitled to two senators on the floor of the senate of the United States. If we, in Pennsylvania, were to be governed in our senate, entirely by population, he would ask gentlemen, before they made up their minds to that, to look to the last enumeration of taxables. They should be careful how they opened the door to this innovation, for every portion of the state was greatly interested in the senate, as at present constituted. The power of that body would be frittered away We would refuse to send senators to it, because under such an arrangement, we should have one senator representing three or four counties, A man representing a territory, could have but little personal knowledge of the district in which he resided, and yet he would have to act upon all the appointments made by the governor.

He would ask gentlemen if they were prepared to vote for any amendment which would deprive the people of being represented, as they ought to be, on the floor of the senate of Pennsylvania? He sincerely trusted, that it would be long before such an amendment as that which was pending, would be adopted by the convention. He could not believe that the members from the city and county of Philadelphia would do such manifest injustice to any portion of the people of this commonwealth.

He had not risen to make an argument, but merely to say that he trusted the proposition of the gentleman from Franklin, (Mr. Dunlop) would be adopted, and that his, Mr. F's., constituents would be put on something like an equal and fair footing with the city and county of Philadelphia.

Mr. MEREDITH, and Mr. BROWN, of Philadelphia, having both risen at the same time, the former gave way, and

Mr. BROWN proceeded to say that had he seen his *ursine* friend—as he had been called by the gentleman from Franklin—rising, he, Mr. B. would not have risen, because he had not forgotten the unbecoming manner in which that *ursine* friend had been treated by the delegate from Adams and others.   Besides, he knew that it was only necessary for the gentleman, (Mr. Meredith) to grapple with the subject, to dispose of it at once.

The delegate from Franklin might as well have called the gentleman *ursa major*.   What was this proposition of his?   The delegate said he loved the city: what he wanted to do, however, was, to prevent the voice of the county from being fully represented.   Now, this was a matter which concerned not the city and county only, but other parts of the state.   It was a case of justice on one side, and injustice on the other, and of right against wrong.   We had already adopted a fixed principle of representation, and that was, population and taxation.   But, it seemed a new principle was to be introduced.

The gentleman from Franklin would have acres—territory as the basis of representation.   Were they, whose soil happened to be rich, to be allowed any preference over those whose land was poor?   Were acres and not taxation to entitle a man to vote?   Surely the gentleman did not mean that, and would repudiate such an extraordinary notion.

What! were trees to be represented?   Were we to be told, that the assessors must go and seek for wolves and bears, in order to value them?   Were they to go to the county of Franklin, to hunt and count the foxes?   Were they to go to Lebanon in order to ascertain the quantity of bushels of grain grown there?

Let the gentleman reflect, for a moment, what would be the demand of the city and county of Philadelphia, if the basis of representation was property, and not population.   Whatever the city and county might have done to provoke the ire of the delegate from Franklin, he, Mr. B. would tell him that their representatives had contributed their support to obtain from the legislature, what the people of the interior desired, and which was at all calculated to promote the best interests of the community, generally, throughout the state.   He would maintain, that the only safe principle we could adopt, in reference to representation, was taxation.   These complaints of the gentleman, as well as his proposition, came from him with a bad grace.   What was now called the city and county, was once the city of Philadelphia only.   And, had they not done much towards improving the interior ?   Certainly they had.

Although he was one of those who, in the legislature of Pennsylvania, voted against the York and Chambersburg railroad, yet he did not regret it, because he believed the whole state of Pennsylvania was concerned, and that the road would not be made.   It had required all the aid that the commonwealth could gather, to carry into operation the internal improvement system.   Therefore, it behooved the legislature to be particularly cautious how they acted, lest they might alienate any portion of the state from lending their support to it.   He, and others who voted with him, were actuated by higher motives than giving their votes against the bill, because it would benefit that portion of the state from which the gentlemen from Franklin and Adams came.

On consulting the journals of the legislature, it would be found that the members from the city and county of Philadelphia, had voted for internal improvements in various parts of the state, and with which they had little or no connexion, and from which they expected to derive little, if any benefit.   They had voted only from a desire to promote the prosperity and welfare of the state.   He knew it to be perfectly useless to enter into a long argument at this time ; indeed, it was entirely unnecessary to detain the convention, by saying one word on the subject, inasmuch as it had been discussed some time ago.   He felt quite satisfied that this first, of a series of propositions, would be voted down.   He hoped that the gentleman from Franklin, himself, would vote against it, marked, as it undoubtedly was, with the most flagrant injustice.   And, he trusted, too, that the votes on this amendment would unequivocally show, that it was not to be entertained either now, or at any other time.

Mr. CRAWFORD, of Westmoreland, demanded the previous question ; which was sustained.

And on the question, " Shall the main question be now put ?"

Mr. WOODWARD, of Luzerne, asked for the yeas and nays; which being taken, the question was decided in the affirmative,—yeas 65, nays 49.

YEAS—Messrs. Banks, Barclay, Barndollar, Biddle, Bigelow Bonham, Brown, of Lancaster, Brown, of Northampton, Clarke, of Beaver, Clark, of Dauphin, Cleavinger, Cline, Cochran, Craig, Crain, Crawford, Crum, Cummin, Cunningham, Curll, Darlington, Darrah, Dickerson, Dillinger, Donnell, Earle, Foulkrod, Fry, Gearhart, Gilmore, Harris, Hayhurst, Helffenstein, Henderson, of Allegheny, Hiester, High, Houpt, Keim, Kennedy, Kerr, Krebs, Maclay, Mann, M'Call, M'Sherry, Meredith, Merkel, Miller, Montgomery, Pennypacker, Pollock, Porter, of Northampton, Ritter, Saeger, Scheetz, Sellers, Seltzer, Serrill, Shellito, Smith, of Columbia, Snively, Sterigere, Stickel, Taggart, Weaver—65.

NAYS—Messrs. Agnew, Baldwin, Bell, Brown, of Philadelphia, Carey, Chambers, Chandler, of Philadelphia, Chauncey, Clarke, of Indiana. Coates, Cope, Cox, Denny, Dickey, Donagan, Dunlop, Farrelly, Fleming, Forward, Fuller, Gamble, Grenell,

Hastings, Hays, Hopkinson, Hyde, Ingersoll, Jenks, Konigmacher, Long, Magee, Martin, M'Cahen, M'Dowell, Porter, of Lancaster, Purviance, Read, Riter, Royer, Russell, Scott, Sill, Smyth. of Centre, Sturdevant, Todd, Weidman, Woodward, Young, Sergeant, *President*—49.

The main question being on agreeing with the committee of the whole, in their report upon the seventh section, it was taken and was decided in the negative, yeas 52, nays 61, as follow :

YEAS—Messrs. Baldwin, Banks, Bigelow, Bonham, Brown, of Northampton, Brown, of Philadelphia, Clarke, of Beaver, Clarke, of Indiana, Cline, Cope, Craig, Crawford, Cummin, Darlington, Darrah, Dillinger, Donnell, Earle, Farrelly, Forward, Foulkrod, Fry, Hastings, Helffenstein, Henderson, of Allegheny, Hiester, High, Ingersoll, Keim, Kennedy, Krebs, Magee, Mann, Martin, M'Cahen, M'Dowell, Miller, Montgomery, Pennypacker, Pollock, Porter, of Northampton, Read, Riter, Ritter, Scheetz, Serrill, Sellers, Shellito, Smith, of Columbia, Sterigere, Stickel, Weaver—52.

NAYS—Messrs. Agnew, Barclay, Barndollar, Bell, Biddle,, Brown, of Lancaster, Carey, Chambers, Chandler, of Philadelphia, Chauncey, Clark, of Dauphin, Cleavinger, Coates, Cochran, Cox, Crain, Crum, Cunningham, Curll, Denny, Dickey, Dickerson, Donagan, Fleming, Fuller, Gamble, Gearhart, Gilmore, Grenell, Harris, Hayhurst, Hays, Hopkinson, Houpt, Hyde, Jenks, Kerr, Konigmacher, Long, Maclay, M'Call, M'Sherry, Meredith, Merkel, Porter, of Lancaster, Purviance, Royer, Russell, Saeger, Scott, Seltzer, Sill, Smyth, of Centre, Snively, Sturdevant, Taggart, Todd, Weidman, Woodward, Young, Sergeant, *President*—61.

Mr. READ moved to amend, by striking out the words " within the city of Philadelphia nor any," and inserting in lieu thereof, " no." The effect of this amendment, he said, would be to make the clause in the constitution read as at present, as far as the word " adjoining," and then to add the restriction that " no county shall be divided in forming a district." This part of the section would then read as follows : " when a district shall be composed of two or more counties, they shall be adjoining, no county shall be divided in forming a district."

The question was taken on the amendment, and it was negatived.

Mr. WOODWARD moved to amend by striking out " four," and inserting " three," so as to read as follows : " but no city or county shall be entitled to more than three senators."

Mr. BELL said he would move an amendment to the amendment of the gentleman from Luzerne, with a view to obtain the sentiment of the convention upon the subject of the amendment which he had formerly offered, and which had been ruled out of order.

The PRESIDENT decided that the motion was not now in order.

Mr. EARLE hoped, he said, that the amendment offered by the gentleman from Luzerne, (Mr. Woodward) would not prevail, for this reason that he considered it essential to adopt something to prevent gerrymandering. The motion of the gentleman from Luzerne, would not effect this object. He wanted some thing that would show how strong was the sense of the convention against the practice of carving out districts for political effect. The opinion of the convention had been heretofore strongly expressed on that subject. The vote in favor of such an amendment as would prevent gerrymandering, was eighty-three, while the regative vote was thirty-three, in the committee of the whole. The same amendment which had just been negatived, was agreed to in the committee of the whole, by that large vote. That amendment was adopted for the purpose of preventing gerrymandering, and it was rejected because it contained no limitation upon the number of senators which a large city or county might elect. He hoped, therefore, the gentleman from Luzerne would withdraw his amendment, and suffer the gentleman from Chester, (Mr. Bell) to offer his motion. If the amendment was not withdrawn, he hoped it would be rejected for the purpose of adopting something much better, and which would entirely remove the present difficulty. He was prepared to show that an amendment which he had himself drawn up would remedy the difficulty entirely, answering the purpose of preventing gerrymandering, and also restricting the number of members from each county. Either his amendment, or that which the gentleman from Chester had offered, would answer the object, and would be greatly preferable to that proposed by the gentleman from Luzerne. The amendment which he would offer would prevent any city or county from having more than four senators.

Mr. HOPKINSON was, he said, gratified at the disposition manifested on this subject. He had voted against the unrestricted right of the city, or of the several counties, to elect senators; but he thought it would be extremely unjust to fix the limit below what it was fifty years ago, when the population of the city and county was so much less than what it now is. He was willing that the limitation fixed by the present constitution should be retained.

Mr. AGNEW had opposed, he said, the amendment which had been rejected, on the ground that it fixed no restriction on the representation in the senate, of the cities and counties. But he had now risen to do himself the justice to say that it was never his desire nor intention to fix the limitation of the number of senators from Philadelphia, at less than it was in 1789. He did not wish to revive the controversy between the city of Philadelphia and the counties, and he had no prejudice against the city to gratify. He was now opposed to the motion of the gentleman from Luzerne, because he thought it was illiberal towards the city of Philadelphia. That amendment would reduce the number of senators from Philadelphia city and the county of Philadelphia very unreasonably. He was willing that they should have one-fourth of the whole number of senators but not more. It was not from any hostility to the city or county of Philadelphia, that he had opposed the former amendment, but he was in favor of some restriction.

Mr. FORWARD said the effect of his amendment would be to restrict the whole number of senators from the city of Philhdelphia, or from any county to three. He must vote against this. He would ask the gentleman from Luzerne, who offered the amendment, upon what principle he proposed to base the representation in the senate? Shall we take property as the basis? That principle would be spurned by every one here. What is the true principle of representation? What is that principle which we have always adhered to and approved? There must be some principle to guide us in relation to this important subject, and it must be a uniform, universal, and settled principle. Gentlemen when they come to look into the matter, will find great difficulty in departing from the principle of taxable population as the basis of senatorial representation. It is proposed by the amendment, that no city or county shall have the right to elect more than three senators, whatever may be the number of their representatives. If we can restrict the city or a county from electing more than three senators, what shall prevent us from restricting them to the election of one senator? What, indeed, shall prevent us from saying that they shall elect no senator at all? If we have no principle to govern us in settling the representation, we may fix the representation of each county and of the city arbitrarily, and may say that only this or that county shall have any representation at all. We must either take a fixed and universal basis of representation in the senate, or else involve ourselves in the absurdity of arrogating to ourselves the power to disfranchise any city or county. As to himself, he was content to stand upon the basis of taxable population. No better basis than that had been suggested or could be devised? That was the basis which had been uniformly approved in this state, and it was the only basis upon which free representation could rest. We must have some basis, or else we can take away all political power from one or more districts altogether, and no basis is preferable to that of taxable population. If you can abridge the number of representatives to which a district is entitled by its population, you may take away their representation altogether. There is no end to this absurdity.

Let gentlemen put their finger on the point where they will stop, if they depart from the just, true and uniform basis of population. You may regulate the right to vote and say what age or what property shall entitle a man to vote. But you cannot apply one rule to one district, and another to another. Ile would like to know on what principle any discrimination would be made between the basis of representation fixed for one county or district and that which we adopted for another. If we carried out this principle, it would lead to total disfranchisement. We must have a fixed and universal principle, applying alike to every district. What hinders us from putting the ban of disfranchisement upon the minority? What prevents us from disfranchising those districts which, in party times, may be in the minority? Nothing but the uniform and impartial system of representation. Let the gentleman from Luzerne fix his principle of representation, and stand by it; and not attempt to make one rule for one district and another for other districts. Another matter in relation to this subject deserved consideration. This commonwealth ought to be considered as a unit for all great purposes. It should be looked to as a whole. Who is to assume that any particular city or county will be hostile to the common interests, and endeavor to subvert them? Who is to presume that any one district will exert its legislative influence to the disadvantage and ruin of other districts? We have no right to act upon any such presumption. We must look to the state as a body bound together by the ties of a common interest, and a common government. Can we assume these local jealousies as principles for guiding us in settling organic laws? But here is a local jealously against a district founded upon its number of taxables inhabitants. What right had we to assume that these inhabitants were hostile to the common interests? What right had we to judge at all of their sentiments? Have they not a right to freedom of thought and action, as free citizens. How shall we arraign them, and undertake to disfranchise them, because we suppose that their opinions may differ from ours? He must, he said, repudiate all his notions of republicanism, before he could undertake to assume that the people of Philadelphia would be hostile to the common interests, and act upon this assumption. It was truly an extraordinary doctrine, that the inhabitants of any part of the commonwealth, were to be deprived of their due relative share in the representation, because a jealousy existed against them, on account of their numbers. What has been and ought to be the basis of free representation, but numbers? No other basis can be devised, and when that fails, representative government must fail. We can never act upon the principle that local influence will be exerted to aggrandize one part of the state at the expense of another. In regard to the districts whose rights the amendment was intended to abridge, there was a jealousy not only of them, but between them. There existed local jealousies between the city and the county of Philadelphia. Such jealousies must always exist, under any form of government.

On motion of Mr. READ, the convention here took the usual recess.

THURSDAY AFTERNOON, JANUARY 4, 1838.

FIRST ARTICLE.

The convention resumed the second reading of the report of the committee, to whom was referred the first article of the constitution, as reported by the committee of the whole.

The seventh section of the said first article of the constitution, being again under consideration,

The question recurred upon the motion of Mr. WOODWARD, to amend the same, by striking therefrom, in the third line, the word "four," and inserting in lieu thereof, the word "three," so as to read as follows: "The senators shall be chosen in districts, to be formed by the legislature, each district containing such a number of taxable inhabitants, as shall be entitled to elect not more than three senators."

Mr. FORWARD resumed the floor, but gave way, in order to afford an opportunity to the gentleman from Luzerne, to explain his amendment.

Mr. WOODWARD said, he would avail himself of the opportunity thus presented, to say a few words on the amendment which he had offered, and which he had designed to submit, without remark.

He felt, he said, that he had discharged his duty, by offering the amendment, and that it was calculated to remedy some of the objections urged against the section as it now stands, without doing any real injustice to any part of the commonwealth. While he said this, he wished also to do himself the justice to declare, that he considered the entire and uniform principle of representation based on taxable population, as a just and sound one, in view of the general organization of the state government; and, in conformity with this principle, when the gentleman from Adams proposed to limit the representation of the city and county, to a certain number, he opposed it, and voted against it.

In relation to representation in the house of representatives, the principle of taxable population prevailed, without any limitation, and he was not disposed to interrupt, or in any way, to limit the application of that principle, so far as the more popular branch of the legislature was concerned.

But, sir, (said Mr. Woodward) the principle of popular representation never did prevail, in regard to the senate. The constitution of 1790 did not apply that principle to representation in the senate. That constitution contemplated geographical and territorial interests, in fixing the representation in the senate, and did not, as in regard to the other house, look solely to taxable population, as the basis of representation.

We find, in the old constitution, this limitation upon that principle, in regard to senatorial representation. The constitution provides, that no district shall be entitled to elect more than four senators. It was quite possible, that the population of some districts might, in the course of time, become so large, in proportion to that of other parts of the state, as to entitle them to elect more than four senators; and, in contemplation of this contingency, the framers of the present constitution, provided that no district should elect more than four senators.

This was a departure from the principle, that representation should be based on numbers, though that principle was rigidly adhered to, in regard to the other branch of the legislature. Beyond a certain limit, which this constitution fixes, the principle of population was not to regulate the number of senators from each district.

In relation to the constitution of the United States, we find a similar qualification. The senatorial representation is not based on the principle of federal numbers, like that in the other house, but upon the several states of the union, as distinct communities.

In the organization of the general government, we find the principle of population prevailing without limitation, in regard to representation in one branch of congress; and, in regard to the senate, we find the principle of locality prevailing. Each state sends to the national senate the same number of representatives. That local principle was not adopted to the same extent, in the constitution of this state; but we had gone so far as to restrict the application of the popular principle.

The amendment which he proposed, did not violate any principle which was to be found in the constitution of Pennsylvania. It carried out a principle which was already in it. The amendment was a further qualification upon a principle which our constitution had already qualified. Heretofore each district was restricted from electing more than four senators, and it is now proposed further to restrict the districts in this respect, by providing that no district shall elect more than three senators. There was no principle of republican government which would be violated by this provision, and no principle of our government, as it was formed by the present constitution, would be violated by it.

The object of this amendment was precisely the same with that provision of the present constitution, which restricted the number of senators from each district to four, whatever might be their relative population. The object was to counteract local influence upon legislation, and to give weight to geographical interests as such.

From all the reflection which he had given to the subject, he had been led to the conclusion, that the amendment which he had offered, would promote the true and permanent interests of this commonwealth. It would, he believed, promote and secure the general interests, by guarding against the danger of the commanding influence of particular localities, upon legislation.

Allow me, (said Mr. Woodward) to say that, whatever may have been said by others on this floor, or elsewhere, in regard to local jealousies, I do not myself feel any thing of the narrow prejudice against the city and county of Philadelphia, which other gentlemen here have made a merit in divesting themselves of; nor do I, on the other hand, stand here for the purpose of eulogizing any particular portion of the people of Pennsylvania. I view them all as brethren of the same family, as citizens of the same great community; and, when necessary, I can speak of the great merits of the people of every section of the commonwealth as they deserve; but, I do not claim for any one portion, a superiority over other portions, in point of patriotism, or intelligence, or virtue, or attachment to the common interests of the state.

The city of Philadelphia is a great and noble city, and I am too much of a Pennsylvanian, not to take pleasure and pride in claiming her as a part and portion of my native state.

At the same time, there is here, as in all other large cities, an amount of crime and of poverty that cannot be found in the country, among the same number of people. This is true of large and crowded towns, vice and misery hang upon the skirts of dense population, let the people be collected wherever they may.

Every large town necessarily draws to itself a large amount of low and depraved population, and these are not as good citizens, nor as well qualified to judge of the public interests, as the ordinary population of the country.

The agricultural pursuits of the people of the country are unfavorable to a dense population, but give to the inhabitants of our mountains and vallies, the advantage of industry, comfort, independence and good morals Ought there not to be some check upon the influence of city population upon our legislation? Should the towns and cities that may grow up in the state, have a predominant legislative influence over those districts, whose pursuits render their population less dense, though, as a body, better entitled to influence in legislation?

The framers of the constitution of 1790 judged that a restriction upon the representation of numbers in towns and cities was necessary, and they adopted a provision accordingly, which met with the sanction of the people.

They limited the number of senators to be elected from each district to four, and I submit whether we ought not, for the same reasons which influenced the framers of the present constitution, now to reduce the integer to three.

The city and county of Philadelphia, Mr. President, have exerted a great influence upon the legislation of this state, and that influence has been exerted in favor of their own local interests, to the disparagement of other interests. This is perfectly fair, and in conformity with the instincts of our nature, which are selfish, and I do not complain of it.

But, is there not danger that this local influence will become too powerful upon state legislation, if it be left unrestrained? Does it not behoove us, in providing for the interests of all, to guard against the accumulating influence of the numbers crowded into particular districts?

Look, for instance, upon the influence of towns and cities, upon our internal improvement and revenue system. The capital for all private incorporations, for making rail roads and canals, is necessarily drawn from the towns and cities. Such rail roads and canals, are incorporated every year by the legislature, through the influence of the cities, and they are authorized to be built alongside of those which the commonwealth has built out of the money of the whole people.

In this manner, sir, are the public revenues diverted from their proper channels, into the pockets of private capitalists, in our towns and cities. This, sir, is one of the results of the overshadowing influence of towns and cities upon the legislature of the state.

They will also contrive, through legislation, to give the capital of the cities, a direction which is more favorable to them than to the interests of the people at large.

Now, Mr. President, if the large cities are to have not only their full representation in the house of representatives, according to their population, but also one-fourth, or more, of the senate, what security do we retain for our internal improvement system, which has cost the state so many millions?

The city influence in the legislature, acting under the influence of city capital, will be able to deprive the state of nearly its whole revenue, arising from its works of internal improvement; and, these great works, which are as much the boast of Pennsylvania as any city within her limits, will become a tax upon her citizens, and be abandoned as profit-less and expensive, while the vast revenues which the state ought to derive from them, go to enrich the cities and their rich capitalists. I may be charged with an unreasonable jealousy of towns but I disclaim it. I would give them the whole of their due share of influence. Because we come from the mountains and the wild woods, will it be supposed that we wish to extinguish the great light of Philadelphia? No. We would glory in it, and seek to cherish and defend it, and to promote its true interests.

But, we cannot give up every thing in the commonwealth to the accu-mulated influence of numbers and capital in these cities. If we look calmly at the subject, will we not come to the conclusion, that the interests of this little locality are amply provided for, by allowing to it its full share of representation in the house of representatives, according to numbers, and giving to it besides, one-sixth of the representation in the senate. Is this not enough to give to this little territory? The money borrowed for the prosecution of our internal improvement system must be paid, and it must be drawn from every part of the state.

If you allow this narrow district, with all its narrow feelings, and for its own purposes, to obtain incorporations for their own benefit, and break up your internal improvement system, by building canals and railroads alongside of them, are you not, by such a course, surrendering the rights of the whole people of the commonwealth to a few? Are you not, by this means, giving an undue and unjust preponderance to one section of the commonwealth over every other section? Are not the interests of the whole to be provided for and secured, as well as the interests of the few?

I have said that there is necessarily a large mass of depravity in all great cities, and a large portion of their population consists of persons who have not feelings in common with the great body of intelligent and patriotic citizens. I do not say that "great cities are great sores." But, I speak of a well-known fact, when I say that we find great numbers in all large towns, who are ignorant and depraved.

Are such people to form the basis of a large and overpowering representation in the state legislature, which is to break down the interests of our farmers? Is the agricultural interests,—are the farmers, who are the bone and sinew of the state, to be subjected to the rule of such a population?

It is undoubtedly our duty and interest to protect and guard the interests of the city, and I have supposed that the city and county of Philadelphia, with three senators each, and one-sixth of the whole senate, and a full numerical representation in the house of representatives, would be fully protected. I still believe that it would abundantly protect the interests of the city and county, and at the same time give a due share of influence to the representation of the rural population of the country. Something like a fair equipoise would be established between town and country influence in the legislature. It was with the firm belief that equal and exact justice would be done to every part of the commonwealth, by this amendment that I have offered it.

Mr. BROWN, of the county of Philadelphia, said, when he heard of an amendment for the purpose of abridging the rights of Philadelphia, coming from the gentleman from Franklin, (Mr. Dunlop) he was not so much surprised, but when he saw a proposition of this kind coming from a gentleman who possessed democratic principles, he confessed that he was struck with astonishment.

The gentleman began by telling us that he did not wish the few to govern the many, yet, he brings forward a proposition, the very object of which strikes at the root of democratic principles, and gives the few the right to govern the many. This was the effect of the gentleman's amendment; because, whenever you take from a portion of the state, a part of their representation, and give it to another part of the state, which has not a number of inhabitants as large as that from which the representative was taken, then you give the few the right to govern the many. If you take from the county of Philadelphia, with twenty-five thousand taxable inhabitants, two of her senators, and give them to counties with not more than ten or twelve thousand taxables, he would ask, if that would be in accordance with democratic principles? If so, he confessed he had yet to learn the first lesson in those principles. Never was any such principle as that intended by the framers of the constitution of 1790. He was no lawyer, but he took upon himself to say, that no such principle was embraced in the constitution of 1790, either in letter or spirit. He believed it never was intended that any portion of the people of this state should be deprived of their representatives, in order that those representatives might be given to another district, or to other districts.

Section six of the constitution, which referred to this matter, read as follows:

"The number of senators shall, at the several periods of making the enumeration, before mentioned, be fixed by the legislature, and apportioned among the districts formed, as hereinafter directed, *according to the number of taxable inhabitants in each.*"

There was no limitation here laid down, and the principles of representation and taxation here, go together. Then the next section went on to say, that the " senators shall be chosen in districts, to be formed by the legislature, each district containing such a number of taxable inhabitants, as shall be entitled to elect not more than four senators; when a district shall be composed of two or more counties, they shall be adjoining; neither the city of Philadelphia, nor any county, shall be divided in forming a district."

When this constitution was formed, it never was supposed that any county in the state, according to her ratio of representation, would be entitled to more than four senators, and under that supposition, it was declared that no county should be divided to form a district. That was the sole intention, and it never was intended to limit any county. All our apportionments have been based upon taxable inhabitants, and upon nothing else, and it never was intended by any provision in the constitution, to limit any county. It was contrary to all democratic principles, that it should be so, and he trusted he should always advocate sound democratic principles here and elsewhere.

But the gentleman from Luzerne has found out that the character of the citizens of the city and county of Philadelphia, is not equal to that of the interior counties of the state, and that, in consequence of this, they ought to be deprived of some of their rights. He has found out that there was a want of common feeling on the part of the citizens of the city and county, for the rest of the state.

Now, Mr. B. denied the truth of both these positions. He denied that the citizens of this part of the commonwealth, were any less deficient in interest for the general welfare of the whole state, than any other portion of it. The gentleman again says, that there is a want of knowledge of the interests of the state, by the citizens of the city and county of Philadelphia; and, that many of them, are totally ignorant of the number of miles of canal and rail road, which had been constructed by the state.

Why, he, Mr. B., might just as easily speak in this way of Luzerne, or any other county, for he presumed there were many citizens of that county, and every other county in the state who were uninformed as to the extent of the internal improvements of the state. This proved nothing. But he would assert that there was as much intelligence in the city and county of Philadelphia, as among the same number of persons in any other portion of the state. He would ask the gentleman to go to the small farmers of the county of Philadelphia, and see if they were not as intelligent as any other farmers in the state. He would ask the gentleman to go into the workshops of the mechanics, and see if they were not as intelligent as the mechanics or the farmers of Luzerne. Mr. B. ventured to assert that the gentleman would find as much intelligence on the smallest farm in the county of Philadelphia, as he would upon the largest in the county of Luzerne. This assumption of the gentleman's showed a want of knowledge of the people, whom he was about to deprive of their rights.

The gentleman asks where the revenue of the state is drawn from, and says that it is not drawn from Philadelphia, but from the consumers. Mr. B. would tell the gentleman that much of our revenue was not drawn even from Pennsylvania, immediately. When the merchants of Ohio, and the south-western states, come to Philadelphia, and purchase goods of our merchants, and have them transported along our rail roads and canals, he would ask if they were paying a portion of the revenue of our state and bringing substantial wealth to the soil of Pennsylvania? Pennsylvania draws a revenue from nearly every state in the Union. Even assuming that it is the consumers who pay the revenue, and the gentleman will find that much, very much of it, is paid by merchants out of what they have drawn from the merchants and consumers of the other states. Pennsylvania draws revenue from New Orleans through the vast valley of the Mississippi, in consequence of her internal improvements. Pennsylvania draws wealth from Delaware, New Jersey, Maryland, Virginia, and all the southern states. Well, sir, the means of drawing this wealth from the other states, is concentrated in the city and county of Philadelphia, and was she to be deprived of a voice in the councils of the nation, because her citizens were not so pure, as the gentleman alleges, as the people of the interior ?

Was this the love the gentleman had for Philadelphia ? If so, he trusted he should long be saved from the embraces of such affection. He did hope this morning, that this question would not again be brought upon us. Any attempt to deprive Philadelphia of her equal rights, or to disparage the character of her citizens, must beget unpleasant feelings, and he should say that any man who would sit quietly by, and hear the character of his fellow citizens traduced in this way, was unworthy to be called a Pennsylvanian. He should never submit to it, and the moment it was done, he should defend his fellow citizens to the best of his ability.

Mr. MCAHEN moved to insert after the words " three senators,' the words " unless a city or county shall be entitled to more."

The CHAIR ruled this amendment to be out of order

Mr. M'CAHEN had hoped that the amendment made in committee of the whole, would have been retained, but unfortunately the views of the gentleman from Franklin, in this instance, prevailed.

IIe, Mr. M'C. could readily perceive, that by this amendment the city might not be injured, while the county of Philadelphia would be deprived of her rights. The city of Philadelphia being confined within narrow limits, will, perhaps, never be entitled to four senators, but the county of Philadelphia, being some thirty or forty miles in circumference may increase in population, in a short time, to be entitled to more than four senators; consequently, it would only be the county of Philadelphia which would be injured by the amendment.

The amendment of the gentleman from Luzerne, would make it still worse, and he was sorry that that gentleman had thought proper to intro· duce this amendment. He should be sorry to see any other county in the state deprived of its just representation in the senate of the state, and he hoped that the county of Philadelphia would be permitted to retain what she was entitled to by the number of her taxable inhabitants. He looked upon the senate of the state as a part of the legislature, and derived from the same source with the popular branch. He took it for granted that we were to be represented according to taxation, and not according to territory. It was one of the established principles of our government that representation shall have its basis on taxation, and he did hope that gentlemen would reflect well on this subject before they gave their votes for the amendment of the gentleman from Luzerne; and he hoped the convention, in this act, would not do injustice to a portion of their fellow-citizens in Pennsylvania, who had the interests of Pennsylvania as much at heart as any other portion of her citizens. The city and county were entitled to a large representation, because they paid a large tax, and contributed largely to the support of the government. There was a vast amount of the revenue of the state derived from the city and county of Philadelphia, and why should they be deprived of having a proper weight in the senate of your state? The city and county were very much interested in this question, and he hoped their interests would not be disregarded in this body. He hoped also, that this convention would not follow the aristocratic example of the constitution of the United States in this respect, which gave to Delaware as great a voice in the senate of the United States, as New York. Delaware, Arkansas, Michigan, and Missouri, united perhaps, did not contain a population equal to that of New York; yet those states in the senate of the United States, had four times as much weight as New York; but he trusted that no such doctrine would be advocated, in relation to a Pennsylvania senate. We wish to stand here upon the republican principle of equal representation, and we hope equal justice will be dealt out to all men, and to all parts of the state. We ask for equal representation in every branch of the government, and we ask for no more.

It had been suggested, however, that the party now in power in the county, might, in the course of time, be out of power, and therefore, we ought not to advocate our cause so strenuously. This he hoped never to see realized, but even if it should, he would still be unwilling to submit to the injustice which would be done the county. Whatever party was in power, he wished her to have her full weight in the halls of legislation, both state and federal. He hoped, therefore, that the amendment would not prevail; but if it should, he gave notice now, that he would present the amendment he had suggested at the commencement of his remarks, in order that the county of Philadelphia may obtain her just rights.

Mr. Earle said, that it seemed we were to have every thing acted over again here, which we acted in Harrisburg. We had there abundance of party discussions, and discussions in relation to the city and county, and had the county of Philadelphia attacked and abused, and now the same thing was to be done over again. We had hardly taken our seats at Harrisburg, before the county of Philadelphia was attacked. Now, he was one of those persons who never meddled in those sectional attacks, and he only spoke when it was necessary to make defence, and he would not now have risen, had it not been to express his abhorrence of the doctrines advanced by the gentleman from Luzerne, and to call the attention of the convention to the consequences to which those doctrines would lead, if we adhere to them. He would tell the gentleman, that if he adhered to those doctrines, he would be precisely where the gentleman from Northampton, the other day, predicted he would be.

What are the principles upon which the doctrines of the gentleman from Luzerne are founded? They are the very principles on which the aristocracies of Greece and Rome were established. His principle is, that the best men shall govern, and this was the aristocratic principle of ancient governments. Well, how are we to know who are the best men? The gentleman denies that my constituents are entitled to as great privileges in our legislative halls as his own constituents, because his constituents are wiser and more moral than mine. Who invested the gentleman from Luzerne, with authority to decide upon the morals and the intelligence of the people of Philadelphia? If the gentleman would take the trouble to cross the state line, into some of the neighboring states, he would find plenty of persons who would join him in saying that there was a great deal of ignorance and want of education in Pennsylvania, but ask the citizens of those states where that ignorance was, would they say it was in Philadelphia? He thought not. He took it, they would say it was in the interior of the country, among the mountains of Luzerne, or in some other interior settlements; and he would find no where any person to assert that there was a greater mass of ignorance in Philadelphia, than in other portions of the state. Mr. E. did not charge any other portion of the state with being more ignorant than Philadelphia, but the gentleman from Luzerne, would find that this was the prevailing opinion throughout the United States.

In relation to the morality of Philadelphia, he believed the people here were just as moral as they were in any other portion of the state. He did not say that they were more so, but he would not admit that they were any less moral. But the gentleman says that some of my constituents do not know the number of miles of canal and rail road in Pennsylvania. Now he expected if the gentleman was to put this question to many of his own constituents, he would find them just as ignorant on this point, as any citizens of Philadelphia. Furthermore, he believed if the gentleman were to rest his election upon those who were best informed, on the subject of canals and rail roads, that he would always be defeated, because he expected the political party opposed to him, were better informed on this subject than his own party. The opposition party in the gentleman's county, he suspected had more book learning than the party which supported him. But in case the county of Philadelphia increased in numbers, so as to entitle her to ten senators, would the gentleman say that she must not have more than three, and that the other seven must be given to counties with not the-one twentieth part of the taxable inhabitants? This was an unsound and anti-democratic principle, which never could prevail in this country.

The influence of wealth is not to be entirely restrained, and any thing else is just as much entitled to influence as barren acres. If mere territory is to be the basis of representation, let us see what the principle would lead us to, if carried out. The acres of rocks and barren soil, without any people, would be represented, instead of the towns, villages and cities, which are teeming with life, energy and resources. The true principle of representation is to be found in the old constitution of 1776. That constitution is founded upon the doctrines of the patriots of 1776. Their principle was, that man is man; and when we depart from that, the true republican principle, we can no longer possess a free representative government. Man is man, and all are equally entitled to protection, though some may not have so much wealth, or so much learning as others. The principle of representation, according to population, is dear to freemen, and to republicans. The federalists have endeavored to dispute, but he hoped no one possessing republican principles, will ever maintain, any thing contrary to this doctrine. We have hung high our banner of equal rights, and manfully maintained our principles, through so many trials, and so many contests, we will not now easily surrender them.

John Adams, Mr. Webster, Mr. Everett, and others of the federal school, went for the principle of representation according to property. He had never heard that this principle was maintained by any except the federal party. The doctrine had prevailed, not only in Massachusetts, but in New York and elsewhere. It had been advanced by Chancellor Kent, and Judge Spencer, and had been also ably supported by Alexander Hamilton, and Robert Morris, in the convention which sat in this city. I deny that wealth ought to confer upon a man any more or any less influence, than other men without wealth, are entitled to. I deny, too, that the people who live in woods and mountains, are any better entitled to the franchises of free men, than those who pursue their avocations in the cities. The city of Philadelphia, now believes herself to have been deprived of one senator, to which she was fairly entitled; and by this act, both the city and the county of Philadelphia are to be in future deprived of the fair proportion of senatorial representatives, to which they will be entitled by their population. The rule of population, if just, must be applicable to every district in the state. It will be impossible and unjust to make one rule for one district, in one part of the state, and another rule for another district, in another part of the state. The same principle of representation must be applied to all districts, whether composed of rural or city population. I ask for the city and county of Philadelphia, only their due share of representation, according to their population, and this they are entitled to, only unless you fix some other basis of representation than population. But there is no other basis which will receive the assent of republicans. I ask, then, for the city and county of Philadelphia only their due share of legislative influence, and that, and no more; I hope they will obtain. We shall be obliged, after all, to come to some system that will prevent an unfair distribution of representatives; and he was willing, in regard to the limitation of the number of senators, to be elected from each district, that it should stand where the old constitution has put it. He was willing that the number should be restricted to four, provided some clause were adopted, to prevent gerrymandering.

Mr. Woodward would not, he said, have risen again, but to explain the principle on which the amendment had been offered. He had never, he said, advocated the principle of representation according to territory. On the contrary, he had expressly stated he was in favor of the principle of taxable population, as the basis of representation. But, as to the senate, he had shown that the principle of popular representation had been modified and qualified by the present constitution, and he had, for the same reasons which actuated the framers of the present constitution, proposed some additional modification of the principle. He wished, also, to disclaim all party sympathy in regard to this question. His friends from the county of Philadelphia must excuse him, if he declined acting here as the partizan of the whig party, or of the democratic party. They must excuse him for not yielding to the force of party appeals on this subject. He had moved the amendment under the sincere belief that it was right, according to the principles of the present constitution, the principles of true republicanism, and the interests of the whole people of the commonwealth, for which we are bound to provide. The gentlemen who have opposed it, had better convince him that it was wrong in principle, than merely to denounce it. I took that course in this matter, which seemed right in my own judgment and conscience, and not that course which I supposed would best suit the politicians of the country or those elsewhere.

Mr. Porter, of Northampton, said, his friend from Philadelphia county, had brought him in rather oddly. He had represented him as being opposed to the rearing up of Manchesters and Birminghams. Northampton might turn out a few of them, and perhaps he might, therefore, be in favor of them. He had supported the principle that every man was entitled to equal rights in the government of the state, and for that reason, he was opposed to the proposition now before the convention.

Mr. Biddle said, he was sorry that the gentlemen who had introduced and supported this proposition were now weary of the debate. The principles of the discussion were too important not to call forth some further reply to what had been said.

He regretted that the gentleman from Luzerne did not rest satisfied with the decision of the morning. But the delegates from Philadelphia, now ask to be heard on a question which so deeply affects her rights and interests. The gentleman asked whence Philadelphia derived her strength? He says from the state. I cordially concur with him that the interests of the city and the state are so bound up together, that what gives a blow to one, injuriously affects the other. But the argument went to shew a common interest, and no reason why Philadelphia should be excluded from her fair share of representation. What rule does the gentleman propose, by which large cities and populous counties shall be represented? Has he any other rule than taxation and representation? What rule does the gentleman propose? Property? That he disclaims. Intellect? There is no measure for it. He proposes an arbitrary and partial rule. If we are to have a new rule of representation, let us have a permanent, and equal, and just one.

The arbitrary rule of reducing the representation of certain districts, which he suggests, is not one of that equal and universal character which can be adopted for the government of a great commonwealth like this. The principle was well considered and settled this morning. Gentlemen have given us no new rule, and the old rule of taxation and population is a just and equal one, and I trust the convention will stand by it. After what has been said in disparagement of the people of large towns, I cannot take my seat without bearing testimony to the orderly and quiet manners and virtuous habits of the people of the city and county of Philadelphia. I trust that no one will descend so low as to make this a party question.

Mr. FULLER, of Fayette, said he would congratulate the gentlemen from the city and the county of Philadelphia on the probability of their coming together, at last, upon one question. He did not consider that there was any principle involved in the question now presented by the amendment offered by the gentleman from Luzerne.

The question was merely whether the limitation should be three senators for each district or four? The constitution of 1790, restricts the number to four, and gentlemen who oppose the amendment are willing to let it stand at four. Whether the restriction should be reduced to three or not was, therefore, one of expediency merely, and not of principle. No district can, if the section remain unaltered, elect more than one senator. There was more plausibility in the proposition of the gentleman from Luzerne than the gentlemen from the city and county were disposed to admit. It appeared to him that, as the city and county of Philadelphia would have no fractions in the apportionment, and as they were compact, and well known by their representatives, they could be adequately represented by a less number of representatives, in proportion to the population, than a large and thinly peopled district. Some districts were from one to two hundred miles in extent, and it was very difficult for one man to represent them satisfactorily and impartially. One senator could hardly be acquainted with all the interests and concerns of a large district. It has been urged, therefore, that the districts ought to be made smaller, in order that they may be satisfactorily represented. The district of Centre and Lycoming is from one to two hundred miles in extent, and was inadequately represented in comparison with Philadelphia

Another advantage which the city and county had in their senatorial representation was, that the fractions lost in the districts which were composed of two or more counties, were there saved. The aggregate of the fractions lost by the northern and western counties, was very large; and, as the city and county lost nothing in this way, it followed that they had the advantage in the representation now over the northern and western counties.

There was, therefore, some ground for the proposition to reduce the limitation of the senatorial representation from four to three senators for each district. He was not, however, going to advocate the doctrine that territory ought to be represented. The amendment presented precisely the same principles with the provision of the present constitution, and there appeared to be very plausible reasons in favor of its adoption. He was disposed to vote for it; and, whether it prevailed or not, he did hope that we should take the vote, and pass to the next section.

Mr. FLEMING, of Lycoming, said, if the proposition of the gentleman from Luzerne went to decrease the size of the senatorial districts, he would vote for it. It did appear to him, that it was necessary and proper to take this step. The senatorial district which he represented was composed of no less than six counties. It was utterly impossible, as he had heretofore taken occasion to say, for one senator to become acquainted with the local wants and interests of so large a district. Look at the territory of this district. It comprises one-fourth of the commonwealth. Is it the business of a single week or of a month to become acquainted with the concerns of so many and such large counties? He was confident that the senatorial districts were not so framed as to conduce to the best interests of the people. If we reduced the size of the senatorial districts, it would place the north-eastern counties on a much better footing, in proportion to the city than the eastern counties. With respect to the character of the people of the city and county, he had nothing to do with that subject. He had found the people both of the city and county intelligent, kind and patriotic, but not more so than the people in the country. He would not concede to the inhabitants of the city or of any of the eastern counties, a claim for any superiority in these respects.

It had been urged, on this floor, that on account of the dense population of the county, and the enormous sums they pay in the shape of taxes, they ought to have advantages in reference to representation. They had had them already, although some gentlemen denied the fact. Now, if gentlemen would take the trouble to look back to the different apportionment bills, they would find that the eastern counties had, at all times, a greater share of representation, in proportion to numbers, than other portions of the commonwealth—than the north-western counties. All he desired was, that all the counties might be put on an equal footing. At present, he felt that this advantage would continue over the counties to which he had referred. They felt that their destiny was in the hands of the eastern portion of the state.

In the legislative halls we must act with the members from the city and county, if we wished to get any thing. It was found impossible to carry any measure in the councils of the state, without the aid of the eastern counties. We had been told that the city and county had stepped forward and assisted us—that it was to them we should be grateful in the matter of public improvements. Without desiring to disparage the motives of the citizens of the city and county, he would venture to say, that they never lost sight of their own interests. No doubt, their representatives acted quite independently, on many occasions, in voting for improvements in which they had no direct interest. And, while he said this, and wished to attribute no other than good motives to them, he, at the same time, could not give his assent to the city and county having a greater representation in the legislature than they were really and justly entitled to. He trusted that as facts had been brought home to the convention, showing that the counties of Lycoming, Centre, and others, had not heretofore had their proportionate share of representation, while other portions of the commonwealth had, that justice would now be done them.

Mr. CHANDLER, of Philadelphia, said he trusted that the convention would now see who it was that entertained so wonderful a regard for the "democracy of numbers." It had been charged here that the city and county of Philadelphia manifested a desire to obtain a representation beyond what they were really entitled to. He disclaimed any such wish on the part of the city; and with respect to the county, the charge had been fully refuted and shown to be entirely unfounded. He was sure there was not a man in the city or county that would wish to represent either, unless he was satisfied that those who elected him were entitled to send him to the legislature. It had been said, that the counties in the western and northern parts of the state were not properly represented. He could not say that any injustice had been done to them and thought that his friend from Lycoming, (Mr. Fleming) must have made an inaccurate calculation with respect to the proportion of representatives to which the city and county and the other counties of the state, were now entitled. The citizens of Philadelphia claimed no extraordinary intelligence or honesty above other portions of the state; but, on the contrary, were proud to be held in the same estimation.

He was astonished, and much regretted that, any delegate should have attempted to draw any distinction between the morality of the citizens of Philadelphia and those living in the interior. He (Mr. C.) asked to make no such invidious distinction, nor did he desire that any should be drawn. A gentleman who had preceded the delegate from Lycoming, suggested that three representatives would represent any county or city in the state quite as well as four.

Now, he (Mr. C.) would admit that if three of the most eloquent men were to be selected, and the question to be decided by their eloquence, then three would be equal to four. He, however, should not like to see any distinction of that sort made. The people had a right to elect whom they thought proper, whether he was a speaker or not. The man who did not possess the faculty of speaking, might, nevertheless, render his constituents great service by the use of his vote. This was the first time, in his life, that he had ever heard that social intercourse—that a combination of numbers produced narrow feeling. If that was the case then the whole current of life must have changed. If the eastern part of the state joined with the southern, as doubtless they did, it was to be presumed they acted for the best interests of the commonwealth. Philadelphia has done all that has been required of her, all that could be asked of her, in promoting the internal improvements and interests of the commonwealth, not by any means for her own exclusive benefit, but for the good of the whole state.

He apprehended that nothing would be more dangerous to the commonwealth than that it should be represented by territory instead of numbers. It certainly could not be right that the wilds of Warren, Tioga, &c. should be represented in preference to mind and intellect. He trusted that the advocates of representation by territory would not, after this, charge their opponents with being influenced by narrow views and local prejudices. Every Philadelphian would be found to be a Pennsylvanian in heart and feeling.

Mr. C. asked for the yeas and nays ; which were ordered.

The question was taken on the amendment, and it was decided in the negative—yeas 15 ; nays 99.

YEAS—Messrs. Barclay, Bedford, Crain, Cummin, Fleming, Grenell, Keim, Scheetz, Sellers, Smith, of Columbia, Smyth, of Centre, Sterigere, Stickel, Sturde-vant, Woodward—15.

NAYS—Messrs. Agnew, Baldwin, Banks, Barndollar, Bell, Biddle, Bigelow, Bonham, Brown, of Lancaster, Brown, of Northampton, Brown, of Philadelphia, Carey, Chambers, Chandler, of Chester, Chandler, of Philadelphia, Chauncey, Clark,of Dauphin, Carke, of Indiana, Cleavinger, Cline, Coates, Cochran, Cope, Craig, Crawford, Crum, Cunningham, Curll, Darlington, Darrah, Denny, Dickey, Dickerson, Dillinger, Donagan, Donnell, Doran, Earle, Farrelly, Forward, Foulkrod, Fry, Fuller, Gamble, Gearhart, Gilmore, Harris, Hastings, Hayhurst, Hays, Hen-derson, of Allegheny, Hiester, High, Hopkinson, Houpt, Hyde, Jenks, Kennedy, Kerr, Konigmacher, Krebs, Long, Lyons, Maclay, Magee, Mann, Martin, M'Cahen, M'Call, M'Dowell, M'Sherry, Meredith, Merkel, Miller, Pennypacker, Pollock, Porter, of Lancaster, Porter, of Northampton, Purviance, Read, Riter, Ritter, Royer, Russell, Saeger, Scott, Seltzer, Serrill, Shellito, Sill, Snively, Taggart, Thomas, Todd, Weaver, Wiedman, White, Young, Sergeant, *President*—99.

Mr. BELL moved to amend the section by striking therefrom, after the word " legislature," in the second line, the words "each district contain-ing such a number of taxable inhabitants, as shall be entitled to elect not more than four senators," and inserting in lieu thereof the following, viz : " but no district shall be so formed as to entitle it to elect more than two senators, unless the number of taxable inhabitants in any city or county shall, at any time, be such as to entitle it to elect more than two ; but, no city or county shall be entitled to elect more than four senators "

The PRESIDENT said it was his opinion that this was contrary to what had been decided by the convention, and he, therefore, decided it to be out of order.

Mr. BELL said that with perfect respect for the opinion of the Chair, and in order to obtain the sense of the convention on this important ques-tion, he would beg leave to appeal.

The PRESIDENT stated the question, and said that his decision was that the motion was not in order, because it was directly contrary to what had been decided by the convention.

Mr. READ moved an adjournment. Lost.

Mr. STERIGERE said he thought the mode of proceeding very unimpor-tant in this case ; but, he suggested the withdrawing of the appeal, and putting it to the sense of the convention whether the amendment should be offered or not.

Mr. BELL said it was of little consequence in what way the sense of the convention was reached. If a majority of the convention was in favor of having the amendment offered they would sustain the appeal.

Mr. BELL spoke in support of the appeal.

Mr. STERIGERE made some remarks on the same side. The gentleman in his opinion, was clearly entitled to have the amendment received.

Mr. READ expressed his opinion that the motion was in order, and gave his reasons in support of this opinion. ·

The PRESIDENT further explained the grounds of the decision, and, without taking the question,

On motion of Mr. CHAMBERS,

The convention adjourned.

FRIDAY, JANUARY 5, 1838.

UNFINISHED BUSINESS.

The convention resumed the consideration of the memorial presented from twenty-three citizens of Berks county, constituting the grand jury of that county, at the present court of quarter sessions, praying that the convention do adjourn forthwith, *sine die.*

The question being on the motion of Mr. PURVIANCE, of Butler, that the said memorial be rejected.

Mr. DICKEY, of Beaver, resumed his remarks. In looking over the petition, he saw that it purported to be from citizens of Berks county. If hese citizens are acting in the capacity of grand inquest of the county, or not, he did not know. This had nothing to do with the endorsement. The signers came from the body of the inhabitants, and had a right, not to be disputed, to petition for the redress of grievances. There was no just ground, if the allegations are true, for the rejection of the memorial. It was only yesterday that he had seen a notice which had been published by the secretary calling on all those persons who had accounts against the convention to send them in for examination. So extravagant had been the expenditures of this body, that the disbursing officer no longer knew who had claims against it. And what will our labours amount to? We see one unrighteous proposition submitted after another, until the whole will be so unpalatable, that when the amendments come before the people, they will be rejected on account of the radical character of the propositions inserted by this convention—propositions which are brought forward here, clothed with the authority of a caucus recommendation. After the gentleman from Susquehanna had discussed the subject of the banks, and the propositions he brought forward, with a view to political and party effect, he sent his speech throughout the state in English and German. And after they had been the subject of debate for five or six weeks here,—he ha finally withdrawn, after previously modifying, them so as completely to change their character. The petitioners have a right to think, because the whole country thinks, that our course of proceedings will have a deleterious effect on the business interests of Pennsylvania. They say—"the resolution which has been adopted, there is reason to expect may be rescinded." They have a right to say so, because there has been already an attempt to rescind it.

They have a right to tell us to adjourn, and we have a right to reject their petition. If their language is respectful, they have a right to send their petition here: and he would call on the gentleman from Berks, (Mr. Keim) to say if the petitioners are not respectable, or of what complexion they are. It was suggested by that gentleman that this was a packed jury.

Mr. KEIM begged leave to explain. He denied that he had applied the phrase to this jury. He found that there was a fraud on the face of the petition. It purported to be from the grand inquest of the county: yet he found, on reference, that it had not the names of those persons who were on the grand jury. He was not bound to defend such a paper.

Mr. DICKEY resumed. If he was in error in designating that the gentleman had applied this language to the grand jury, he had erred with many others, and with the reporters for the daily newspapers. How do gentlemen desire this petition to be treated? Is the record on the journal to be *expunged*, after the fashion of the United States Senate? Is it to be circumscribed by black lines, and written across? Because to reject the petition would be useless. Gentlemen ask us to reject the petition, in order to sustain the dignity of the convention. The best mode would be to receive the petition. Its language is more respectful than that of the people of Pittsburg which was received; and will you treat the respectable citizens of Berks worse than you treated the people of Pittsburg?

Mr. M'DOWELL, of Bucks, said he felt no great difficulty about this petition, or to any thing which was contained in the paper: and he did not know why the convention should be so sensitive in receiving, or disposing of, a paper said to reflect on this body. He had heard the petition read twice, and it did not appear to him to be one-fortieth so bad in its language as that which members use daily on this floor, in reference to each other. It becomes a matter of dignity if we slander each other, but the people are not to be permitted to send back an echo to it. Even the gentleman from Beaver (and I suspect, said Mr. M'D. he suggested their paper!) finds here the same language which he addressed to the convention some six weeks ago, and no wonder he is in favor of the petition. This is a bill of indictment sent by the grand inquest and all we have to do is to answer it—he was not bound to point out how we should answer. The gentleman from Beaver need not be so anxious to receive the petition, for he will be the first to be convicted. But there was a difficulty arising out of the explanation of the gentleman from Berks, and which might make it proper that the petition should not be received. Are these persons not the grand inquest of the county?

Mr. KEIM replied that there were names attached to it which were not in the list of the grand jury.

Mr. M'DOWELL. Then it is a fraud, and intended as such, and ought not to be received.

Mr. PORTER of Northampton, said he would read the letter inclosing the petition, which he had already shown to the two delegates of Berks, who had stated that it was from a respectable source. [Mr. Porter then read the letter.] He was told that the writer of this letter was a respectable citizen of Reading, and a member of the grand jury. That it was no hoax, he had satisfied himself. But he had not seen any list of the grand jury.

Mr. DARLINGTON, of Chester. The question was, if the petition should be rejected? His vote would depend on certain facts which he wished to understand. It purported to be from the grand jury. The delegate from Berks had said, they are not all names of persons on the grand jury. He would be glad if that gentleman would point out such names as are on the grand jury. He had not been able to discover any thing disrespectful in the language of the petition. Why should the gentleman from Butler, (Mr. Purviance,) and the gentleman from Susquehanna (Mr. Read) wish to reject the petition, and thus to show to the people that we are testy and ill-tempered? We should better sustain our dignity by pursuing a different course. He did not desire to occupy the time of the convention. Would the gentleman from Berks say what names are not on the grand jury?

Mr. COX, of Somerset, said he did not know if gentlemen signed this petition who are not members of the grand jury. There was a gentleman, who was a near relation of the gentleman from Berks, here yesterday, who had said these were the names of the grand inquest, and that it spoke the sense of a majority of the citizens of the respectable county of Berks. The petition said nothing about grand jurors. The body of the petition is all he cared about. If the signers are freemen of Berks and American citizens, they had a right to memorialize the convention. They had a constitutional right to do what was essential to the rights of the people; and if we despise their petition, would it not be assuming constitutional right on the subject of dignity? Are we to reject a petition because it is not pleasing to every body? No man will assume that there is any thing untrue in the petition—that time has not been uselessly expended on the bank question—that tens of thousands have not been wasted on what the movers knew would be rejected. Will any gentleman say it is undignified to receive this petition because it contains solemn truths? Shall we reject it, because the endorsement on the back states that it is from the grand inquest of the county, when there is not a word in the body of the petition that indicates such to be the fact? He agreed with the gentleman from Chester, that to reject the petition would be to set ourselves up as masters of the people. He would not consent to receive any memorial which was disrespectful in its language, but this was not obnoxious to any such objection.

Mr. HIESTER, of Lancaster, could not, he said, but express his surprise at the motion of the gentleman from Butler, (Mr. Purviance) to reject the memorial, and the motion of the gentleman from the county of Philadelphia, (Mr. Martin) to throw it under the table. The right of petition was a sacred and inviolable right, and had been so held by the people of this commonwealth. The people were secured in the right of peaceably assembling together and addressing petitions and memorials to their constituted bodies. As long as those petitions were couched in decorous language, we were compelled to receive them and treat them with consideration and respect. The right of petition was granted both by the constitution of the United States and of the state of Pennsylvania. Under the constitution of this state the people have a right to apply to those invested with the power of government for redress of grievances or other proper purposes, by petition address, or remonstrance ; and for the convention, while revising this constitution, to treat a right so sacred with contempt, would be very extraordinary. The members of this convention have exerted their very right as citizens since they assembled here.

He had seen some petitions to congress signed by members of this body. While we claimed the right for ourselves, we ought to allow it, in its proper extent, to others. It is said that the petition does not come from a responsible and respectable quarter, and that it is disrespectful to the convention. What is the fact? It is said that there is nothing in the body of the petition indicating the source from which it comes. But that is not strictly the case, because it purports to come from the grand jury of Berks county. On the back of the paper is an endorsement stating that the paper is the petition of the grand jury of the county of Berks, in the commonwealth of Pennsylvania. The reason that the petition came not from a responsible and known source, therefore failed altogether. We know the men who signed it as holding the responsible situation of a grand jury in an intelligent and respectable county in this state, and unless we had some other reason for rejecting the petition or treating it with contempt, it was incumbent upon us to receive it and give it a proper consideration. Again, it is charged that the memorial is couched in disrespectful terms. What there is disrespectful in it towards this body I cannot see. If there is any thing disrespectful in it, I request the gentlemen who make the objection, to point it out, as I have not been able to find it. It appears to me that the memorial is objectionable to gentlemen on account of its truth. That is probably the true reason why it is so offensive to this body. This is generally the case with those who refuse to receive petitions. The idea of rejecting or contemptuously treating a petition was never heard of in this country till lately, and it first came from some of our high-toned southern friends, who heard through some memorials addressed to congress, truths which were offensive to their ears. They took the ground that the petitioners had no right to argue upon the subject, or make any statements about it. But such a doctrine is a very novel one for Pennsylvania. I took the memorial to the gentleman from Berks, who had knowledge of the facts concerning it, and ascertained from him that twenty-two of the signers of the memorial are members of the grand jury, and two are not. It had been said that there was something fraudulent in the manner of getting up and addressing the petition, but it does not appear that this is a fact. It is a fact that twenty-two grand jurors signed the paper, according to its purport. In regard to the responsibility of the signers, I have the pleasure of knowing the majority of them, and can safely assure the convention of their entire respectability. Some of them are doctors, other merchants, iron-makers, and farmers. As to the political complexion of the signers, when analyzed, it would be found, that twelve of the signers were in favor of the election of govern____ ___ and that eight were for Van Buren. The politics of the other ___ ___ not known here. Can gentlemen then call them a packed ___ ___ party men or men unknown or irresponsible? No ___ respectable men of the county and are made up of all parties. I can see no reason, therefore, why their petition should not receive all that respect and attention which the constitution guaranties to petitions, addresses, and remonstrances sent from citizens to their constituted authorities, for the redress of grievances, or upon any proper subject.

Mr. FULLER regretted, he said, to see so much of the valuable time of this body spent upon so profitless a subject as this, at this late period of the session of this convention, and he hoped the discussion would be brought to a speedy close. Inasmuch as the petition has been received by this body, and made the subject of consideration, it cannot be now rejected. Though the doubts entertained as to the genuineness of the petition were proved to be well founded, yet if it appeared that the petitioners were citizens, their petition must be received. Whether they are actually what they represent themselves to be, the members of the grand jury of Berks county or not, we are well assured that they are citizens of Berks county, and, as such, they have a right to address any public body constituted by the citizens. The petition ought not to be rejected nor treated with contempt, as some have proposed to do, whether its sentiments were agreeable to us as a body or not.

He regretted that the gentleman from Beaver, (Mr. Dickey) who had always expressed a strong disposition to terminate the labor of this body, had contributed to prolong this discussion, at the expense of the time of the convention, by the introduction into it of the subject of politics. If every individual matter brought before us is to be discussed as a party question, there can be no end to unnecessary and protracted debate. The gentleman from Beaver is no doubt in earnest when he expresses a strong desire to bring the session to a close, but he must be sensible that his course tends strongly to the unnecessary protraction of the session. We must vote more and speak less, if we wish to hasten the day of adjournment. I move, sir, the indefinite postponement of the whole subject.

Mr. READ moved the previous question, and the main question was ordered to be put.

The main question, "shall the petition be rejected," was then put, and decided in the negative, yeas 9, nays 103, as follow :

YEAS—Messrs. Bell, Bigelow, Cummin, Magee, Mann, Meredith, Purviance, Read, Sturdevant—9.

NAYS—Messrs. Agnew, Baldwin, Banks, Barclay, Barndollar, Bedford, Biddle, Bonham, Brown, of Lancaster, Brown, of Northampton, Brown, of Philadelphia, Carey, Chambers, Chandler, of Chester, Chandler, of Philadelphia, Chauncey, Clarke, of Beaver, Clark, of Dauphin, Clarke, of Indiana, Cleavinger, Cline, Coates, Cope, Cox, Craig, Crain, Crawford, Crum, Cunningham, Curll, Darlington, Darrah, Denny, Dickey, Dickerson, Dillinger, Donagan, Donnell, Earle, Forward, Foulkrod, Fry, Fuller, Gamble, Gearhart, Grenell, Harris, Hastings, Hayhurst, Hays, Helffenstein, Henderson, of Allegheny, Henderson, of Dauphin, Hiester, High, Hopkinson, Houpt, Hyde, Ingersoll, Jenks, Keim, Kennedy, Kerr, Konigmacher, Krebs, Long, Lyons, Maclay, M'Cahen, M'Call, M'Dowell, M'Sherry, Merkel, Miller, Montgomery, Pennypacker, Pollock, Porter, of Lancaster, Porter, of Northampton, Riter, Ritter, Royer, Russell, Saeger, Scott, Seller, Seltzer, Serrill, Shellito, Sill, Smith, of Columbia, Smyth, of Centre, Snively, Sterigere, Stickel, Taggart, Thomas, Todd, Weaver, Weidman, Woodward, Young, Sergeant, President—103.

So the question was determined in the negative.

Mr. MEREDITH presented a memorial from citizens of Philadelphia, praying that the word "white" may be inserted in the constitution, so as to confine the elective franchise exclusively to the whites.

Mr. SELLERS presented three memorials from citizens of Montgomery county., praying that measures may be taken effectually to prevent all amalgamation between the white and coloured population, in regard to the government of this state.

And the said memorials were laid on the table.

Mr. WOODWARD asked leave to make an explanation upon a subject which had been before the convention. He had seen it stated, he said, that when a memorial which had been disposed of was presented, he said that he wished it withdrawn " as the petition of some bl·ckguards in his county." He must have applied the term blackguard to the petition and not to the petitioners.

Mr. KEIM also begged leave to make an explanation as to some remarks which had been attributed to him, by one of the newspaper reports of the proceedings, upon the petition from Berks county.

The remarks attributed to him did not convey his ideas and had a tendency to destroy his standing at home. The United States Gazette, as containing the report to which he alluded, and the accuracy of that report he denied. He hoped the gentleman connected with that respectable print would correct the erroneous statement of his remarks.

The PRESIDENT stated that the petition from Luzerne county came to the Chair, and upon looking at it, the Chair entertained no doubt that it was unfit to present, being in terms and in substance disrespectful to the convention. The minutes did not shew that it had been introduced. He presented it to the delegate from Luzerne, who, as well as others, concurred with him as to the impropriety of presenting it.

The memorial was on the President's table, and was at any gentleman's service, if he chose to present it.

Mr. CHANDLER, of the city of Philadelphia, remarked that the words attributed to the gentleman from Luzerne, and disavowed by him, were such as met his view ; but as the gentleman denied them, he was bound to suppose that he did not make them.

Mr. WOODWARD did not, he said, deny that he said the words or something like them, which might have made the impression upon others such as they did upon the reporters. But he did not recollect the words, and was certain that the approbious epithet attributed to him must have been applied to the character of the petition.

Mr. KEIM remarked that, in regard to the report of his remarks, they were so garbled as to present a very different meaning from that which he conveyed.

FIRST ARTICLE.

The convention resumed the second reading of the report of the committee to whom was referred the first article of the constitution, as reported by the committee of the whole.

The seventh section being still under consideration,

The question recurred upon the appeal taken by Mr. BELL from the decision of the President on Thursday, by which his motion to amend the seventh section was decided to be out of order.

Mr. MEREDITH said as the discussion of the question of order would necessarily occupy some time, he would suggest, though he believed the decision of the Chair to be correct, that the gentleman from Chester had better withdraw the appeal and leave the question to the house.

Mr. BELL then withdrew the appeal, expressing the hope that the Chair would submit the question.

The PRESIDENT put the question to the convention whether the amendment proposed to be offered by the gentleman from Chester should be received.

It was decided in the affirmative.

Mr. BELL then moved to amend the section by striking therefrom after the word "legislature," in the second line, the words " each district containing such a number of taxable inhabitants, as shall be entitled to elect not more than four senators," and inserting in lieu thereof the following, viz: "but no district shall be so formed as to entitle it to elect more than two senators, unless the number of taxable inhabitants in any city or county shall, at any time, be such as to entitle it to elect more than two ; but no city or county shall be entitled to elect more than four senators."

Mr. BELL said it would be perceived that the object of his amendment was to reduce the number of senators to be elected from each district, and to restrict the number from any district to four, no matter how great might become its population. The old constitutional restriction as to the number of senators to be chosen from any one district, would thus be preserved.

Much had been said in this debate as to the comparative intelligence and integrity of the rural population and the inhabitants of cities ; but, in general, it would be found that on the whole, men were much on a par in these respects. As to the interests of town and country, which had also been brought into the discussion, they could never be hostile to each other in point of fact, neither their interests nor their opinions could be hostile without the operation of prejudice upon them. The intelligence of a community was to be measured by its liberality, for prejudice was the result of ignorance. Both ignorance and prejudice would soon give way, so far as the interests of town and country in this state were concerned. This would be one of the great results of the interchange of opinion and intelligence produced by the system of internal improvement, now carried on by the combined strength of the state. These im'provements, while they bring the remotest sections of the state into close communication, will do away with those natural prejudices which have been the disgrace of Pennsylvania. What is the question now before us! It is simply whether, in one branch of the state legislature, one part of the state shall have the same political voice with other parts of the state, in proportion to its taxable population. We find that many sections of the state will join in resesting any partiality towards one section or any incroachment upon any one section. There was a kind of political equilibrium which it was necessary to maintain between different parts of the state. No one could look at the vast resources and interests of this great state without perceiving the importance of maintaining this equilibrium. We are not composed of a people of different interests and policy, but we form one great commonwealth. The interest of one section is the interest of all. How shall we best cherish and promote that system of policy and those feelings which will but tend to bring out and cherish our great resources, and prevent sectional jealousy and hostility? My proposition is simply this : that hereafter, as now, no senatorial district shall be entitled to elect more than four senators. The county of Philadelphia according to the present ratio, might, with its great and increasing population, be entitled to and send more than four. But it is evident that the ratio must hereafter be greatly increased both in the city and the county of Philadelphia and in the country districts. When the amount of the ratio was increased, it was not to be expected that Philadelphia city and county would suffer any inconvenience from the proposition now offered. It was not to be expected that the population of these districts would ever be so vastly increased as to be entitled, under the increased ratio, to more than four senators. No injustice could therefore be done by the proposed restriction to the city and county of Philadelphia, but it afforded a guaranty to the country districts that they should not, by any great accumulation of population in the city and county of Philadelphia, be made subject to their predominating influence in the senate as well as in the house of representatives. I pledge myself (said Mr. Bell,) to show that this proposition is nothing more than the plan proposed and intended by the framers of the constitution of 1790.

It was objected to, however, by some gentlemen from the county of Philadelphia and why? Why because their population might increase so that they would be entitled to more than four senators. If this ever should be the case, it must be at a very remote period from this. He cared not how fast the population of the county of Philadelphia increased, and he hoped it would increase much ; still it would not increase in so much greater proportion to the county, to give it that number of senators for a very considerable time. Gentlemen must recollect that we can have but thirty-three senators under the constitution. Then, as the number of taxable inhabitants increase, so must the ratio of representation increase ; and the county of Philadelphia must increase rapidly, indeed, to give her the number of senators which some gentlemen here seem to expect. It was not to be expected, in any event, that this would be the case. But, sir, what has the county of Philadelphia to complain of, even supposing that the convention does agree to the proposed amendment? Under every kind of circumstances with reference to population, the county of Philadelphia as connected with the city, will always have a very large representation in the hall of your Legislature, and they will always be able to prevent the adoption of any measures adverse to their interests. But again, suppose the population of the county of Philadelphia increases so rapidly, that within a few years, she will be entitled to more than four senators, she would be no loser by it, because in that case it would become her interest to have a division made of her territory. If it should so happen that she ever had inhabitants sufficient to entitle her to that number of senators, then a division of the county would become inevitable. Then, under no circumstances whatever, can the county of Philadelphia be injured by this amendment, as they will always have a large and overpowering representation in your legislative halls. Now, sir, on what grounds is this proposition rested? and what is proposed to be effected by it? Why, in the first place he proposed to engraft on the constitution of Pennsylvania a provision that no district composed of more than one county shall be entitled to elect more than two senators. Well, what was the object of this? Why, we have all heard a vast deal of complaint issuing from the people in different portions of the state through their representatives here, in relation to the last enumeration of representatives being a vicious and a bad enumeration. We have heard it asserted here, that the rights of the people, in many cases, were sacrificed; that districts were arranged to suit the political partisans then in power; and that, in short, thestate was gerrymandered; as we understand the term. The very district he represented was arranged in this way, with a view that the democratic vote of Montgomery county might be overwhelmed by the federal votes of Chester and Delaware; but unfortunately for the parties who made the arrangement the democratic vote of Montgomery overwhelmed the federal votes of the other counties. Now, this matter of gerrymandering was a thing said to have been done on more than one occasion, and the great object of his amendment was to prevent this from being done in future by either political party. This matter of gerrymandering was a thing which he knew little about, but he had been assured by gentlemen who held seats in the legislature of Pennsylvania, that it had been practiced there to an incredible extent; and it was not only believed to have taken place by a large majority of the members of this body, but nine-tenths of the people of Pennsylvania believed that the state had been gerrymandered. Then what did his amendment propose? It proposed, in some degree, to take it out of the power of the legislature of Pennsylvania to act dishonestly, if they ever have acted dishonestly in the appointment of senators of the state. It proposes that no district composed of more than one county shall elect more than two senators. By this means you prevent the throwing together of these counties, as the counties of Montgomery, Chester and Delaware, had been thrown together, for the purpose of sending to the senate of Pennsylvania, three senators of a particular party cast: and he was sure there could be no difficulty on this subject. In committee of the whole, he believed a similar provision received the vote of a large number of the members of the body, and he could not see how an objection could be raised against it from any quarter of the house on this ground, or in relation to this part of the amendment. He would then pass to the other branch of the amendment; that is, that no county shall be represented by more than four senators in the senate of the state. Well, what is the objection to this? Why, it is argued that it is anti-republican. This, however, Mr. B. denied.

Again: it was said to be unjust, with regard to some districts in the state. This he also denied, and pledged himself to prove that it was neither anti-republican, nor unjust. Gentlemen had argued stoutly that this proposition was anti-democratic in its character and unjust in its tendency; but he would prove by a reference to our own legislative bodies, and to the constitutions of the other states of this Union, that it was neither anti-democratic, nor unjust. What is our system and how is it made up? Why, gentlemen have told us that taxation is the basis of representation, and that we cannot depart from it, under any circumstances, without parting from what they are pleased to call a fundamental republican principle.

Now, he would say that our system was not, in reference to all bodies and under all circumstances, made up in this way. Our system is a system of checks and balances, and this had been said so often, and been so often proved here, that it was not necessary for him, also, to go into an argument to prove it. Our system, then, is a system of checks and balances ; and it was a want of those checks and balances which was a main objection against the constitution of 1776. The representation of Pennsylvania under the constitution of 1776, was based on taxation and population ; and because there was no check upon the popular branch, the people became dissatisfied with the system, and appointed a convention for the purpose of amending that constitution. That convention was called for the purpose of introducing into the system another body differing from the popular branch. The result of the labors of that convention was the adoption of the constitution of 1790, and by that constitution a select body was introduced into the government of the state to act as a check upon the sudden infatuations of the popular branch of your legislature. The object of creating this body was to act as a check upon the sudden ebulitions of passion or feeling, which might exist in the other branch of your legislature. Well, was he to be told that there was any thing anti-democratic in introducing that provision in the constitution, which provided a check upon the popular branch of the legislature ? Why was it that the senators had a term given them by the old constitution of four years, while the representatives had but one year ? Why, it was to remove them from the people, and to enable them to act as a check upon the other body. Well, was there any thing anti-democratic in this ? If so, then we have an anti-democratic feature in the constitution of Pennsylvania. If then, this was an anti-democratic feature in that constitution, why does not some gentleman move to strike it out, and have the senators elected for but one year ? Sir, no delegate who has proposed this and no man has the audacity to propose it. Then, this is not an anti-democratic feature, and the senate does differ from the popular branch of the legislature. It differs from it in being a more select body, and it differs from it in being elected for a longer term ; and the object of this is that it may form a check upon the other body. Is, then, the senate of Pennsylvania necessarily, and under all circumstances, to be based upon population and taxation ? He confessed that at present the legislature were known to consult the number of taxable inhabitants in making up their senatorial districts : but sir, the framers of the constitution of 1790, had an eye to a state of things when this system should be abandoned. The framers of the existing constitution had an eye to circumstances which might arise when it would be expedient to proper and depart from the basis of population and taxation in making up the number which were to compose the senate of Pennsylvania. In the first place, is it anti-democratic, under any circumstances, to depart from this basis ? If so, he would give up the point he was contending for, because he had always professed and practised upon democratic principles ever since he knew any thing of the science of politics and government. For the purpose of ascertaining the truth in relation to this matter, let us look at the provisions in the constitutions of other states, known to be republican and democratic in their formation ;

and in this respect she must not be told that other states were less democratic than Pennsylvania.

Sir, the constitutions of other states, upon this subject, as upon other
subjects of constitutional law, are safe authorities; and the experience of
other states, will be a safe guide for us.   In the state of New Hampshire,
taxation alone was the basis of their senatorial representatives, and not
population and taxation, as is said to be the basis in Pennsylvania.   The
state, by the constitution, was directed to be divided into twelve senatorial districts, and in making this division they were to be governed by the
number of taxable inhabitants. It was, therefore, not population and taxation which formed the senatorial basis in New Hampshire, but it was
taxation alone which formed the basis.   Well, again, in the constitution
of Delaw re, recently formed, the counties sent senators without any
reference to the number of taxables, or the amount of their population.
Well, is Delaware less democratic than Pennsylvania? In Virginia, in
the western portion of the state, one number of taxables entitle it to a senator, and in the eastern portion another number elects a senator.   In North
Carolina, each county is entitled to one representative, without reference to
taxation and without reference to population.   In South Carolina, the
districts were fixed in the constitution itself, without reference to taxation
or population : and in Georgia, there is one representative for every county.

Now, there were other constitutions which contained similar principles
to these but he presumed he had referred to a sufficient number to show
that this was neither a new nor an anti-democratic principle. How was it
in Pennsylvania, which was certainly a democratic state ?   Did any one
suppose that the framers of the constitution of 1790 never contemplated
that there should be a representation in the senate of the state, based upon
any thing except population ? He would undertake to show under the
constitution as it now existed and as it had existed for the last forty-seven
years, that it was anticipated that a state of things might arise when a
particular district should not be entitled to representation in proportion to
population.   By the sixth section of the existing constitution, it is provided that " the number of senators shall, at the several periods of making
the enumeration before mentioned, be fixed by the legislature and apportioned among the districts, formed as hereinafter directed, according to
the number of taxable inhabitants in each."

Now, if we were to take this provision alone, he admitted that the argument might be somewhat against him ; but when we come to construe a
constitution, we must take it as a whole.   Then, by the seventh section
immediately following, it is provided that " the senators shall be chosen
in districts, to be formed by the legislature, each district containing such
a number of taxable inhabitants, as shall be entitled to elect not more than
four senators."

If he were to stop here, he might, perhaps, have but little ground
for his argument, because the districts might be so divided as to avoid the
necessity of having more than four senators in a district ; and a city and
county which might have more inhabitants than would entitle it to more
than four senators, might be divided, but when you take the subsequent
part of the section, in connection with the preceding one, there could not
be a doubt as to the meaning of the framers of the constitution of 1790.
The subsequent part of the seventh section is as follows :

" When a district shall be composed of two or more counties, they shall be adjoining ; neither the city of Philadelphia, nor any county shall be divided in forming a district."

Look at the language of this clause, and then say whether it is not conclusive that it looked to a period when representation in the senate should not be in proportion to population.   At the time that provision was adopted, it was known that the population of the city and county of Philadelphia might increase to such an extent that they would be entitled to more than four senators.   But, with this knowledge, they declared that neither the city of Philadelphia nor any county shall be divided in forming a district.   Then, was it not evident that the framers of the constitution did contemplate a period when representation in the senate should not be based upon population ?

Well, sir, how was it with regard to the popular branch ?   You find with regard to the lower house, that there is a provision which compels the legislature, in apportionments, to look to population alone as the basis of representation.   There was no such provision in relation to the lower house as there was with respect to the senate.   Taking all the circumstances into consideration he, would submit to the convention whether the framers of the existing constitution did not look to a time when the basis of representation in the senate should not be population alone.   He trusted, therefore, that his amendment might be adopted, as his only object was to prevent gerrymandering of the state, and, to have all interests properly represented in her councils.

Mr. STERIGERE called for the yeas and nays on Mr. Bell's amendment; which were ordered, and were yeas 68, nays 48, as follow, viz :

YEAS—Messrs. Banks, Barclay, Bedford, Bell, Bigelow, Bonham, Brown, of Northampton, Brown, of Philadelphia, Chandler, of Chester, Clarke, of Indiana, Cleavinger, Cline, Crain, Crawford, Crum, Cummin, Curll, Darlington, Darrah, Dillinger, Donagan, Donnell, Doran, Earle, Fleming, Foulkrod, Fry, Fuller, Gamble, Gearhart, Gilmore, Grenell, Harris, Hastings, Hayhurst, Helffenstein, Hiester, High. Hyde, Ingersoll, Keim, Kennedy, Krebs, Long, Lyons, Magee, Mann, Martin, M'Cahen, Miller, Pennypacker, Porter, of Northampton, Purviance, Read, Riter. Ritter, Scheetz, Sellers, Shellito. Smith, of Columbia, Smyth, of Centre, Sterigere, Stickel, Sturdevant, Taggart, Thomas, White, Woodward—68.

NAYS—Messrs. Agnew, Baldwin, Barndollar, Biddle, Brown, of Lancaster, Carey, Chambers, Chandler, of Philadelphia, Chauncey, Clark, of Dauphin, Cochran, Cope, Cox, Craig, Denny Dickey, Dickerson, Farrelly, Forward, Hays, Henderson, of Allegheny, Henderson, of Dauphin, Hopkinson, Houpt, Jenks, Kerr, Konigmacher, Maclay, M'Call, M'Dowell, M'Sherry, Meredith, Merkel, Montgomery, Pollock, Porter, of Lancaster, Royer, Russell, Saeger, Scott, Seltzer, Serrill, Sill, Snively, Todd, Weidman, Young, Sergeant, President—48.

So the amendment was agreed to.

The question then recurred on the section as amended.

Mr. DICKEY hoped the section, as amended, would not be adopted. Although the vote upon the amendment was large, he was firmly impressed that the section ought not to be adopted as amended.   Without adverting to the position in which we might find ourselves placed by this amendment, he might say that the only alteration which was proposed by it from the old constitution, was in the formation of senatorial districts it providing that hereafter no counties should be connected so as to create a district entitled to more than two senators. And the reasons set forth by the gentleman from Chester in support of this were, that it will prevent gerrymandering; and that it will cure the defects, if any defects there were in the last apportionment bill.

Now, there were but two senatorial districts out of the city and county of Philadelphia, formed by that bill, which were entitled to more than two senators. The first one being Montgomery, Chester and Delaware; and the next Lancaster and York. All the other districts were limited to two, and this would be the only effect which the gentleman's amendment would have—to require these two districts to be divided.

The gentleman from Lycoming, the other day, made great complaint against the last apportionment bill because his district was not more fully represented.

Now, the rule which always governed the legislative body in the apportionment of representatives was, to divide the whole of the taxable inhabitants in the commonwealth by one hundred for the representative ratio, and by thirty-three for the senatorial ratio. These districts had to be formed, and after they were formed, there would always be fractions; and the great object of the legislature always was to reduce the fractions to the lowest denomination. Representatives then had to be given upon these fractions, and the largest fractions always got the representatives, whether senatorial representetives or otherwise. Now, he had before stated, and he would again repeat, that the last apportionment bill was the fairest bill and the fractions were reduced to the lowest denomination of any apportionment bill which was ever made in Pennsylvania.

The principle was, that the greatest fractions should always be entitled to the preference. And, in the cases mentioned, the counties that had the largest fractions got the representation. It would have been impossible to arrange the fractions among the districts better than they were, and the aggregate amount of the fractions was less than in some former years. The districts always had been, and always would be arranged with a view to favor the political party which might be in power. The democratic legislature in 1828 did this. They arranged the districts for political effect. The representative to which Delaware was entitled, they gave to Lycoming. The fractions were always so managed that the party in power would lose nothing by them. The amendment now offered by the gentleman from Chester, would not prevent gerrymandering. It would still leave to the legislature the power of using the fractions as they pleased. It went to favor the union of counties, in the adjustment of the representation, so as to enable them to elect three or four senators in counties entitled to but two.

Mr. FLEMING said, it was given as a reason against the amendment, that the fractions were always arranged for political effect. That was the sum and substance of the objection. The gentleman had given his own experience on the subject on both sides of the political parties to which he had been attached. He had no doubt the gentleman was much experienced in the arrangement of such matters, but he did not wish to look to the political results which partizans might bring about by the adroit arrangement of fractions. That is a subordinate consideration, and the parties in the legislature in making the distribution may, as the gentleman says they will, make the most of the little latitude which the constitution gives them. But, we are here to provide for the general interests of the state, and to afford to each part of the commonwealth an opportunity to obtain an equal participation in the management of the government. We wish to put a stop to some prominent evils that have been complained of. We wish to give the northwestern counties a 'fair opportunity to be represented. The gentleman has given us no reason against the adoption of the amendment, except that the districts have been heretofore arranged for political advantage; and there is no occasion for the repetition of the assertion again and again, that the last apportionment was the best ever made in the commonwealth. I labor under the opinion that it was not the most judicious arrangement that could have been made for the purpose of giving effect to the representation of the popular will. He would not keep his seat when that apportionment was held up as the pink of honesty and fairness. It was true that the gentleman shewed us the manner and effect of the arrangement, and declared that it was all fair enough; but there was some misfiguring in the gentleman's calculations, his friend from Bucks (Mr. M'Dowell) not being here to do the cyphering. There were some errors in the calculations. It did not, after all, prove that his part of the state had its full share in the representation in the legislature. It would be seen, at once, that the north-eastern counties had not their fair and proper share in the representation, in proportion to their number of taxables. He had not the journal here; and, if he had, he would not now go into a statement of the operation of the last apportionment upon his part of the state. But, he would ask the gentleman from Beaver to refer to that apportionment, and see whether all parts of the state had their full share of representatives under it.

Mr. STERIGERE said he rose to say that the statements of the gentleman from Beaver were incorrect. He could show that they were based on an assumption that could not be sustained. This amendment precluded any county from having any more than four senators, and, in that respect, it corresponded with the old constitution. It also secures a fair arrangement of the districts.

In regard to the arrangement of the districts, the last apportionment provided for such an arrangement as defeated the voice of one county and gave it to another. It was said that Montgomery was not entitled to a senator; but this was incorrect. Montgomery had a larger number of taxables than the senatorial ratio. She had 9774. Westmoreland county had only 8223. This being the case, why should the senator have been given to Westmoreland rather than to Montgomery. The statement of the gentleman from Beaver on this subject was, therefore, unsustained by facts. He forgot to look at the book before he made his assertion. The object of the arrangement was to give effect to the political opinions of Chester and Delaware. Lancaster was not put with York, for the object was to control the voice of York county. He had voted for the proposition to diminish the size of the districts. He would have greatly preferred smaller districts; but, as the proposition to reduce them was rejected, he must submit to it, and make the best of it. The argument had been fully gone into by the gentleman from Chester. If the convention wished to secure a full and fair representation in the senate, and to defeat all attempts at party arrangement of the districts, they would support the amendment. The journal would contradict the statement of the gentleman from Beaver as to the character of the last apportionment; and the reason which he gave for the arrangement which was made of some of the districts, was not the true reason.

Mr. SMYTH, of Centre, had, he said, listened to the remarks of the gentleman from Beaver, and the editorial gentleman from Philadelphia, and he thought they were under some mistake about the matter. They had certainly made some miscalculations. He asked them to turn to page 291 of the journal and calculate for themselves, so that there could be no mistake. Taking the true returns of the different counties, it would be seen that something was done that was not fair. According to the gentleman from Beaver the representative ratio was three thousand. The whole number of taxables returned in the state was 309,421. Now, Philadelphia had seven representatives and two senators. The number of taxables returned from Philadelphia was 14,419. But multiplying the ratio by the number of her representatives, we shall see that her number of taxables ought to have been 21,000 in order to entitle her to seven representatives in the lower house of the legislature. There was a just ground of complaint from the county of Centre. While Centre was deprived of her full and fair proportion of representatives, Philadelphia had two more than she was justly entitled to.

One gentleman from Philadelphia said there was a mistake as to the number of taxables in that city, and that he asked the legislature for a new enumeration which was refused. But he estimated the whole number of taxables in Philadelphia at only 18,000; and even according to that estimate, Philadelphia had one more representative than she was entitled to. Centre and Lycoming together were allowed one senator, and they had good ground for complaining of that. Centre was entitled to a senator, without any fraction at all.

The gentleman from Beaver alleged that this was the fairest apportionment ever made in the state—an apportionment which gave Philadelphia seven representatives for fourteen thousand taxables, when she was entitled to but four representatives, with a remaining fraction of two-thirds of a ratio. He wished to know how the gentleman could allege that this was the fairest apportionment ever made? He could not conceive how he could call it fair.

Mr. DICKEY said he would endeavor to explain the matter. He would show that he was correct, both in regard to Centre and Lycoming and Montgomery. He would correct an error into which he had fallen as to Montgomery. That county had a little more than enough for one senator.

In relation to the returns of the city and county of Philadelphia, he would state the reason why the apportionment made upon them, exceeded the number which the returns called for. These returns were fraudulent and illegal. They were made out contrary to law, and by persons not appointed under the law, but by the county commissioners. It was also believed, and represented, that they were extremely incorrect and unfair, and intended to do injustice to the people of Philadelphia. These returns were set aside by the legislature. As an honest legislature they could do no less than to set them aside as fraudulent returns. They were set aside as unworthy of any consideration. A new enumeration, which was applied for by Philadelphia, was refused. It could not be granted. But the legislature, acting in good faith towards that city, and not recognizing the fraudulent returns, could not apportion the representatives to that city under those returns. They felt bound, in justice to Philadelphia, to allow her to disregard the returns, and allow her the same number of representatives to which she had been entitled under the former apportionment, in 1828. This was done upon the presumption which was believed now to be a fair one, that the taxable population of Philadelphia had increased, in seven years, at the same rate of increase with the taxable population of other parts of the state, and thus left her number of representatives stationary.

That would explain to the gentleman from Centre the reason why Philadelphia was allowed seven representatives. Philadelphia was also entitled to the senatorial representation allowed to her. He had remarked that the apportionments were generally made with a view to political effect, but he meant to say that the late apportionment was made with a view not to party effect, but to the interests of the state and its several parts, considered as one political body.

Beaver was attached to Mercer, because these two counties were united in interest. They were placed where they ought to be placed politically. Identity of interest was consulted in the late apportionment, and that was what he meant in saying that it was made for political effect. We will find, then, in the arrangement of the senatorial districts, that those counties that were united in interest were united in senatorial districts. Chester, Montgomery and Delaware were united closely in interest, and they were put together for political, and not party effect. He asked if it was not right to enlarge the districts, in order to carry out this identity of interest, and enable a district to elect three or four senators? What harm was there in doing this? If the districts were diminished in size, the large counties would gain and the small ones lose their fractions.

Mr. STERIGERE said he would add a few words, to show that the reason given, in relation to the arrangement of Montgomery in the senatorial district, was not the true reason. Chester, Delaware and Berks would have filled up the senatorial ratio much better. If the object had been the interest of the counties, without regard to party interest, that would have been the arrangement.

Mr. EARLE, of the county of Philadelphia, said, if the gentleman from Beaver, (Mr. Dickey) went on with his topic of party discussion every day as he had done, we should never witness an end to our labors. The 2d of February, when, according to his motion, we were to adjourn, was not so far off but that the gentleman would occupy the whole interval in these unimportant party discussions. All reasonable objections to the amendment have been fully met and overthrown, and there is no reason why the debate should not cease and the vote be taken. I ───── vious question.

The motion for the previous question was seconded ───── question was ordered to be put.

The main question on agreeing to the report of the committee of the whole, as to the seventh section of the first article, as amended, was taken, and decided in the affirmative, yeas 66, nays 50.

YEAS—Messrs. Banks, Barclay, Bedford, Bell, Bigelow, Bonham, Brown, of Northampton, Chandler, of Chester, Clarke, of Indiana, Cleavinger, Cline, Cruin, Crawford, Crum, Cummin, Curll, Darlington, Dairah, Dillinger, Donagan, Donnell, Doran, Earle, Foulkrod, Fry, Fuller, Gamble, Gearhart, Gilmore, Grenell, Harris, Hastings, Hayhurst, Helffenstein, Hiester, High, Houpt, Hyde, Ingersoll, Keim, Kennedy, Krebs, Lyons, Magee, Mann, M'Cahen, Miller, Pennypacker, Porter, of Northampton, Purviance, Read, Ritter, Scheetz, Sellers, Seltzer, Serrill Shellito, Smith, of Columbia, Smyth, of Centre, Sterigere, Stickel, Sturdevant, Taggart, Thomas, White, Woodward—66.

NAYS—Messrs. Agnew, Baldwin, Barndollar, Biddle, Brown, of Lancaster, Brown, of Philadelphia, Carey, Chambers, Chandler, of Philadelphia, Chauncey, Clark, of Dauphin, Coates, Cochran, Cope, Cox, Craig, Cunningham, Denny, Dickey, Dickerson, Farrelly, Hays, Henderson, of Allegheny, Henderson, of Dauphin, Hopkinson, Jenks, Kerr, Konigmacher, Long, Maclay, Martin, M'Call, M'Dowell, M'Sherry, Meredith, Merkel, Montgome,y, Pollock, Porter, of Lancaster, Riter, Royer, Russell, Seager, Scott, Sill, Snively, Todd, Weidman, Young, Sergeant, *President*—50.

So the question was determined in the affirmative.

The convention next proceeded to the consideration of the following section, as reported by the committee of the whole:

"SECTION 8. No person shall be a senator who shall not have attained the age of twenty-five years, and have been a citizen and inhabitant of the state four years next before his election, and the last year thereof an inhabitant of the district for which he shall be chosen, unless he shall have been absent on the public business of the United States, or of this state, or unless he shall have been previously a qualified elector in this state; in which case he shall be eligible upon one year's residence."

Mr. FULLER, of Fayette, moved to amend by striking out all the amendment of the committee of the whole, and inserting the following:

" And no person elected as aforesaid shall hold said office after he shall have removed from such district "

Mr. F. believed that the amendment which he had just offered, was a very proper provision to be inserted in the constitution; and the statement he was about to make, he thought, would sustain him in the view which he took of the matter. It would be recollected that the constitution contained no provision, that a senator shall be bound to reside in the district which he represents. His opinion, however was, that such a provision was absolutely necessary. A senator had been elected some years ago from the county of Fayette, and after the first year he removed from the county, and did not again return, although he continued to represent Fayette. The people did not know exactly how to act in the case, and the senator was permitted to serve out his time. They conceived that their business and interests were not so well attended to, as they might be if their senator lived under their own eye. To prevent a similar occurrence, and for the purpose of meeting the views of his constituents, he had introduced the provision which had just been read.

Mr. DARLINGTON, of Chester, said, that he hoped the amendment would not be agreed to. He could see no good reason why the individual elected, should be compelled to reside in the district which he was to represent. If the gentleman removed, and the people were willing to trust him, why should he be compelled to reside in the district? Why, under those circumstances, should there be a constitutional provision to restrain him from going elsewhere? Such cases had frequently occurred, and he (Mr. D.) had not heard of any inconvenience having been felt. He would ask, whether the delegate from Fayette, meant to cast censure on his colleague who sat next but one to him, and who resided in another county? That gentleman's constituents were satisfied with his services; then why should we insert a provision, the effect of which, would be to prevent him and others from living out of the county, although their constituents entertained no objection to their doing so?

Mr. FULLER observed, that the remarks which had fallen from the gentleman from Chester, made no impression on his (Mr. F's.) mind.

Mr. EARLE, of Philadelphia county, thought the phraseology of the amendment rather vague, and suggested that it would be better to say, " District he shall have been elected to represent."

The question was then taken on the amendment offered by Mr. FULLER, and it was agreed to.

A division being asked, the ayes were 61 ; noes, not counted.

Mr. STURDEVANT, of Luzerne, moved to amend the section as amended, so as to make it read " twenty-one years, instead of twenty-five."

Mr. S. said, he would not detain the convention long, as he had but very few remarks to make. He was at a loss to know why the electors and freeholders of a district might not elect any freeholder a senator or representative, no matter what was his age ; provided, however, he was competent to the discharge of the duties which would devolve upon him. In looking at the constitutions of several other states of the Union, and among them, Massachusetts and North Carolina, he found no restrictions with respect to age—that men were eligible, at least, to the station of representative on arriving at twenty-one years of age. They did make it necessary that a man should have reached a certain number of years beyond his majority, before being entitled to hold the office of senator. All that was required was, that he should be a freeholder. And until he (Mr. Sturdevant) heard some better and more sufficient reason given, why a man should not be eligible until he had attained the age of twenty-five years, he could not vote for the section. If the people of a district preferred selecting a young man, a freeholder, although under twenty-five years old, yet fully competent to fill the station of senator, he (Mr. S.) saw no substantial objection, why they ought not to be allowed to gratify thier wishes.

The adoption of a principle of this kind, had doubtless, in many instances, the effect of keeping back young men of promising talents, who might have distinguished themselves, and done credit to those who brought them into public life. It might be said that experience was necessary. He admitted that it was, in many instances, a requisite to entitle a man to a seat in the senate. But, it was not indispensable. Indeed, there were many men of twenty-two or twenty-three, who were equally as well qualified as men at forty. He (Mr. S.) regarded this matter as one that should be left to the judgment and discretion of those who were to be represented.

Mr. SHELLITO, of Crawford, hoped that the section would not be altered, so as to conform to the notions of the gentleman from Luzerne, (Mr. Sturdevant.) He wished every aged man in this body, to take a retrospective view of what was his own character, at the age of twenty-one —a giddy boy, lifted up with high notions, his head filled with nonsense, just coming into the world, full of ambitious ideas, and wholly inexperienced. He (Mr. S.) trusted that the constitution would be allowed to remain unaltered. Young people fancy old people are fools; but old people *know* them to be so.

Mr. MARTIN, of Philadelphia county, said that he had not been able to understand the argument of the delegate from Luzerne, though he fully comprehended the object of his amendment. He understood the delegate to say, it was hard that a young man twenty-five years of age, and a freeholder, too, should be cut off from being elected a senator. He (Mr. M.) did not know why a freeholder should have a preference over other citizens; but he was not aware that there was any restriction in the constitution, in regard to freeholders. A freehold was not the test of intellect or capacity, for the office of senator.

Mr. SURDEVANT disclaimed any such idea, that, because a man was a freeholder, he was therefore to have a preference over his fellow-citizens.

Mr. MARTIN expressed a hope that the gentleman would withdraw his argument, if he did not his amendment.

Mr. CHANDLER, of Philadelphia, wished the delegate from Luzerne, had well weighed the amendment before offering it, as he was in the habit of doing in respect to the propositions he brought before this body. But, he appeared to have overlooked the constitution as it now stood, and the fact, that all the language was well weighed by the framers of that instrument, before being inserted. Doubtless the provision in question was well considered by the convention that framed the constitution. It was true, as had been remarked by the delegate from Luzerne, that there were young men possessed of extraordinary talents—who were distinguished for some remarkable precocity.

But he (Mr. C.) conceived that it was not that kind of precocity, which was indispensable. They required experience and wisdom, not learning, to qualify them for the discharge of their legislative duties. He should hope that those who became senators, previously understood something of ordinary legislation. He was a great stickler for words, and the propriety and necessity of attending to their meaning. If he understood the definition of " senator," it meant an old man, and was derived from the Latin word " *senex*." Therefore, sending *young* men to the senate, would be a contradiction in terms. He implored gentlemen not to touch the little that was left of the constitution, and hoped they would suffer our young men to tarry at Jericho a short time longer, because they might be called upon to vote for a speaker of the senate, who would, in the event of the death of the governor, fill that office.

Then, in whose hands would be the office of governor? Probably in those of a young man, only twenty-one years of age, and he would have the appointment of the judges and other officers!

Mr. M'CAHEN. of Philadelphia county, said, he did not apprehend any danger from the proposed amendment, if it should be agreed to. It was not probable that a very young man would be chosen to fill either the office of speaker or governor. He, however, would leave the people free and unrestrained in their choice. They should be at liberty to choose as young a man as was liable to be called upon to defend his country, or had to contribute to the support of the government. He could not agree with the delegate from Philadelphia, that a senator ought to be a " potent, grave and reverend seignior." It was not necessary that a man should be so grave or so old. The remark might be generally correct, that a young man was not so wise as his elders; but, nevertheless, as he had already said, the people should be left to select whom they thought proper. There were young men who, if not so wise as their seniors, yet had done as great actions, and distinguished themselves as much. Every delegate would recollect the gallant and heroic conduct of Major Crogan, at Sandusky, during the late war. That distinguished officer was under twenty-one years of age, and showed as much skill and bravery as General Harrison, his commander. Napoleon Bonaparte was young when he entered the service of France, and every one knew what he had risen to be. Regarding the amendment in every point of view as unobjectionable, he would vote for it.

Mr. SMYTH, of Centre, said, that if the amendment prevailed, it would be necessary to amend the fourth section of the second article, which provides, that the governor shall be at least thirty years of age. It might happen, as had been said by the gentleman from Philadelphia, (Mr. Chandler) that a young man might become speaker or governor, according to the amendment now under consideration.

Mr. M'DOWELL, of Bucks, hoped that the amendment would not be adopted. When this subject was under discussion at Harrisburg, the delegate from Indiana, (Mr. Clarke) offered an amendment providing that a man twenty-eight years of age, shall be eligible to a seat in the senate, and a man who had reached the age of twenty-five, can become a member of the house of representatives.

He (Mr. M'D.) would be glad if the gentleman would renew his amendment now. The delegate had said that the opposition made to his amendment was only an indication of the aristocratic feeling which prevailed in this body. If it was so, he (Mr. M'D.) was very willing to take his share of the responsibility. For his own part, he had no idea of sending boys to the legislature "muling and puking from their nurses arms." Let a man's character and knowledge and genius be what they might, he was not competent, to represent this great commonwealth in the legislature, immediately after quitting the schools or colleges of Pennsylvania. A man might possess the most extraordinary talents, and what then? What could he possibly know of the legislative history of the state? What practical knowledge would he have of the great interests of Pennsylvania? Had he ever given them a thought? No.

He (Mr. M'D.) would rather have an old man of reputed ignorance, than a young man of the most splendid talents, without experience, to make laws for him. He would repeat, that he had never entertained any such notion as that of sending boys to the legislature. It was true, as was observed by the gentleman from Luzerne, that the people would judge of that matter. Why, then, should they not judge of every other matter?

Gentlemen had said that a restriction was arbitrary and anti-democratic, and that the people ought to be left at liberty to select men of whatever age they deemed right. Why, he asked, was it provided in our constitution, that a man shall not hold office, unless he is of age? Why, fix upon twenty-one years of age? It was an arbitrary matter—a general rule laid down, that a man shall not act for himself, until he arrives at that age. Was it not known that a man could not make a will, if under twenty-one? A young man might not have discretion enough to take care of his own affairs, and yet he was to be sent to the senate to make laws for the people! There were some boys of fifteen, who knew more than many old men; whilst, on the contrary, there were some who had no sense at fifteen years old, and never would have any. It was not necessary that he should say a word about the dignity of the senate; the people might be happy where the king was a fool. So with regard to a governor; the state might have wise laws, and yet he be a fool.

He (Mr. M'D.) would rather vote for an amendment providing that men of twenty-five shall be eligible to the house of representatives, and at twenty-eight to the senate. He thought the constitution very defective in this respect, that it made a seat in the lower house quite a common matter. Fixing the age, would have, in his opinion, a tendency to elevate the character of the body, as no man could have a seat in it who had not, at least, arrived at the years of discretion. Genius, talents, and inexperience were not wanted. Young men, just from college, went to Harrisburg, knowing nothing about the internal improvements, the banking institutions, nor any thing else connected with the welfare of the state of Pennsylvania. Now, this was not the class of men required to transact the business of this commonwealth; they were men well acquainted with the business operations and interests of the community, and could see, at a glance, what would promote the welfare and prosperity of the state.

Mr. WOODWARD, of Luzerne, would say a word or two on the subject. He regarded the introduction of this provision in the constitution as a very salutary regulation with respect to the young men themselves. He did not think political station the principal object for which young men should seek—the great end of life. He conceived that it would be infinitely better, henceforth, that young men should properly qualify themselves for the duties they would have to discharge as representatives of the people of this great commonwealth. He looked upon this amendment, therefore, as a sort of shield for their protection against the vices and temptations of political life. For these reasons, then, he would vote for the incorporation of the amendment in the constitution of Pennsylvania.

Mr. STURDEVANT wished to say a word or two, to explain why he— a young man—had dared to offer this amendment. He had hoped that other gentlemen would have offered reasons in its favor, which would have rendered it unnecessary for him to obtrude himself on the convention. It has been said that the legislature is likely to be corrupt. Does it require more ability to fill a place in the senate, than in the house of representatives? If the people choose a young man, they are fully competent to select whom they desire. There are some of us here, in this convention, who are young men; and if the people would trust us here, to amend the constitution of Pennsylvania—admitted to be sound by all—might they not safely admit us into the halls of legislation? Does it require more ability to fill a seat in the legislature, than to fill one in this convention? Are we not as likely to do our duty honestly, as if we were more advanced in years? There is no good reason for the distinction made between a member of the house of representatives and a senator. It had been said, by the gentleman from Philadelphia, that because the word senator is derived from *senex*, a senator ought to be old. He admitted that the word was so derived; but this was no reason why we are to be compelled to arrive at the age of twenty-five, before we are entitled to the appellation of *senex*. At twenty-three we might be as well qualified. If the people of the district choose to send a young man, they are the best qualified to judge of the propriety of the act.

His colleague (Mr. Woodward) desired to prevent young men from going into the senate, and to keep them at home for the sake of attaining experience. May I be preserved from such prevention! Young men should be sent to the senate, and should remain there until they become old. Young men of twenty-two, may have acquired as much experience as many who are forty. The young man may have a mind as capable of discriminating and judging; he is certainly as active, as the man who is more advanced in years; and why shall he not be entitled to be elected to office? There is no reason why young men should stay at home until they are twenty-five, any stronger than there is for them staying until they are thirty. If they have not experience at twenty-five, they will not have it at thirty. There are some young men at sixteen, who are better fitted for public life, than others are at thirty or fifty.

Here you require a precise number of years as a qualification, and if a person be twenty-four years and ten months, he is not regarded as qualified. He believed that there were young men in this convention, who were as much qualified for the situation at twenty-three or twenty-eight, as others were at fifty and sixty. He saw no reason why the matter should not be left to the people. It is the people who are to be the judges. They are to suffer if any injury shall arise. If the people choose to send boys, let them send them. He would guaranty, that young men would make as good legislators, as men who were more advanced in life.

Mr. PORTER, of Northampton, wished to say but a single word. The amendment of the gentleman from Luzerne, was predicated on two grounds: 1st. That it is wrong to restrict the people; and, 2d. That age is not requisite to qualify for a senator. Every constitution was for the purpose of controlling the people; therefore, that argument could not avail him, for reasons very obvious and proper. The gentleman from the county of Philadelphia, said this amendment should prevail, because Colonel Croghan behaved gallantly. If we were called on to choose for soldiers, he would not be sure that it might not be proper to prefer young men. It was urged that William Pitt entered parliament when a very young man. But this was not an illustration of the rule, but rather an exception to it. Where are we to find another William Pitt? It is said some have greater experience at twenty-five, than others have at fifty. But we must settle this matter by some general rule. He knew many young men of great talent and experience at twenty-one. But he would ask any gentleman to look back and see if, at the age of twenty-one, men were generally found qualified to take charge of the interests of a whole people, and to regulate the machinery of government. For himself, he would wish to be governed by experience, in preference to youth.

The question was then taken, and the amendment was decided in the negative.

The Convention then adjourned.

————

FRIDAY AFTERNOON, January 5, 1838.

ORDER OF THE DAY.

The convention resumed the second reading of the report of the committee, to whom was referred the first article of the constitution, as reported by the committee of the whole.

The eighth section, as amended, being again under consideration,

Mr. CLARK, of Indiana, moved to amend the section, by striking therefrom the word "twenty-five," and inserting in lieu thereof, the word "thirty."

After what he had stated this morning, (Mr. C. said) it would be expected that he should renew his amendment. He would not otherwise have offered it, as he had once obtained an expression of the sense of the convention, and found it against the proposition.

The subject had, however, been agitated this morning by the gentleman from Luzerne, (Mr. Sturdevant) and as his friend from Berks, (Mr. Keim) and other gentlemen, wished for an opportunity to record their votes, he again submitted his amendment. He disclaimed any ill-will towards the young men. Few there are, who liked young men better than he did. In regard to the honesty of young men, he would freely concede the point, that young men were more honest than old men. Their hearts were warm, they were unsuspicious, and unskilled in the ways of the world. But they were deficient in experience, in law-making. He would be desirous to have young men in all offices, but those of the executive and the law-makers, which required age.   The whole field of ambition is open to them.

The gentleman from Luzerne laid great stress on the point that the people should do as they pleased.   That assertion holds good, as regards county officers, but the legislature legislates for the whole people, and should embody the age, experience and wisdom of gentlemen from all parts of the state; and, it was his wish to protect his constituents against young men exercising the powers of legislation.

That was the reason for the limitation which was imposed, because it is requisite, in reference to those who are to make the laws for the whole state; and differs from those offices which only affect particular sections of the state, which ought to be filled by the voice of the constituents, who are immediately interested.   Besides all these county offices, young men have the army, navy, and the militia, open to them.

He would rather see them filling other offices.   Let them take wives, and then get families.   He wished to see the senate, a staid, sober, deliberate body.   What measures may originate, or pass through the other house, let the senate deliberate on, and mature.   He would not take up any more of the time of the convention, except to ask for the yeas and nays on the question.

The call being seconded, the yeas and nays were ordered accordingly.

The question was then taken on the amendment of Mr. CLARKE, and decided in the negative, by the following vote, viz :

YEAS—Messrs. Clarke, of Indiana, Lyons, M'Dowell, Nevin, Shellito—5.

NAYS—Messrs. Agnew, Baldwin, Banks, Barclay, Barndollar, Bedford, Bell, Biddle, Bigelow, Brown, of Lancaster, Brown, of Northampton, Brown, of Philadelphia, Carey, Chambers, Chandler, of Chester, Chandler, of Philadelphia, Chauncey, Clarke, of Beaver, Clark, of Dauphin, Cleaving r, Cline, Coates, Cochran, Cox, Craig, Crain, Crawford, Crum, Cummin, Curll, Darlington, Darrah, Denny, Dickey, Dickerson, Dillinger, Donnell, Earle, Farrelly, Fleming, Foulkrod, Fuller, Gearhart, Grenell, Harris, Hastings, Hayhurst, Hays, Helffenstein, Henderson, of Allegheny, Henderson, of Dauphin, Hiester, High, Hopkinson, Houpt, Hyde, Ingersoll, Jenks, Keim, Kennedy, Kerr, Konigmacher, Krebs, Long, Maclay, Magee, Mann, Martin, M'Cahen, M'Call, M'Sherry, Merkel, Miller, Montgomery, Pennypacker, Pollock, Porter, of Lancaster, Read, Riter, Ritter, Royer, Russell, Saeger, Scheetz, Scott, Sellers, Seltzer, Serrill, Sill, Smith, of Columbia, Smyth, of Centre, Snively, Sterigere, Stickel, Sturdevant, Taggart, Thomas, Todd, Weaver, Weidman, Woodward, Young, Sergeant, President—103.

Mr. JENKS moved to strike out twenty-five, and insert twenty-seven. He thought, he said, that the age at which a person, in ordinary cases, should be eligible to the office of senator, ought to be greater than twenty-five.

He did not consider, that for that grave and responsible station. a person of an age under thirty ought to be chosen, unless in some extraordinary cases, which he admitted, had happened, though they ought to be considered as exceptions to the general rule, and not as contradictions to it.   He was of opinion, that as the gentleman from Indiana had well remarked, the senate ought to be made a little more patriarchal than i was.   He was aware that the opinion of the convention was opposed to any change.   They had, while in committee, if he recollected aright, rejected the motion of the gentleman from Indiana, (Mr. Clarke) to increase the age to thirty or to twenty-eight.

It was very true, therefore, that there was a disposition in this body, not to carry the ineligibility of persons to the senate, beyond the age of twenty-five years.

But, if we considered the additional duties imposed upon the senate, by the new constitution, there would be found in that consideration, a strong reason for increasing the age, which could not have occurred to the members, at the time of their former decision.

The senate was now made a much more important body, than it ever was before; and, in addition to their legislative duties, which were very heavy, they shared with the governor, the appointment of some of the highest executive officers.

He would ask whether the duty of making important appointments, should be conferred upon those whose age forbid the idea of their having acquired the experience necessary to enable them to exercise their duty judiciously? It required much experience and observation, and much mental discrimination, to exercise that power in a proper manner. The judgments of persons of five-and-twenty are not, in the majority of cases, matured. When they enter upon public life, with their minds unimproved by experience, they cannot be well fitted for the discharge of its high and responsible duties.

We look upon the senate, as a body which is to act as a check upon the imprudence of the other house, and correct any errors which might occur in legislation, from the want of experience, wisdom and prudence. Therefore it is that we make a distinction as to the age and the term of service of the two bodies, and also, as to their number.

The senate is intended to correct the mistakes of the more popular branch of the legislature. He had never witnessed any material benefit from sending very young men, either to the senate or the house. It was true, that there were exceptions, but they were very rare. Young men were ardent and ambitious, and, in legislation, they were apt to be hasty and indiscreet. They were better fitted for active, than for sober reflec_tion, and were more trust-worthy in the council than in the field.

The gentleman from Indiana had shewn his discrimination and practi_cal knowledge of legislative matters, and the concerns of government, by bringing forward this proposition in committee. He (Mr. J.) was now decidedly in favor of it, though he did not vote for it at the time, in con_sequence of the manifest indisposition of the body to adopt it. But, he thought that, though the committee had refused to fix the age at thirty, and at twenty-eight, the convention might agree to fix it at twenty-seven, instead of twenty-five, in consideration of the new responsibilities imposed upon the senate.

Few, he thought, would disagree with him as to this—that the age of twenty-seven was not too great, as the age at which eligibility to the senate should commence. By the adoption of the amendment, our legis_lation would be rendered more correct and enlightened than it now was. He flattered himself that his proposition would meet with a favorable reception.

The motion to amend was put and decided in the negative.

Mr. FLEMING moved to strike out all after the word "state," in the fifth line.

The PRESIDENT decided that the motion was not in order.

Mr. FLEMING withdrew the motion.

Mr. EARLE said, the present constitution required one year's residence of the district, for which he is elected, before a person could be elected to the senate. He thought the amendment of importance, and he trusted there would be no doubt of its passage. He asked for the yeas and nays upon the adoption of the amendment.

The question was taken on agreeing to the report of the committee, as to the eighth section, as amended, and decided in the affirmative—yeas, 59; nays, 56; as follow:

YEAS.—Messrs. Banks, Bedford, Bell, Bigelow, Brown, of Northampton, Brown, of Philadelphia, Clarke, of Indiana, Cleavinger, Crain, Crawford, Crum, Cummin, Curll, Darrah, Donagan, Donnell, Doran, Earle, Foulkrod, Fry, Fuller, Gamble, Gearhart, Gilmore, Grenell, Harris, Hastings, Hayhurst, Helffenstein, Hiester, High. Hyde, Ingersoll, Keim, Kennedy, Krebs, Lyons, Magee, Mann, Martin, M'Cahen, M'Dowell, Miller, Nevin, Porter, of Northampton, Read, Riter, Ritter, Scheetz, Sellers, Shellito, Smith, of Columbia, Smyth, of Centre, Sterigere, Stickel, Taggart, Thomas, Weaver, Woodward—59.

NAYS—Messrs. Agnew, Baldwin, Barndollar, Biddle, Brown, of Lancaster, Carey, Chambers. Chandler, of Chester, Chandler, of Philadelphia, Chauncey, Clark, of Dauphin, Cline, Coates, Cochran, Cope, Cox, Craig, Darlington, Denny, Dickey, Dickerson, Dunlop, Farrelly, Fleming, Forward, Hays, Henderson, of Allegheny, Henderson, of Dauphin, Hopkinson, Houpt, Jenks, Kerr, Konigmacher, Long, Maclay, M'Call, M'Sherry, Meredith, Merkel, Montgomery, Pennypacker, Pollock, Porter, of Lancaster, Royer, Russell, Saeger, Scott, Seltzer, Serrill, Sill, Snively, Sturdevant, Todd, Weidman, Young, Sergeant, President—56.

So the question was determined in the affirmative.

The convention then took up that part of the report of the committee of the whole, which proposed to strike out the ninth section of the old constitution, and insert the following:

"SECTION 9.—At the expiration of the term of any class of the present senators, successors shall be elected for the term of three years. The senators who may be elected in the year one thousand eight hundred and forty-one, shall be divided by lot, into three classes; the seats of the senators of the first class, shall be vacated at the expiration of the first year, of the second class, at the expiration of the second year, and of the third class, at the expiration of the third year; so that thereafter one-third might be chosen every year."

Mr. DARLINGTON wished to call the attention of the convention to the condition in which this section had been left by the committee of the whole.

It must be recollected, that we have made a change in relation to the senatorial term, from four to three years, and we are to classify our senators in a different manner from the old constitution. Well, then, let us look at the provisions of this amendment. It provides that at the expiration of the first class of senators, others are to be elected for a term of three years; but, we must recollect, that the first class is only one-fourth of the senate; at the expiration of the second class, senators are to be elected also for a term of three years, and so of the third class; so that you will have three distinct classes of new senators. Then provision is made, that the senators who may be elected in the year eighteen hundred and forty-one, shall be divided into three classes by lot. It was not those who might be representatives at that time, but those who were elected in 1841, which were to be divided into three classes, and how many would they be? Why, only one-fourth of your senators. Nine senators were to be divided into three classes, and the term of the first class was to expire in one year; of the second, in two years; and of the third, in three years.

Now, he would ask gentlemen to look into this matter, and see if it was what they desired to have adopted. When the constitution of 1790 went into operation, we had no senate. The whole of the senators were therefore elected together, so that the old section, on this subject, was plain and easily understood. They being all elected together, it was an easy matter to divide them into four classes, and then have their seats vacated in successive years.

It seemed, however, now to be a difficult matter to adopt a system which would work properly in classifying the senators, unless the whole of the senators were elected anew, when the constitution went into operation. Then there would be thirty-three senators only to be divided into three classes.

He confessed that he saw a difficulty in the way of adopting this section, and he thought it would be better if the convention were resolved to reduce the term of senators, from four to three years, to declare the seats of all the senators to be vacated, when the constitution went into operation, and have an entire new senate elected. Then, there would be no difficulty in classifying them properly.

He had, therefore, with a view of meeting this case, prepared an amendment, which he thought would answer the purpose.

Mr. D. then moved to strike out the section, proposed by the committee of the whole, and insert the following:

"At the first election, subsequent to the next enumeration, the whole number of senators which shall then have been fixed by the legislature, shall be elected in the respective districts into which the state shall then be divided. Immediately after the senators shall be assembled, in consequence of such election, they shall be divided by lot, as equally as may be, into three classes. The seats of the senators of the first class, shall be vacated at the expiration of the first year; of the second class, at the expiration of the second year; and of the third class, at the expiration of the third year: so that one-third may be chosen every year."

Mr. STERIGERE said, if the gentleman from Chester (Mr. Darlington) had acted on the advice he had given to others—to read the amendment —he would not have favored the convention with the speech he had delivered. The difficulties that gentlemen apprehended existed in his own imagination, and not in the amendment. Mr. S. then read the amendment as follows:

"Section 9.   At the expiration of the term of any class of the present senators, successors shall be elected for the term of three years.   The senators who may be elected in the year 1841, shall be divided by lot into three classes.   The seats of the senators of the first class shall be vacated at the expiration of the first year—of the second class at the expiration of the second year—and of the third class at the expiration of the third year ; so that thereafter one-third may be chosen every year.

This amendment is predicated on the idea that the amendment, if adopted by the people, will go into operation before the annual election in 1838. This will depend on what this convention may finally do in relation to this matter.   If the convention provides for submitting the new constitution to the people in May or June next, and provides for its enactment before October next, the amendment is correct.   On the contrary, if the new constitution should not go into operation before that time—the time mentioned for the classification must be postponed one year, viz : to 1842. This will be mere form—and can be easily arranged in the end, to be adapted to what may be provided respecting submitting the amendments to the people.

The senate, under the present constitution, is divided into four classes, one of which is elected annually for four years.   The first part of the amendment provides for the continuation in office of the present senators for the term for which they were elected, and for the choice of their successors.   The term of the senators who were elected in 1837, under the present constitution, and those who may be elected in 1838 under the new one, if it should be adopted by the people, will expire in 1841.   Consequently, two classes—a fourth, equal to seventeen senators, will be elected in 1841. The class of senators who may be elected in 1839, will expire in 1842— and will in 1841 have only *one* year to serve.   The class who may be elected in 1840, will expire in 1843 ; and in 1841, will have *two* years to serve.   Three of the senators who may be elected in 1841, will, under the amendment, be added to the class of eight senators whose time will expire in 1842, and their seats will be vacated at the expiration of the *first year*. Three more of them will be added to the class of eight, whose term will expire in 1843—and their seats will be vacated at the expiration of the *second* year.   The seats of the remaining eleven of the senators elected in 1841, will be vacated at the expiration of the *third* year, or in 1844.   The senate at the session succeeding the election of 1841, will be divided into three classes, of eleven senators each, and thereafter one-third, or eleven, will be chosen every year.

This amendment occupies the same place that a similar provision does in the constitution of 1790, and only varies from it so much as is necessary, to provide for the continuance in office of the present senators during the time the people have chosen them—on an equal classification of the senators, some of whom held for four, and others for three years.   The provision was as plain and simple as could be wished.   No doubt other schemes could be presented—every delegate might submit one different from this.   I might also require less phraseology to provide for the classification of the senators, if the present one were swept overboard, and an entire new senate elected when the new constitution went into operation.   To which war opposed.   He thought it unnecessary to explain the report.

tee further, as any gentleman would understand it, if he was disposed to do so.

Mr. Agnew thought there were some objections to this amendment which had not been alluded to either by the gentleman from Chester or the gentleman from Montgomery. As he viewed the amendment, it would place us in the predicament of having but twenty-four or twenty-five senators in the year 1841, instead of thirty-three. This was obvious, as he calculated. Mr. A. went into a calculation to show that this must inevitably be the result; therefore he took it that there must be some mistake about the calculation of the gentleman from Montgomery.

Mr. Sterigere said he meant no disrespect to the delegate from Chester in the remarks he had made, when he before addressed the convention, and he hoped the gentleman would not think so. Mr. S. entered into a more minute explanation of the operation of the amendment. He thought it was just as practicable to put the new constitution into operation before the election of 1838, as at any other time. If it could not be, the amendment only required to change the year 1841 to 1842. He was glad to hear that the objections, at first mentioned, had been entirely explained away, and the only one remaining was the year the classification was proposed to be made. He was perfectly willing that it should be changed to 1842. As this was, however, a mere matter of form, and depending on what time the convention might provide for the new constitution going into operation, we had better wait for the final decision of the convention on that subject.

He would be glad if the delegate from Chester county, (Mr. Darlington,) would withdraw his amendment to enable him to prepare an amendment to the report of the committee of the whole, which would remove all the objections urged last evening—[he not complying with this request] Mr. S. said he would then bring into the view of the convention what he proposed viz : to strike out " in the year one thousand eight hundred and forty-one, " and insert " at the next election after the adoption of this constitution. " This was in conformity with a rule in the senate of the United States, upon the admission of new states into the Union, and the introduction of senators from such states.

It would make the classification more certain and better than the report of the committee proposed to do ; and would remove some objections which some of the delegates entertained.

Mr. Dickey said gentlemen seemed to presume that this constitution would be adopted and go into operation before the election of senators in '38. This would not be the case. The law requires the returns of the votes for and against the constitution to be made to the next legislature, who did not meet till December, 1838. The first election under the new constitution must. therefore, be in 1839. The amendment was consequently wrong upon the gentleman's own calculations.

Mr. Porter, of Northampton, said he was not remarkably good at arithmetical calculations, but the delegate from the county of Montgomery might be right. If he was not, he would recommend an application to the gentleman from Bucks, (Mr. M'Dowell) or, if he was not in the way, he would send to Northampton for a large slate of his own manufacture, and see if he could make it out. He did not see, at present, that it would made any odds whether the time fixed was in 1838 or 1839.

Mr. AGNEW said he had made a few figures to explain the matter.   At the expiration of the term of the present senators, their successors would be elected in 1841.   Those last elected would hold their office longest. Those elected after 1838 would hold their office beyond the term of three years.   The last class of the present senators would go out in 1841.   It is evident that the last class of the present senators cannot be in office in 1841, because, elected for this year, their term of four years, under the present constitution, must expire with the session of 1840.   Those, therefore, who are elected at the fall election of 1841, are elected under the new constitution for three years.   This must be clear to the dullest capacity.   If the last class of senators go out in 1841, they cannot be in the senate in 1841.   The periods at which the members of the present senate go out is in 1838, '39, '40, and '41.   Now, I apprehend that four times eight will make thirty-two.   The terms of all the senators who are in office will have expired in 1841.   The next and last election under the old constitution, for senators, will take place next fall, and their terms will expire in 1841.   So, no election can take place under the new constitution before the fall of 1839.

Mr. STERIGERE said, he would be obliged to the gentleman from Bea·ver, (Mr. Agnew) to show him what part of the amendment required that those senators whose terms expire in the year 1841, should be there in the session of 1841-'42.   I regret to say a word because the gentleman cannot believe what he lays down as the right position.   The provision is that those senators, whose terms expire in 1841, shall be succeeded by senators who shall be chosen for three years.   The argument was based on the idea that the constitution would be adopted before the expiration of the year 1838.   When we come to final action on the matter, all that we shall have to do will be to make the term 1841-2.   That will be a mere matter of form.

Mr. BELL said his attention was never called to this matter before now, but it was evident that those gentlemen who had given the most attention to it, could not agree in regard to it.   Afternoon sessions were not often favorable to calculations.   He was not willing to vote in the dark on the subject.   Every gentleman who speaks mystifies the matter more and more.   There is no necessity for passing it now, and I hope we shall pass on to another subject.   I move to postpone this for the present.

Mr. Cox did not think, he said, there was any necessity for postponing it at all.   He understood what the operation of the clause was intended to be; and, as he was not willing to concede that the gentleman from Bucks county, was the only one who could figure out a matter of this sort, he would undertake to show how it was.   It was perfectly plain according to his mode of cyphering.   If the amendments should be adopted before the next election and the senators should be elected in 1838, under this new constitution, then their terms would expire at the session of 1840-41.   Seventeen senators would then go out in 1841. The terms of those elected in 1839 would expire in 1842.   Those who were elected in 1840 would go out in 1843.   Those elected after 1841 will be classified.   Eleven will go out in 1843, and the other eleven three years after.   Eleven will be elected every year after 1843.   This must be the way in which they are classified.   I shall vote for the proposition of the gentleman from Chester, so as to have the constitution go into operation in 1842.

The motion to postpone was lost.

Mr. DICKEY said it was admitted that the amendment was based on the supposition that the constitution would go into operation before another election. He called the attention of the convention to the fact that the law required the returns of the votes for, and against, the constitution to be returned to the legislature. Well, suppose we get through by the 2d of February, will it be possible to submit the amendments to the people and return their votes to the legislature before the termination of the present session of the legislature?

Mr. DARLINGTON said the whole of the argument of the gentleman from Montgomery, was based on the supposition that the constitution would go into operation in the year 1838, and that the election under it would take place in October, 1838. He did not believe it possible for this to happen. The first election that could possibly take place under the constitution, would be in 1839. In October, 1839, the first election would take place for senators, for three years. Eight only would be elected, for there would be but eight vacancies, and those then elected would hold their office till 1842. In 1841 the third class would be elected.

He maintained that nothing was to be gained by this complex mode of proceeding. The gentleman from Montgomery, (Mr. Sterigere) had argued that there would be impropriety in turning a senator out before the expiration of the four years' term for which he was elected. He (Mr. D.) insisted that the amendment he had proposed, would not do injustice to any individual, and that the delegate had entirely mistaken the effect of it. The senators could not be classified till 1843, and no individual could be deprived of his office before his term expired. The plan which he (Mr. D.) had proposed, was in accordance with the principle laid down in the constitution of 1790.

Mr. STERIGERE had a word or two to say. The argument of the delegate from Somerset, (Mr. Cox) made the question so plain, that all opposition on that point ought to be abandoned. The argument of the delegate from Beaver, (Mr. Dickey) and that of the gentleman who had just taken his seat, seemed to be predicated on the assumption that the amendments to the constitution were not to be submitted to the people this year. He considered that it was by no means so improbable, as the gentleman from Beaver seemed to suppose, that the constitution would not go into' operaton till 1839. He (Mr. S.) thought that when the convention came to its final action on the amendment, that they would find some difficulty in changing the figure from 1841 to 1842. The convention should provide, if the amendments were adopted, that the governor might convene the legislature to do what was necessary.

Mr. DARLINGTON asked for the yeas and nays; which were ordered.

On motion of Mr. PORTER, of Northampton,

The convention adjourned.

SATURDAY, January 6, 1838.

Mr. Biddle presented the memorial of Charles W. Gardner and Frederick A. Hinton, in behalf of the people of colour in the city and county of Philadelphia, praying that no alteration may be made in the present constitution in regard to the rights of citizenship and suffrage.

Mr. Biddle moved that this memorial be printed. The subject was one of importance. It would be premature to go into the discussion of it at this time. Similar documents had been ordered to be printed, and among them, one which was adverse in its tone to the prayer of this petition. He hoped, therefore, that the convention would agree to his motion, and order the memorial to be printed. On this question he would call for the yeas and nays,

The yeas and nays being ordered, the question was then taken and decided in the negative by the following vote, viz:

Yeas—Messrs. Agnew, Baldwin, Barnitz, Biddle, Brown, of Philadelphia, Carey, Chambers, Chandler of Chester, Chandler, of Philadelphia, Chauncey, Clarke, of Beaver, Clark, of Dauphin, Cline, Coats, Cochran, Cope, Craig, Crain, Cunningham, Darlington, Denny, Dickey, Dickerson, Earle, Forward, Hays, Henderson, of Dauphin, Hiester, Kerr, Konigmacher, Long, Maclay, M'Cahen, M'Call, M'Dowell, Montgomery, Pennypacker, Porter, of Lancaster, Purviance, Royer, Saeger, Scott, Serrill, Sill, Sterigere, Thomas, Todd, Weidman, Young, Sergeant, *President*—50.

Nays—Messrs. Banks, Barclay, Barndollar, Bedford, Bigelow, Brown, of Lancaster, Brown, of Northampton, Clarke, of Indiana. Cleavinger, Crawford, Crum, Cummin, Curll, Darrah, Dillinger, Donagan, Donnell, Fleming, Foulkrod, Fry, Fuller, Gamble, Gearhart, Gilmore, Grenell. Harris, Hastings, Hayhurst, Henderson of Allegheny, High, Hopkinson, Houpt, Hyde, Ingersoll, Keim, Kennedy. Krebs, Lyons, Magee, Mann, M'Sherry, Merkel, Miller, Pollock, Read, Riter, Ritter, Russell. Scheatz, Sellers, Seltzer, Shellito, Smith, of Columbia, Smyth, of Centre, Snively, Stickel, Sturdevant, Taggert, Weaver, White, Woodward—61.

So the question was determined in the negative.

Mr. Carey presented a memorial from citizens of Bucks county, praying that no alteration may be made in the present constitution in regard to the rights of citizenship and suffrage.

Mr. Darlington presented a memorial of like import, from citizens of Chester county.

. Mr. Clark, of Dauphin, presented a memorial of like import, from citizens of Dauphin county.

Mr. Sellers presented two memorials from citizens of Montgomery county, praying that measures may be adopted effectually to prevent all amalgamation between the white and coloured population, in regard to the government of this state.

Mr. Stickel presented a memorial of like import from citizens of York county.

Mr. CLARK, of Dauphin, presented four memorials from citizens of Dauphin county, praying that the sixth section of the ninth article of the constitution of this state, may be amended to read as follows: " The trial by jury shall be as heretofore, and in questions affecting life or liberty shall be extended to every human being, and the right thereof shall remain inviolate."

And the said memorials were laid on the table.

Mr. COPE, from the committee on accounts, reported the following resolution, viz:

Resolved, That the President draw his warrant on the State Treasurer, in favor of Samuel Shoch, secretary, for the sum of two thousand dollars, to be accounted for in the settlement of his accounts.

This resolution was then read a second time, considered and agreed to.

FIRST ARTICLE.

The convention proceeded to the consideration of the following amendment, offered yesterday, by Mr. DARLINGTON of Chester, in lieu of the ninth section of the first article, as amended by the committee of the whole:

" At the first election subsequent to the next enumeration, the whole number of senators which shall then have been fixed by the legislature shall be elected in the respective districts into which the state shall then be divided; immediately after the senators shall be assembled in consequence of such election, they shall be divided by lot as equally as may be, into three classes. The seats of the senators of the first class shall be vacated at the expiration of the first year; of the second class, at the expiration of the second year; and of the third class, at the expiration of the third year, so that one-third may be chosen every year."

Mr. CLARKE, of Indiana, moved to amend the section by substituting the following:

" The senators who may be elected at the first general election under the amendments to the constitution, shall be divided by lot into three classes: the seats of the senators of the first class shall be vacated at the expiration of the first year; of the second class at the expiration of the second year; and of the third class at the expiration of the third year; so that thereafter one-third of the whole number of senators may be chosen every year. The senators elected before the amendments shall be in operation, shall hold their offices during the terms for which they shall respectively have been elected."

The PRESIDENT: The amendment cannot be received at this time, it being an amendment to an amendment.

Mr. CLARKE proceeded to explain the object of his amendment. It would be perceived that by the original report of the committee, a particular year was fixed, without knowing whether the constitution would be adopted by the people. In order to bring the section into operation, it would require seventeen senators to be elected in one year. That he regarded as an objectionable feature. With respect to the amendment of the gentleman from Chester, it contemplates that all the senators are to be newly elected, after the next enumeration shall have been made and divided into classes, so that they shall go out in rotation, and one-third of the senators be chosen every year. The amendment that he (Mr. C.) had brought to the notice of the convention, he conceived, would obviate many of the objections which attached to the section, as reported by the committee of the whole, as well as to the amendment of the delegate from Chester. He (Mr. Clarke) had been told by those whom he respected, that having brought forward an amendment he had a right to explain its meaning. He would do so. At the first election, after the new constitution shall have gone into effect, there would be eight senators to elect. There were three classes; the term of the first class would expire one year subsequent to the constitution going into operation. The second, the second year; and the third, the third year. His amendment would not unsettle any of the seats of the senators holding for the time being. The whole arrangement was simply taking the class that was left, and distributing it among the rest, which would not disturb the remaining senators. . He thought the simplicty of the amendment would recommend it to the favorable attention of the convention.

Mr. STERIGERE would inform the gentleman from Indiana, that he was going to move to strike out the year, and say the first election after the adoption of the constitution.

The PRESIDENT said the motion would not be in order.

Mr. MEREDITH, of Philadelphia, said it seemed to have been forgotten that this section was introduced as a substitute, in the expectation that the new constitution would be voted for at the last fall election. The difficulty at present in the way, could be very easily removed, and that was simply by changing the year. The object in view was to obtain a new classification without producing much derangement. The objection taken to the amendment of the gentleman from Chester, (Mr. Darlington) was that we should have to commence with new senators. He (Mr. M.) thought the best mode was that suggested by the report of the committee. The third year after the constitution would have been in operation, the terms of two classes of senators would expire. There would be one class for one year, another for two years, and two classes for three years. It would then be necessary to take two from the three year class, and add them to the one year class, and then three and add them to the two year class. Then a new classification would be made. In 1838, one-fourth of the senators would be elected for four years, whose terms would expire in 1842, and those elected in 1839, under the new constitution, would go out in 1842, also. By arranging the plan in this manner, as suggested, he thought it would be likely to meet the views of the delegates. He considered this a most intricate subject to debate, and he would submit whether it did more properly belong to the schedule.

Mr. CLARKE said he hoped that the gentleman from Philadelphia, (Mr. Meredith) whose judgment he respected, would examine his (Mr. C.'s) proposition, before giving his preference to the mode suggested by the committee, and respecting which he had given his views. Supposing the constitution to go into operation in 1839, the terms of those senators who were elected in 1836, would expire in 1840 ; those in 1837, in 1841; and those in 1838, in 1842. But, the senators elected in 1839, the year the constitution would go into effect, if approved, would by his (Mr. C.'s) amendment, be divided into three classes—the first of which would expire in 1840 ; the second, in 1841 ; and the third, in 1842. His amendment, therefore, created no derangement, and the new section would come into operation without disturbing anything.

Mr. READ, of Susquehanna, rose for the purpose of making a remark or two, which might, perhaps, relieve us from a difficulty on the subject, suggested by the gentleman from Beaver, (Mr. Dickey) which had been stated, he thought, without much reflection, and that was, that we could not hold an election under the new constitution until it was adopted. He (Mr. R.) would say that there was no necessity for postponing the election under the new constitution, in consequence of the provision in the act of assembly to which the gentleman had referred. He appre- hended that the convention would be able to submit the constitution to the people in April or May, at farthest. And, although the act of assembly makes it the duty of the speaker of the senate to open and publish the returns of the election, yet every delegate must be convinced that there was no necessity, for waiting until next December. The convention could direct that the returns should be opened by the state treasurer and governor, or any other officer, in whom they have confidence, before the meeting of the next legislature ; so that if the amendments are approved, the next election might be held under the new constitution.

Mr. DARLINGTON said that, when he first turned his attention to the subject, he saw the difficulty, and without having had any previous reflection, he sat down and drew up an amendment which he thought was calculated to remove it. On subsequent reflection, however, and after having seen the proposition and heard the remarks of the delegate from Indiana, he had made up his mind to accept that gentleman's amendment as a modification of his own. Mr. D. then withdrew his amendment.

Mr. MEREDITH remarked, after reading Mr. Clarke's amendment, that there might hereafter arise a question as to whether those senators elected before the constitution of 1838 went into operation, hold their offices or not. He then suggested, in order to remove all ambiguity, that a clause be inserted in the schedule.

Mr. CLARKE fully acquiesced in the propriety of the course suggested.

Mr. STERIGERE said, that the only difficulty among delegates last evening was, to fix upon the year when the new constitution should go into effect. He (Mr. Sterigere) thought that the provision fully explained itself.

With a view to obviate the objection, which some gentlemen regarded as attaching to the amendment, he had intended this morning to have moved to strike out the fourth or fifth line, so as to strike out the year, and to have inserted the words "after the amendments to this constitution shall have been adopted." The objection to the amendment of the gentleman from Indiana was, that it was susceptible of another construc- tion being put on it, besides the one that he gave to it, and that was, that all the senators—the old as well as the new, shall be chosen at the next election after the adoption of the constitution ; for, there was no pro- vision to prevent the continuance of the old senators in office. So that in fact, we should have the old and new senators in office at the same time. The report of the committee of the whole provided for the successors of the present incumbents. He thought that they should be arranged into classes, and that the first class of eight should serve one year; the second two years; and the third three years; and that the present senators should remain in office till the end of their respective terms. Now, this would be the proper and fair construction, and such an amendment would remove all the difficulty at present in the way. If the amendment pending should be rejected, he would move an amendment to the effect he had indicated.

The question was taken on the amendment, and it was agreed to.

The question was next taken on the report of the committee as amended; which was agreed to, as was also the section, as amended.

The convention next proceeded to the consideration of the fourth section, as amended by the committee of the whole:

Sec. 10. The general assembly shall meet on the first Tuesday of January in every year, unless sooner convened by the governor; and shall adjourn on the first Thursday in April, unless continued longer in session by law for that purpose.

Mr. Fuller, of Fayette, moved to strike out all after the word "shall," in the third line, and insert "not continue in session longer than the first Thursday in April, unless otherwise continued by a joint resolution of both branches of the legislature."

Mr. F. said he had offered this amendment, believing that it would meet the approbation of the convention. He found this language used in the amendment making it obligatory on this body to adjourn on the 1st of April. And, if they could adjourn before, he saw no reason why they should continue in session till that day.

Mr. Darlington moved to amend the amendment by striking out the word "special."

The President said the motion was not in order.

Mr. Darlington would suggest that they had better leave out the word "special," as it might some time be found necessary for the legislature to pass a general law to continue in session longer.

Mr. Fleming was at loss to see the force of the amendment adopted in committee of the whole, and as proposed to be amended by the gentleman from Fayette, (Mr. Fuller.) It was proposed to amend the section by limiting the time that the legislature shall continue in session; while, at the same time, you put it directly in their power to say whether they shall continue longer in session or not. In his opinion, the provision was entirely nugatory—could have no binding effect whatever, and, therefore, it would be better to leave it out. Would gentlemen say tha the governor shall compel them to remain in session? The go would have no influence whatever, over the legislature, as they reject any act of his by a vote of two-thirds of both branches. P some delegates present might be able to show, that the provision in tion would be of service; but, really, he was at loss

would, therefore, move to strike out the amendment of the committee f
the whole, together with that of the delegate from Fayette.

Mr. DUNLOP, of Franklin, did not like the phraseology of the amendment of the committee, or of that of the gentleman from Fayette.   He
had, at one time, thought such a restriction would be a good one ; but, on
further reflection, he had become satisfied, that in was objectionable,
inasmuch as it would throw additional responsibility on the governor,
and prevent the legislature from sitting longer, if the public interest
required that they should do so.   Besides, too, it would be taking away
a democratic feature of the constitution that ought to be preserved.   He
would suggest to the gentleman from Fayette, to modify his amendment
so as to make it read " unless the two houses shall otherwise determine."
The legislature should have it in their power to continue in session,
without the concurrence of the governor, if they deemed that the public
interest required it.   They should be independent of the governor, and
not under his control.   He (Mr. D.) thought that the constitution should
require that the legislature shall adjourn on a particular day, unless the
two houses shall otherwise determine.   He felt sure that no gentlemen
here could wish the governor to interfere, if the legislature considered
that they ought to remain in session longer, for the purpose of disposing
of important public business before them.   It might happen on a particular occasion—in times of high excitement and party feeling, that the
governor and the legislature might differ as to the policy of some bill
under consideration ; then the governor would have it in his power to
adjourn the legislature, although they might wish to continue in session.
He thought the gentleman from Fayette must see that great inconvenience would result from the adoption of such an amendment.   The legislature would have to pass a special act every time they deemed it necessary to sit beyond the period to which they were limited.   It would be
much better that they should remain in session by a joint resolution of the
two houses.

Mr. FULLER said, when the amendment fixing the day of the meeting
of the legislature, was before the committee of the whole, there was no
limit adopted for the length of the session, though one was proposed.
He thought it very necessary to impose a limit to the length of the sessions of the legislature, in order to prevent that body from wasting their
time and increasing greatly, the public expenses.   The time for the
adjournment ought, in his opinion, to be fixed as well as the time of meeting.   The three months from the first of January to the first of April,
was a sufficient time to enable the legislature to bring all their business to
a close; and if there should be a necessity for prolonging the session beyond
that time, then let them take the responsibility of enacting a special law
for the purpose.   If they were properly attentive to their duties from the
commencement of the session, they could, in ordinary times, bring their
current business to a close before the first of April.

But, in times of public emergency, a special law for the continuance
of the session would be very proper.   If the business was left undone
through neglect and delay, as is usually the case, then the legislature
must incur the responsibility, in a direct and plain manner, so that the
people can understand it, of continuing the session and imposing great

expenses upon the public treasury, merely for the purpose of gratifying their own love of ease.

The opinion of many was, that a day of adjournment of the legislature should be fixed. We should, at least, hold out the idea, in the constitution, that three months is long enough for the session. If they sit longer it must be upon the responsibility of a special law made by themselves. He moved to amend the section, so as to provide that the session shall terminate by adjournment on the first day of April, until the legislature shall otherwise determine by special law.

Mr. DUNLOP said, he supposed the meaning of the amendment was that the legislature should adjourn on the first day of April, unless the two houses should otherwise determine. Was that it ?

Mr. FULLER replied in the affirmative. He would propose to strike out all after the word "unless," and to add the following : "the two houses otherwise determine."

Mr. DICKEY said this was a proposition to lay an injunction upon the legislature to adjourn in April, and if it was adopted, the legislature would be compelled by a constitutional provision to adjourn on the first day of April, unless it should be absolutely necessary, in case of public emergency, to prolong the session. If the act by which the session, in such case, was to be prolonged, should be in the form of a joint resolution or law, the governor must have a negative upon it. He should have the power to prevent the prolongation of the session, unless he thought it proper and necessary. The governor should concur in the extension of the session beyond the constitutional limit. Unless this were the case, the provision would be no effectual restraint upon the length of the legislature, and that body would continue, as heretofore, to fix the day by a joint resolution.

The governor, as a part of the law-making power, should have the right to veto this as well as any other law. If the legislature undertook to protract the session unreasonably and for an unnecesary length of time, the governor should have power to prevent it and enforce the provision of the constitution. Without this, the provision would be of little or no effect. It should be provided also, that the legislature, in case they prolonged the session, beyond the time fixed by the constitution, should do it, by law, and not by concurrent resolution. The governor, it must be admitted, ought to have his negative on this as well as any other law. He hoped the delegate from Fayette would so modify his amendment as to render a law necessary, instead of a mere resolution.

Mr. FLEMING said, if it was the wish of the convention to give the governor the power of adjourning or prolonging the legislature whenever he should see fit ,let them say so in plain terms ; for that will be the effect of the provision, with the modification proposed by the gentleman from Beaver.

When the first of April comes and the legislature find that they have not half completed their work or that many important acts remain unfinished, they will, of course, under this provision, pass a law for the continuance of the session. The governor, if the tenor of the legislation has been such as to displease him, will veto the law. He may veto it and force an immediate adjournment with a view to deprive the legislature of an opportunity to pass laws, which, though wholesome and useful for the commonwealth, may yet be obnoxious to him. It may well be doubted, whether the fast accumulating business of the legislature of this state can hereafter be despatched in a session of three months. Granting that a three months' session will suffice now for the despatch of all the important business, what will be the case when this amount of business is doubled, as it will be, after the lapse of a few years? Is legislation to be hurried and pushed by steam power or any other mechanical process, in order to suit the go-ahead habits of the day? If so, we shall have every year, more and more complaint of hurried, careless and injudicious legislation. The chief complaint against the legislature now is, that the laws are loosely framed, and framed with too little reflection and consideration. How often does it happen that a law of the utmost importance to the whole state, and which is to affect its interests for many years, is passed through in a hurried manner towards the close of the session? It often happens too, that laws pass in this way which would not pass, if sufficient delay were allowed to enable the popular sentiment on the subject to bear upon the legislature. The effect of the constitutional provision now proposed, would be to hurry legislation, and drive it, helter-skelter, through its various stages, to the end of the session. More and more steam would be put on, as the business of the body accumulated. This would be one effect of the provision.

But, after all the hurry, the first of April might still find the business of the session incomplete, and the legislature, having a proper regard for the public interests, might pass a law to prolong it. The governor must then approve or veto this law. So, it will rest with him to decide whether the legislature shall continue on or not. This will, in effect give the governor the power to prorogue the legislature, if he please. He had no idea of conferring such a power as this upon the governor. It was unheard of in this country, since republican institutions were established here.

The governor, in all the states, may convoke the legislature on special occasions; but, on no occasion, in any state of the Union, can he dissolve it. The provision would be a decided innovation, and a most mischievous one, upon the republican principles of our government.

Mr. Darlington said, he thought it advisable to fix the day of adjournment of the legislature, as well as the day of meeting. The whole experience of the legislative action of this state clearly shewed the necessity of this. When a day of adjournment is fixed, a long way in advance, the members work up to it and in reference to it, and are very likely, by increasing their industry, to get through the business, by the time fixed. At the same time, it may be necessary to allow a majority to take the responsibility of prolonging the session beyond the time fixed.

Another reason why it was proper to fix a day of adjournment was, that the legislature was in the habit of wasting much time, particularly in the early stages of the session. They made their sessions much longer than was necessary, and put the commonwealth to a great and unnecessary expense in this way. The longer they sit, the greater always becomes the accumulation of business before them. The time spent in profitable discussion is always very small. After all, no matter how long may be the session, the greater part of the work is crowded into a few last days or weeks of the session, after the day of adjournment has been fixed. This is always the case. There is almost always more business done in the last fortnight of the session than in all the preceding fortnights put together, because the members see the necessity of beginning to do the business, or else of leaving it undone. The time employed by the committees in acting upon the subjects referred to them, and in making their reports, was well spent. But, all this was generally done in the earlier part of the session. The rest of the business was ordinarily crowded into the two or three last weeks. For these reasons, he thought it would have a good effect to limit the continuance of the session to the first of April, allowing the legislature, however, to prolong the session, by resolution, should they see proper to take upon themselves that responsibility.

But, he was entirely opposed to giving the governor the power to veto the law or resolution for the continuance of the session. It was true, as the gentleman from Lycoming (Mr. Fleming) had remarked, that this would be virtually giving the governor the power of dissolving the legislature at his pleasure. This is, perhaps, one of the most unpalatable of all the prerogatives ever exercised by any of the royal governors of the American colonies, and was a constant source of vexation and complaint on the part of many of the colonies, whose governors were invested with this power. It was also a fruitful and perpetual source of irritation and dispute between the crown and the commons in England. Such a provision as the gentleman from Beaver proposes would be in effect a provision that the governor shall have the power to dissolve the legislature, after a certain day of the session. To that provision he was entirely opposed, as anti-republican and arbitrary, and wholly unnecessary.

Mr. MARTIN said, the more he had reflected upon this subject, the more had he become convinced, in his own mind, that we had better not insert this provision in the constitution. He was convinced that it would do no good, and that it might do an infinite deal of mischief to the public interests. When the subject was carefully examined, the proposition would appear absurd. How is it that the legislature should not know when they ought to adjourn as well as we do, or better than we do? We were not limited by law to so many weeks, and the legislature took it for granted that it was safe and proper to leave that matter to our own discretion. If such a discretion was to be left to a body which was assembled specially, and for a specific purpose, how much more proper must it be to allow the same discretion to a permanent body, which is annually assembled, and charged with the multifarious legislative concerns of a great commonwealth? If the legislature was fit to be trusted to do any thing, it was to be trusted to fix the time of its adjournment. If the people thought they sat too long, they have the same remedy that they have against injudicious legislation.

The responsibility of the representative and annual elections, are the true and the efficient remedy for all errors or misconduct of the legislature. The people, if they will it, can elect men who will, like the Rhode Island legislature, in past years, meet in the morning, sit till dinner time, and then adjourn, *sine die*. If, on the other hand, the people wish to have longer sessions, with a view to allow a reasonable time for the careful despatch of business, they can elect men who will carry out their views. The proposed restraint was vexatious and unnecessary, and would, without doubt, be found extremely mischievous. As to the time of meeting, he had no doubt that December would continue to be found the most convenient time for the farming interest and for all interests. On the whole, he could not see that any thing was to be gained by fixing upon January, instead of December, for the commencement of the session. Why should we pass over the month of December, a season of the year when the farmers are most at leasure? The reason and only reason given for it was, in his opinion, insufficient, if not contemptible.

It was a reason wholly unworthy of this body—viz : that the members of the legislature adjourned over the holidays. He was not for putting down the holidays of Christmas and new-years, nor for shaping the constitution of the state in reference to them. The observation or non-observation of them was to be left to the choice of each individual. If the legislature did not choose to do business at that particular time, it was not a matter for grave complaint against them, nor a reason for cutting off the most convenient month of the year for legislative business, from the sessions of our legislature. We have no power to prevent the adjournment of the legislature for a few days at any time. If we avoid the holidays by commencing the session on the first of January, the legislature may still, if they please, take a recess in January, if a recess they choose to take at all. The alteration would be unavailing, if it was intended to confine the legislature, against their will, to their business every day, and day in and day out, from the beginning to the end of their session. I have served many years in the legislature, and it was the universal practice for that body to adjourn for a few days during the Christmas holidays, and that it was of any disadvantage to the public interests, I am not prepared to say. I do not believe that it was. The time of the short recess was generally not lost by the members. They conversed with each other upon the subjects before them, made themselves acquainted with the official documents connected with their business, and had time to consider upon the many matters which were to be acted upon and to make up their minds in regard to them. They fixed their minds perhaps, after due reflection and study, upon what it was proper to do in regard to particular subjects.

The legislature had always a great deal of matter to reflect upon. To act without preparation and mature consideration, would neither be wise nor safe. He hoped the convention would be satisfied to go back to the first Tuesday in December, as the most fit and convenient time for the meeting of the legislature. The legislature would then have the whole winter before them, in which to discharge their duties, and would always be able to adjourn in March. The only reason, he repeated, which had been given for postponing the meeting of the legislature, till the first of January, was that it would avoid the holidays. It was urged that members took a few days then to themselves at the public expense. It was a poor reason for the proposed alteration. To decide such a matter in reference to a few dollars and cents, was unbecoming a great state like this. There would be no advantage gained by this pitiful and vexatious course ın regard to economy in the despatch of business. He should vote against the whole amendment as reported from the committee, and stand upon the provision of the old constitution. He was opposed also to the proposed amendments to the report of the committee. To limit the duration of the sessions, as he had already attempted to show, would be derogatory to the just rights of the legislature and their constituents, to whom they were responsible for the discharge of their duties. But the proposition to confer upon the governor the monarchical prerogative of dissolving the legislature, was still more extraordinary. Such a provision could never meet the approbation of a people who understood, and were attached to, a free representative government. He would throw as much power, perhaps, into the hands of the governor, as we have taken from him. He hoped the convention would abandon all these mischievous, and as it appeared to him, absurd projects, and go back to the original provision on this subject in the constitution of 1790, viz: "the general assembly shall meet on the first Tuesday of December, in every year, unless sooner convened by the governor."

Mr. SMYTH, of Centre, said nothing which was recommended by the committee on this subject, met his approbation to a greater extent than the proposed alteration of the time of the meeting of the legislature. He heartily approved the amendment, fixing upon the first day of January, instead of the first Tuesday of December, as the day for the annual meeting of the legislature. There was, he well knew, a strong sentiment among the people against the time now fixed. By nothing, could this convention more injure the popularity of their action on the chance of the adoption of their proposed amendments, than by continuing the present time of meeting, viz : the first Tuesday in December. It had been a complaint among the people, for many years, that the legislature, after meeting in December, spent a great deal of their time in idleness and festivity, during the continuance of the Christmas and Newyears holidays. While they were idling their time, they were still drawing their pay, and the expenses of the body were going on. The people had long regarded this as a great abuse, and they expected from this body, some attempt to prevent it. The best, and perhaps the only means to prevent it would be found in the proposed change of the time of meeting. The members from the eastern counties in the state, knew too well the feeling of their constituents on this subject, to oppose a change so salutary, and which was so much desired. He hoped the amendment reported by the committee would be adopted.

Mr. SHELLITO said, it is truly a very fine thing for members of the legislature to get their three dollars a day for work that they do not attend to, and all under the pretence of staying at home for a few days to prepare their minds by reflection, and get knowledge. They had better get their knowledge beforehand, and when they go to the legislature, go there for the purpose of doing the public business. How is it with the members of the northern parts of the state, who cannot go home during the holidays, on account of the great distance? They, I suppose, can get no wisdom during the holidays. If they have to go home for it, like the members from the neighborhood, they cannot. Is it just and right for the members to take money to frolic on, from the public treasury, in this way? Is it proper that they should have money from the people, for which they do not labor ? Would any gentleman here give a person a dollar a day to do his work and then let him go and play ? I am surprised that any one here should oppose the reasonable proposition of the committee, to prevent the members of the legislature from frolicing on the public money during the holidays. To think that the legislature should take ten thousand dollars every year to frolic with, without rendering one scrap of work in lieu of it, is abominable. I hope the amendment will pass and that this abuse will cease. I care but little for that part of the section which proposes to limit the duration of the session to the first day of April, because when spring arrives, the farmers will all be anxious to go home and attend to their private concerns, and will do so, unless the public business should be very pressing. If the members of the legislature want to frolic, let them do it on their own money, and not on the people's money.

Mr. Hiester said he hoped we should strike out all but that part of the clause which fixes the day of meeting. Any restriction as to the time of adjournment would be unmeaning, and would avail nothing. The people would expect the day of meeting to be fixed ; but it would be useless to require that the legislature should adjourn on such a day, or else pass a resolution continuing the session. That would amount to nothing, unless we went farther, and gave the governor the prerogative of dissolving the legislature. if he did not choose to approve of the resolution for continuing the session. The legislature could pass a mere resolution to prolong the session, just as well as they could pass a resolution to adjourn.

It appears to me that we are disposed to arrogate too much to ourselves in this matter. The legislature are a part of the people and are responsible to them, and it is improper for us to make provisions of a nature so trifling and so disrespectful as this, in regard to the legislature. If they conduct their business in an improper manner in any respect, the people ' to whom they are responsible, will see that the abuse is corrected.

Every one must be aware, too, that the legislature, composed as it is, to a great extent, of men of business, and especially of farmers, would not willingly prolong the session after the first of April, if the public interest would permit an adjournment. He should vote against the amendment of the gentleman from Fayette, and all amendments to this section, except one fixing the time of the meeting of the legislature.

Mr. Sturdevant said it appeared to him that we were too much disposed to restrict the action of the legislature. We ought to leave to their discretion and responsibility, the length of their sessions. They were certainly better able than we, to judge how long it would take them to dispose of their business, and we could not assume that they would prolong the sessions unnecessarily.

The proposition assumed that the legislature, consisting, as it did, of men twenty-one years of age and over; and selected by the people as their representatives, and as men qualified to do their business, did not really know when their sessions ought to be terminated. If we limited the sessions, the legislature, by a special law, would lengthen them ; so, the provision would be utterly useless. The restriction would not prevent the legislature from sitting as long as they pleased. If they choose to spend the summer in Harrisburg, they would be responsible for it to the people, their constituents, who would judge whether their session was continued unnecessarily or not.

The circumstances which gentlemen now suppose to govern the length of the sessions, may greatly change. If a session, lasting till the first day of April, be long enough, under present circumstances, there may be circumstances, hereafter, which will render a longer session proper and necessary.

It was not at all impossible that the press of business and the exigencies of the times might become such, as, on some occasions, to require the continuance of the session till the month of August, or of July. But why is it now proposed to restrict the legislature, as to the length of the sessions. Do the people require or expect any amendment of this sort? Not a single individual, among the people, ever asked or suggested such a change of the constitution. No complaint, in reference to this matter, had ever reached us from any quarter.

Some gentlemen say that the legislature do not get along quite so fast as they should do, with the public business; but it has never been pretended that the legislature is not always ready to adjourn as soon as their business is accomplished. It is objected to the section, as it stands, that the legislature meets in December and adjourns over the holidays. Of that there has been some complaint, on account of the waste of time, and it has, therefore, been wished by some to postpone the day of meeting till after the holidays. But, he had never heard of any wish, on the part of the public, for a limitation of the length of the sessions.

Mr. DARLINGTON hoped, he said, that the convention would reject the amendment and the whole report of the committee now under consideration.

What, he would ask, was the great evil complained of, and which we ought to redress? That the legislature take a short holiday at Christmas and New-years. What was the objection to this? No particular inconvenience resulted from it to the public business. But, it is said the expense is an objection. The members of the legislature, it is said, receive three dollars a day, for the time which they pass in holidays. The only objection then, is, that the state cannot afford this vast expense. What is the amount of the whole expense thus incurred? About ten thousand dollars some gentlemen say. That sum divided among over three hundred thousand taxables, will be but three cents each. It will cost but a few mills to each of our inhabitants. But, he would leave this matter for his friend from Bucks county to figure out. This was the amount of the whole inconvenience, if any there was, in the practice of adjournments by the legislature over the holidays. Did the people of Pennsylvania complain of this practice as a grievance? Did they wish to make a constitutional provision for the purpose of avoiding it? Was that one of their objects in incurring the expense of a convention? He thought not. But, if the people so much objected to the practice, their course was a very plain one. They could easily put a stop to it, by saying to their representatives, you must not spend the public money in your own pleasure and business. You must reduce your wages, by the amount of the sum which is allowed you during the holidays.

He considered the proposition to postpone the day of the meeting of the legislature as highly inexpedient. If any change was to be made in regard to that matter, an earlier instead of a later day, should be agreed upon. He thought the most suitable and convenient time for the meeting of the legislature, was the first week in November. Experience had shown that the legislative business of this state, could not be done in a less time than four months. The most convenient time for the adjournment would be in March. If the session be prolonged into the spring, it becomes extremely inconvenient for the farming interest, and, indeed, for every other interest. If we make any change at all in the time of meeting, he hoped we should fix upon the first of November, when the farmers could leave their business with convenience.

Mr. MARTIN said, he could not concur with those who proposed to fix upon January instead of December, as the time for the meeting of the legislature. The objections urged against the present time of meeting, had no force, in his opinion.

The gentleman from Crawford, (Mr. Shellito) urges that the public money is wasted by the short holidays taken by the legislature at Christmas and New-years.

Now, sir, (said Mr. Martin) I examined that matter when I was in the legislature ; and I always found that the objections to the holidays, whenever it was made, was made by those who were in search of popularity traps. With these men the objections to holidays originated, and not with the people.

He had never heard his constituents complain of the holidays, and he had never been informed that the people, generally, objected to them. All this hue and cry about the expense of the legislature, and the waste of public time in holidays, was got up as a popularity trap. The fact is— and the people generally are aware of it—that the time spent in holidays, is not lost to the public.

The members of the legislature do not know what is to be their business, until the committees are appointed. After the legislature is organized, the committees are appointed. Each member then knows what business he must attend to', and he must give some time to the examination of the subjects upon which he is to act.

Where is the harm or the loss of time in a member's going home, for a few days, to consult his constituents, and to prepare himself for acting on the subjects to be committed to his care? There is a gain of time in proceeding deliberately and advisedly with such business.

A member, who has just taken his seat, for the first time, in the legislature, and to whom the subjects committed to his charge, in parcelling out the business, is new, cannot be expected to proceed hastily and without due consideration. in the discharge of his duties. The brief recess afforded by the holidays, allows him this time, and he resumes his seat, fully prepared for the discharge of the business devolved upon him. I believe that all the clamor which we have heard against the practice of adjourning over the holidays, began, not with the people, but with those who wished, by this means, to win a little popularity.

The legislature ought certainly to have the power of fixing upon the day of adjournment. They were more able to judge upon what day they could adjourn, in reference to the state of the public business, than we were. If the legislature was not competent to fix the day, surely this convention was not.

Every member of the legislature knows, that if they waste the winter months, they must trench upon the spring, when their business requires their attention at home. A large portion of the legislature always consists of farmers and others, who find it extremely inconvenient to remain in session during the spring. When the spring opens, they can no longer confine themselves to the business of the session. This is alone a security that the legislature will always adjourn as soon as the state of the public business will allow them to do it, and also, that they will not idle away the winter months, so as to render it necessary for them to prolong the session, after the opening of spring.

Sir, this hue and cry about wasting the public time and money, in holidays and long sessions, always originates with some small popularity seeker; and it would never be heard of among the people, unless it originated in the legislature and here. The people scorn to look at this subject in the light in which it is held up to them. They are not so mean and miserly, as to begrudge a few dimes or cents, in the compensation allowed to their representatives.

I hope, sir, we shall not hear it alleged again, that the people demand this change, and we shall, I trust, leave it to the legislature to fix their day of adjournment themselves.

Mr. CURLL said, his friend on his right, who had just taken his seat, was, he thought, mistaken in supposing that the people wished no change in reference to this matter. The people, to his knowledge, had complained very much of the practice of the legislature in taking holidays and going home to spend their time, while they were paid by the public. It was unfair also, in regard to those members from a distance, who could not go home and return after the holidays. Only a few of the members could avail themselves of the privilege; and the farmers from a distance were kept here in the spring, greatly to their inconvenience, in consequence of this waste of time during the holidays. The western and northern members must stay at Harrisburg, while those living in the vicinity are enjoying New-years' and Christmas with their families at home. It was important, he thought, that the members of the legislature should attend to their business, while they were receiving pay as members. The expense of the holidays had been calculated by the gentleman from Butler at forty thousand dollars. He could not consider this as a paltry sum, even in the revenue of this commonwealth. It would in a few years, amount to a sum equal to the expenses of this convention, about which such a hue and cry had been raised here and elsewhere, for popular effect only. The people had always complained of the waste of time by the legislature. He did not feel any disposition to restrict the legislature as to the time of their adjournment. He was willing to strike out that portion of the amendment, but he would willingly support it, should he be convinced of its propriety. But, he did hope that the amendment fixing the first Tuesday in January, as the day for the meeting of the legislature, instead of the first Tuesday in December, would prevail.

Mr. FULLER said, that the gentleman from Lycoming and the gentleman from Philadelphia county, had both alleged that the people never asked for this amendment. He, however, would state to the convention, that there had been much complaint among the people, in relation to the members of the legislature not attending more closely to their duties, and with respect to the protracted sessions of that body. This very matter had been a great cause of complaint in his district, and it had been stated by members on this floor, that it had been complained of throughout the state.

With the view of remedying this evil, the amendment was adopted by the committee, which was now before the convention. The gentleman from the county of Phiadelphia must know, that the legislative bodies of Pennsylvania, do but very little business during the first month of their session. He had been in the legislature with the gentleman from the county of Philadelphia, some two or three sessions, and he spoke from experience on this subject, as the gentleman knew, when he said that their sessions had been unnecessarily protracted, which caused very great complaint among the people.

He believed that three months' legislation in the year, was as much as the people of Pennsylvania needed, and he believed that that would have been sufficient time for our legislature to sit in any year, for the last twenty years. He had no doubt but even in our greatest internal improvement struggles, that three months would have been ample time, yet some of those sessions had been protracted to five months. It was in the legislature as in this convention, very difficult at times to get any business at all done. At other times the members became anxious to have business done, and are very industrious in the business of the people. But if the time of adjournment was fixed by a constitutional provision, they knowing that they must have the business which comes before them completed in a specified time, he ventured to say, that they would be more active and industrious than they had been in former legislatures, and there would be as much business done in a month's time less than was occupied in former sessions. The amendment he had proposed did not make it imperative on the legislature to adjourn on the first Thursday in April, as some gentlemen had intimated; but it fixed that as a proper adjourning time in the opinion of this convention, and then if they were not prepared and could not adjourn at that time, with safety to the public interest, they would show it by passing a resolution extending the time. This would be throwing upon them a proper responsibility, and if the public business will justify it, they will always be willing to incur this responsibility; but, on the contrary, if there is nothing of very urgent necessity before them, it will bring their sessions to an early close. This proposition, in his opinion, would operate as a strong check upon the legislative body, and with this view he had offered; it and he thought that every gentleman here, who had been a member of the legislature, must see the propriety of adopting it. If the legislature can show to the people of the commonwealth, that the business of the people require such an extension of their session, they can extend it by resolution; and this they will always do in such cases. As to the propriety of striking out the whole of the report of the committee of the whole, he hoped no gentleman of the reform party would think of such a thing. He trusted that

the course of this body would be onward, and that it would not retro-
grade; because he believed there was no amendment which we would
make, that would receive a more universal approval of the people than
this one.   As long as his recollection served him, the legislature of Pennsylvania had taken for themselves a month, or very nearly a month's holidays, or at least they did but very little business in that time.   Then, as
to this point of the amendment, he could not see how any one could object
to it.   In relation to that part fixing the day of adjournment, he apprehended that it was entirely proper, and that no inconvenience would
result from it.   He trusted, therefore, that the amendment would be
adopted.

Mr. BIDDLE said, that the more we examine, and the more we attempt
to amend the old constitution, the better it appears, and the more perfect
did it present itself to our view.   It appears now, that the changes which
it was believed proper to make a few months ago, since we have come to
pass upon them again, all require modification and amendment either
in substance or in terms.   What was this calculated to teach us?   If the
work of our own hands, in favor of which we are naturally prepossessed,
after so short a time has elapsed, requires in our own estimation, in almost
every instance true to be changed, how can we expect that others who may
come after us will be able to construe it and act under it?   If it be
time that our amendments, which were made only a few months ago at
Harrisburg, were not now understood by ourselves, does it not teach us
the great necessity which exists to be careful in making every change
in this instrument, which has existed for near fifty years, without ever
leading to any difficulty in its construction?   But further than this, he
was afraid that when the people saw us, the ardent advocates of short sessions; and when they found us strenuously in favor of economizing time,
that they would point to our own session and our own work. If we were
to consult those out of doors, we might be told that we have been too long
in session for the amount of work we have done.   He imagined that we
were now engaged in an effort to prevent others from doing the very thing
which we ourselves have been guilty of.   He took up this argument, not
as his own, but he took it up that we might not impute to others faults
which we ourselves have been guilty of.   He should therefore, unless
some stronger reason was adduced in favor of this amendment, stronger
than any he had yet, heard be in favor of leaving it to the legislature to
exercise their own wisdom in relation to this matter of adjournments.
We have heard much of the supremacy of the people, and that they
would not be restricted by paper constitutions; the omnipotence of the
legislature, with some, has been a favorite theme of declamation.   Are
we then about to impose in the constitution a useless and unnecessary
restriction on those who are to come after us; because restrictions on the
legislature are restrictions on the people.   In many instances, restrictions
ought to be imposed, but they ought to be such as the permanent welfare
of the community require.   All others are calculated to impair the
strength of the instrument that contains them.   He was, therefore, not
prepared to vote for this amendment, because he was not satisfied that it
would be of any benefit to have it incorporated in the constitution.

Mr. BROWN, of the county of Philadelphia, was in favor of the principles contained in both branches of the amendment.   The first portion

of it proposing not to meet until the first Tuesday of January, and the second to adjourn early in April.

He did not believe, with the gentleman from the city, who had just taken his seat, that this proposition was a restriction upon the people; but he believed it to be quite the reverse. The present constitutional provision refuses to either branch of the legislature, the right to adjourn for a longer period than three days, without the consent of the other; thus placing it in the power of one branch of the legislature to keep the other in session for a year, if it sees proper. He thought if the two branches of the legislature disagreed, it ought not to be in the power of one branch to cause the other to continue in session; therefore, some period ought to be fixed, beyond which, to continue in session, should require the joint action of the two bodies.

If the time should ever come, when the one branch of the legislature had a favorite measure under consideration, which they wanted to pass, and the other was opposed to it, he considered that the best tribunal to refer the matter to, was the people, at the next election.

Sir, there is no restriction in this amendment, but it is a freedom from restriction; because, when the public good requires that the legislature should continue in session longer than the day named in the amendment, it gives them power to extend the time. He would go for this amendment, because he believed it to be one of the evils of this country, that we had too much legislation throughout the United States. When we look around, and see twenty-six legislatures of the different states, legislating for three and four months every year; and the congress of the United States legislating for six months in each year, it must strike every one, he thought, that we had more legislation than the good of the country demanded.

If any man would take the trouble to look at the list of bills which are reported to our legislature, every session, and never passed, he must see that much of the time of the legislature is taken up in that kind of legislation which never arrives at maturity; and which was, in many cases, merely agitated with a view of having an effect in particular localities. If, however, there was a limitation placed on the legislature, they would first proceed to the performance of those public duties which were called for by the people of the whole state, and which would operate for the good of the whole community.

He thought also, that all laws that were necessary to be passed in a legislative body, in a country where all power sprung from the people, should be originated with the people and considered by them, before the legislature met; and that they should not be originated in the body, without the knowledge of the people, and passed through in that hasty manner in which laws were frequently passed.

His opinion on this subject was, that the people should propose such laws as were necessary for their safety and happiness, and that the members of the legislature should take their seats, with a knowledge of the laws which the people of the state required; and not meet for the purpose of seeking what laws were wanted, without consulting the people in relation to them.

He thought that part of the amendment which required that the legis- lature should meet on the first Tuesday in January, would find but few opponents here; because, every one who had any knowledge of the man- ner in which business was conducted in the legislature of Pennsylvania, must have seen that one month of their time, if it was not wasted, in the business which was done, was not worth the fatigue which the member experienced in getting there.

If then, you give them more time between the day of their election and the day of the meeting of the legislature, as was proposed to be done by this amendment, they would have a better opportunity of consulting with their constituents, in order to obtain a knowledge of the business which they ought to perform, when they went to the seat of government.

He took it, therefore, that that portion of the amendment, in relation to the meeting of the legislature, at a later day, was a salutary provision; and the latter part, designating a day for adjournment, was equally necessary, unless there should be some good reason for their continuing in session, and in such cases, they would always take the responsibility of prolong- ing the session, by a law for that purpose.

Mr. PORTER, of Northampton, was in favor of the resolution, so far as the fact in relation to the meeting of the legislature, in January, was concerned; and, would go for striking out that part of it, in relation to their adjournment in April. He should vote in favor of the first part of the resolution, because he believed that all that was done in the legislature, prior to that time, was of very little importance. As to the amount spent by the body before the first of January, he apprehended that the gentleman from Chester labored under some mistake in his calcu- lation. He believed the expenses of the legislature to be about equal to the expenses of this convention, about a thousand dollars a day, so that ten days' holidays would amount to about ten thousand dollars. Then, in the course of ten years, this would make a very large sum, which would enable us to improve the mental faculties of the children of our common- wealth, or to add much to our system of internal improvements.

He thought that all former experience had shewn that there was more legislative business transacted in the last two or three weeks of the ses- sion, than in the whole of the preceding period.

So far, therefore, as the first part of the amendment was concerned, he should vote for it.

With regard to that part, fixing a day of adjournment, he should vote against it, for two reasons. In the first place, he had not so much fear about the legislature abusing the trusts committed to their hands, and this might be because he had never been a member of the legislature; but, he did not believe that there was so much fear of members of the legislature of Pennsylvania, abusing their trusts, as some gentlemen apprehended. He believed there was as much honesty in the senate of Pennsylvania, as in any other thirty-three men which you could find. But really he was afraid that some of those gentlemen who had been members of the legisla- ture, from their continual intimations in relation to this matter, would persuade the public that they were not the most honest set of persons in the world.

Mr. FULLER said, if the gentleman had understood him as saying that the members of the legislature were dishonest, he had entirely mistaken him.

Mr. PORTER resumed.   He was aware that there was one way of conveying evidence to a person's mind, without expressing it direct, and there was another, by an express declaration.

The gentleman did not say that the members of the legislature were dishonest but he took great pains to prove it. It reminded him very much of one of Junius's letters, in which the writer said : "I will neither call you rogue, rascal, nor liar ; but with the utmost good humor, I will prove you to be all three."

He was sure that self-interest would induce the members of the legislature to adjourn by the first week in April.   As self-interest is the ruling principle with men, you cannot have a better guaranty for their early adjournment in the spring than this.   They will not remain away from their occupations in that season of the year, when there is most call for them to be at home.   This thing called patriotism, is a very good thing, and ought to be cherished, encouraged, and preserved ; but, there are but few of us who will serve our country long, at the expense of our own individual convenience and profit. This convention, perhaps, might be an exception, as many of us have got into the scrape and cannot get out of it.   Circumstances, too, might occur that would induce the legislature to adjourn earlier, and we ought to leave them to exercise their own sound discretion in relation to the matter.

A constitutional provision to compel them to adjourn on a particular day, he feared, would be attended with great inconvenience; and he hoped, therefore, that we might change the time of meeting of the legislature, and allow them to adjourn when they pleased.

The gentleman from Philadelphia county, however, thinks that we ought not to say a word about the length of the sessions of the legislature, because of our own protracted sessions. The gentleman, however, ought to know that the doctrine has always been, to do as I say, and not do as I do ; others should not do wrong, because we had done wrong. He should be disposed to have the legislature commence their session on the first Tuesday in January, and his word for it, they would not continue in session very long in the spring.

He, like the gentleman from the county of Philadelphia, (Mr. Brown) was not for having too much legislation in the constitution; and he should be for leaving the matter of carrying out the different provisions of the constitution to legislative action.

He knew very well that there were many provisions of the constitution, which were thought by the framers of the instrument, to be very difficult to carry out, which were referred to the legislature, and carried out by that body without any difficulty.   That body has carried out many of the provisions of the existing constitution, in such manner that they have worked well in practice, and the people are perfectly satisfied with them.

Mr. FULLER then modified his amendment, by striking out all after the word " shall," in the second line, and inserting " not continue in session longer than the first Tuesday in April, unless by a joint resolution of both branches of the legislature, passed for that purpose."

Mr. CHANDLER said, this matter of the members of this body censuring the legislature for long sessions, reminded him of the old proverb, of a certain person, rebuking a certain thing, which he need not repeat here, as it would be well understood. He did not believe that so much injury had resulted to the public, and the public interests, from the multiplicity of legislation, as the gentleman from the county of Philadelphia supposed ; nor did he believe we had suffered much from the holidays occasionally taken by the members of the legislature. It was not the mere matter of money which we should regard when we were legislating for the whole people of a state. It was well known, that the first thing to be done after the organization of the legislature, was the appointment of the committees. Then, it was necessary after this, that the persons thus thrown together from different sections of the state, should become acquainted with each other, and ascertain from an interchange of opinions, the will and wishes of the people of the different sections of the state. This would require some time, and he knew of no better time to do this, than the time which members of the legislature now have.

Too much legislation was not the fault that we had most to complain of in this country. Too hasty legislation was what was most to be guarded against ; and, it was to be apprehended that we would have too much hasty legislation, by fixing the day of meeting for the legislature, on the first Tuesday of January, and compelling them to adjourn on the first Thursday in April.

He never had the honor of being a member of the legislature ; but, he was once placed on the floor of the legislature, in a situation that satisfied him, that there was great danger to be apprehended from too hasty legislation ; and, he believed that that act which placed him in that position, originated, and was carried to maturity, by too hasty legislation. Our legislative bodies, should be deliberative bodies, and not bodies to pass matters without proper consideration and reflection and discussion.

The gentleman from the county, (Mr. Brown) had deprecated the idea of one branch of the legislature being compelled to wait on the other. He (Mr. C.) however, imagined, if one house had the power of adjourning without the other, that whenever a measure might be before one house, which the other house was desirous of rejecting, they might adjourn, and leave the body remaining in session inoperative ; and then we would have something to complain of.

He would ask those gentlemen who had been members of the legislature, whether, when they first became so, they did not derive great advantages from the experience of those with whom they were associated during the first months of the session, and, more than compensated for the apparent loss of time ? If then, this, was the case, the time was not lost , and it would prevent the inconsiderate action of the body in many cases.

He would not occupy the attention of the convention longer, but would merely express the hope, that if we had adopted a hasty amendment, which was not likely to be of any benefit to the people at large, that we might now retrace our steps, and leave the old constitution as it now existed in this particular.

Mr. DUNLOP was very much afraid that the gentleman from Fayette had spoiled his amendment, by its last modification. The gentleman will recollect, that all joint resolutions require the signature of the governor, and this introduces the very difficulty which the gentleman in the first place endeavored to avoid.

He hoped the gentleman would be kind enough to put it back to what it was before; and if he did not do so, Mr. D. must say that he would be compelled to vote against it. He knew the difficulty which presented itself to the gentleman's mind; but that, he thought, could be obviated hereafter, in a separate amendment. If the resolution, or bill, to prolong the session of the legislature, requires the signature of the governor, it will be placing it in his power to veto it, and say they shall adjourn, when perhaps the public service may require that they should continue longer in session. If it was necessary that their sessions should be prolonged, it ought not to be in the power of the governor to say that they should adjourn. He hoped, therefore, that the gentleman from Fayette would remove this objection.

M. STERIGERE presumed that every gentleman's mind was made up on this subject; but as he could not vote for either of the amendments pending, he desired to say a word or two in explanation of his views. The object of the first part of this proposition was, to avoid the holiday adjournments. Now, he undertook to say that the meeting of the legislature on the first Tuesday in January, would not prevent this occurrence. Every legislature that ever assembled, had their holidays; and so it would be with every one that was to assemble in future. This convention, which met in May last, had its holidays; and it was in vain to attempt to prevent a legislature from taking holidays, by a constitutional provision. In his opinion, there was an erroneous impression in the public mind in relation to this matter. When the legislature organized, committees have to be appointed, and they must have some time to get acquainted with the wishes of the people in the different portions of the state, and to mature business for the action of the house. This must all be done before the house is able to proceed intelligently and understandingly to business; and thus, while the legislature was, apparently, doing no business, its members were most arduously engaged in committees making examinations, and preparing business for the action of the legislature. He made this statement from some little experience on the subject. There may be some few who leave the seat of government, when the legislature adjourns over for a week or ten days; but a larger portion do not leave, and are engaged during that time in an interchange of sentiment, and in obtaining information which will be of the utmost importance to them, in the prosecution of their business. He thought we had better leave this section as it stood in the old constitution, and leave it to be a matter between the members of the legislature and their constituents, if they did not perform their duties in as prompt a manner as they ought to do. He agreed with the gentleman from Northampton, that the members of the legislature were about as honest as the members of this convention, and he presumed they were about as patriotic. For all their acts, however, they were responsible to their constituents, and with them was he disposed to leave those gentlemen, without any interference on our part, in this respect.

The gentleman from the county of Philadelphia, (Mr. Brown) has told us that three months was long enough for the legislature to continue in session, to transact all the business which the people required. This, however, was but the gentleman's opinion; and he presumed if that gentleman had been asked before this body met, how long it ought to have remained in session, that he would have said that three months would have been long enough for it, but instead of that, we have been nearly six months in session. It was, in his opinion, highly improper, to place such restrictions as these upon the legislature, because much greater evils were to be apprehended from hurrying measures through the legislature, than from the time which was spent by the body, as it was thought by many in doing nothing.

He thought the argument of the gentleman from the city of Philadelphia, (Mr. Chandler) on this subject, was conclusive. It was deliberate legislation which the people want, and not hasty legislation. Give the legislature time, and let them do that which they are assembled to do, well, and the people will be more benefited by it than the difference in the expense will injure them.

The gentleman from Northampton has told us, that he has never seen that there has been much done in the legislature for the first two or three weeks. Well, the reason of this, was, because, during that time, the members were engaged on committees, maturing business for the action of the house, and this must be done when they meet in January, just as well as when they meet in December. He would rather vote to have the legislature meet in November than in January, because he believed that more good would result from it.

Mr. M'CAHEN moved the previous question, which was seconded by eighteen members rising in their places.

Mr. M'CAHEN called for a division of the question, so as to take the question first upon the first clause of the section, ending with the word " governor."

The question was then taken—" Will the convention agree to the first division ?" viz :

" The general assembly shall meet on the first Tuesday of January in every year, unless sooner convened by the governor ?"

The yeas and nays were required by Mr. EARLE, and Mr. GRENELL, and are as follow, viz :

YEAS—Messrs. Agnew, Banks, Barclay, Barndollar, Barnitz, Bedford, Bigelow, Brown, of Lancaster, Brown, of Northampton, Brown, of Philadelphia, Carey, Chambers, Chandler of Chester, Clarke, of Beaver, Clark, of Dauphin, Clarke, of Indiana, Cleavinger, Cline, Cochran, Cox, Craig, Crain, Crawford, Crum, Cummin, Cunningham, Curll, Darrah, Denny, Dickey, Dickerson, Dillinger, Donagan, Donnell, Doran, Dunlop, Earle, Fleming, Foulkrod, Fry, Fuller, Gamble, Gearhart, Gilmore, Grenell, Harris, Hastings, Hayhurst, Hays. Helffenstein, Henderson, of Allegheny, Henderson, of Dauphin, Hiester, High, Houpt, Hyde, Ingersoll, Keim, Kennedy, Kerr, Krebs, Lyons, Maclay, M'Cahen, M'Call, M'Sherry, Merkel, Miller, Montgomery, Pollock, Porter, of Lancaster, Porter, of Northampton, Purviance, Read, Ritter, Royer, Russell, Seeger, Schoets, Sellers, Seltzer, Serrill, Shellito, Sill, Smith, of Columbia, Smyth, of Centre, Snively, Stickel, Sturdevant, Taggart, Thomas, Todd, Weaver, White, Young—98.

NAYS—Messrs. Baldwin, Biddle, Chandler, of Philadelphia, Chauncey, Coates, Cope, Darlington, Hopkinson, Meredith, Sterigere, Weidman, Sergeant, *President*—12.

So the question was determined in the affirmative.

And on the question. "Will the convention agree to the second division," viz :

"And shall adjourn on the first Thursday in April, unless continued longer in session by law for that purpose?"

The yeas and nays were required by Mr. DICKEY, and Mr. AGNEW, and are as follow, viz :

YEAS—Messrs. Banks, Barndollar, Brown, of Philadelphia, Carey, Clarke, of Beaver. Cox, Crain, Crawford, Crum, Cummin, Darrah, Dickey, Dillinger, Dunlop, Fry, Fuller, Gamble, Gearhart, Gilmore, Grenell, Hays, High, Hyde, Ingersoll, Kelin, Krebs, Lyons, M'Cahen, Merkel, Miller, Purviance, Read, Ritter, Royer, Seager, Shellito, Smith, of Columbia, Stickel, Taggart, White, Woodward—41.

NAYS—Messrs. Agnew, Baldwin, Barclay, Barnitz, Bedford, Biddle, Bigelow, Bown, of Lancaster, Brown, of Northampton, Chambers, Chandler, of Chester, Chandler, of Philadelphia, Chauncey, Clark, of Dauphin, Clarke, of Indiana, Cleavinger, Clino, Coates, Cochran, Cope, Craig, Cunningham, Curll, Darlington, Denny, Dickerson, Donagan, Donnell, Doran, Earle, Fleming, Foulkrod, Harris, Hastings, Hayhurst, Helffenstein, Henderson, of Allegheny, Henderson, of Dauphin, Hiester, Hopkinson, Houpt, Kennedy, Kerr, Long, Maclay, Magee, Mann, Martin, M'Call, M'Dowell, M'Sherry, Meredith, Montgomery, Pollock, Porter, of Lancaster, Porter, of Northampton, Russell, Schoetz, Sellers, Seltzer, Serrill, Sill, Smyth, of Centre, Snively, Sterigere, Sturdevant, Thomas, Todd, Weaver, Weidman, Young, Sergeant, *President*—72.

So the question was determined in the negative.

Mr. READ moved to amend the section as amended, by adding thereto the following, viz :

"And shall not continue in session longer than the first Tuesday of April, unless continued by a vote of two-thirds of each house."

He offered this amendment, he said, because he was satisfied, from his observation and experience, that three months was ample time, and that even two months was long enough to complete the business of each session.. He trusted that members would see the propriety of agreeing to this amendment. Under the present mode of conducting the business of the legislature, the mass of the public business was thrown upon the last three weeks, and this would be the case, whatever might be the length of time allowed for the sessions. He was anxious to see some restriction placed upon this waste of public time by the legislature.

Mr. CUNNINGHAM said, the amendment was not in order. No amendment could apply to the report of the committee, and as the original section of the constitution was not before us, no amendment could apply to that.

Mr. MARTIN said, he hoped the amendment would not prevail. We have now, by confirming the report of the committee of the whole, agreed that the legislature shall meet on the first Tuesday in January. If we now restrict the session to the first Tuesday of April, we shall require the legislature then to adjourn, no matter what may be the state of their business. This will put it in the power of a minority to close the session at that time, for the amendment requires that the session shall not be continued longer than the first Tuesday of April, without the concurrent votes of two-thirds of both houses. Any minority, perhaps a party minority, a factious minority, might thus have it in their power to defeat all the chief acts of the session. Every one acquainted with legislative proceedings, knows that the most important business of every session, is generally finished near the close of the session. Any vigorous opposition to a measure, especially if it was a subject of much deliberation and discussion, will defer its final passage through both houses, till near the close of the session. Thus it is plain that, by this amendment, we put it in the power of a small faction, consisting of only one-third of either house, to defeat the most important business of every session, and to render impotent the will of a large majority of both houses. A more unsafe measure, and one better calculated to defeat the expression of the public will, through the legislature, could not be devised. He believed that the first weeks of the session were, generally, most carefully employed in carving out and maturing the business, by the standing committees. But in the latter part of the session, there is always much hasty legislation, and much log-rolling. A great many bills fall through, and lie over, as unfinished business, and many more are hastily passed without due consideration. The proposition to limit the session, would, in his opinion, have the effect to increase the hurry and confusion attending the close of a session, and, at the same time, to prevent the legislature from proceeding in its usual and proper course in the early part of the session.

The question was then taken on the amendment, offered by Mr. Read, and it was decided in the negative; yeas 41, nays 69, as follow, viz:

Yeas—Messrs. Banks, Barndollar, Bigelow, Clarke, of Beaver, Cleavinger, Cox, Crain, Crawford, Crum, Cummin, Darrah, Dickey, Dillinger, Dunlop, Fry, Fuller, Gamble, Gearhart, Gilmore, Grenell, Hayhurst, High, Ingersoll, Keim, Kiebs, Magee, M'Cahen, Merkel, Miller, Purviance, Read, Ritter, Royer, Shellito, Smith, of Columbia, Smyth, of Centre, Snively, Stickel, Taggart, White, Woodward—41.

Nays—Messrs. Agnew, Baldwin, Barclay, Barnitz, Bedford, Biddle, Brown, of Lancaster, Brown, of Northampton, Carey, Chambers, Chandler, of Chester, Chandler, of Philadelphia, Chauncey, Clark, of Dauphin, Clarke, of Indiana, Cline, Coates, Cochran, Cope, Craig, Cunningham, Curll, Darlington, Denny, Dickerson, Donagan, Donnell, Fleming, Foulkrod, Harris, Hastings, Hays, Helffenstein, Henderson, of Allegheny, Henderson, of Dauphin, Hiester, Hopkinson, Houpt, Hyde, Kennedy, Kerr, Long, Maclay, Mann, Martin, M'Call, M'Dowell, M'Sherry, Meredith, Montgomery, Pollock, Porter, of Lancaster, Porter, of Northampton, Russell, Saeger, Scheetz, Scott, Sellers, Seltzer, Serrill, Sill, Sterigere, Sturdevant, Thomas, Todd, Weaver, Weidman, Young, Sergeant, President—69.

The section as amended was then agreed to.

Mr. Meredith suggested the expediency of taking the question on the remaining sections of the article without reading them; if no amendments were to be proposed.

Mr. Porter, of Northampton, said, he wished to offer an amendment to the next section, allowing the house to elect a speaker *pro tempore*, in the absence of the speaker. Much inconvenience had been felt in the house for the want of such a person.

On motion of Mr. SERGEANT,

The Convention then adjourned.

APPENDIX

TO THE

EIGHTH VOLUME.

APPENDIX.

Mr. STERIGERE,* of Montgomery county, rose and said :

Mr. Chairman, it is with extreme reluctance that I rise to say any thing on a subject which has already been discussed in this body for so many successive weeks. My reluctance arises, in a great measure, from the consciousness which I feel of my own inability to do justice to a subject which has been so ably debated on both sides of the house. Fifteen of the twenty delegates from Philadelphia city and county, have made seventeen speeches. I hope the committee will pardon one of the other one hundred and thirteen for trespassing on their time a brief period.

Sir, I am free to confess that this question is one which requires more deliberation and more talent, than I shall be enabled to bring into its discussion ; and I must also say, that the reluctance with which I enter it, at all, is enhanced by the consideration that, after other gentlemen have been allowed the privilege of addressing the committee for one, or two or three days, in explanation of the views they may entertain, I am to be confined, under the operation of the rule which has very recently been adopted, to the space of a single hour.

It seems to me, that this does not afford sufficient time, even to glance at the various matters which have been introduced, much less to attempt a discussion of them.

I had entertained some hopes, frem the course which this debate has taken, for the last two or three days, that we were at least about to come directly to the subject, upon which we have to act ; but I think that it has again been departed from by the remarks which have been made by the gentleman from the city of Philadelphia—who last addressed the committee, (Mr. Cope). Of all the gentlemen who constitute this body, I should have thought that he would have been the very last to introduce political topics, here or elsewhere, which he must have known could not have failed to excite a strong feeling among us.

But, Mr. Chairman, the lingering feeling of hostility which still exists against the great chief who has recently retired from public life, to enjoy that repose at the hermitage which his advanced years and his glorious public services render so essential to him, still exists, I regret to see, in the minds of some of the members of this body, as well as in the minds of many beyond these walls, and inclines them to introduce topics which have no relevancy here, and to make comments upon them which, to my mind, are as improper as they are ill-timed and out of place.

The gentleman from the city of Philadelphia, (Mr Cope) has been pleased to attribute things to General Jackson, of the authority for which I am entirely in ignorance. In this, he has followed the example of other delegates who have addressed the committee on this subject. The late chief magistrate has been reviled and calumniated, and charges have been brought against him, in the course of this debate, which, I feel satisfied, have no foundation in truth. Among other offensive things which have been said against him, the gentleman from the city of Philadelphia, in his remarks this morning has compared him to a cock-fighter. Sir, I think that the members of this body will agree with me that, on a question of such grave importance as that now before the committee, language of such a character is not such as to give dignity or reputation to our proceedings. Such language is too low for this floor.

But, Mr. Chairman, it appears to me that the position assumed by the gentleman from the city of Philadelphia, is of a very extraordinary character. He has stated that, according to a calculation which he has recently made, the sum of six hundred and twenty millions of dollars, would be required annually to pay the expenses incurred annually by the citizens of the United States. Archimedes is reported to have said, "give me a place upon which to set my foot, and I will move the world." And so it is with these gentlemen; give them a place to stand upon, and they can prove any thing which they may set out to prove. But, unfortunately for their own argument, they endeavor to prove too much; and it would require a greater stretch of credulity than they can hope for, to believe that the positions which they attempt to maintain are sound, or capable of being proved to the satisfaction of any intelligent and unprejudiced mind.

The only idea which the gentleman from the city seems to hold out, is this: that when any man incurred a debt to the amount of so many dollars, and paid it, that amount of money was to remain inactive for the whole period of a year. On no other ground can the gentleman hope to make good the ground he has taken. In a day, a single dollar may pay hundreds—in a week, thousands.

I have taken some pains, Mr. Chairman, to investigate the subject, in order that I might be the better able to perform the duties which I am sent here to discharge; but it will be impossible to lay before the committee the results of that investigation in the short space of time, during which I shall be permitted to retain the floor. I shall therefore, glance very briefly at them, and pass through them as rapidly as I can. I would not now trouble the committee with them, did I not feel that I had a serious duty to perform, and that there are those at home, to whom I am to answer for the course I may pursue in this convention. I am aware that I shall give some votes which may be called in question by my political friends there, as well as here, and I am desirous to justify myself, as I believe I shall be able to do, both here and elsewhere.

It is not my purpose to enter into a discussion of these ten thousand matters which have been introduced into this debate, and which have no sort of connexion with the question now to be decided. Nor is it my purpose to hunt up musty and long forgotten words, in order that I may justify my own feelings by exhibiting to the view of this committee the votes which have been given, at other times and in other places, by the members of this body. I do not intend to follow the example which has been set before us by the learned president of this convention, and to take you to China that I may shew you what are the laws which prevail in relation to the currency there. Nor will I go back to the days of knight-errantry to learn what was the state of trade and commerce in those times. I will travel into no such distant regions for any argument which I may have to offer, first, because I think that we shall find nothing applicable to the subject; and, secondly, because, if we could, I should feel myself incompetent to the performance of so arduous and extraordinary a task. I think, as I have before intimated, that the debate has been of an improper character, und that topics have been introduced which, inasmuch as they had no connexion with the question before us, ought to have been excluded. I think that a political character has been given to it, which was entirely unsuited to the occasion. The party with which I act in this body, is accused of having been the first to introduce these political topics; but, even if this is the case, I think it must be admitted that the course which we have pursued has been forced upon us, and that we could not, consistently with the duty which we owe to our constituents, have pursued any other.

As a justification of some of the arguments which have been introduced by gentlemen on the other side of the question, it has been said that we have made a severe and unwarranted attack upon the banks, and that those who conduct them have been made the subjects of illegitimate and unjust observation.

The questions which it is our duty here to decide, are of the most grave and important character—involving the rights and the interests of a million and a half of people, not for a few days—a few months—a few years—but for a long series of years to come—and all that we do here, is to be submitted to the people for their examination and approbation, or rejection. For my own part, therefore, I feel disposed to treat this subject with all the deliberation and gravity which its importance deserves. I am disposed to consider it, as the learned judge from the city of Philadelphia (Mr. Hopkinson) has very properly said, in a spirit of conciliation and peace—and not to entangle myself in a political difficulty with any member of this body. I fear, however, that the remarks of the gentleman from the city of Philadelphia, were much less conciliating in their tone and temper, than the observation just referred to, would naturally have led us to anticipate. The gentleman, among other things, observed that he saw around him some honest faces, the fragments of a party to which the government was indebted for almost every thing valuable in it. I presume by this the gentleman intended to place his own friends in contrast with the members of another party here present, who have been denounced as a party ready to join their leaders at Washington to put down the institutions and the liberties of the country, and to destroy every thing that was valuable and desirable in them.

The gentleman has also been pleased to say, that the remarks of some of the members of this body, became important from the situations which they occupied ; as though to insinuate that they were entitled to consideration or respect, only because they came to us endorsed with all the weight of official dignity. Sir, in that particular the learned judge possesses a pre-eminent advantage over us ; since we all know how important a station he does himself hold under the government of his country. I cannot claim to have any importance on this account with the learned judge. But, Mr. Chairman. notwithstanding all remarks of this kind, we have a duty to perform to our constituents, according to the best ability we may possess, and I, for one, shall not be turned aside from it.

It was my intention to have given some little attention to the observations which have fallen from the gentleman from Washington county, (Mr. Craig) and who infused into these observations so much of political spirit and political rancour as to render them deserving of comments which I shall not at this time condescend to bestow upon them. He read extracts from certain documents with a view to convict a distinguished officer of government of inconsistency, and as acting in opposition to the people of the state. I shall not enter into this subject now. If gentlemen will examine it for themselves, they will find that there is very little evidence to support the position which the delegate has taken, and how little regard should be paid to it.

The gentleman, also, introduced a report on the subject of banks, with a view to shew, that the legislature of Pennsylvania were in favor of them, at the time General Jackson was in opposition to them. In reply to this argument, I have to say, that that report was made by a high individual, Mr. Leaming, the federal representative from the city of Philadelphia, who was chairman of the committee, and that the report was never acted on, nor sanctioned by that body. The messages which have been read, are no endorsers, because some were on one side and some on the other.

We have been told, over and over, that there is a party in this body which is opposed to all banks—that we are waging an interminable and insane war against all the banking institutions of the country, and observations and projects of this kind are laid to our charge, for the purpose of affording gentlemen on the other side of the question, a better opportunity of extending their remarks to any latitude which they may think proper. These charges were improper, and these purposes have been again and again disclaimed, and it is an act of great injustice that such imputations shall be sent forth against a certain portion of this body. Let gentlemen tell me, if they can, who have proposed to abolish the banks ? Who has proposed to destroy them ? Who has proposed to break up the banking system by the roots ? or who in this convention has made any observations, to justify the inference that the party with which I act, is in favor of prostrating these institutions ? Sir, I know of none such, I have heard of none such, and repeat, that it is unfair in gentlemen to pursue this course towards men who honestly differ with them in opinion. Gentlemen are altogether mistaken. They set out by assuming facts which they must be aware, are not susceptible of proof, nor founded in truth. The object held in view by those who are here regarded as the opponents of the banking system, is not, as has been assumed, to destroy or up-root that system or the institutions which have been created under it, but it is to regulate and restrain their operations, in order that we may be enabled to secure all the good purposes for which they were created, and to prevent any evils from their improper administration. Every gentleman on this floor, so far as I have yet heard, is in favor of a properly regulated banking system; every gentleman, so far as I have heard, is in favor of a proper and secure kind of bank-paper; that is to say, paper convertible at all times into gold and silver. This is the doctrine which all our bank charters uphold and sustain: and none of them contemplate allowing the banks to issue any paper which is not at all times convertible into gold and silver. This is the doctrine of our legislature, and this is the doctrine for which we are contending in this body, and who among us, of any party, wishes to go further? Who among us, of any party, wishes that the banks should have the privilege to issue paper which is not at all times convertible into gold and silver? If there be any, he has not been bold enough to avow his wishes. I believe that there are none here who entertain such views. We have heard some warm panegyrics, in the progress of this discussion, on the banking institutions, and on the benefits of the blessings which they were said to have bestowed upon us. To them has been attributed all the prosperity which it has been our happy lot to enjoy. If we could bring ourselves to believe all that has been said in relation to them by some gentlemen who have addressed the committee, we should come at once to the conclusion, that the banking system was the only element of prosperity in this great and growing state of Pennsylvania. That they are the very heart blood of security.

If we believe all we have heard in favor of the banks, we must come to the conclusion that all the energy, and the skill, and the industry, and the enterprise of our people, amounted to nothing, when put in the scale with the banking system. Nay, that even our charities were dependent upon the liberality and the kindness of the banks. We have been told by the gentleman from Allegheny, (Mr. Forward) of the great wonders which have been wrought by the banks in the section of the state in which he resides; and he has thought proper to introduce the opinion of a distinguished citizen of this commonwealth, in favor of banking institutions. I allude to Mr. Carey. I do not know that the opinion of that gentleman can be of any service to us in deciding upon the question under consideration, but happening to observe an opinion which was delivered by that gentleman on the same subject some time ago, I will, with the permission of the committee, read it for the information of the members. I find it in a publication against banking institutions, made by Mr. Carey in the year 1816.

In that publication he says: "Previous to commencing this pamphlet and during its progression in my hands, prudence and discretion have been constantly exerting themselves to repress my zeal and to deter me from the undertaking. They have constantly spread before my eyes the risk of offending these powerful bodies, the directors of the banks, who have so many opportunities of making their indignation be felt, and some of whom may not be above the mean and malignant desire of availing themselves of these opportunities.

"To the soundness of these suggestions, (of prudence and discretion) I must freely assent. This plan is practicable, and were I to consult my own personal advantage or comfort, I should bow down in humble submission to their authority. I am well aware of the risk I run. I know if there be at any of the boards any practice of malice or resentment, (and were can there twelve men assemble together without malice orresent ment?) it will be roused into action to persecute the man who has dared to arraign those institutions at the bar of the public, and to accuse them of gross errors, which have produced a fertile crop of misfortunes and distress to our citizens.

"Another consequence equally clear is present to my view. One bank director, actuated by malice and resentment, would do me more injury in a day, than one hundred of those, whose cause I undertake to defend, would do me good in seven years. The malice of the one, would be strong, lasting, insatiable, and as vigilant as Argus, with his hundred eyes to gratify his spleen. The friendship or the gratitude of the others, would be cold, torpid and lifeless."

Such, resumed Mr. S., were the deliberate opinions of Matthew Carey concerning banks and bank directors. Has not time and experience confirmed their soundness? Where is the man whose observations and experience has not convinced him this is all too true?

If the opinion of this gentleman was of any consequence in a debate here, we find that some years ago he entertained opinions in relation to the banking system, which differed very widely from those which have been referred to by the gentleman from Allegheny, as the opinions expressed at the present time. I cannot, however, for my own part, see what this has to do with the matter under discussion,

The gentleman from Allegheny, in his zeal, has also told us, in prophecy, that the time will come before long, when the banks will be so popular that those who opposed them would be denounced as tories. Sir, this is history already and not prophecy. Those who oppose the banks, are denounced as tories even at this time, and this is done by the descendants of tories and refugees of the American revolution.

But, Mr. Chairman, the prejudice which exists against banks, is a very vehement prejudice. The people who see the crisis to which the affairs of this nation have been brought—when they recurred to the immense profits which were made out of these banking institutions—when they saw that the banking capital of this state which, in the year 1814, amounted only to seven millions and a half, suddenly increased to the amount, I believe, of something like seventy-four millions of dollars,— when they saw that over-trading and over-banking produced such pernicious results as those which we have experienced and do still experience, they became naturally excited against these institutions.

Previous to the year 1814, there were but four banks in the state of Pennsylvania, with a capital of seven millions and a quarter of dollars.

In the year 1814, forty-one banks were added to the number, and the banking capital of the state increased to the sum of seventeen millions. We now have in this state, seventy-eight banks, with an authorized capital of $74,051,000,—$58,174,336 of which has been paid in. These have now in circulation notes amounting to $23,648,770. Their discounts are seventy-eight millions of dollars, and their liabilities one hundred and eighty-three millions.

In the United States, in 1831, there were three hundred and thirty banks, with one hundred and ten millions of capital.

In 1834, five hundred and six banks, with two hundred and five and a quarter millions of capital. In two years before 1836, the banking capital increased from two hundred, to two hundred and fifty-one millions. Bank notes, from ninety-five to one hundred and ten millions, and bank liabilities from three hundred and twenty-four millions, to four hundred and fifty-seven millions.

When these things were observed by the people, it was natural that a great prejudice against them, by those which they supposed had produced such ruinous consequences to their integrity, should exist. The explosion of the banks shewed the people how little security they did in fact possess for their notes, which they might get into their possession.

I have before me a statement which I have made out from some documents in relation to the condition of the Bank of England and the Bank of the United States; and the result was that, for the period of twenty-seven years, previous to the year 1805, the specie of the Bank of England towards its circulation, was two and three to one, and so long as eleven years, previous to 1826, it was eleven to one.

According to the report of the secretary of the treasury on the deposit banks in the United States, their notes in circulation were about five times the amount of specie in their vaults; and this would be found to be about the condition of the banks of the state of Pennsylvania at this time.

According to a report made to us by the auditor general, it appears that the United States bank had in circulation about nine millions of dollars of her own notes, and for the redemption of this vast amount of notes, she had only about three millions of dollars in specie. That institution has been drawing in her own notes for a long time, and has been paying out the notes of the old Bank of the United States. This is a fact which can be proved at any time, and it appears, therefore, that they have not given us a true account of the amount of notes which they have issued.

A short time previous to the period alluded to, the amount of notes in circulation was thirty millions of dollars and upwards; and I presume that the whole amount of notes at this time in circulation, including the notes of the old United States bank and of the present United States bank, will not fall far short of that amount. It is impossible to know what is the amount of the issues of this bank, in consequence of the issue of the notes of the old bank, in the place of the notes of the new United States bank. We have no means of obtaining accurate information.

From all the observations which we are able to make, and from all the investigation of which the subject is susceptible, it is evident that almost all the debts of the banks in the United States, are debts of honor; and that, for the payment of the immense amount of notes which they have in circulation, and for their liabilities of all description, they have nothing to offer that would redeem them to any considerable extent. These things are apparent—they admit of no evasion—they are facts which can not be got rid of. And here it is that the disposition is becoming more and more strong, not only in the community in which we live, but among the people in every part of the United States, to throw some restraint upon the management of these banking institutions. This is a natural disposition, and has grown out of the nature of circumstances by which we have been surrounded.

What may have been the immediate causes of the calamities under which we are now suffering it is useless to inquire, except so far as an inquiry into the causes may lead us to a remedy for these calamities. Beyond this, no good can result from such an investigation.

Some gentlemen have attributed the present condition of things, to the specie circular issued under the administration of the late chief magistrate of the United States. Some have attributed it to the manner in which the bill to regulate the public deposits was executed by the secretary of the treasury ; while others have attributed it to " the ruthless and insane war," as it has been termed, upon the Bank of the United States.

For my own part, Mr. Chairman, I do not believe that the existing state of things is to be attributed to any or all of these particular causes. I believe it is to be wholly attributed to the charter of the Bank of the United States by the legislature of Pennsylvania. This is my deliberate opinion. It has been known, for the period of twenty years, that the charter granted by the Congress of the United States to that institution, would expire on the fourth of March, 1836 ; and for many years before that charter expired, it was notorious to the people of this country, that Congress would not consent to its renewal. The bank began to curtail its issues, so as to wind up its affairs with safety to the business interests of the community ; and all the other banks throught the Union began to regulate their business in such a manner as to conform to the proceedings of the bank of the United States.

Every man who was engaged largely in business, was also arranging his affairs in the same manner, and when it became certain that Congress would not renew the charter of the bank, the amount of business and of bank accommodation had been reduced to a very safe limit. If this had been allowed to remain as it was, none of the over-trading and over-issues and speculation which followed the re-charter of that institution by the legislature of this state, would have taken place. But, unfortunately, for the business and the prospects of this country, such was not the case.

The United States bank was looked upon by the party in power, as a great balance wheel, capable, as it was said, of regulating and controlling the general currency of the country, and the very moment it received its charter at the hands of the legislature, it began to expand its issues and its accommodations. All the other banks in the Union followed the example ; and every business man, finding the facility with which loans of money could be obtained, began to extend his business in the same proportion. A man who had a capital of $1,000, would be found increasing his business to $10,000, or more ; and a man with a capital of $20,000, would be found increasing his business to $50,000 or $100,000.

They ran largely into debt—large importations were made—heavy debts were contracted, and ruin was the consequence.

I am fully convinced, that to the re-charter of the United States Bank, by the legislature of Pennsylvania, is fairly and truly to be attributed all our distress, all our calamity. If the time allotted me, would permit, I could shew by documents not to be disputed, that the accommodations afforded by the banking institutions in this state, in 1835, at a time when it was evident that the Bank of the United States would not be re-chartered by congress, amounted to $27,323,000. The amount afforded by the sixteen Philadelphia banks, was $20,182,000. And by the twenty-five county banks, $7,141,000. The notes of the Philadelphia banks then in circulation, amounted to $3,943,000. Those of the county banks, to $3,420,000. In less than one year after the Bank of the United States was chartered by this state, the notes in circulation, of the Philadelphia banks, had increased to $6,034,600, nearly seventy per cent, and their accommodations to $29,632,000, nearly fifty per cent, and in the same time, the notes of the county banks, had increased to $6,746,000, nearly one hundred per cent, and their accommodations to $12,480,000, nearly eighty per cent. In this short period, the increase of the circulation of bank notes in this state, was upwards of seventy per cent, and the increase of bank accommodations, fifty-five per cent. This was the consequence of the chartering of the Bank of the United States. From the time when the people were brought to the impression that that institution would be re-chartered, down to the time of the suspension of specie payments, bank accommodation increased so much as to lead inevitably to the results which we now experience.

Mr. Chairman, it has been denied here by a gentleman of high respectability and standing, (Mr. Sergeant) that the importation of foreign goods was the cause of the vast foreign debt which we owed; and he asserts that that debt was created by the importation of specie!! This assertion, whatever credit we may award to it, on the score of ingenuity, will not be sufficient, I think, to satisfy any candid man in this convention, or elsewhere, that the fact is as it is stated to be. If we consider the amount of specie in the vaults of the banks, at the time they suspended specie payments, compared with what it was a year before that event occurred, we shall find that it had not increased to any great extent. If the sum of thirty millions of dollars—the amount of the foreign debt—had been imported into the United States, it certainly would have been found somewhere in the country, and would have superceded the necessity of the suspension of specie payments on the part of our banks. To my mind, this seems to be a most extraordinary and unaccountable argument. The difficulty under which the people labor here, and which they desire to be corrected with as little delay as possible, is the existence of an institution in this city, and in this state, which has been established in open and direct violation of the public will, and in direct opposition to the public interest, and the public welfare. The people desire to be freed from this incubus; they desire to get rid of an institution, embracing, as the Bank of the United States does, a capital greater than all the other banks of the state of Pennsylvania, put together. The people also desire that they should be provided with some security against the over issues of the banks of the state generally; they desire that some limits should be placed upon the accommodations or facilities afforded by the banks, for the purposes of speculation and foreign trade. They desire, also, to be furnished with some security for the redemption of the notes issued by these institutions.

This, sir, it appears to me, is the amount of what is required by those who are generally supposed to have arrayed themselves in opposition to the banking system. I do sincerely believe that a large majority of the people of this commonwealth, desire to see the charter of the United States Bank of Pennsylvania abolished. I believe that a large majority of the people, desire to see a limit placed upon the amount of bank capital, bank issues and bank accommodations, and that they desire to have a better security than that which they now possess, for the redemption of the notes of these institutions.

If this is the fact, and I have not, myself, a doubt upon the subject, we were naturally led to the inquiry, what measures should be proposed to secure these desirable objects, and to prevent a recurrence of the alarming evils, under which the country is suffering at the present time. Several plans have been proposed. One of them, has been to make the stockholders liable for all the debts of the institutions, to which they may belong. Other propositions of a different kind have been made, some requiring the legislature to place upon the banks, such wholesome restrictions, as may, from time to time, seem to them to be expedient and proper; others, prohibiting the banks from issuing notes of a less denomination than ten dollars; and others, prohibiting the granting of a bank charter, unless by the vote of two successive legislatures. It is probable I may differ from a large majority of my political friends on this floor, but I am compelled to acknowledge that, from the best reflection which I have been able to give to the subject, I look upon all these propositions as being inefficacious and delusive.

I was not at Harrisburg at the time the vote was taken on the proposition, to render the stockholders of those institutions personally liable ; but, if I had been present, I should certainly have voted against it. And while I am on the floor, I will state briefly the reasons which, would have swayed my mind in the course I should have adopted. I look upon it as being altogether unjust and impolitic, that an individual who might possibly hold only a single share of the stock of any of these institutions, should be held liable in all his property for the whole debts of that institution, however those debts might have been incurred. I cannot reconcile such a provision, in my own mind, with any standard of right and justice.

We have been told that a large portion of the banking capital of this commonwealth, is held in small amounts. If this is the fact, you would find many individuals, interested, only, perhaps, to the amount of a single share, and yet, it is proposed to make them liable in the whole amount of their property. Where is the justice of this? Is it just, is it right, is it equitable that a guardian, a trustee, or any other person, holding stock to the amount of one hundred dollars, should be held liable, in all his property, for the whole debts of the institution?

But again, Mr. Chairman. I believe it would be impracticable to carry such a provision into effect. I have heard myself of no plan by which this could be accomplished. Would you say that an individual who became originally a stockholder, should be liable in every emergency, if he had transferred and sold the amount of his stock? Surely, no sane man would ever invest his money in so perilous a project. If you propose to limit this liability, only to the time during which he may be a stockholder, the provision would amount to nothing at all; because the moment he had reason to expect that difficulty of any kind was about to arise, he would sell out without loss of time, and, in all probability, to a man who might have no responsibility. And if every man to whom the stock may, from time to time be transferred, is to be held perpetually liable, the absurdity of the proposition becomes still more apparent. The consequence of such provisions in bank charters, would be, that no man of character or responsibility—no man in the possession of his sound senses, would ever own a share of stock; and the end of it would be, that all moral restraints which men of character and respectability impose when interested, would be removed, and that so far from giving any additional security, we should take away all the security which now exists. The security of character and integrity, which is now, I hope, to be found in the majority of the bank directors of this state, would be entirely removed, and these institutions would fall into the hands of mere swindlers, and irresponsible speculators in stocks. So far, then, from being a proposition which will increase the security the people now have, I repeat, it is my opinion, that it is a proposition which would take away even that security which we now possess.

Of the forty-one banks chartered by the legislature of Pennsylvania, in the year 1814, thirty-nine received charters—thirty-seven went into operation—eleven forfeited their charters, and one wound up its concerns; the year 1822, only twenty-two of these banks were in existence as specie paying banks. There were six hundred banks incorporated in the various states of the Union; about two hundred of which, were broken, and fifty suspended. From 1821, to 1830, one hundred and sixty-five banks broke, which had thirty millions of capital. I attribute these results to such kind of persons, as I say would be brought into those institutions, if the stockholders were made individually liable for the debts of the corporation. I believe it was owing to such causes that those banks have failed, and hereafter, this would be the history of the banking system throughout the United States, if such provision were a part of their charters. Are we prepared to impose upon the people of this commonwealth provisions which must lead to such disastrous results? I hope not—I trust not. I, for one, entertaining the honest conviction that such a provision would be improper, impolitic, unjust—yes, sir, and impracticable.

Another proposition which it is not worth while to discuss here, but which has given rise to an almost interminable debate, has been introduced. I allude to that offered by the gentleman from Adams, (Mr. Stevens) rendering it the duty of the legislature "to provide wholesome restrictions on all banking institutions within this commonwealth, so as to promote the best interests of all the people."

This is an amendment so extremely convenient in its nature, and so well calculated to tally with the conscience of a man, whether his conscience be long or short, that it would have suited any kind of case which could have occurred. It would have done for a charter with a capital of one million, or with a capital of one hundred millions; it would have done for a charter which had one year, or a hundred years to run; it would have done for a charter, giving permission to issue notes without redeeming them in specie; or it would have done equally well for a charter, requiring a corporation to issue no more notes than would be equivalent to the amount of specie in its vaults.

To all these uses, the provision of the gentleman from Adams might, with equal facility, have been applied. It would enable the legislature to do any thing or every thing, and in the end, it would amount to nothing. But, as that proposition is not now before us, it is of no use for me to make any further comment upon it, except to say, that I should never vote in its favor, because there is nothing obligatory about it. It has no force in it; it can remedy no evil, and can produce no good.

The proposition now pending before the Chair, is a proposition to confine the banks of this commonwealth, to the issue of notes not under the denomination of ten dollars. This, it seems, is regarded as a great and mighty thing, which is about to remedy all the evils, and to heal all the disasters, under which the community is now laboring.

This has been the subject of debate for several weeks, and but little, after all, had been said on the immediate question. I regard the scheme as perfectly Eutopian—as affording no remedy whatever, and as just such a proposition as might have come from the friends of banks. It is unworthy our party and our cause. The play is not worth the candle. It is a shadow without substance. I candidly confess, that had I not known the quarter whence it originated, I should have thought it a tub thrown to the whale, and should have given the credit of it to gentlemen on the other side.

Believing, then, as I sincerely do, that no practical good would result from the adoption of the proposition, I shall feel myself compelled to record my vote against it.

I would inquire of gentlemen around me, whether it afforded the community an opportunity of getting rid of the institution, to which I had just referred, if such was their desire? Does it prevent the banks from making over issues? Does it restrain them from granting accommodations too freely? Does it afford any security whatever to the people for the debts and notes of the banks? Does this in fact, present any remedy for any of these complaints? If it did not, why should gentlemen vote for it? The only effect of the proposition, in my opinion, would be to put out of circulation, all notes under ten dollars.

Now, I will undertake to say, that the banks had no great objection to that. The only individuals that would dislike the operation of the provision, would be those who derive some benefit from the circulation of five dollar notes, and who prefer them to larger ones.

I think the people will not like the provision of the gentleman from Susquehanna, (Mr. Read) inasmuch as it would operate injuriously to their convenience. When it was first introduced, and knowing the favor which it would receive from some of my political friends here, I felt some degree of pain at witnessing the opposition that was made to it, and was about to reconcile myself to vote for it. But, upon examination, I convinced myself of its entire inutility, as a remedy, and, that it therefore, ought not to be adopted.

I think it would be better to leave to the legislature the regulation, as to what notes shall be issued by the banks, especially, as in my opinion, all charters are repealable. It would be improper for this convention, as I had already stated, to incorporate in the constitution, as a *permanent* provision, a proposition such as that of the delegate from Susquehanna, even if proper in itself, because a time might arrive when circumstances would require an issue of small notes.

The act of 1814, prohibited the banks from issuing notes under five dollars; but, the legislature, by the exigencies of the times, was obliged to suspend its operation from time to time, till October, 1817. What man, he asked, would undertake to say that the same necessity might not exist even before the ratification or rejection of the constitution by the people of Pennsylvania? If it were proper in itself, he would not vote to put this provision in the constitution, because a necessity might arise, requiring the issue of smaller notes, than those of the denomination of five dollars.

For myself, I would much rather see bank notes, under five dollars, in circulation, than the notes of the numerous petty corporations in the commonwealth. The amount of five dollar notes, throughout the United States, was supposed to amount to between eight and ten millions, of which there was, perhaps, a million and a half in circulation in Pennsylvania, and issued by our banks. To this extent, then, would be the circulation of ten dollar notes to five. If it was thought advisable to try the experiment, the legislature might incorporate a bank for that purpose, and if the experiment proved beneficial, they could continue the circulation of notes of the denomination of ten dollars.

Now, I will seriously ask every delegate present, who was in favor of restricting the banks, and affording the community security against the evils complained of, whether they really believe the proposition of the gentleman from Susquehanna will effect those objects?

If so, then I confess that I am unable to see it. I am free to admit that the proposition contained some wholesome *principles;* but, nevertheless, I should feel myself compelled to vote against it.

This proposition, in some particulars, goes too far, while in others, it does not go far enough. For instance, the delegate would not permit any acts of incorporation to be passed, except with the concurrence of two successive legislatures. Now, (said Mr. Sterigere)it might happen that a community, in some part or other of the state, might deem the immediate establishment of a small bank among them, very desirable, and much to their interest; but, should the provision of the gentleman be adopted, they would have to forego whatever advantage they might otherwise have reaped, until the action of two successive legislatures. I cannot but regard this restriction as altogether useless,—therefore could not support it. This provision not only extended to bank, but to other corporations. There had been no corporations more obnoxious to the public feelings, than many of the railroads which had been established, the directors of which had entered upon the lands of private individuals, and in many cases, paid no damages.

Many reasons might be assigned, why there should be restrictions introduced in reference to these corporations, as well as to banks. The proposition was also confined to charters hereafter granted. Now, I am not one of those—right or wrong—who believed that a bank charter once granted to a company, could not be repealed thereafter. I am, therefore, disposed to vote for that proposition of the delegate, which makes every bank charter now in existence, or which may be hereafter granted, subject to repeal or modification.

I will advert, very briefly, to some propositions that have been suggested by the governor of this state, in his late message to the legislature, because they have a connexion with the subject under consideration. The governor recommends :

1. That the profits of dividends, payable to the stockholders, be forever restricted to seven per cent, per annum, on the capital actually paid in.

His excellency went on to suggest, in another part of his message, that the excess beyond eight per cent, shall be paid into the state treasury. The proposition or suggestion, made by the governor, appear- to me entirely impracticable and perfectly delusive. They seemed to argue an ignorance of the subjects on which he spoke, and a want of that proper and due reflection which ought to have been given to them. I regard them as absurd, so far as respects their operation. If, for instance, the profits of a bank were restrained to seven per cent, it required but little reflection not to see that such a provision would be entirely delusive and inoperative.

There have been many charters granted with similar restrictions. I believe that the Schuylkill canal company are realizing, at this moment, no less than twenty-five per cent profit. No company, in the city of Philadelphia, has ever paid any thing above the profits to which it was limited. There is no instance of the kind to be found in the report of the auditor general. I have not been able to discover that a single cent has been deposited in the treasury, on account of the excess of profit made by any corporation. And why ? Because, when the profits amount to the maximum allowed by law, the excess was taken to make repairs, or improvements, instead of being paid into the state treasury.

The Schuylkill navigation company were, at this time, making very costly improvements, so that they manage to keep the excess over the profits, in their own hands; and the consequence is, the company's works are becoming more and more valuable.

I am borne out in this statement relative to banks, and other corporations, that have been in successful operation. The success of most of them, is the result of some one man's talents and exertions; and, when a company perceives that they are making large profits, and are approaching their maximum, they naturally remember him, to whose talents and exertions they are indebted, and feel inclined to pay him with the money which was intended to go into the coffers of the state. He is made a president, or other officer, with a large salary—or the office and salary may be made to rotate, till each stockholder gets his share of the excess in this way.

You cannot prevent this. We know companies are permitted, or will manage matters in their own way, and by some such mode as I have mentioned, nine times out of ten, a very considerable profit is secured to the stockholders, over and above what it was intended they should receive, and thus they dispose of what otherwise would be an excess, to be deposited in the treasury of the state. I have heard of some very amusing instances of this kind in the eastern states.

Now, I will appeal to every man who knew and had observed the operation of these things, whether they were not likely to take place again. A proposition like that which the governor had suggested, although it might look very well on paper, is, practically, utterly nugatory and useless.

[The CHAIR here announced that the hour had elapsed, which had been allotted to members to address the committee, at one time.

Mr. CHAUNCEY then addressed the committee, until the President announced the expiration of the hour; when

Mr. STERIGERE resumed his remarks.]

Mr. Chairman at the expiration of my hour, when I before addressed the convention, I was considering the restrictions which the governor in his late message, has recommended to be imposed on banking institutions and banking operations, and had just concluded my remarks on the first proposition.

His next is :

2. That the notes in circulation be still further reduced, in proportion to the amount of capital stock paid in. It may, by the present laws, be double that amount.

This recommendation is the result of gross ignorance. It will appear by the returns of the banks, that th amount of notes ine circulation has scarcely ever exceeded the capital stock, and that, on an average, the amount is below the amount of capital stock. There has been no evil arising from this cause, and there is no remedy needed. The circulations has never exceeded what the governor proposed to limit it at. The evil and mischief lies in the excessive amount of accommodations, and is effected by putting drafts, checks and the like into circulation, instead of notes. This is what needs a restraint. But on this subject the governor is perfectly silent.

The governor's third proposition is :

3. That whenever the specie of any bank shall fall below a fixed proportion to the notes in circulation, all increase of circulation shall be strictly prohibited and summarily punished, until the proportion required by law shall be restored.

A suspension of specie payments, when each gets to the proportion fixed on, would seem another exception for the penalty of this provision. The mode of securing punishment is not pointed out. Then by whom it is to be inflicted, whether by one officer or another, by the United States Bank, or by the governor or his deputy, he has not informed us.

The next proposition is:

That no loan shall be made to any broker or other person engaged in dealing in money, notes, bills, or other evidences of debt, until persons engaged in other business, and presenting equal security, shall be first accommodated; nor any loan be made on pledge of stock, nor on any security, except that which is usually demanded. And that loans to directors, directly or indirectly, shall be placed under similar restrictions with those to brokers.

This is improper, and indeed impracticable. The governor is thus attempting to proscribe certain individuals. If he thought these were injurious to the community, it would have been better for him to have them indicted under the statute against vice and immorality. The next difficulty would be this, the officers of the bank must have inquired into every man's business, to see what was the nature of his transactions, and for what purpose he desired to borrow money. This was not a course which every individual would be willing to pursue. The recommendation prohibiting loans to directors is utterly impracticable. It could not be carried into effect. There are so many institutions, that if a man could not borrow from one, he would be enabled to obtain what he wanted from another, and there would be an arrangement among the different boards of directors, so all could get what they wished.

The governor recommends:

5. That the amount of loans to any individual or firm, whether as drawer or endorser, or both, shall not be permitted to exceed a certain sum fixed by law, except with the consent of three-fourths of the directors.

It would be as difficult for the legislature to fix a standard of safety, as it would be absurd, unless an arbitrary rule were established. Who ever before dreamed of such a means of fixing the responsibility of individuals? Besides, if this was practicable, it must and would be evaded, for what a man could not get at one bank he would at another, unless there should be a board of directors made up of delegates for each board of bank directors in the state.

He also recommends;

6. That the excess of annual profit, beyond six per cent, shall be invested by the officers of each bank, in such manner as shall be approved by the state treasurer, until it reach a certain amount to be fixed by law, in proportion to the capital paid in, as a separate fund to secure the safety of the bank, and to redeem its notes in case of accident. The fund to be under the direction of the stockholders, who shall be permitted, after its completion, to receive all the earnings of the bank, until they shall be reimbursed for such portions of the dividends between six and seven per cent, as were therein invested. But after they shall have been thus repaid, all excess of dividend over seven per cent shall be periodically paid into the state treasury for the use of the commonwealth, together with the fund itself, at the expiration of the charter and discontinuance of the bank.

The safety fund system, is the next recommendation of his excellency, as a substitute for our present banking system. It is to be sure, recommended to secure a portion of the profits of the banks for the use of the state. I do not (said Mr. S.) pretend to understand this system exactly. It was first established in the state of New York, upon the recommendation of now one of the most distinguished senators in congress, a man in whose judgment in such matters, I would place as much confidence as that of any man in the United States, I mean Silas Wright, of New York. The governor has chosen to say in his message, that he does not recommend the safety fund system. But the leading principles of his substitute are the same. If they are not, I do not comprehend it nor approve it.

The next recommendation of governor Ritner is:

7. That every bank in the state shall be compelled to keep its notes at par in Harrisburg, Philadelphia and Pittsburg, the one the capital, and the others the great commercial emporiums of the commonwealth, or be summarily liable to the holder for any discount incurred.

This is Pandoras' box itself. Such a provision in a bank charter would create more shaving shops in various parts of the state, than any state has yet been cursed with. It would also introduce a spirit of litigation, heretofore unknown, by authorizing the usury of discounts paid. It would also operate most severely on the small banks, and most beneficially on the mammoth institutions. This matter should be entirely left to the character and credit of the banks themselves.

He further recommends:

8. That a law be passed fixing a period, not more distant than three four or five years from the present, for the expulsion from circulation of all notes of a lower denomination than ten dollars.

9. That the president and directors for the year during which a suspension of specie payments shall occur in any bank, shall be individually liable for its notes, and for all other claims against it.

I would not approve of the first, because I am confident it can afford no remedy to the public for any evil or danger, and would be more injuriously felt by the people, than the banks. The next would be a matter of such monstrous injustice, in many instances, and the consequence would be that the best men would keep out of the directions of banks, and the worst and most irresponsible would manage these corporations. Suspensions generally spring from causes not under the control of the generality of banks, or any but mammoth institutions. But for all matters within their control, directors should be answerable.

The other two propositions of the governor contain nothing new or worth notice. I had intended to have gone more fully into these propositions, to show their delusive character, but the time allowed to me will not admit of this. One grand objection to all of them, is that they are not to operate on the present banks, they are only recommended to be incorporated in charters to be granted. The present banking system is to be continued, and the present institutions are to be allowed to pursue their own course. I have no confidence in the plan of making stockholders liable, or of crippling notes under ten dollars, for circulation. or in the schemes of the governor, as a remedy for the evils now complained of, or as a security to the public against future suspensions. I am opposed to all these, and for a plan which will at once strike at the root of present evils—or for nothing, I am for placing a restraint in granting charters to banking and other corporations, which may interfere with the property, interests or liberties of the people, and for granting full authority to repeal any law heretofore passed or which may hereafter be passed, for the incorporation of powerful moneyed institutions, capable of producing panics and pressure, and of shaking the commonwealth to its very centre, when feeling power, and forgetting right, they shall attempt acts, or measures injurious to the community. If I succeed, I am sure it will satisfy public opinion—if I fail, I have the consolation of believing that the object was worthy of the effort.

Mr. Chairman, I repeat the opinion which I have before expressed, that the charter of the United States Bank, by the legislature of Pennsylvania, was an act done in violation of the will of the people. I believe that the public interests require that it should be placed in the power of the legislature, to repeal the charter, when that repeal is called for. I would not now vote for its repeal, because I think such an act, at this time, might be attended with injurious consequences. But, I would put it upon its good behaviour; so that if it was ascertained to be injurious to the public welfare, it might be removed, and that if it was ascertained to be beneficial to these interests, it might be retained. For my own part, I regard this institution as dangerous to the liberties of the people, and as dangerous to every institution of the same character in the state.

When, in the year 1819, an investigation into the affairs of the United States Bank took place, the president of the bank declared that "there were very few banks which might not have been destroyed by the exercise of the power of this bank, that they made the banks shape their business according to their means."

If this is so, and I incline strongly to the belief that it is, it must exercise a power over the people, and the property, and the interests of the country, which is too great to be left in the hands of any twenty-five men, directors of any bank in the United States. The amount of its capital is larger than the capital of all the other seventy-seven banks in the state, put together; and the duration of its charter three times as long as that of any other institution. This will contract a combination with the other banks. In the language of the legislature of 1785, such an institution "is injurious to the welfare of the state, and incompatible with the public safety."

We have seen the career, and felt the bitter fruits of a United States Bank, chartered by congress; we have seen that, for a series of years, there have been great complaints and much excitement throughout the country, on the ground that that institution was detrimental to the public interests.

Sir, there can be no doubt, that such an institution, established in this commonwealth, will give rise to such complaints; it must be so; it has already done so, as we are all aware, and the question now, in almost every county, of a political character, is between the advocates of that bank, and those who are opposed to it.

I am aware of the fact, that the power to repeal charters has been denied to the legislature, and also to this convention. For my own part, I do not entertain a doubt of the right of the legislature to exercise that power, whenever it may choose to do so. I say, I do not entertain a doubt on that point. The power has been exercised in various instances. A charter is but a law, and a law may be repealed. It has been called a contract, but while it depends on an act of assembly, which is a law, it may be repealed in the same manner as all other laws may be repealed. This doctrine has been sustained by some of the first men in the nation. It is inculcated in every book that treats upon the subject, that one legislature cannot bind another.

The legislature of this state did repeal a charter granted to the Bank of North America, which was first chartered by congress, and then by the commonwealth of Pennsylvania, in the year 1782. It had a perpetual charter, with a capital of three millions of dollars. Three years afterwards, in the year 1785, the charter was repealed.

Thus we see, that one of the most valuable charters, and for a large amount of money, and unlimited in duration, was repealed, and the contest arose in regard to the right of the legislature to repeal it. It is one of the firmest principles of your government—a principle which lies at the very root of all your institutions—that when a government becomes injurious or oppressive to the people, it is the duty and the right of the people, to alter it, so as to secure their safety and their rights. If the legislature has no right to repeal a charter, this convention, whose proceedings are to be submitted to the people, that they may pass their judgment upon them, may undoubtedly settle that point beyond the possibility of further dispute. It is a most extraordinary position, and one which cannot fail to challenge our wonder, that any legislature can pass a law, granting a charter, which law cannot, at any subsequent time, be repealed. If this principle is to prevail, there is no end to the abuses which might grow up under it.

But, Mr. Chairman, this objection has been fully answeered, by the fact, to which I have referred—that is to say, that the legislature of Pennsylvania actually did repeal a charter granted to the Bank of North America—which charter was perpetual in its character, and that the power to do so was never contested. I think, looking to it as a matter of public benefit, it would be proper that this power should be given to the legislature, because every bank in the state would then be put upon the good behaviour principle—knowing, at the same time, that there would be no interference with it, so long as its affairs were properly administered, and so long as it confined its operations to the objects contemplated by the charter. There can be no fear, that such a power would be prejudicial to the banks, because we have the experience of twenty-three years, to convince us, that it could not be so.

Every bank in the commonwealth, with two exceptions, has a clause inserted in its charter, giving to the legislature the right of repeal. The banks have accepted their charters with these provisions inserted, and we have never yet discovered that it was prejudicial, either to them, or to the community in which they were placed. The manner in which the banks have conducted their business, has been such, as, generally speaking, to recommend that this provision should be inserted hereafter.

It is impossible for any administration to exist, in opposition to the will of the people. Neither can any bank exist, in opposition to the will of the people, among whom it is situated. It seems to me, therefore, that it would be a matter of policy, on the part of the banks, to have a provision of this kind placed in the constitution—because, that would restore them to the favor of the public, and remove that jealousy which exists in the public mind against them. I think gentlemen must have seen many evidences, that the feeling existing in the community, against those institutions, was very deep, indeed; and I agree with the gentleman from Luzerne, (Mr. Woodward) that, if something of this kind is not done, before long, we will have a struggle between the banking institutions of the country, and the people of the country. Not by mobs, as the delegate from Washington, (Mr. Craig) has said, but that the legislature, operated upon and controlled by the will of their constituents, would exercise the power of repealing their charters, and, in this way, a struggle will ensue, in which the people must and will prevail, and the banking institutions will be prostrated.

I am in favor of prohibiting the legislature, in consideration of a bonus, from granting a charter to any banking institution. This had a more injurious effect, than almost any thing else. It was almost impossible for a representative to oppose a charter to a bank, when a large bonus was offered, which would, perhaps go to make some improvements in the immediate vicinity of his constituents. In such cases, a member can hardly resist the importunity of his constituents, and I know of no better manner of preventing evils being done in this way, than by prohibiting the legislature from granting charters, in consideration of bonuses to be paid. In this matter, I am happy to have the governor with me. Thus far, I think the convention ought to go,—because no action of the legislature would be binding upon future legislatures. Before the year 1832, I believe there were but two banks (the Bank of North America, and the Farmers' and Mechanics' Bank) which had paid bonuses; and since that time, there had been upwards of six millions of dollars paid in this way. This shows that the evil is of recent origin, and has grown up in this country but very recently. The governor has seen the bad effects of it since. he has come into office, as the most of these bonuses had been paid since that time ; therefore, his recommendation on this subject was entitled to some weight. If, then, we make a provision in the constitution, that no banking institution shall be incorporated, in consideration of a bonus granted, it will relieve the people from having so many of these banking institutions forced upon them, which act so injuriously to their interests.

I am, also in favor of requiring, for the passage of some charters, more than the votes of a bare majority of the members of the legislature, but, at the same time, I should be opposed to having it require two successive legislatures to agree to the passage of a law, granting a charter to a small banking institution ; because, if the people, in any particular district, wanted a bank of small capital, which would be beneficial to them, it ought to be granted to them, and go into operation as soon as possible. But, where the institutions were to have large capitals, and would be able to exercise an influence over the whole state, or a considerable part of it, and beyond the state, and could control and regulate our money affairs at pleasure, and make money scarce or plenty, at will, I would require the votes of two-thirds of the legislature to pass a charter.

Mr. S. here gave way to]

Mr. STEVENS, who moved that the committee rise. Lost. Ayes 43, noes 56.]

Mr. STERIGERE resumed:

I feel very reluctant to trespass on the time of the committee at this time of night, but as the subject was an important one, I feel it to be my duty to give my views upon it.

In stating to the convention the propositions and restrictions for which I would be disposed to vote, I am free to declare that I have as much confidence in the legislature of our commonwealth, as any man on this floor. I am by no means disposed to call in question their integrity or honesty; but there are times when the legislature do not express the public will; and erroneous legislation sometimes takes place from improper motives, and sometimes from proper motives. If one legislature act faithlessly, fraudulently, or even improvidently, there should be a remedy. I am, therefore, disposed to give a power to the legislature, to correct all bad legislation, so that the public will may be carried into effect, when it is ascertained that previous acts of the legislature have been injurious to the public interest. We cannot trust to mere restrictions in the charters of banks, for they are too easily evaded. Let them, therefore, be put upon the good behaviour principle. Every one knows the restrictions which were placed in the charter of the United States Bank, in 1816, and every one recollects its proceedings under that charter, and how little they were regarded. This is one example of the inefficiency of mere restrictions. Nothing can control these institutions so well as a visitorial power in the legislature.

No man could have believed it possible that the restrictions imposed on the directors of the banks, at that time, would have been so shamefully evaded, as they were. They were most shamefully disregarded, as any one who has taken any notice of the report made on that subject, must know. I am not disposed to make charges against the directors of any bank. The remarks I make, are intended to apply to the system. I know nothing of the directors; all their proceedings are secret, and there are no means, generally, of knowing whether they are proper or not. How far it is proper to throw the veil of secrecy over their proceedings, is, to my mind, a matter of much doubt. We all know that there once was a time, when it was thought to be improper that any man should know any thing about bank proceedings. Such, however, is not the case at this time. All the banks are now compelled to throw open their books to the stockholders; but still they are prohibited from throwing open the private accounts of the stockholders. This, I think, is an erroneous idea; although, I am free to say, that my mind is not entirely settled on that point. There is no doubt, however, that the favors granted to individuals, have been beyond all the limits of sound discretion, and I look upon it as necessary that the amounts of the discounts to individuals, should be limited. This, I think, will be a better means of restraining the banks from making improper loans, than would the suggestion contained in the recent message of the governor, to the legislature of this state, to take their property into the state coffers.

Mr Chairman, I have now come to a conclusion with my remarks on this very important question. I am aware that my argument has been an irregular one; but the rule by which we are now bound down to a given space of time, and that space, too, so very brief, imposed a difficulty as to the course I had chalked out, in addition to the difficulty which I naturally feel in discussing such intricate topics.

I am disposed to go at once to the root of the evil, because I believe that banking institutions, unless properly regulated and restrained, are injurious to the best interests of the country. I shall, therefore, vote in favor of all such propositions as I believe calculated to promote the public welfare, and to secure the public liberties. I shall, however, vote against the proposition now before the Chair.

I close by reading a proposition, which I now give notice, I intend to offer for the adoption of the committee at a proper opportunity, and which I desire to see made part of the present provision of the constitution.

It is as follows:

"The legislature shall have power to repeal, or alter, any charter which has been, or may be, granted to any bank, whenever, in their opinion, the same is injurious to the citizens of the commonwealth; but no such alteration shall be binding on any bank, unless the same be assented to by a majority of the stockholders, certified in such manner as may be proscribed by law: And in case the bank, whose charter may be altered, shall neglect, or refuse, to assent to such alteration, within the time fixed by law, the chartered privileges granted to such bank, shall thenceforth cease and determine, except so far, and for so long a time, as may be necessary to collect its debts and wind up its concerns, not exceeding two years. Provided: that when any bank charter shall be repealed or altered, or shall cease, as aforesaid, in case any bonus or sum of money, other than a tax on the stock, or annual profits of the bank, may have been paid to the state by such bank, for the privileges granted to it, the state shall retain, for the privileges enjoyed, only so much of such bonus or sum, as will be a just proportion of the bonus, or sum, such bank was to pay for the privileges granted—having a due regard to the amount of capital, and the duration of the charter, to be determined in such manner as may be provided by law.

" No bank, rail road company, navigation company, or canal company, shall be chartered, unless three-fifths of all the members of each branch of the legislature, concur therein. No bank shall be chartered with a capital of more than two hundred thousand dollars, unless two-thirds of all the members of each branch of the legislature, concur therein; nor any bank, with a capital of more than five hundred thousand dollars, unless three-fourths of all the members of each branch concur therein.

" Nor shall any bank be chartered with a capital greater than one million of dollars, nor for a longer period than ten years, unless the law chartering the same, be passed by three-fourths of all the members of each branch of the legislature, at two successive sessions, and be approved by the governor.

"And the bill which may be passed the first session, shall be published, with the laws enacted at such session. No bonus shall be required, or allowed to be paid by any bank, for the corporate privileges granted to it; and every law chartering or re-chartering a bank, which provides for the payment of any such bonus, shall be wholly void; but all sums of money required to be paid by any bank, for such privileges, shall be a yearly, or half yearly, tax on the stock or the profits of the company."

With these remarks, said Mr. S., thrown together in this crude and hasty manner, I leave the subject.

Mr. WOODWARD,* of Luzerne, moved to amend the amendment by adding to the end thereof the words following, viz:

"And the legislature may repeal, change, or modify the charters of all banks heretofore incorporated, or which may hereafter be incorporated in this commonwealth, whether the power to repeal, change, or modify, be reserved in such charters or not; but when the legislature shall repeal the charter of any bank, or reserve any of its corporate privileges, they shall provide adequate and sufficient compensation to the stockholders of such bank."

Mr. WOODWARD moved that the committee rise, report progress, and ask leave to sit again; which motion was decided in the negative.

Mr. WOODWARD said, he had a few remarks to make on the subject of his proposition; and if the committee wished to hear them at this time, he would proceed. He had introduced this amendment with reluctance. In the present temper of the convention, he would not have brought it forward, but for certain resolutions, which were adopted by the convention in Harrisburg, before the adjournment to this city. He was fully aware of the difficulties against which he had to contend. He might be told that he was going against the expressed will of the majority of this body, in which, it was, at all times, his pleasure to acquiesce. These resolutions, however, seemed to make it necessary that there should be some amendment to the constitution, in reference to this subject. They would not have any influence on the legislature, except a moral influence. But, whatever influence they were calculated to bring to bear in this commonwealth, it would be contrary to the genius and object of our institutions, and subversive of the liberties of the people. With this conviction impressed on his mind, deeply impressed as any honest conviction could be, he should consider himself recreant to his duty, if he did not attempt to obtain some amendment which would counteract the effect of these resolutions.

[Mr. M'CAHEN—Mr. Woodward having yielded the floor—moved that the committee rise, report progress, and ask leave to sit again, which was decided in the negative—ayes 43, noes 49.]

Mr. WOODWARD resumed. The resolution to which he particularly referred, was in the following words :

" *Resolved,* That it is the sense of the convention, that a charter duly granted, under an act of assembly, to a bank or other private corporation, is, when accepted, a contract with the parties to whom the grant is made; and. if such charter be unduly granted, or subsequently misused, it may be avoided by the judgment of a court of justice in due course of law, and not otherwise, unless, in pursuance of a power expressly reserved in the charter itself."

The phraseology of this resolution, seemed to him to be obscure and uncertain. He did not clearly understand it. A charter " *duly*" granted is, when accepted a contract. but if " *such*" charter be " *unduly* granted" or misused, it may be avoided by the courts, &c. There may be undue circumstances attending the grant of a charter, which will call most loudly for executive and legislative interposition, and for which the courts could afford no adequate remedy ; and does the resolution mean to affirm that every charter to a bank, under whatever circumstances granted, is beyond legislative reach, and not to be repealed? It means this, if any thing. To such a proposition he could not be brought to assent.

On the 25th of March, 1821, the legislature passed a law to re-charter certain banks, and they reserved the power to revoke, alter, or annul the charter of any of the banks, thereby chartered, whenever the public interest should require it. and all the acts in corporating banks, since that period, with one exception, have expressly reserved the same power, as extended and applied to the new bank the restrictions, limitations, and penalties of the general act of 1824, so that there is now only one bank in Pennsylvania, whose charter is not liable to be revoked, altered, or annulled by the legislature.

The United States Bank of Pennsylvania. is the only exception. In its charter, there is no such reservation expressed, and nothing referring it to the general bank law. That bank, therefore, is the only one, to whose charter the doctrine of this resolution is applicable.

[Mr. MARTIN—Mr. Woodward having yielded the floor for the purpose —moved that the committee rise, report progress, and ask leave to sit again ; which motion was decided in the negative—ayes 42, noes 57.]

Mr. WOODWARD resumed :

The object, then, of this resolution, I take to be, to assert that the United States Bank—because no other bank can be the subject of such an assertion—is entirely independent of all legislative action, so long as, in the judgment of a court of justice, it does not violate the terms and conditions of its charter.

[Mr. W. here gave way to Mr. INGERSOLL, who moved that the committee now rise.

And on the question,

Will the committee of the whole agree to the motion?

The yeas and nays were required by Mr. INGERSOLL, and nineteen others, and are as follow, viz :

YEAS—Messrs. Ayres, Banks, Barclay, Bedford, Bell, Bonham, Carey, Clarke, of Indiana, Coates, Craig, Crain, Cummin, Curll, Dillinger, Doran, Dunlop, Earle, Fleming, Foulkrod, Fry, Fuller, Gamble, Grenell, Helffenstein, Houpt, Ingersoll, Jenks, Keim, Krebs, Maclay, Magee, Martin, M'Cahen, M'Dowell, Nevin, Read, Ritter,

Scheets, Sellers, Seltzer, Shellito, Smith, of Columbia, Sterigere, Stickel, Sturdevant, Taggart, Weaver, Weidman, Woodward—49.

Nays—Messrs. Agnew, Baldwin, Barndollar, Barnitz, Biddle, Bigelow, Brown, of Northampton, Brown, of Philadelphia, Chambers, Chandler, of Philadelphia, Chauncey, Clarke, of Beaver, Clark, of Dauphin, Cleavinger, Cline, Cochran, Cope, Cox, Crawford, Crum, Cunningham, Darlington, Darrah, Denny, Dickey, Dickerson, Forward, Gearhart, Gilmore, Harris, Hayhurst, Hays, Henderson, of Dauphin, Hiester, Hopkinson, Kennedy, Kerr, Konigmacher, Mann, M'Call, M'Sherry, Meredith, Merkel, Miller, Montgomery, Overfield, Pennypacker, Pollock, Porter, of Lancaster, Porter, of Northampton, Purviance, Reigart, Royer, Russell, Saeger, Scott, Serrill, Sill, Smyth, of Centre, Snively, Stevens, Thomas, Todd, Young, Sergeant, *President*—65.

So the committee refused to rise.]

Mr. Woodward resumed :

On the 18th of February, 1836, the law passed, re-chartering the Bank of the United States—he said re-chartering, because it was, in fact, re-chartering it,—and there was no such provision contained in its charter in relation to leaving the power in the hands of the legislature, to modify, and repeal it, as was contained in the other bank charters in Pennsylvania. Then he wished to say, that if this resolution which he had read, was to be understood by the public, as the mover of it, and that majority who adopted it, intended that it should be understood, it only embraces that one bank—the Bank of the United States—which has a capital of thirty-five millions, and which has the power of controling all the interests of Pennsylvania. The resolution places that bank entirely beyond the legislature of the commonwealth, which created it, and beyond the power of the people of the commonwealth, who have a right to re-model their form of government when they please. The people of Pennsylvania, have an acknowledged right, both by the constitution of the United States, and the constitution of their own state, to alter, modify, and reform their government; but according to this resolution, they have not a right to touch this institution, which is to remain sacred for thirty years.

Sir, we have an institution, created on the soil of Pennsylvania, more powerful than the Queen of England in her own dominions; more powerful than the King of France, or the Emperor of Russia. Yes, sir, it is an institution which can exercise a greater influence, for good or for evil, over the people of this commonwealth, than either of these sovereigns can exercise over their subjects. It concentrates more power than the government of Pennsylvania, or that of the whole Union. It may make war or peace—preserve or destroy the constitutional currency—give value to every man's property and labor, and control our whole political system. Such an institution has been established in Pennsylvania, and it is now declared to be beyond the reach of the popular arm. Whatever may be its influence on a million and a half of people, their representatives are to have no power to control or modify, in any manner, its action. He apprehended that this was the most fatal blow, ever yet aimed at our liberties. It is calculated to lay those liberties low, and if the gentleman who moved this resolution, and his friends who supported it, will consent to submit the proposition to the people, they shall see with what indignant scorn it will be rejected. Why, sir, ought not such a proposition as this to be submitted to the people ? Is a principle like that of the to be incorporated in our constitution, and to become law, without their having any voice in its adoption? The resolution, as such, cannot go to them, but his amendment could, and if they adopt the amendment, they reject the sentiment of the resolution. He wished to see this subject properly settled, and this had induced him to bring forward the amendment, which, if we adopt it, will be submitted to a vote of the freemen of the commonwealth, and will give them an opportunity to decide, whether they have surrendered their rights to corporations, or whether they mean to retain the power of controling and restraining corporations, such as the Bank of the United States. He wished the appeal to be made to the ultimate tribunal, which, in this case, was the only proper tribunal. He wished the doctrine of that resolution, applicable as it is, solely to that bank, to be brought to the test of the ballot box, and he would cheerfully abide the issue.

He now proposed examining whether this charter was, in fact, a contract or not, and, in doing so, he intended to leave out of view, for the present, all the decisions of courts on this subject. He intended to take a plain common sense view of the question, and to look at it, precisely as he believed the people of Pennsylvania would look at it; independently of those decisions, which it had been contended, settled the whole question. He was not unmindful of those decisions, but he should pass over them for the present, and if time was allowed him hereafter, he would notice them, before he took his seat, in a proper manner.

This act, approved on the 18th day of February, 1836, he said, was not a contract, but it was a law, according to the common understanding of the terms, and he asserted that there was a wide difference between a law and a contract. It is a law in all its forms and features. It was passed by the law making power. It was an act passed in the ordinary form, in which laws were made. It is called a law. It has sections and parts, just as all laws have. The first section went to repeal a law, and that he took to be a law. It was passed by that department of the government whose especial duty it was to make laws, and not contracts.

The people never conferred such a power upon the legislature, and they could not have it. Members of the legislature were not elected for that purpose. They are not elected for the purpose of selling the rights of the people, and pawning out their liberties to those who will give most money for them. This law was not a contract, because it had nothing of the form of a contract. The language of a contract is, " I will, or I will not." That of a law is, "thou shalt, or thou shalt not." There was also a consideration necessary to every contract. But he denied that this law, which was called a contract, had any consideration at all. He was perfectly aware that one section of the law, authorizes the stockholders to pay into the treasury a sum of money, called a bonus; and he was aware that that was called a consideration. But he denied that the legislature could pass a law, in consideration of a certain sum of money paid. The legislature cannot sell law. It is a violation of their trust;—it is a violation of the constitution, to make law a vendible article. If it be true that the legislature can bargain away a law, then the members of the legislature are but the market men of the people, and then it follows as a necessary consequence that the men who have the most money, will have the most law, and the best law.

For every such man goes to market, at all times, with the advantage over him who has less means within his control. And, where—I ask again—where in our system of government, do you find ground for the idea, that the legislature may part with any portion of the sovereignty of the people, in consideration of money, in that sense in which you part with a house or a farm, in consideration of money paid to you?

The fact then, Mr. Chairman, that the treasury of the commonwealth has been replenished by virtue of this act of assembly, by which the charter was granted to the United States Bank of Pennsylvania, does not, in any sense, make this a consideration of a contract. It surely cannot be so regarded. It would be derogatory to the legislature of the common- wealth, and subversive of the constitution of the land, and of the liberties of the people. It is not a contract, furthermore, because it admits of no remedy as a contract.

Suppose that the legislature of Pennsylvania should, during the present session—and I wish they would do so, as well on grounds of general state policy, as to bring the question to a test—suppose, I say, that they should pass a law repealing this act; or, suppose they should deprive this insti- tution of certain privileges. In what court could it cite the state to appear? What court has been provided for the purpose of asserting the rights of a contract, such as this is said to be? Where is the remedy? And, where is the court of justice in which the commonwealth would be answerable to this corporation?

But, sir, there is another reason why it is not a contract.

[Mr. W. here read an extract from Judge Story, on the subject of con- tracts, sustaining him in the argument he had advanced.]

It would, continued Mr. W., be a fraud in the legislature, to grant any other kind of charter.

For these reasons, Mr. Chairman, as well as for many other reasons which refer to the subject, I say, that this act of assembly is a law, and not a contract; and, of consequence, that it does not fall within the mean- ing or spirit of that provision in the constitution of the United States, which declares, " that no state shall pass any law impairing the obliga- tion of contracts."

Surely, there is no constitutional provision, which forbids a legislature to repeal a law. If the charter of the United States Bank of Pennsyl- vania is a law, it is undoubtedly repealable. And, why shall we not say so? It does not come, I repeat, within the meaning or spirit of the con- stitution.

At the adoption of the federal constitution, the word "contract" was understood to mean precisely what it is understood to mean at this day. It is a word of universal import and employment; no word in our whole language is better understood—and none, as I apprehend, less capable of misconstruction.

Thus much, Mr. Chairman, in relation to the character of this act of assembly.

But, sir, I am aware that many of the courts, as well federal as state, have decided that a charter, granted by the legislature, is in the nature of a contract, where it is accepted ; and, for the purposes of this argument, I do not object to admit that such an act of assembly is, according to these decisions, a contract.

The question, then, is, whether it falls within the scope of that clause in the federal constitution, which forbids a state to pass any law impairing the obligation of contracts.   It has been asserted, that it does come within the scope of that provision; and I suppose that the resolution rests on the idea, that this being a contract, the legislatue cannot, without a violation of the constitution of the United States, pass a law impairing its obligations.

Probably, there is not, in the entire constitution of the United States, a more wise provision, than that which secures private rights, under ordinary contracts, between man and man.   But it is denied that this act of assembly is a contract embraced by the provision of the federal constitution, to which I have adverted.   I know not how better to defend this position, than by considering briefly, the principles on which our government is founded.

The just objects of all civil governments, are the protection and happiness of all the subjects.   For these ends were governments instituted, and in this country, the better to attain these ends, we make our constitutions and laws to depend on the will of the people.   The force of laws consist in the fact, that the people have assented to them—that they sprang from them and are according to their will, and since the people cannot be presumed to assent to laws which have not a tendency to promote their welfare, the objects of all laws are the happiness or welfare of the mass of the people—the many—the great body—a majority of the citizens.

But, to promote and accomplish these objects, legislation must change, from time to time, with the ever varying circumstances of the people. Laws which were wise and salutary, when they were enacted, become, by events, unsuitable to the people, and must give way to such as may be thought better adapted to the great ends and aims of popular government—the welfare and happiness of the mass of the people.   With such views and for such purposes, was our complex system of government adopted.

Here, were separate communities, self-existing and perfectly independent of all superiors—states that were perfectly sovereign within their own limits, and capable of passing and repealing laws, as their best interests should from time to time require, and better calculated than any other power on earth to regulate and control all their internal affairs. But, for their protection from exterior dangers, the people of these separate and independent states, confederate and establish a new power—a Union— to which they impart enough of their own rights and powers, to make it effectual for their protection.

"The state government is a beautiful structure.   It is situated, however, on the naked beach.   The Union is the dyke to fence out the flood." It was mainly to protect themselves from the inundation, to " fence out the flood," that the people gave up any thing to the Union—it was not at all for the purpose of disabling themselves from regulating their domestic interests, and controling their internal relations, that they came into the compact. No—into this compact, like those which formed them into separate communities, the people came for their own better protection and security, and the same objects precisely were in view, in adopting the constitution of the Union, which are sought for by every constitution and law to which the people actually, or by implication, assent. In this instrument they are to be understood as aiming at the attainment of these objects—their own security, welfare and happiness, and since these objects forbid fixed and irrepealable legislation, and require wholesome changes of laws, can it be presumed that the people mean to give up the power to repeal any law they might pass? Is it true that the people of Pennsylqania, in assenting to the constitution of the United States, parted with their right to repeal a law establishing a base born bank? Whatever may be the public necessity—hewever sternly the welfare of the many may demand the repeal—how cruel and oppressive soever this monster may become, we the people of Pennsylvania may not move hand or foot to remove the scourge, and to abate the nuisance, because we have so stipulated in the bond! Having in view all the while our own good, we have forsaken the right to promote it by repealing such a law, we have given it away, unasked and uncalled for, and when painful experience drives us to search for it, we find that it is gone—not torn from us by a conquering enemy, but given away freely and foolishly. I do not believe it. Such is not the right construction of the federal constitution.

Mr. Dunlop—Mr. W. having yielded the floor—moved that the committee rise, report progress, and ask leave to sit again.

Mr. Agnew asked for the yeas and nays on this motion, and they were ordered.

The question was then taken on the motion of Mr. Dunlop, and decided in the negative, by the following vote, viz :

Yeas—Messr. Ayres. Banks, Barclay, Bedford, Bell, Bonham, Brown, of Philadelphia, Clarke, of Indiana, Crain, Cummin, Curll, Dillinger, Doran, Dunlop, Fleming, Foulkrod, Fry, Fuller, Gamble, Gearhart, Gilmore, Grenell, Hastings, Helffenstein, Houpt, Hyde, Ingersoll, Keim, Krebs, Maclay, Magee, Martin, M'Cahen, M'Dowell, Nevin, Read, Ritter, Scheetz, Seller-, Seltzer Shellito, Smith, of Columbia, Sturdevant, Taggart, Weaver, Woodward—46.

Nays—Messrs. Agnew, Baldwin, Barndollar, Barnitz, Biddle, Bigelow, Brown, of Northampton, Chambers, Chandler, of Philadelphia, Chauncey, Clarke, of Beaver, Clark, of Dauphin, Cleavinger, Cline, Cochran, Cope, Cox, Crawford, Crum, Cunningham, Darlington, Darrah, Denny, Dickey, Dickerson, Forward, Harris, Hayhurst, Hays, Henderson, of Dauphin, Hiester, Hopkinson, Jenks, Kennedy, Kerr, Konigmacher, Mann, M'Call, M'Sherry, Meredith, Merkel, Miller, Montgomery, Overfield, Pennypacker, Pollock, Porter, of Lancaster, Porter, of North. ampton, Purviance, Reigart, Royer, Russell, Saeger, Scott, Serrill, Sill, Smyth, of Centre, Snively, Sterigere, Stevens, Thomas, Todd, Weidman, Young, Sergeant, President—65.

Mr. Woodward, resumed as follows :

Sir, the states agreed, in ratifying the constitution of the United States, to surrender some portion of their power, and they assented, undoubt. edly, to some limitations on their original and inherent powers of legisla. tion. These restrictions are specified and set down in the constitution, and any man may read and understand them, and among them is this provision, that no state shall pass a law impairing the obligation of contracts. I have said that the word contract is a word of universal use, and perfectly well understood, and that it was used and understood in the same sense by the framers of the constitution, that it is by us. Be it that a bank charter is a contract, what had the constitution of the United States to do with bank charters? Did the convention which refused to give congress the power to grant one, take away from the states the power of repealing theirs? No, sir, they dreamed not of an immunity such as this to bank corporations, when they said, wisely, that states should not annul or impair contracts. They looked to a preservation of the rule of sound morality in the dealings between man and man, and made the good faith of such dealings sacred.

This was another security for the welfare of the people, and it taught them that if their own representatives should forget their duties, or unwittingly pass a law, which would destroy confidence between men, their act should be void. It furnished, and will continue to furnish, ground for popular confidence in our governments, and in that feeling, sir, consists our great security, for if the people see and feel that their government protects them in all their dealings, they will protect their government in all its perils.

But the states, in agreeing to some restrictions upon their own powers, reserved to themselves some rights which were to be inviolable. Such are the rights to alter and change their government, to regulate the administration of justice, to establish internal improvements, and common schools, and especially to regulate the paper currency of the states. Banking, in all its principles, operations and results, is exclusively a state system, and if there is any subject in reference to which state legislation is untrammelled, it is this; and if there is any subject more than all others which requires vigilant caution and frequent legislation, it is this. We have spent weeks here in this body, endeavoring to devise some new checks and limitations on the legislative power over this subject, which should operate to the public advantage—the public mind is bent anxiously to it, and we all feel our responsibility to do something which may prevent future evils, if it cannot remedy past ones.

What I am now doing, is in performance of my duty to my constituents on this subject—feebly and imperfectly enough, to be sure, but the duty must be performed, whether the committee will hear me or not. I am sorry for the impatience of the committee, and sorry that I have been driven into this discussion at a late hour, unexpectedly, and without any of the materials around me, which I had laid away for this discussion, and to this circumstance they must attribute somewhat of my tediousness. I do not, however, mean to weary them long.

The right to regulate and control the paper currency of the state, I take it, is complete and absolute, and any construction of the federal constitution, which abridges, restrains or denies this right, must be vicious, because it would be subversive of the great ends of human government. The United States Bank has a capital of $35,000,000 and power to issue paper money without limit. It is claimed for it, that it can supply the people with a currency, and its admirers call it the "Regulator" of the currency. In the pride and plentitude of its power, it has, through its President, boasted that it can destroy the other banks of the state, and this I believe. Now, sir, is there any thing in the constitution of the United States to prevent the people, through their representatives, from regulating this "Regulator"? May they not restrain its power, or curtail its proportions, when their highest interests demand it? What, sir, is banking a state right, and the regulation of paper currency a state duty, and yet the state is not to question the action of this bank of banks? Is it to be left to go on in its career of mischief and injury, however it may crush the public interests, and however the million and a half of freemen in this state may wish it to be restrained—mocking the popular fears and defying the legislative arm?

Sir, if it is so to be, some better reason must be found out than that the framers of the federal constitution wrote it down that a state may not impair contracts. If the state erected such an institution, so powerful and so inviolable, and endowed it with an indefeasible existence, there, in *that* act, was the violation of the great first contract which brought men into society. It impaired not, for it dissolved utterly, the obligations of this primal bond, and violated, aye, *annihilated* the vested rights of a nation of freemen to govern themselves. Such an institution, as it is now claimed this bank is, cannot be erected without an overthrow of all our constitutions, and it is vain to appeal to them for its defence. Our government may be taken down and put up anew—whatever we call ancient and permanent in our civil institutions may be changed, but we may not touch this bank. Sir, it cannot be so. The only legitimate existence which that institution can claim, is, and must be, by the assent of the popular will, directed to the attainment of the popular good, and if it came thus into existence, then all reason and law authorize the popular will, still pursuing the public good, to put it out of existence. I do not advocate any wild, ill defined or licentious power. Even that which I believe exists in our legislature, I would have prudently exercised. I would not repeal the United States Bank charter wantonly, nor in such manner as to take away one dollar of the property which individuals have invested there, and I would only repeal it on some great and pressing emergency, when the public interests demanded it, unless indeed it should become necessary to repeal it in order to vindicate the right to do so. But rather than have one of our highest rights struck out of existence, and rather than see the marble pile down Chestnut street become a monument of one atom of departed freedom, I would exercise the repealing power at once, without waiting for occasion. If the struggle is to be brought on between corporate and popular power by the denial of all responsibility on the part of this bank to the people, let it come. It may as well be determined now as ever. But if it is desirable to avoid such a struggle, let the truth be recorded, that the people may alter or repeal its charter, and there let the contest end, until public necessity demand the exercise of the admitted power.

On the subject of the constitutional provision, which is supposed to be the shield of this bank, I beg leave to refer gentlemen to the forty-fourth number of the Federalist, written by James Madison, in which he calls this provision "a bulwark in favor of private rights," and speaks of it as a restraint on that kind of legislation that disturbs the private affairs of society. Not a word falls from this great expositor which indicates an opinion that that provision was ever to restrain a state from taking all such measures in behalf of their currency, and internal commerce, as they should deem wise and salutary. Least of all are his terms an apology for corporations. And, sir, do you believe the people of Pennsylvania would ever have assented to the constitutional provision, if they had anticipated its application to such a subject? Would they have trusted their representatives to concentrate the money power of the country in one corporate institution under the direction of a few individuals, if they had understood, when this was done, that they should have no control over it. No, sir, I have no doubt they would have disabled, by an express provision in our own constitution, their legislature from making such a contract—from selling into irredeemable bondage their liberties. But they did not so understand the contracts referred to in the constitution, and they do not now so understand them.

What, then, is this resolution but a denial of a right, which the people of Pennsylvania ever possessed and have never given up—a right which came down to us from the revolution, which is ours, and which I wish to make part of the inheritance of my children. If the resolution be true, and this right of controling this bank be gone from us, then it is in vain we labor to devise restrictions for other banks. We may tie them up never so closely, but whilst this monster is permitted to run at large, and is taught that he cannot be restrained, you have not made one step of advance towards reform. Indeed you do but serve him when you crush others, and when all is done, reform is nothing, absolutely nothing, unless it leave to the people their privilege to protect themselves from this worst, because the greatest of corporations.

The CHAIR here interrupted Mr. W., and announced that the hour allowed by the rule, had expired.

Mr. WOODWARD inquired, if the time consumed in the call of the yeas and nays, had been deducted?

The CHAIR replied in the affirmative.

Mr. WOODWARD then said;—I feel exceedingly anxious, Mr. Chairman, to get out something like my views on this very important subject. I am ready to take my seat, if the committee say so. I trust, however, that I shall be considered as entitled to the same courtesy which has been extended to other gentlemen; and, that a vote may be taken on giving me leave to proceed, I move that in this instance the rule be dispensed with, and that I have leave to proceed with my remarks.

Mr. PORTER, of Northampton, seconded the motion.

And on the question being put, it was decided in the negative—yeas 40, nays 67.

THURSDAY AFTERNOON, DECEMBER 28, 1838.

Mr. WOODWARD resumed the remarks he had commenced yesterday.

He would proceed now, first, to say, and then, to prove, that the corporation created by the act to which he had referred, was a public, and not a private, corporation.

There is a wide difference between public corporations, and those of a strictly private nature, and the right to repeal charters, is made, by the courts, to depend on this difference. It might be said that, if a corporation possess any share of political power, or if it was erected mainly for the convenience and welfare of the public, who can participate in its "objects, uses and purposes, by right," it was a public corporation. And he apprehended, the public or private character of a corporation, was to be decided, rather by the objects and purposes of it, than by the character of the funds employed by it.

He observed, in casting his eye over the speech of the gentleman from Northampton, (Mr. Porter) which he had not the pleasure of listening to, and which he had only had opportunity to glance at, since it was in print, that he relies on the distinction taken by Judge Story, who, it must be remarked, uses stronger, and apparently less cautious, language, on this subject, than any of the other judges; but he would endeavor to show, presently, that Judge Story himself considered the Dartmouth college a private corporation, because of the exclusively private character of its objects and purposes.

Judge Baldwin states the distinction clearly, in the case of Buonaparte vs. the Camden and Amboy rail road company, reported in the first volume of Baldwin's Reports. The question in that case, turned on the character of the corporation, and it shall be seen that Judge Baldwin looked not to the private ownership of the stock, but to the uses of the corporation, and the right of the public to participate in them.

The act of assembly incorporating that company, provides that the rail road shall remain a public highway, but the company were allowed to charge toll to such amount, as to make it almost an exclusive monopoly.

Judge Baldwin, as he had already said, delivered the opinion of the court, as to whether it was a public or private corporation.

He says:

"Generally speaking, public corporations are towns, cities, counties, parishes, existing for public purposes; private corporations are for banks, insurance, roads, canals, bridges, &c., where the stock is owned by individuals, but their use may be public.—4 *Wheat.*, 664.

" A road or canal constructed by the public, or a corporation, is a public highway, for the public benefit, if the public have a right of passage thereon, by a reasonable, stipulated, uniform toll; its exaction does not make its use private. If the public can pass, and repass, and enjoy its benefits by right, it matters not whether the toll is due to the public, or a private corporation; the true condition is, whether the objects, uses and purposes of the corporation, are for public convenience or private emolument, and whether the public can participate in them by right, or only by permission. To ascertain this, the provisions of the law must be examined."

Now, although banks might sometimes be private, still they might be public corporations. All that he had to do, on the present occasion, was to show that the Bank of the United States was a public, and not a private corporation.

The question, according to the argument of Judge Baldwin, was—was the bank established for public convenience, or only for private emolument?

That question had been frequently answered on this floor, during our deliberations.

The grounds on which all had put the passage of the bill, were, that it was necessary to carry out the internal improvement system—to aid in placing the common schools on a firmer basis, and to sustain the credit of the state.   Public necessity and public convenience had induced the establishment of that corporation.

Was the Bank of the United States incorporated for individual emolument—for the benefit of individual stockholders?   He had never heard such an allegation, from its friends or advocates.   He presumed there was not a member of the legislature who voted for the bill, that entertained such an idea.   The grounds on which the measure had always been justified, were, that the public interests required it, and that it was adapted to the public necessities.

Now, if that was the principal object—the main end in view, then he apprehended that it became necessarily a public corporation; and the fact that private means are invested and employed by it, did not at all change the character of the corporation, nor take from it its public use. He would ask whether the public can participate in it by right?   Have they any interest in the existence of the bank, by authority of law—by the charter itself?   Undoubtedly they have.

The bank is required to loan money to the commonwealth at different times, by the act of assembly itself.   It is obliged to contribute its funds to the treasury of the state, to carry out the great objects of the commonwealth.   It is obliged to contribute $100,000, per annum, to the common school fund.

In this way, said Mr. W., the public, by the terms of the charter, have a right to a participation in its means, and the enjoyment of its privileges.   They had an interest in it, and could participate in its wealth—in its resources, not by the permission of the bank, but by right.   This was another characteristic of a public corporation.

Again:—The present bank was the same institution as the United States Bank, in all its features, except that the general government was formerly a stockholder, and that bank was a public, and not a private corporation, as was decided in the case of Osborne vs. the United States Bank—9th Wheaton, p. 859.

That bank though founded chiefly on private means, was a public corporation, and let it be remembered, that in deciding that it was so, Chief Justice Marshall, looked to the general reasons and purposes of its institution which (Mr. W.) contended, were the proper criteria of public corporations.

It was true, Judge Story had said a bank founded on private means, was a private corporation, but, in the case just referred to, the supreme court of the United States had decided that an institution, four-fifths of whose capital was of private contribution, was a public corporation, and that the congress could establish no other than such a corporation.   And, sir, if it was a public corporation, under its charter from congress, has it ceased to be so, under its present charter, with the same capital, and more intimately than ever associated with the general interests of the state, and the public welfare? Having the absolute control of the paper currency of the state, the auxiliary of internal improvements, common schools, and the general revenues, who will say that the present corporation is not quite as public in all its aspects, as when it was only the fiscal agent of the general government?

[Here Mr. PORTER, of Northampton, rose and asked the gentleman from Luzerne, (Mr. Woodward) to read the authority, as he, Mr. P., had no recollection of any such decision having been made.]

Mr. W. replied, that he had not the book at hand, but merely extracts. Having procured the book, Mr. W. read the following:

Osborn vs. United States Bank, 9th Wheaton, p. 859—Chief Justice Marshall says:

" The foundation of the argument in favor of the right of a state to tax the bank, is laid in the supposed character of that institution. The argument supposes the corporation to have been originated for the management of an individual concern, to be founded upon contract between individuals, having private trade and private profit for its great end and principal object."

He then goes on to shew that if these premises were true, the right of a state to tax the bank would follow necessarily.

" But the premises are not true. The bank is not considered as a private corporation, whose principal object is individual trade and individual profit; but as a public corporation, created for public and national purposes. That the mere business of banking is, in its own nature, a private business, and may be carried on by individuals or companies, having no political connexion with the government, is admitted; but the bank is not such an individual or company. It was not created for its own sake, or for private purposes. It has never been supposed that congress could create such a corporation. The whole opinion of the court in the case of M'Culloch vs. the state of Maryland, is founded on, and sustained by the idea that the bank is an instrument which is " necessary and proper for carrying into effect the powers vested in the government of the United States." It is not an instrument which the government found ready made, and has supposed to be adopted to its purposes; but one which was created in the form in which it now appears, for national purposes only."

Such was the opinion of Chief Justice Marshall, in the case to which he had referred. Now, if that great and good man were on the bench, and the question should come before him, whether a bank, created by act of assembly, was a public or private corporation, would he not look at the object and purposes for which it was established—at the end, purposes, and design of that institution? And when he discovered that it was established to answer public necessity—to aid the commonwealth in carrying out its various purposes, would he not admit—would he not decide, as he (Mr. Woodward) believed the supreme court of the United States would decide, when the question should come before it, that it is a public institution?

The only case to which the gentleman from Northampton, (Mr. Porter) had referred, on the subject of charters, was that of the Dartmouth college ; and that was the only case he (Mr. W.) had had time to look into. There might be other cases, relating to private grants of land, but he had not had an opportunity of looking into them. But what was the Dartmouth college case?

That college was deemed, like other colleges of private foundation, to be a private eleemsoynary institution, endowed by its charter with a capacity to take and hold property *unconnected with the government.* It was a private institution for general charity.

Judge Story, in his commentaries on constitutional law, vol. 3, p. 262, gives that account of it. Would the gentleman from Northampton, able and distinguished as he was known to be, or any other lawyer, draw an argument from this, as if applicable to the bank. Was there, he asked, any analogy between the two cases? Was not the Bank of the United States a partner with the government of the commonwealth, in carrying into effect the great purposes she had in contemplation, or now in progress? If this was a public corporation, as he had endeavored to show it was, then, what, he would ask, was there to prevent the legislature from repealing its charter? There was nothing.—And for truth's sake we ought to say, that the only bank charter about which the question can arise, is repealable.

The Dartmouth college was a case precisely in point. Chief Justice Marshall had asserted it to be in the power of a legislature to repeal, or alter, or control the charter of a public corporation. He (Mr. W.) believed that the gentleman from Northampton denied the correctness of the decision in the very first paragraph of his printed speech.

Mr. W. then cited the opinion of the chief justice, as follows :

" I do not think the principle correct, that all charters of incorporation are beyond legislative control. Those which are of a public or political character, such as municipal corporations and the like, not partaking of the nature of contracts, are subject to the supervision of the legislature, which has the power to alter, remodel, and repeal the same as the exigencies of the state and a regard for the public good may require. It is, in my judgment, to private corporations, that the principle is applicable and the position true, that a charter is a contract, and cannot be altered by one of the parties to it, without the assent of the other."

If, then, the bank was a public corporation, as he (Mr. Woodward) affirmed it to be, its charter might be repealed by the legislature. Again, sir, the legislature could not arbitrarily sacrifice the rights of property, but they might take private property for public purposes. This was a principle which was universally known, and had been settled over and over again. They could not take the property of one man and give it to another; nor could they take private property for private purposes. The delegate from Adams (Mr. Stevens) asked, the other day, whether banks did not hold their privileges by the same tenure as the farmer holds his land? Suppose they did, did it follow that the legislature might not repeal their charters when the public necessity required? The legislature might take the gentleman's property and devote it to public purposes. So that if the banks did hold their charters on the same principle that an *individual* held his land, he was bound to give it up for the convenience and benefit of the public. It was only when the public convenience rendered such a course necessary, that he would give the power to the legislature to resume these charters of privileges. When a franchise is resumed, when a charter was repealed, compensation must follow; a very adequate and ample compensation must be provided by law. That was done every day. Compensation must be made in some form or way. The amendment he would submit would embrace that object. Now when that was done—when the commonwealth of Pennsylvania made due and adequate compensation for property taken, whether it was in the form of a farm, or in the peculiar privileges of a bank, he wished to know what constitutional provision was violated?

He desired to know what contract and what vested right was violated? He would contend that no contract was violated, because the citizen held his property expressly on the condition that he should surrender it for an adequate compensation, when the public good required it. No man's rights were violated, because they were held on this condition.

What, he asked, was to restrain the legislature from taking possession of these rights, when the public good required that they should be surrendered, the proprietor receiving a proper compensation in lieu thereof?

He fully admitted that vested rights were sacred; and no man in this convention had a more sincere regard for them, and a greater desire that they should be respected, than he had. He would do nothing that had the remotest tendency to impair vested rights.

But, let us examine what they are. Some gentlemen here had said that the granting of a charter was a contract, and that it could not be broken without the assent of the party to whom it was given. Let gentlemen (continued Mr. W.) examine what constitutes a contract; and then let them say, if they could, that a contract entered into with the state does not necessarily possess this inherent quality—that is, the right of the commonwealth to take back what she has granted, on making a suitable compensation for so doing. That compensation may be a mere return of compensation, or bonus; or, it may be more or less. A compensation, however, in money, must be made. And, when that is made—what contract is violated? I deny that any contract is violated, because it is made with the express condition that it must be surrendered, if deemed necessary, to the state. A man's rights are subject to all the conditions expressed in the contract, or bond. They are subject, moreover, to that ever controling, and ever present condition, the right of the legislature to remove whatever they have granted, when public necessity requires it. I beg leave to refer to the same case from which I have already cited some views bearing on this subject. In page 220, Judge Baldwin says:

"It is a settled principle of American jurisprudence, that the transcendant powers of parliament devolved on the people of the several states by the revolution, 4 Wheat. 651; 8 Wheat. 584; 2 Peters, 656; it necessarily follows, that the only restraint on their legislative power, is that imposed by their own, or the constitution of the United States, 2 Peters, 410, 414. That of New Jersey contains no bill of rights, or any other restriction on the legislative power, the only article, which has been referred to; of course .... if the right of trial by jury is

APPENDIX.

preserved inviolate in the cases contemplated by the constitution. It is silent on the subject now before us, for an obvious reason, it is an incident to the sovereignty of every government, that it may take private property for public use; of the necessity or expediency of which, the government must judge, but the obligation to make just compensation is concomitant with the right. Vatt. 112; Ruth. 43; Burl. 150; Puff. 829; Gro. 333.

"Though the divesting of vested rights of property, is no violation *per se* of the constitution of the United States, 2 Peters, 412, 413; yet when those rights are vested by a contract, its obligation cannot be impaired by a state law, 6 Cranch. 137; 7 Cranch. 164; 9 Cranch. 45; 4 Wheat. 625. In this case the complainant by his contract of purchase, authorized by the law of the state, comes so far within this protection, that his property cannot be transferred to the defendants without his consent, by mere legislative power. To make such transfer valid, it must be an appropriation to a public use, in virtue of the inherent sovereignty of the states, which carries with it the obligation to make compensation.

" When this is done, no contract is impaired, as all persons hold their property subject to requisitions for public service, it is protected only against arbitrary seizure, not when it is taken or appropriated by public right for public use; compensation must indeed be made, but no particular mode is prescribed by which its amount shall be ascertained.

It is a principle of Magna Charta, recognized in all the states, that no man shall be disseized or dispossessed of his property without due process of law, or legal process, or the judgment of a jury; 2 Co. Just. 45; but if either mode is pursued, the principle is unimpaired. A law which authorizes the appropriation of property to public use, and prescribes a mode of proceeding by which compensation shall be ascertained and made, is not obnoxious to Magna Charta, or its construction in England or this State."

This is the doctrine in relation to private property. Will any gentleman on this floor, state the distinction clearly and satisfactorily, between private property and that kind of property which a stockholder of the United States Bank has, in the charter of that institution? Will any gentleman tell me that it is but property? What have they acquired from the commonwealth, but a right to do certain acts with their own property? And is there any distinction between the principle to which I have alluded, as applicable to private property, and such a franchise or right as the stockholders have in the Bank of the United States? I apprehend that no distinction can be shown, and that the principle applies to all species of rights and property, which a citizen may acquire and hold under a contract with his government.

Then, sir, if I have been disposed to concede for the purpose of the argument, that a charter be a contract—if, as the gentlemen will have it—it be a contract, although much may be said against that view of the subject—if this be a contract and the rights be vested—it is still subject to this condition—that is to say, to the right of the commonwealth to resume whatever was granted at any time when the public necessity might require it, and upon providing a proper compensation. Is there any thing in the case of the Dartmouth college, to conflict with this view of the —I know of nothing. And, if not, is there any other case reported which is applicable to it? I will not undertake to say, surrounded as I am, on every side, by judges and lawyers of far more experience than myself, that there is not another case, but I do say, that I have never been able to find,—and that I have never seen, a case, in which the principle I have defended here, was regarded in any view inconsistent with that which I have expressed.

Here then, let me say, that to my mind, there seems to be nothing in the federal constitution to prevent the repeal of the charter in question, because, the contracts to which inviolability is guarantied by that instrument, do not comprehend this charter; but if they do, then I insist that such contracts made with a sovereign, bound at all times to retain and use the powers, necessary to the welfare of the people, are attended inseparably by the implied condition, that that sovereign may resume the grant when the great object of government—the welfare of the people—requires the resumption. This condition must enter into, and qualify the contract, or it will be subversive of the first principles of our government, and in derogation of popular rights, and therefore void. And if this condition do pertain to, and qualify the contract, then it may be annulled by its own admission, and a repeal, so far from violating, would be consonant to the contract. Of course, compensation must be made, and when it is, the right to repeal is perfect, and there is no ground of complaint, because, the repeal is according to the stipulation of the parties.

On what other principle is the state justified, for taking the lands and personal property of the citizen for public use, stipulating such compensation as its own sense of justice, or the tribunals of its own creation may prescribe? He has bought his property, perhaps of the state, and paid the price demanded, and received a charter, which should be as sacred as any human transaction. He has, perhaps, expended years of his labor on the property so purchased, and taught his children to expect it as their future inheritance. Yet this may be taken from him, and all the associated hopes disappointed, and he obliged to be content with such a pecuniary equivalent, as the state is pleased to give.

Still, no vested rights are violated, no obligations of the contract impaired, and the citizen must acquiesce in uncomplaining silence. Why? Because, the state has only done that, which it was agreed she might do, in a particular contingency. Because, she is to provide for the welfare of the whole people, and her contract cannot stand in the way of this great primary object—the citizen knew, or was bound to know, it could not, and when he made the bargain, it was his business to remember, that it must be controled and expounded on these principles.

Now, sir, I call on gentlemen to show me the foundation in any sound principle, for the distinction which is attempted to be made in favor of this bank. What is there in the spirit or letter of our constitutions, that clothes such an artificial, soulless being, with immunities which you deny to the free citizens of this commonwealth? What is the peculiarity which makes the bank's title to an incorporeal hereditament granted them by the state, so absolute and indefeasible, while our titles to corporeal things, have to yield to the demands of the public?

I believe sir, the distinction exists only in imagination, and has no foundation in reason or law, even if the bank claims to exist by contract.

If it will plead a contract let it be content to stand on the same footing with the republicans of the commonwealth, in respect, to their acquired rights. Against its assuming or holding any higher or exclusive grounds, I enter my most emphatic protest. Many reasons concur why it should not be admitted to the dignified equality which the argument concedes to it. Its immense power, its avarice, its distance from popular influences, its aristocratic tendencies and its anti American sympathies, are circumstances which admonish us to preserve a more rigid and vigalent control over it, than we extend to the concerns and interests of citizens. But above all things, we should never admit that we can strip the citizen of all he possesses for the general good, but cannot, whatever be the emergency, touch this corporation.

I pass to another subject. The bill of rights which forms a part of our constitution secures to the people the right of self-government, and recognizes their power to alter, reform or abolish their government in such manner as they may think proper. Can the state legislature make a contract in restraint of this right? Is it not just as true now, as it was before the recharter of the United States bank, that the people of Pennsylvania may so alter their government as to declare that no bank whatever shall exist? Unless it be so, we have erected a power greater than ourselves. But if it be so, what application has the provision of the federal constitution in regard to contracts, to this case? Does that provision restrain the states from altering and abolishing their internal institutions? If it does, it seems to me it is inconsistent with our own bill of rights, which affords ample authority for the proposition I contend for. And the bill of rights contemplates changes of government when the safety, happiness and welfare of the people require them. How much rather should mere laws be subject to change when the same reasons justify it. Why sir, some gentlemen have objected strongly to any constitutional provision relative to banks, because it would be too permanent. They tell us that every thing around us is changeable and changing, and that they prefer leaving it to the legislature to adopt measures to every new circumstance and condition of the people, and they argue that the representatives of the people should not be restrained by a constitutional provision from making such wholesome and necessary alterations relative to banks, as from time to time may become necessary. Why then should not those representatives have power to remodel the United States Bank, when the exegency comes? I propose to place in the constitution, the assertion that they have the power. I do not propose to confer it, for they already possess it, but only to say they possess it, so that when necessity demands its exercise, it may be prudently and properly employed without any dispute about its existence. This is the whole scope of my amendment,

[After a few more observations from Mr. W. the Chairman interrupted him, and stated the hour had expired. Mr. W. then took his seat.]

Mr. MEREDITH* rose and said :

Mr. Chairman, I should not have spoken on a question which I took to have been long since definitely settled, but for the fact that the gentleman from Luzerne, (Mr. Woodward) has made this an occasion for a general assault upon certain resolutions on the inviolability of contracts, which were passed by a very large majority of this body, at Harrisburg, and which, I had myself the honor of moving. We had heard from the gentleman from Luzerne, (Mr. Woodward) as we are in the habit of hearing from that gentleman, the most formidable argument to be expected, in support of the doctrines held by his political friends in this body, and if his argument be satisfactorily refuted, it will scarcely be necessary to notice any other upon that side.

I could not but congratulate myself, when I found the gentleman from Luzerne turning from the discussion of the great principles here involved, to vent certain hypercriticisms upon the resolutions before mentioned. He is not much given to small disquisitions on supposed verbal inaccuracies, and I am sure would not have entered on them, if he had felt his usual confidence in the strength of his more important positions.

His objections to the wording of the resolutions are two-fold :

1. That the second resolution declares that a charter granted by act of assembly, is a contract with the parties to whom that grant is made, but does not state who is the other party to that contract.

2. That the same resolution declares that a charter duly granted to a private corporation is a contract, and then proceeds to declare that if *such* charter be *unduly* granted, &c., that is, (says the gentleman) " if a charter *duly* granted, de *unduly* granted."

As to the first objection, I shall only say that the parties to a grant are the grantor and grantee, and if the grant is a contract, the grantor and grantee are necessarily the parties to it. A grant made by act of assembly, is a grant by the commonwealth, in the most solemn and authentic form—and the grantees being one party to the contract, spoken of in the resolution, the commonwealth is necessarily the other.

As to the second objection, I would observe that the phrase " *such* charter," does not refer to the phrase " *duly granted*" but to the kind of charter, viz : a charter to a private corporation.

I will not do so much injustice to the gentleman from Luzerne, as to suppose that he was even in doubt, of the meaning of the resolution, and I will only add that a very moderate acquaintance with the idioms and grammatical construction of our language, is sufficient to reform his opinions to its phraseology.

He, Mr. M., intended to condense all he had to say, so as to come within the hour prescribed by the rule. He considered it to be his duty to enter his protest, if no other gentleman did so, against the proposition which had been introduced by the gentleman from Luzerne, (Mr. Woodward.) He, Mr. M., had listened with peculiar pleasure, on this as on former occasions, to the legal argument which had been presented by the gentleman from Northampton, (Mr. Porter.)

* See page 70.

But, said Mr. M., it is not my intention to look to this question in the light of a legal or a technical question, as other gentlemen have done. I should be sorry indeed, that, on a question of so vital importance to the liberties of all—it should be thought necessary that those who speak, should be lawyers alone, who are acquainted with technical cases. I believe there is written upon the heart of every man, that principle which, without reference to courts, will aid in the sustenance of our credit and character—that principle which existed before judicial decisions were made, and where none such have been had, and which, in every free government, has been regarded as a principle most sound and important.

Nor shall I dwell particularly upon the restrictions imposed upon us, in this respect, to the constitution of the United States. I rise principally for the purpose of making some remarks on another part of the argument which has not hitherto been touched. I admit the conclusion of those doctrines which have been stated, that, so long as the constitution of the United States stands with its authority—where ever political parties are drawn—so long as that constitution remains, we are bound by it, and can not go beyond it.

But, sir, I do not wish that the opinion should go abroad, that the commonwealth of Pennsylvania, is restrained from the violation of the faith of contracts only by a positive law. I appeal indignantly to the history of the country, to shew the contrary ; and I do not wish it to be understood that, except for the obligation imposed by the provision in the constitution of the United States, she would sunder the bonds by which she has voluntarily bound herself.

I will shew that the commonwealth of Pennsylvania, in her assembly, which has been charged on one day, with not being fit to be trusted, and which on the next day, it is proposed to set up as a tribunal, to violate the faith of the commonwealth by annulling contracts, has not the power to do so; that these are judicial questions; that the parliament of Great Britain has refused to exercise that power; that it has preferred to leave judicial questions to be settled by the judicial tribunals; and that they are there fully sensible of the impropriety of a deliberative body sitting in judgment upon private right.

Much has been said, in the course of this debate, as to whether, according to the decided cases, a private charter is, or is not a contract. These cases have been cited, and I do not propose to touch that question. But I speak to gentlemen of common sense, and I ask whether there is not written in the heart of every man a belief, that when the commonwealth passes a law declaring that if certain individuals, foreign as well as native, will put their capital together for certain purposes, and for a given period of time, the state will guaranty to them certain privileges as a body, that law becomes a contract?

Mr. M. alluded to the conditions upon which bank charters were granted and founded.

If a contract means that by which one party agrees to do one thing—and, in consideration of that, another party agree to do another—if a thing is a contract when certain things have been agreed upon by both parties, and have been exercised by one or the other—I ask if a bank charter does not become a contract?

I say there is fixed in the heart of every man, a belief—however his party spirit may have blinded his intelligence, or warped his judgment—or however he may attempt with his conscience, to wind it up in the difficulties of decided cases—there is written a sacred feeling in the heart of every man, that, after all, this must be something more than a mere law which is subject at every moment to repealing, without a breach of faith. I say the legislature has the power to grant a charter of this kind; and, if so, what authority have you to take it way?

The amendment now proposed, admits the power of the legislature;—and because they may have acted beyond their authority, it is not necessary for us to give them more power. The reason applies as well to one charter as to the other—although one institution, being unpopular, is singled out as the object of attack.

If it be true that if the legislature has not the power to grant such a corporation, why give the power to retake it? But where is the doubt that there is the power, and that the legislature of the commonwealth is no where restricted from its exercise by the constitution or the bill of rights? Where is it said that they should not exercise power in relation to certain particulars? We differ in this respect from the congress of the United States, where there is a body elected with limited powers, and where it is declared they should exercise no powers but such as are expressly given, whereas, in our legislature, they exercise all power, from the exercise of which, they are not expressly excluded.

It is true, that in the constitution of 1776, an enumeration of the powers was attempted, and that the enumeration included a power to grant corporations, to pass bills and laws—and all such powers, it goes on to say, as are necessary for the existence of a free government—thus, in fact, declaring that this power to erect corporations—to do that which was necessary for the people, to authorize the aggregation of capital, is recognized as a power necessary to a free people. And, in the year 1790, instead of enumeration, they give them the whole legislative power, controlled only by the bill of rights, and such other clauses of the constitution as relate to the exercise of it.

I will not stop here to debate this, because it is rather a technical question than otherwise. I do not believe, as I have said, that this is a question for lawyers alone; it comes home to the mind of every man of common sense; and fatal would it be to the success of our republican institutions, if the settlement of this question depended on lawyers alone.

I do not stop to inquire, Mr. Chairman, whether this is a law or a contract. I believe that it is both; and I call upon gentlemen to shew me, if they can, that a law may not be a law as well as a contract, and yet it seems to be supposed that a public contract, sanctioned by all the authority of the state, is no law. If it were not a law, it would not be a contract. No individual has a right to bind the faith of the commonwealth. In order to do that, there must be a law passed, and there must be a contract: and when that law has been so passed, and has been acted upon, it is a contract as well as a law. How, I would ask, are we to appear—I do not mean in the view of the world, but to the citizens of this commonwealth, if we are to proclaim the doctrine that a law is not a contract?

How are we to appear to the citizens of foreign countries who are authorizing loans, and advancing capital to the amount of twenty-four or twenty five millions of dollars, upon the faith of the commonwealth, if what is now said be true—that this is a mere law and not a contract, and that it can be at any moment repealed? A mere law connected with public affairs! I may be asked, suppose the legislature should give a perpetual charter of this kind—should give up the money interests of the country—should divest themselves of all power of questions of public importance, what would you do? Does not the argument apply as well to works of public improvement? You must put faith in your legislature, if you mean to do any thing at all.

Mr. M. then adverted to the foreign capital employed in this commonwealth, and to the sources of revenue thereby created.

The state, said he, is pledged to pay interest to foreigners, and the whole argument goes as much to the demolition of faith upon loans, as upon the grant of a charter. And, if this were so, with what responsibility would any man deal? In what situation would any man be, who would rise and declare that the legislature has no power to make contracts, that they are appointed only for the purpose of passing laws, that these are nothing more then laws, that they partake of nothing in the nature of contracts, and that they may contain repealing clauses, to be enforced at any time. If such were the state of things here, a legislature might make a loan of twenty millions of dollars, might pledge the whole property of the state for the payment of the interest and principal, and might then put the money in their pockets and run away. No man would be received with patience, if he were to advance such an argument as this; and yet, this argument is to be applied to one case as well as the other, though it would fall with much more force in the one instance, than in the other.

These corporations have a right to lend their own money. Is that an injury to the commonwealth? They have a right to issue paper money to be taken only by those who choose to trust them. Is this an injury to the commonwealth? And they have a right to take on deposit the money of those who choose to confide it to their care. Is this an injury to the commonwealth?

It has been said however, and the gentleman from Luzerne, (Mr. Woodward) has laid much stress upon that argument, that, although this charter may be admitted to be a contract, still that it ca not be a contract, because there is no remedy in case of its violation.

Suppose that a man should sell a locomotive engine to the agent of the state. Is he not correct in saying that the faith of the commonwealth is pledged for the payment of the sum stipulated for the purchase? We are all aware of the fact that a private individual has never a remedy against a sovereign state. We all know that there is no remedy, but that moral obligation which has, up to this period of the world's existence, been found sufficient for the purpose, because upon this, it is known, that the true interests of the government itself depend. There can be no remedy here by action against the commonwealth; nor, in Great Britain, for any act of the parliament, by way of a breach of contract. Yet, in what point of view, has this matter heen considered in England? I beg gentlemen for a moment, to turn their eye to those governments which have adhered

to their plighted faith, and have recognized the doctrine of the inviola-
bilty of their own contracts, and who have declared that their faith should
be maintained at any and every sacrifice. They will find, as the result
of their investigations, that such governments have been always the most
free, and that they have done the most to promote the interests and the
prosperity of their people.

Let them east their eyes to Great Britain! a country where there is no
written constitution—where the parliament is omnipotent, and where the
legislative body is in session nearly the whole year round—and which, at
one sweep, may destroy the liberty and prosperity of any man in the
land! What, let me ask, has been the result there? Where has the government of that, or any other free country, violated its plighted faith?
Let them shew me an instance if they can. Let them point me to a case
where a man who has applied to the British parliament for a contract, has
been sneeringly asked, where was his remedy; and has been told that,
unless he could bring it into a court of justice, there is no remedy for the
violation of the contract? On the other hand, let us see with what sacred-
ness they have complied with their contracts, and by means of which
they have been enabled to command the wealth of their people to any
extent. It was by means of the reliance on that faith which had never
been shaken, that England was brought safely through that perilous
struggle with Napoleon, who had subjugated almost all the nations of
Europe, and whose whole soul was bent upon making England add one'
more to the number of his conquests. He was baffled by the nation's
faith. At the period when the whole taxation of the country was scarcely
sufficient to pay the interest of the national debt, over and above the
expenses of the government, there never was a time when the subjects
of Great Britain, or foreigners from other parts of Europe, hesitated to
put their money into the funds, under a certain condition that contracts
would be complied with. These have been the fruits arising from this
principle; and this too, in a country where they held only by the imperfect title of good faith; where they hold the doctrine that in ordinary contracts a man is not to be held bound beyond the amount in the contract.

And are we, because the constitution of the United States contains a
positive provision on the subject—are we, because this great principle
is sanctioned by positive law—are we, I ask, to forget—the principle
itself which lays at the bottom of all law, and to declare that, but for that
law, the state of Pennsylvania would be found acting in violation of the
faith of contracts? Sir, I do not believe it, and when I look back to our
history, I find it impossible to believe it. And I assert that whereever
this great principle has been violated, it has been followed by ignominy
to the nation and, eventually, by destruction to the government itself.

Mr. M. adverted to the position assumed by Mr Woodward, as to the
course of the state of Pennsylvania in certain cases of charters repealed;
and then proceeded.

Let the gentlemun shew me an instance where a charter has been violated
by act of assembly in this state where, within a year or two, there has not
been a re-enactment. Allusion has been made to the case of the Bank
of North America. It is true that the charter of that bank, under the

inflictions of the fierce spirit of party, was repealed; and yet within a year or two, to the great honor of certain parties, that very bank which had been weighed down by its own unpopularity, was re-chartered. Do gentlemen want a stronger argument than this, to show what has been the spirit of Pennsylvania on the subject of the violation of charters?

When the doctrine as to the expediency of repealing charters in this commonwealth, came into existence, how was it to be enforced? By setting up a clause to repeal charters or laws? No—but by inserting in the several acts of incorporation an express clause, that the legislature should have that power—thus making the power a part of the contract itself. The question itself never was raised in the legislature of this state—I believe down to this very hour, it never has been seriously raised there. I never heard of it being debated, except, probably, at the last session of the legislature. But they shewed their unanimous sense on the subject even in a stronger manner than by a decision, and, instead of asserting that they had the power already, they made it, on the other hand, an express provision of the contract. The whole of those proceedings, from beginning to end, demonstrate that this idea of the repeal of charters is a new light which has but recently dawned upon the commonwealth; and I hope it will be met by the freemen of the commonwealth in such a manner as that this will be the last time we shall hear of it.

But, sir, more than this, I will shew what has been the course pursued in our former history, within the last ten or twelve years, and when they have had the whole authority to repeal charters, if they thought proper to resort to it. A charter was granted to a company in the neighborhood of Harrisburg, giving to the company authority to take water out of the Susquehanna, at a point about six miles above Harrisburg. The members of the company not having complied with the provisions necessary to obtain the charter, waited till the legislature of Pennsylvania, authorized the construction of a canal across the Susquehanna, over that very interval and at that point where, in consequence of the peculiar nature of the country, it was difficult, though not impossible, to locate more than one canal between the river and the hills. At that time, and after the engineers had been sent for, the gentlemen authorized by the charter, professed to have complied with the provisions necessary to obtain the charter, presented themselves and claimed to receive their charter. And they did receive it. They employed their own engineers to go upon that very line, which it was known, would be taken by the state, although nothing had been done upon the line; and they marked out their own line of canal in defiance of the commonwealth, and claimed, and had the right to claim this land—it belonged to them, and it could not be taken except it was paid for.

Here was a case, which happened in the heat and fury of internal improvement; at a time when, on every question having reference to internal improvement, the difficulty was, not to urge, but to restrain it; and this outrage, as it purported to be, was committed under the very eye of the legislature. That was also a case, in which the legislature reserved the power to repeal the act of incorporation, and stood there with their ████ ████, like the parliament of Great Britain, except by their own objection, and upon the great principles of moral obligation, except, in short, by the moral law.

What course did the legislature in that instance pursue? Where was the remedy which the Harrisburg water company had, if the legislature had chosen to step in, and as a judicial body, had taken away their charter and their property? Where, I ask, was their remedy? They had none; but, by their charter, they had agreed to submit themselves to the magnanimity and justice of the legislature of their country. They had no remedy, sir, because, with the faith, and honor, and justice of Pennsylvanians, they had said in the charter, that for them and their state, it was not necessary that the constitution of the United States should be held as a rod over their representatives, because, with a confidence of a generous people, which had never yet been denied, and which had led to the grant of almost innumerable charters—they had relied on the magnanimity and the justice of their country.

What, I ask, did the legislature do? A joint committee was appointed; and that committee reported, that upon an investigation of the facts, they were satisfied not only that the company had abused their charter—that they had perverted it to improper and illegal purposes, but that they had not complied with the conditions, and had, therefore, never in fact obtained their charter—that is to say, that the charter had been granted unduly —that the conditions which the legislature had imposed, had not been complied with, and that, therefore, having authority under the express provision of the act of assembly, they recommended the repeal of the whole charter. Well, sir, what followed? On reference to the journal of the senate of Pennsylvania, of the session of 1825-6, page 527, you will find the following opinion expressed:

"On the question of subsequent forfeiture by misuser, your committee will offer a few remarks: By the 4th section of the act of assembly which has been already referred to, the president and managers of the company to be incorporated under that act, are authorized to cause a navigable canal, with such locks and other works as shall be necessary, to be made, "commencing at the east side of the river Susquehanna, *between the house of the late John Carson, Esq. and the end of the second Kittatiny mountain,* from thence along or through the east side of the borough of Harrisburg to the said river, at the mouth of Paxton creek, or at some point between the same and Mulberry street, in the town of Harrisburg." It is in evidence, from the minutes of the company and the testimony of their engineer, that the president and managers have instructed their engineer to make the necessary surveys and levels for locating a canal *from the mouth of Stony creek in Middle Paxton,* to the borough of Harrisburg; that the engineer has accordingly surveyed and placed a line for a canal from the mouth of Stony creek, that the upper point of the canal is not yet precisely determined, but that it is intended by the company to be fixed as soon as the state of the river will permit, and between the mouth of Stony creek and the house of James Armstrong, about 100 perches farther down the river. In the opinion of your committee, this assumption of an authority to make a canal to *the mouth of Stony creek, which* is believed to be at a considerable distance above *the end of the second Kittatiny mountain,* and the actual commencement of their operations for this purpose by the company, afford evidence of an assumption and misuser on the part of the company, of a violation of the spirit and letter of their charter, and that they have thereby subjected themselves to a forfeiture of their corporate franchises, if they ever were legally vested with them.

"Your committee regret to observe in the acts and resolutions of the company, a disposition to occupy the ground for their canal in such a mode as to preclude the canal commissioners from exercising the right to the priority of location, which the state should certainly not relinquish.

"Extracts of the material parts of the minutes of the board of managers are submitted with this report, and the senate will find in them, and especially in the resolutions of the board of managers of the 8th and 11th of March, evidences of feelings and intentions which the committee have no disposition to comment on, or to characterise.

"Your committee are entirely satisfied that if the company should be permitted to persist in their present course, the result must be an increase of delay, expense and embarrassment to the state, in the prosecution of the great system of improvement, on which she has now at length happily entered, and the execution of which is already begun.

"Under these circumstances, it behooves the legislature to take immediate measures for protecting the rights and interest of the commonwealth. They should act prudently, temperately and constitutionally, with no unnecessary harshness, but at the same time *firmly and promptly*: By the 25th section of the act of assembly already referred to, the right is reserved to the legislature of resuming the franchises of the company, in case they should at any time misuse or abuse their chartered privileges. Your committee believe that such misuser has already taken place. But they are not disposed to recommend to the senate an immediate and unqualified exercise of the power reserved to the legislature in such circumstances; they prefer leaving the rights of the company to be adjusted in the forms of law, and by the ordinary tribunals of the country. A bill is herewith submitted for effecting these objects:

"1. By authorizing the supreme court to entertain proceedings to be instituted by the attorney general, for testing the original validity of the letters patent granted by the governor, and ascertaining whether the charter of the company has been forfeited by misuser or otherwise.

"2. By suspending, revoking and annuling for the time being, all the corporate rights, powers, liberties and franchises of the company whatsoever, until the proceedings thus to be instituted shall have been brought to a determination.

"3. By providing for the indemnification of the company, for any damages which they shall have sustained by the construction of the Pennsylvania canal, in case the legal proceedings should result in a decision that their charter was not invalid in its inception, and has not been subjected to forfeiture by subsequent misuser.

"4. Providing however, That no proceedings against the company shall be instituted by virtue of this act, if an agreement should be made between the canal commissioners and the company, under the 11th section of the Pennsylvania canal law, before the first day of June next, but in that case the company shall have full power to carry such agreement into effect."

This, continued Mr. M. was the opinion of the legislature in a case where they had the power, and where, being a case of such extreme grossness, they might have resolved themselves into a judicical tribunal, and wrested from the company their rights and property, by the strong arm of power. I say of power, and not of right, because, although the clause to which I have adverted, removes the obligation of a positive law in the constitution of the United States, it does not, it cannot, remove the obligation of the public faith, which is the life and soul of all such instruments. This must always remain. It holds good as well in public corporations as in private ; and although, in technical terms, it may be asserted, that the right to do this does not exist, yet it may be affirmed, in any government whose example is worthy of respect, that they have not the moral right, except there be a case which justifies it—that you cannot do it through mere caprice, and then ask the party aggrieved, to point you to a law which gives a remedy in a court of justice for the violation of a contract.

In conformity with the recommendation of this committee, an act was passed, which, while it established the right of the public, at the same time left the right of the company, and the amount of compensation, to be decided upon by a court of justice. It was an act of magnanimity.

Leaving this part of the subject, I will say a word on the only remaining branch on which I have to speak; and I am admonished that my remarks must be brief, because, although I may not conclude all I might wish to say, within the hour prescribed, still, I will not condescend to ask permission to extend my observations beyond that period of time.

The other point is that, admitting this to be a contract, a right beyond the reach of the legislature, still, that under the clause of the constitution which authorizes the taking of private property for public use, the legislature have a right to resume the whole, whenever they may please. I maintain that the rights of all holders of contracts, under the state, are all based upon the same foundation. and must all be shaken, if this be removed.

Although in this very charter, there is a clause authorizing the repeal, in certain cases, still, the gentleman from Luzerne, (Mr. Woodward) contends that they have still a right to take it for public purposes.

Now, he had been considered, ever since he was in public life, until very recently, an anti-corporation man, and he had never been in favor of conferring very extensive powers upon corporations, and he was never opposed to reasonable restrictions upon them, where they were necessary; therefore, he was in favor of treating the Harrisburg water company, as he would have treated individuals. He was in favor of taking their property, and paying them a compensation for it.

He did not now, however, wish to be pushed into the situation that he, or any one who acted with him, held to the doctrine that chartered privileges were so sacred that the commonweath could not take their land from them, for public use, the same as they could take the land of individuals He did not wish to be placed in the position of claiming for these corpora tions, that you could not run a street, a canal, or a rail road, througl their property. He held no such doctrine at all, and he held that their property could be taken for public use, just in the same manner as any other property.

But what a strange confusion of terms it was, for gentlemen to hold that, because you could take private property for public use, that you could take the rights of corporations, which was no property, for no use at all.

What possible use could be made of the rights of a corporation for banking purposes, by the public? An individual has a right to his credit, and if persons will deposit money with him, and entrust him with it, because of his credit, he has a right to make of it what he can. Well, would you go to this man, and say that he must deliver up his credit, when it can be of no use to any one? You have a right to take his land for pub- lic use, but you have no right to take from him his credit, which would be of no use at all to the public.

Well, you pass an act of assembly, declaring that a merchant shall not issue notes, and have a credit. He had that right by a law, and not by a contract. If we pass this law, depriving him of these rights, where is his remedy?—for we all know that there can be no law, without its rem- edy.

You tell Mr. A. that you not only claim the right of taking his property for public use, but that you also claim the right of taking from him his credit; you will deprive him of holding, receiving and lending the money of others—and why do you do this? Do you take this from him for public use? Certainly not. Can you make any use of it? Not at all. Why, if it was not that he knew the gentleman to be incapable of it, he would say that this argument was the greatest piece of sophistry which he had ever heard.

We all know that it is a settled principle, that private property may be taken for public use. You may enter upon the lands of an individual, in making a public road; or, in time of war and public emergency, you may take his grain and cattle for the use of the army—and the same prin- ciple applies to the property of corporations; but there was a great dis- tinction between this and the taking away the privileges of a corporation, or the credit of an individual.

If he possessed property, the commonwealth might take it whenever they chose, for public use; but they had no right to take his credit, or any thing else, which they could make no use of whatever. What excuse could you make, when you resume a bank charter? Could you say that you wanted it for public use, or that you could make any use of it? Sir, you would not even have the tyrant's plea, necessity, to sup- port you.

Then, again, let us come round to the question, whether there is, or is not, a public faith. This was a question which was not to be lightly treated. We must ask ourselves whether there is not at stake a public faith, and whether that was to be lightly violated. Whatever might be the power, even with the repealing clause in the charter, and with the clause in the constitution of the United States, in relation to the violation of contracts, stricken out, we must not advance a step in the matter, beyond the public feeling. You might have more power by such provisions, but the question would still rise, whether you had more right; and he considered that it would be entirely improper for the legislature to act in matters of this kind in a legal capacity. He believed the time never had been in this state, when the legislature of this state considered it safe to take upon itself, in a legal capacity, or exercise the proper functions of a judicial tribunal of the country, to decide questions between individuals. The people of this country would stand upon their rights, whatever the power of your government may be.

We come from a stock who stood upon their rights whenever they were encroached upon by power even as far back as before the revolution of 1688. The people even at that early day stood upon their rights. There were then to be sure political oppressions, political injuries, and wrongs done against general principles; but in a question of private right the people resisted all power.

As long ago as the time of James I, when judges held their places at the pleasure of the crown, a circumstance occurred which showed the spirit of these people. At that time the king granted to one of the barons of the exchequer, a commission not in the ordinary manner at that time, but to be held during good behaviour. He supposed the monarch thought that his power was sufficient to make him yield up his commission at any time, and it was little matter what kind of commission the baron held. The king afterward, for some reason, required of him to surrender up his place; but the baron stood upon his private rights, and challenged the power of the monarch to deprive him of his place. He did not take his seat afterwards on the bench, but he held his place until his death, and the king never attempted to deprive him of it, because he knew there was a matter of private right involved in it which never could have been touched without raising a flame in his kingdom that would not easily have been extinguished.

It is on this great principle that all your rights ultimately rest. It is on that principle that your inferior corporations and all your institutions rest secure; and destroy this and there will be nothing but oppression and wrong. It is this great principle which secures confidence to your government, and keeps it on its onward course.

Your government is continually changing hands, but the public faith is always kept in view by all who come into it. In the course of five years, perhaps, there is not a single member remaining on the floor of your legislature; but the foreigner or the native, the stranger or the citizen, knows that when he deals with the government, knows that he deals with those who never violate their public faith. If this was not the case, individuals would have no chance to contend with the multiplied power of the government.

If, however, this question of private right is yielded up and the government have power to violate it at will, no man is safe, no man is secure, and the people remain in a worse condition than the subjects of a European monarch.

But he apprehended no danger from this crusade against corporate rights. Whenever men come to vote on questions of this description, right will prevail over political feeling. This matter is all well enough, and is raised out of doors for the purpose of obtaining, or maintaining political power; but the moment these men come to act on their responsibility to the people in the legislative halls, they concede the point they contended for out of doors, and do not attempt to violate this great and overruling principle.

INDEX

INDEX

A.

C.

G.

H.

J.

K.

L.

M.

T

W

END OF VOLUME VIII.

Lightning Source UK Ltd.
Milton Keynes UK
UKHW020311220119
335963UK00014B/1295/P